RECONSTRUCTING ELIADE

RECONSTRUCTING

ELIADE

Making Sense of Religion

by
BRYAN S. RENNIE

Foreword by Mac Linscott Ricketts

STATE UNIVERSITY OF NEW YORK PRESS

Published by
State University of New York Press, Albany

© 1996 State University of New York

For information, address State University of New York Press,
State University Plaza, Albany, N.Y., 12246

Production by Cathleen Collins
Marketing by Theresa Abad Swierzowski

Library of Congress Cataloging in Publication Data

Rennie, Bryan S., 1954–
    Reconstructing Eliade : making sense of religion / by Bryan S.
Rennie ; foreword by Mac Linscott Ricketts.
        p.   cm.
    Includes bibliographical references and index.
    ISBN 0-7914-2763-3 (alk. paper). — ISBN 0-7914-2764-1 (pbk. :
alk. paper)
    1. Eliade, Mircea, 1907–1986. 2. Religion—Study and teaching—
History—20th century. I. Title.
BL43.E4R45   1996
200'.92—dc20   95-12358
                                                        CIP

10 9 8 7 6 5 4 3 2 1

Contents

PART THREE. BEYOND ELIADE

Foreword

I first met Bryan Rennie in the fall of 1990 when he was in the early stages of writing his doctoral dissertation for the University of Edinburgh, ultimately titled *Mircea Eliade: Making Sense of Religion*, of which this book is a revised version. His bright, cheerful personality and spontaneous wit attracted me immediately, but above all I was impressed by his superb mastery of a large part of the vast Eliadean corpus. Moreover, this mastery, I discovered, had been achieved in a relatively short time, during which he also had read and digested all the books and most of the articles written about Eliade. What he had to say to me then—and in portions of his dissertation he sent me subsequently—about Eliade's thought disclosed an exceptional measure of understanding and depth of insight. When his dissertation was finished (and the degree granted), I urged him to publish it as quickly as possible. Wisely, he proceeded with caution, allowing himself time to reflect on what he had written under considerable pressure and to revise the work with a larger audience than a doctoral committee in mind. This book is the happy result.

Eliade once said in an interview:

> It is only the totality of my writings that can reveal the meaning of my work. . . . I have never managed to write a book that expresses me totally. (*Ordeal by Labyrinth*, 187)

Unfortunately for the scholar who desires to learn the meaning of Eliade's work, his bibliography amounts to more than 1,500 separate items—books and articles (excluding translations and republications), plus many important works that remain in manuscript only, sealed in a special collection at the Regenstein Library of the University of Chicago. Moreover, Eliade was not a "systematic" writer or thinker; being gifted or cursed with a literary style of exposition, he never succeeded in expressing his theoretical views in a logical and rigorously ordered form. He recognized this failing, and in a journal entry for 24 June 1968, after having participated in a colloquium at Boston College on "Methodology in Religious Studies" in which he had spoken about his hermeneutics, he wrote: "It now remains for me or for another to systematize this hermeneutics" (*No Souvenirs*, 313). Of course, it is not only Eliade's hermeneutics that needs systematizing, but his thought in general. And it is to this task that Bryan Rennie has set himself in this book.

To be sure, Dr. Rennie has not read *everything* written by Eliade, but he has read very extensively and, more importantly, he has *understood* what he has read. He has, properly, concentrated on the writings of Eliade's maturity, those written between 1945 and his death in 1986; but he has also learned as much as he could without knowing Romanian about his early works from the 1930s. Additionally he has a good acquaintance with Eliade's literary writings (novels, short stories, and plays). In all these diverse writings Dr. Rennie has found a consistency, an implied system, which he elaborates in this book.

The author brings to his task a keen mind solidly grounded in both philosophy and the history of religions. With skill and familiarity he ranges among philosophies ancient, modern, and postmodern. He understands structuralism, phenomenology, linguistic analysis, and philosophies of science and mathematics, as well as the subtleties of the various competing methodologies of *Religionswissenschaft*. He has studied religions of India and Christianity. No lesser preparation would suffice for one who would undertake to comprehend the underlying principles implicit in Eliade's unintentionally obscure *oeuvre*. I believe Dr. Rennie has seen more clearly what Eliade meant to say than has any previous interpreter of the distinguished scholar. His interpretations of the sacred, history, *homo religiosus*, and modern man, and, by extension, his definition of religion, constitute Dr. Rennie's most original contributions and most significant insights. Added to these are his penetrating and persuasive critiques of Eliade's critics (presented in considerably greater detail in his dissertation than here), whose objections, he finds, arise largely from basic misunderstandings of what Eliade said or from unrecognized personal prejudices. Dr. Rennie's genius here, it seems to me, is his ability to identify and expose the logical flaws in the assumptions and/or reasoning of the critics. It is this same genius for logic that enables him to reconcile what others have seen as inconsistencies in Eliade's writings. Coupled with his logical acumen is an admirable and all-too-rare ability to write well, to express precisely and plainly what others (including Eliade himself) have said confusedly or opaquely.

Anyone who would interpret Eliade positively must inevitably become his apologist. In his early years in Romania, Eliade vigorously engaged in polemics and responded to personal attacks in Bucharestian periodicals, but after 1938 he ceased to defend himself from critics. In 1977 he wrote: "I plan someday to dedicate an entire work to discussing the objections put forth by some of my critics" (foreword to Douglas Allen, *Structure and Creativity*, vii), but no such book ever appeared. Had Eliade answered his critics, or had he written with greater "methodological rigour" as Rennie calls it, a work like this one perhaps would not have been needed. But because he did not, Dr. Rennie's book renders a signal service to Eliade himself and to all who desire to understand him.

Eliade died with several unfinished items on his agenda. One of these was the last volume of his *magnum opus*, his "synthesis," *A History of Religious Ideas*. In the 1975 preface to the first volume he spoke of the conclusion at which he would arrive at the end of the multivolume work:

> It is . . . in this final chapter, in the course of a discussion of the crises brought on by the masters of reductionism—from Marx and Nietzsche to Freud—and of the contributions made by anthropology, the history of religions, phenomenology, and the new hermeneutics, that the reader will be able to judge the sole, but important, creation of the modern world. I refer to the ultimate stage of desacralization. The process is of considerable interest to the historian of religions, for it illustrates the complete camouflage of the "sacred"—more precisely, its identification with the profane. (xvi)

Bryan Rennie believes he understands what Eliade meant by the "sole religious creation of the modern world." If he is right, as I think he is, and if he can persuade his readers that he is right—many of Eliade's critics will be disarmed and Eliade can be read and appreciated in a new light.

Eliade did not leave behind him any well-defined "school" to carry on his program. Those who write about him now are more likely to find fault than to clarify his ideas. One prominent historian of religions has proposed that we are at the "end of the Eliadean era and ready to move on to "new questions and themes" (Smart, review of the *Encyclopedia of Religion*, 197). Another states that Eliade's lifework, which he defines as an attempt to find out "what is religious about religion," was "a failure . . . a magnificent and invaluable failure" (Corless 373).

Neither Bryan Rennie nor I believe these things. If the interpretation of Eliade proposed and convincingly expounded in this book should be accepted, Eliade's thought, far from having become passé, will be seen as still contemporary and able to serve as a guide in religious studies for years to come, in an increasingly secular and postmodern twenty-first century.

MAC LINSCOTT RICKETTS

Acknowledgments

There are many debts which can never be repaid, only acknowledged. Among these are my debts to my parents, Olive and Jim Rennie, who gave me what I needed to be who I am. My high school teacher, Mr. Brampton, and my college professor, Frank Whaling, who gave me the knowledge to acquire knowledge. Mac Linscott Ricketts, who gave me invaluable support and encouragement. Finally, my wife Rachela, who gave me more than either of us know.

I would also like to thank Cambridge University Press for permission to use my article "The Religious Creativity of Modern Humanity: Some Observations on Eliade's Unfinished Thought, *Religious Studies* 31 no. 2 (1995)," and the Academic Press who gave permission for material from my article "The Political Career of Mircea Eliade: a response to Adriana Berger" previously having appeared in *Religion* 22 no. 4 (1992). Thanks are also due to Open Court Publishers for permission to quote from W. W. Bartley's *Retreat to Commitment*, to Scholars Press for permission to use J. J. Kim's "Hierophany and History from the *Journal of the American Academy of Religion* 40 no.3 (1972), to Kluwer Academic Publication for permission for Keith Yandell's "Some Varieties of Relativism" from the *Journal for Philosophy and Religion* 19 no. 1 (1986). The passages from Adriana Berger's "Fascism and Religion in Romania" are quoted with the permission of *Annals of Scholarship*, 6 no. 4 (1989), from which they were taken. Those from Robert Baird's *Category Formation and the History of Religions* are quoted with the permission of Mouton de Gruyter. E. J. Brill kindly gave permission for the quotation from Gregory Alles' "Wach, Eliade, and the Critique from Totality" from *Numen* 35 (1988). The Canadian Corporation for Studies in Religion granted permission for the use of parts of "Eliade on Archaic Religions: Some Old and New Criticisms" by R. F. Brown from *Sciences Religieuses/Studies in Religion* 10 no. 4 (1981). Chicago University Press gave permission for quotation from Douglas

Allen's "Mircea Eliade's Phenomenological Analysis of Religious Experience" from the *Journal of Religion* 52 no.2 (1972). The quotation from "The Myth of the Apolitical Scholar: The Life and Works of Mircea Eliade" by Russell McCutcheon was given with the permission of *Queen's Quarterly* in whose 100th volume, issue no. 3, it appeared. Finally, permission to use material from *Nationalist Ideology and Antisemitism* by Leon Volovici came from Butterworth–Heinemann Ltd.

Thanks are also due to Cathleen Collins and Lois Patton of SUNY Press for their diligence and efficiency. Thanks for the footnotes!

PART ONE

The Implicit Meaning of Religion

INTRODUCTION

The academic study of religion as we know it in the modern West has developed under the influence of two great orthodoxies, Christianity and scientific objectivity. Influential opinions have ranged from the committed Christianity of Wilfred Cantwell Smith, through the pluralist theology of Raimundo Panikkar and the methodological agnosticism of Ninian Smart, to the positively anti-religious sentiments of certain linguistic philosophers for whom all "God-talk" is "meaningless." With such a range of conflicting and mutually exclusive approaches confronting students of religion, it is a task of considerable difficulty to develop a coherent conception of the nature of their subject matter—to make sense of religion.

A scholar of leading stature in the field, Mircea Eliade, produced twenty major books in English on religion as well as acting as editor-in-chief of the 1987 Macmillan *Encyclopedia of Religion*. Subsequent scholarship has disagreed enormously as to whether Eliade has succeeded where others have failed in the task of producing a self-consistent and accurate understanding of his subject. In fact, Eliade has become "a problem: to at least half of today's historians of religion he embodies the discipline; to the other half he is anathema" (Ivan Strenski, "Love and Anarchy in Romania," 391). However, Eliade's books, his articles, his autobiography and journals, and even his less well-known fictional writings are all available to the contemporary reader, as are the deliberations upon them of other scholars. A close inspection of this material should reveal some answer to the question: Does Eliade's work on religion finally make sense? Does it provide today's student with usable concepts for a coherent understanding of the chaotic mass of data which we subsume under the category of religion?

This undertaking is itself problematic. Is it possible to "reconstruct" the thought of the eminent scholar? Interpreting Eliade has become a microcosm of the

1

history of religions itself. As his hermeneutics can be seen as an attempt to reconstruct the realities and the structures of the various religions of the world, so now we attempt to reconstruct his thought through our interpretation of his writings. In the conversation which provided the text for *Ordeal by Labyrinth*, published in 1982, Claude-Henri Rocquet suggested that the scholar of religion, in reading Eliade, is involved in "a hermeneutics without end, since even as we read Eliade, we are interpreting him, just as he himself is interpreting some Iranian symbol" (130). Eliade does not object to this contention and thus accepts that even in his scholarly work he does not transmit a clearly retrievable meaning. He also accepts that the author is not exhaustively aware of the valid implications of his own writings. In this light it is not inaccurate to compare the effort to interpret and understand the work of a scholar such as Eliade with the effort to interpret and understand religion itself.

Eliade himself claims that his work is not systematic, or rather that it has never been systematized (*No Souvenirs,* 313). Yet he affirms that theoretical coherence can prefigure systematic reflection. In an article of 1958 Eliade stated that

> one must not think that theoretical coherence is necessarily the result of systematic reflection; it is already imposed at the stage of the image and the symbol, it is an integral part of mythic thought. ("Bi-unité et Totalité dans la Pensée Indienne," 1 n. 1)[1]

The implication is that theoretical coherence can, and often does, precede clear expression, or even awareness, of any system. This can be compared to the processes of language acquisition in which a "grasp" of a rule-governed system precedes conscious awareness of that system. It can also be compared to Charles Hartshorne's contention that

> the idea of "God" . . . first reaches vivid consciousness in an emotional and practical, not in a logical or analytic, form and that this preanalytic form is not that simple. (*Philosophers Speak of God,* 1)

That Eliade was aware of the systematic nature of his own work is indicated by his complaint that it is a prejudice of the historians of religions that they must turn to other specialists for a worldwide and "systematic" interpretation of religious facts (*Two and the One,* 195). In a "fragment autobiographique" Eliade has said,

---

1. "Il ne faut pas croire que la cohéherence théoretique est nécessairement le resultat d'une réflexion systematique; elle s'impose déjà au stade de l'image et du symbole, elle fait partie intégrante de la pensée mythique." My translation, repeated in *The Two and the One,* 89, n. 1.

I wrote literature for the pleasure (and the necessity) of writing freely, of inventing, of dreaming, of thinking at all, relieved of the strictures of systematic thought.[2]

Hence it seems he did regard his scholarly writings as at least an attempt at systematic thought and a systematic interpretation of religion, although he recognizes that such a systematic nature could issue from pre-reflective thought and subsequently remain only implicit in his work.

I would suggest that Eliade's thought *is* systematic, its internal elements referring to, supported by, and reciprocally supporting its other elements. The rejection of any one element, for whatever reason, can then result in a rejection of the whole. The recognition of a coherent system in Eliade's thought is not particularly new. It is the central theme in Douglas Allen's book, *Structure and Creativity in Religion: Hermeneutics in Mircea Eliade's Phenomenology and New Directions*. Despite the importance of that work, however, I feel that Allen overemphasizes phenomenology. Eliade had other influences aplenty; other writers stress his morphology as opposed to his phenomenology. Also, Allen seeks to subsume under the two headings of the dialectic of the sacred and of symbolism all of the other elements of Eliade's thought. This drive to classify under a reduced number of headings or categories of increased significance is fundamentally foreign to Eliade's approach and hence finally inadequate to the exposition. The actual texts of Eliade's work emphasize *meaning*, not phenomenology (see, for example, *Australian Religions*, 200; "The Sacred in the Secular World," 101). That Allen's emphasis is foreign to Eliade's position is shown by the latter's approving citation of Raffaele Pettazzoni's statement that "the only way to escape the dangers" of a phenomenological interpretation "consists of constantly referring to history" ("Mythology and the History of Religions" 100). It is also valuable to realize that Eliade considered that "Pettazzoni's work seems to us more instructive than his theoretical position" (100). It was evidently Eliade's position to underplay theory in favor of content.

The content of Eliade's *oeuvre* is extensive and its implicit theoretical structure is complex and contentious. Starting, as we always must, from a position of ignorance, it is always debateable to simply *assume* that an expressed opinion must make sense, even to the originator. The misdirections of a hermeneutics of blind faith are as pernicious as the limitations of a hermeneutics of total suspicion. The one leads to a diffuse and ineffectual awe before an incomprehensible mystery of infinite complexity, and the other to a solipsistic arrogance. Yet it seems an acceptable procedural assumption to grant that the originator of a document—

---

2. "Je faisais la littérature pour le plaisir (ou le besoin) d'écrire librement, d'inventer, de rêver, de penser même, mais hors du corset de la pensée systématique." Quoted in the Introduction to *Andronic et le Serpent*, 13, my translation.

literary, religious, or academic—could make at least as much sense out of it as we can. This requires a commitment to discover the internal coherence, to reconstruct the meaning, to *make sense* of the objects of our interpretation *before* we reveal the self-contradictions, deconstruct, and make nonsense out of the views expressed in our texts. Critical analysis is a two-sided coin, one of whose faces is appreciation. Despite the unquestioned importance of critical discrimination, the radically critical, iconoclastic approach of many contemporary scholars can all too easily prevent the comprehension of the central insights of a talented thinker with a web of Lilliputian objections. In order to appreciate fully the thought of a hermeneut such as Eliade I suggest that it is not productive to immediately apply logical criticism of the minutiae, but rather to question the coherence and consistency of the whole.

With such considerations in mind I feel confident that the theoretical coherence underlying Eliade's various expressions—despite the lack of systematization and clear definition—is accessible to reconstruction. In seeking to discover a constant and systematic relation of concepts throughout his writings, I am quite deliberately seeking consistency rather than attempting to disclose inconsistency. I feel further justified in my conclusions since they have been made with reference to a large selection of Eliade's works, scholarly and literary. The consideration of that additional material offers valuable assistance in grasping his theoretical coherence. Eliade lamented that Thomas Altizer, for example,

> relied exclusively on my scholarly studies published in English and French [and] ignored the complementary part of my oeuvre written in Romanian. ("Notes for a Dialogue," 235–36)

Although this Romanian portion of Eliade's writing has become increasingly available, particularly through the translations of Mac Linscott Ricketts, little reference has been made to it in the analysis of Eliade's understanding of religion.

My purpose here is to attempt to appreciate the whole of Eliade's understanding of religions before details are modified or discarded according to criteria which were not his. Secondary scholars have all too often criticized what on closer inspection turns out to be their own interpretations of Eliade's thought rather than his actual thought. Eliade's fiction and some of his journal entries reveal his dismay with the impossibility of the attempt to reveal certain "secrets" no matter how hard one tries. The theme occurs explicitly in *Dayan, A Great Man, Uniformes de Général, Iphigenia, Adio*, and *The Old Man and the Bureaucrats*.

When one is dealing with fundamental categories of thought such as "reality" and "being," fundamental misapprehensions are all too easy to make. I do not believe that we can ever fully escape this. It is a fact of life that what I will describe in this book will never be anything other than my own (creative, I hope) interpretation of the thought of Mircea Eliade. I will attempt to mitigate the possible ill-effects of this fact by referring as often as an acceptable style will allow to the primary sources. Of course, even the primary sources suffer somewhat from the difficulties of translation and the influences of the institutional context. Even so, it is better to read and attempt to analyze what has actually been written than to rely on derived statements of one's own construction. If this has led me to use overly long quotations, it is due to my desire for accuracy and my efforts to avoid the dangers of "paraphraseology."

My approach will also be an attempt to clarify by application Eliade's creative hermeneutics. It may seem unsound to attempt to apply a hermeneutic before one has clarified exactly what that hermeneutic consists of. My point, and, I believe, Eliade's point too, is that interpretation is an iterative and recursive action. One is constantly applying one's understanding in the act of formulating it, and formulating it in the act of its application. Understanding, comprehension, interpretation, is not a precise, step at a time, linear, sequential movement; rather, it is a dynamic, interactive, organic process involving all the coruscations of fractal geometry and the inexplicable leaps of quantum phenomena. While there may be a danger here of simply leaping on a bandwagon of the metaphorical application of fashionable cant, it must be borne in mind that understanding itself is a "metaphorical" process of the application of inexact and partial models, and that until such time as theorists can actually provide us with a consistent, precise, linear, step-by-step, sequential description of what *understanding* and *interpretation* actually are, such suggestive strategies are the most effective mode of communication open to us. Thus, rather than pretending to a linear development in my understanding and my interpretation of the thought of Mircea Eliade, I will openly apply my interpretation in the act of explicating it, in the knowledge that this reflects the actual process by which that understanding came about, and in the hope that this will prove the most effective method of communicating both Eliade's views and my interpretation of them.

Ninian Smart has said that "Eliade's main position is shrouded in ambiguities" (*Science of Religion and the Sociology of Knowledge*, 66). It is my hope that this approach, informed by an extensive and close textual reading will resolve some of these ambiguities and reveal Eliade's main position more clearly. My initial task will be to clarify as much as possible Eliade's vocabulary, to settle on clear definitions of the terminology of his interpretative strategies: "hierophany," "the sacred," "*coincidentia oppositorum*," "*illud tempus*," and so forth. Having suggested distinct applications for these terms I will inspect the implications for the understanding of time and history crucial to Eliade's thought. With these concepts a clearly developed, and hitherto unexplored, interpretation of Eliade's writings will emerge.

My next task will be to inspect the relationship of this new interpretation to established scholarship on Mircea Eliade. How does it fare in revealing an internal coherence, in reducing self-contradictions, in *making sense* of Eliade? And how does it stand against the serious and considerable criticisms which have been brought to bear on the Romanian scholar? Is this interpretation itself free of self-contradictions and incoherences, or is it vulnerable to new criticisms? Finally, if this interpretation be acceptable, what does it imply for further understanding of the phenomena of religion? Can religious humanity be seen in a different light? And is this light any clearer? Can Eliade's thought be taken beyond Eliade, rather than be allowed to stagnate or abandoned in the face of increasingly hostile criticism?

CHAPTER 1

Hierophany

The major themes in Eliade's thought are symbol, myth, and ritual,[1] hierophanies, the sacred and the profane, the *coincidentia oppositorum*, the repetition of archetypal structures,[2] *illud tempus*, and *homo religiosus*. Although by no means an exhaustive index, these concepts provide headings under which the whole of Eliade's thought can be comprehensively arrayed.

As I have suggested the various taxonomic elements of Eliade's thought are mutually dependent. Each one can only be finally understood when the others are grasped. It makes little difference, therefore, in what order I attempt to explicate each concept; the explanation of one of these categories will always partially involve the explanation of all of the others. With this in mind, however, I have attempted to construct an exposition in which the earlier explanations involve the later ones as little as possible, and the later ones increasingly presuppose the earlier. I have found it quite impossible, for example, to discuss the sacred and the *coincidentia oppositorum* without reference to Eliade's concept of "hierophany," and so it is with my attempt to clarify this word that I will begin.

Although it may be strange on first exposure this neologism of Eliade's is deceptively simple. It is compounded, we can easily explain to a freshman student, of the Greek *hiero*, the holy, the sacred, and *phainein*, to show. Thus a "hierophany"

---

1. Throughout this work I have largely ignored the question of ritual as a separate issue. I am assuming ritual to be a dramatic, rather than a narrative, reactualization of mythic structures and symbolic themes. This is mainly because of limitations of space, and I freely admit that it does not do full justice to the issue.

2. These are *not* Jungian archetypes; see 1958 preface to *Cosmos and History*; *Ordeal by Labyrinth*, conversations with Claude-Henri Rocquet, 122; Ricketts, "The Nature and Extent of Eliade's 'Jungianism'," *Union Seminary Quarterly Review* 25, no. 2 (1970): 211–234. The question of the relationship of Eliade's thought to that of C. G. Jung is a complex one requiring further consideration.

is a perception of the sacred. Eliade himself says "the term in its widest sense [means] anything which manifests the sacred" (*Patterns in Comparative Religion*, xiii), and the entry from the *Encyclopedia of Religion* (credited to Eliade and Lawrence Sullivan) insists that "the term involves no further specification" (*Encyclopedia of Religion*, vol. 6, 313). Even so, the matter is far from simple. Completely ignoring for the moment the difficulties raised by the loaded term "sacred" and thus the aporia caused by defining one unknown in terms of another, let me first point out an inherent difficulty. Despite the clear, simple definitions quoted above, the passive form of the verb, *phainesthai*, means "to appear," allowing an interpretation of hierophany as an intransitive action by that which is made manifest—*the sacred manifests itself*. So the ambiguity begins: does the sacred manifest itself, or does some thing manifest the sacred? Of course, this ambiguity is a commonplace in English—it appears to me.

Then there are the difficulties raised by Eliade's actual usage of his term. His first introduction of the word into his text[3] is problematic. "Some hierophanies are not at all clear, are indeed almost cryptic," he states, "in that they only reveal the sacred meanings . . . in part, or, as it were, in code" (*Patterns*, 8). Furthermore,

we must get used to the idea of recognizing hierophanies absolutely everywhere . . . we cannot be sure that there is anything . . . that has not at some time in human history been somewhere transformed into a hierophany. (11)

So, not only are *things* "transformed" into hierophanies, but *anything* can be so transformed, and yet, having been so transformed the hierophany may remain "cryptic." Furthermore, "every hierophany makes manifest the coincidence of contrary essences" (*Patterns*, 29). This is a far cry from the notion of an irresistible and unmistakable self-revelatory, lightning-like manifestation of the divine normally associated with the concept of revelation.

As the *Encyclopedia* goes on to explain, "the appearance of the sacred in a hierophany, however, does not eliminate its profane existence." The implication of this is that

whenever the sacred is manifest, it limits itself. Its appearance forms part of a dialectic that occults other possibilities. By appearing in the concrete form of a rock, plant, or incarnate being, the sacred ceases to be absolute, for the object in which it appears remains part of the worldly environment. In some respect, each hierophany expresses an incomprehensible paradox arising from the great mystery upon which every hierophany is centered: the very fact that the sacred is made manifest at all. . . . The

---

3. See Ricketts, *Romanian Roots*, 877f. on Eliade's earliest use of the word.

same paradox underlies every hierophany: in making itself manifest the sacred limits itself. (*Encyclopedia of Religion*, 314)

Although the term is of crucial importance throughout *Patterns* and makes a considerable contribution to the argument of *The Sacred and the Profane*, it is used only five times in *The Myth of the Eternal Return* and does not occur in *Myths, Dreams and Mysteries, Rites and Symbols of Initiation, Myth and Reality, Zalmoxis, Australian Religions*, nor, most notably, in *A History of Religious Ideas*. Perhaps this indicates a growing dissatisfaction on Eliade's part with either the complexities of the term itself or the reaction which it provoked. Nonetheless, its inclusion in the early works and in the *Encyclopedia* would encourage an attempt to scrutinize it more closely. The light which it casts on the whole structure of Eliade's thought finally makes such an attempt indispensable. To this end I want to consider the history of the usage of the term by Eliade.

As I said, it is not used in his earliest writings but seems to spring fully formed into his vocabulary in *Patterns* in 1949. Mac Ricketts (*Romanian Roots*, 798ff.) points out a pivotal period in Eliade's life toward the end of 1936. Before this date his analysis of religions utilizes a relatively simple structure of polarities. In the published version of his thesis on Yoga, *Essai sur l'origin de la mystique indienne* (1936), for example, he "sought to interpret Yoga in terms of a few basic categories, chiefly two pairs of opposites: 'magical/mystical' and 'abstract/concrete' (*Romanian Roots*, 803). It is only after 1936 that Eliade starts to utilize the terminology and categories of analysis familiar to his Western readers from 1949 onward. His first article published in the English language, "Cosmical Homology and Yoga" (1937, see *Romanian Roots*, 819–25) marks most strongly this development of thought. As Eliade had said in his thesis on yoga, yogic techniques express a tendency toward the concrete, they are empirical in the sense that they emphasize practical, personal experience. The particular empirical experiences which are emphasized are identified as being absolutely "real" in their nature, as experiences of true "Being." Ricketts points out that "this equation of 'concrete experience' with a quest for the metaphysical 'real' is made only once, and without emphasis, in the Yoga thesis" (820), it is tacked on to the last page (311) almost like an afterthought. However, in the 1937 article it is immediately and emphatically stated that

> this tendency toward the concrete, the effort toward the "real," means a way out from daily, profane, insignificant, "illusory" experience in which man lives. ("Cosmical Homology," 188. It is in this same article that Eliade first makes explicit his equation of the real and the sacred, the importance of which will be discussed later in my chapter on the sacred.)

The experience of the real is now further identified as a soteriology, a means of salvation from the profane. Yogins seek to replace their experience of the illusory, the unreal, with experience of the real. Finally their effort "makes Being coincide with Non-being, 'sat' with 'asat'" (202). Evidently this is a prefiguration of what Eliade will later call the *coincidentia oppositorum*.

Previously, in his literature and personal philosophy, Eliade had subscribed to Nae Ionescu's philosophy, often referred to as "*trăirism*" (although not by Ionescu and his followers), the search for and valorization of the "authentic" in and through lived experience (Romanian, *trăire*). In prefiguration of the French existentialists, the Romanian intellectual movement represented by the Criterion group (*Romanian Roots*, 551–65) had stressed actual personal lived-experience or *Erlebnis* as the only source of "authenticity" (*Romanian Roots*, 96f., 98–126; on *trăire* in the thought of Ionescu, see also Sergiu Al-George and Günter Spaltmann). Eliade had militated for "authenticity" in 1932–33 in *Fragmentarium* and in *Oceanografie*. However, in 1936 he published two "notes" on authenticity in the Bucharest journal *Vremea*. In the first note he graduates magic, idealism, and authenticity by the power they ascribe to humanity (magic the most and authenticity the least), and identifies authenticity as "a vulgar popularization of idealism, and both authenticity and idealism are failures of the magical consciousness." In the second, Ricketts describes Eliade as arguing authenticity to be "a reaction against the abstractions of both romanticism and positivism; it is part of a general trend toward the concrete . . . and is the expression of a powerful metaphysical thirst" (982 nn. 55, 56). The implications of the "Cosmical Homology" article are clearly that now Eliade considers normal lived experience to be fundamentally unreal, illusory, and inauthentic. This does not, as it might at first seem, constitute a complete schism from Ionescu's thought. As Eliade made plain in an article assessing Ionescu in 1937, he still considered his philosophy tutor to be the foremost thinker in contemporary Romania. On the contrary, Eliade still subscribes to the concept of *trăire* as the source of authentic experience even though it is paradoxically regarded as simultaneously the source of illusion and the unreal. It would appear that this paradox was made clear to Eliade by the fact that the yogin who has attained to the experience of true Being, the *jīvanmukta*, nevertheless "goes on remaining in 'life,'" even though he "does not partake anymore in the human condition." The whole exercise of the yogin's efforts Eliade sees as an attempt to nullify or escape from the human condition, from the "character *sine qua non* of 'life'" ("Cosmical Homology," 202).

Thus normal, everyday experience is seen as illusory, unreal, profane. Eliade supports this perspective with copious textual examples, but to speak to the general student of religions, he is referring to the fact that the Christian tradition sees the phenomenal world as essentially "fallen," reduced by original sin from its original, divinely intended condition to a vitiated, lesser state; the Buddhist tradition sees the world as *anitya*, impermanent and perishable, and even the human self as negated in the doctrine of *anātman*; to the Hindu the temporal world is produced by *māyā*, the magical power of illusion; for the Moslem "all that dwells upon the earth is perishing, yet still abides the face of thy Lord" (Qu'ran 55:26–27); and so on. Yet that same experience, *when apprehended in a specific way*, when *interpreted* in a certain manner, becomes authentic, real, sacred: it becomes an hierophany. This bears obvious similarities with Nagarjuna's *śūnyatāvāda* in which *nirvāṇa* and *saṃsāra* are equated, a philosophy to which Eliade later referred as "one of the most original ontological creations known to the history of thought" (*History of Religious Ideas*, vol. 2, 225). It also presupposes Eliade's attitude to the *coincidentia oppositorum* as the most profoundly meaningful symbol of the nature of absolute, unconditioned reality.

Precisely what influences or processes made Eliade shift in the late 1930s from the basic notion of lived experience as the source of authenticity to this more subtle, paradoxical conception of the coincidence of the real and the unreal in the experience of human life is not clear. Ricketts' consideration of Eliade's publications from this period are of invaluable assistance, revealing, for example, that "authenticity is no longer a 'cause,' but a 'subject' to be pondered and debated" (983). However, the personal insights of Eliade's journals are unfortunately lacking—the journals which he kept for that period were lost during the war and the autobiography is not helpful on that specific point. His published journals, dating from 1945 onward, make one possibly valuable contribution to this problem. In October 1949 Eliade wrote, "I must divest myself of this remnant of immaturity, this superstition of 'authenticity' at all costs" (*Journal*, I, 99, October 1949). Specifically, he was writing here of his difficulty in speaking from a prepared text. Only the initial confrontation of ideas seemed "inspired" to him, the considered and rehearsed seeming "artificial." Yet, by implication one can detect here the dilution, the doubt, of *trăire* as the only mediator of the authentic. As Eliade began to consider the value of the rehearsed (the artificial in the sense that it had been worked on), to consider that immediate, unmediated experience was not the sole vehicle of the authentic, he was becoming more receptive to the concept of the reworked, mediated meanings of *poesis* as communicative of the real, the authentic; and of the actual lived experience as not *inherently* meaningful at all. Furthermore, he had recognized the thirst to transform ordinary, run-of-the-mill experience into "authentic" experience of the "truly real" as common to both his Criterion friends and the Indian yogins.

This recognition opens out into his doctrine of hierophany: lived experience as simultaneously revealing and concealing the sacred. "Anything man has ever handled, felt, come in contact with or loved can become a hierophany" (*Patterns* 11). Its inherent meaning is quite neutral until it is considered and interpreted. This is simultaneously Kantian and Platonic in structure. The content of sensory experience participates in the sacred which is the source of all meaning, like the Platonic world of Forms, but, like the Kantian noumenal, experience is itself devoid of meaning until it has been "processed" by the interpretative psyche to become the phenomenal world. Lived experience, then, takes the place of the Kantian noumenal. It is not *beyond* all access; it is, on the contrary, immediately present to our senses, and yet its meaning, its significance, is not accessible prior to the perceptual processes of interpretation which identify experience as either sacred or profane. Such an apprehension of the processes of perception and interpretation immediately begins to separate the concept of external actuality from the concept of truth and this inherent reassessment of the constitutive characteristics of truth will be considered further.

This understanding of Eliade's hierophany does not spring immediately from the data but must be finally inferred from the interrelations of the totality of his statements. A more direct and immediate interpretation is given by Jay J. Kim, in his 1972 article "Hierophany and History." Kim's description of what he calls the "ontological locus of hierophany" is so clear and represents the more common understanding so well that I can do no better than to reproduce it *in extenso*.

> According to Eliade's analysis, each locus by its given constitutional nature provides specific meanings to hierophany and circumscribes the range of the possible modal variations of a given hierophany. Let us examine a few examples from Eliade's analysis.
>
> The sky *is* even before man is. The sky is *there* before man, but the sky is not just there. The sky is high, transcendent, infinite, immovable for no other reason than that the sky *is*. As Eliade says,
>
> > let me repeat: even before any religious values have been set upon it the sky reveals its transcendence. The sky "symbolizes" transcendence, power and changelessness simply by being there. It exists because it is high, infinite, immovable, powerful. (*Patterns in Comparative Religion*, 39—I follow Kim's original footnotes)
>
> The essential point is that man does not project or attribute these "qualities" to the sky as a way of apprehending the sky, religiously, mythically, symbolically or otherwise.
>
> > The sky shows itself as it really is: infinite, transcendent. The value of heaven is, more than anything else, "something quite apart" from the tiny thing that is man and his span of life. The symbolism of its transcendence derives from the simple realization of its infinite height. (38f.)
>
> We are aware of and can conceive of infinitude and transcendence only because the sky is there as it is. Our primordial experience of it cannot be otherwise than it is.
>
> Like any other ontological locus of the elementary or central hierophanies, the sky is an inexhaustible source of modal variations and

permutations of the ouranic hierophany. Consequently, anything that happens among the stars or in the upper areas of the atmosphere—the rhythmic revolution of the stars, chasing clouds, thunderbolts, meteors, rainbows—is a moment in that hierophany (40).

Another example is water. Water simply is without modal qualifications, for water has no intrinsic shape of its own. Water cannot be created—given a constitutive form—because "it can never get beyond its own mode of existence—can never express itself *in forms*" (212). Since water cannot be created it always exists. This means that water always and necessarily precedes all creation. And because it precedes all it is not alone. "Water is always germinative, containing the potentiality of all forms in their unbroken unity" (188). It is the necessary matrix of all forms, the necessary basis which upholds all creation. To be created means then to be separated from water. Water can never pass beyond the condition of the potential, of seeds and hidden powers. Everything that has form is manifest above the waters, is separate from them (212).

This primordial nature of water underlies all the innumerable variations on water symbolism. As Eliade emphatically states, "in whatever religious framework it appears the function of water is shown to be the same" (212). The ontological locus of the aquatic hierophany is as inexhaustible as the ouranic but there can be no confusion between them. ("Hierophany and History," 345–46).

What must be considered carefully here is my contention that the hierophany *is dependent* on perception and interpretation as opposed to the insistence that "man does not project or attribute these 'qualities' to the sky as a way of apprehending the sky, religiously, mythically, symbolically or otherwise."

Clearly Eliade's position is that it is the true and accurate nature of the sky, for example, which is apprehended in the "ouranic" hierophany. However, it is equally clear that this nature *need not* be so apprehended. From the totally desacralized point of view the sky is not particularly high, about three miles; it is not particularly transcendent, being a relatively thin blanket of atmospheric gas on the surface of the terrestrial globe; it is not particularly powerful, since modern technology can adequately protect us from the weather, and anyway the human race could (nowadays) blow the atmosphere clean off the planet. Likewise water does not *necessarily* possess, for example, the characteristic of pre-existence attributed to it. Its "formlessness" is merely a characteristic of its normally fluid state and is shared by all fluids, heating or cooling will endow it with other properties; and as a fairly simple compound of hydrogen and oxygen it can be "created" by a number of chemical reactions.

It is not a case of simply apprehending the characteristics manifested by natural phenomena to appreciate the nature of an hierophany, and it is certainly not the case that "we are aware of and can conceive of infinitude and transcendence *only* because the sky is there as it is." If this were the case there would be no possible *new* hierophanies, nor would there be any disagreement as to the nature, meaning, or very existence of hierophanies. Eliade has sought to present his readers with those hierophanies most fundamental to known religious history, those hierophanies most accessible to contemporary humanity, and those hierophanies least likely to cause disagreement. But this has led Kim to oversimplify the relationship of humanity to the hierophany.[4]

While it is true that we do not simply "project" the qualities of infinitude and transcendence onto the sky it is misleading to assume then that we are simply *given* these concepts by our experience of the sky. Rather our experience of the world is a reciprocal affair. Without some pre-existent conception of infinitude we could never recognize the infinitude manifested to us by the sky.[5] Also the specific apprehensions of these sacred qualities, while not simply "projections," are dependent upon our specific embodied condition. Were we not *sighted* beings, would the sky manifest infinitude none the less? Perhaps this is not so compelling an argument in reference to the ouranic hierophany, but consider it in relation to the lunar hierophany, one of Eliade's most frequently cited and extensively elaborated loci of hierophany. Simply stated, the periodic waxing and waning of the moon acquaints humanity with a whole complex of manifestations of the nature of the cosmos: periodicity, cyclicality, the harmony of things celestial with things terrestrial (tides and menstrual cycles). But, of course, the moon does not grow and diminish as countless generations have perceived it to. This is an illusion brought about by the orbital arrangement of the solar system. Were we not sighted beings on the surface of this particular planet with such a satellite body, we would have been vouchsafed no such revelation of the nature of the sacred. The point is that our perceptions are the results of both the external state of affairs *and* our conditioned predispositions and abilities. As Coleridge has said "the world is half created, half perceived." (rendered into poetry in Wordsworth's *Prelude*, II, 258–60.) It is rather typical of Eliade's debt to his Romantic precursors that he should propose a schema anticipated by Coleridge, a Romantic and longtime student of Kant.

One thing finally makes it clear that it *must* be perception which makes the event a hierophany. If all existence is capable of becoming a hierophany, a

---

4. It should also be noted that Kim's analysis seems to be based almost entirely on one book, *Patterns in Comparative Religion*. It is an unfortunate aspect of Eliade's thought that it is rather difficult to grasp without extensive reading.

5. It is by reference to earlier experience that later experiences are classified, hence the attraction of the concept of *anamnesis* for Eliade. Recognition of the hierophany is always a matter of *reacquaintance* with prior revelations of the sacred, hence also his emphasis on eternal return. However, these are elements of Eliade's thought to which I will have to return later.

"manifestation of the sacred," then the difference which separates a profane from a sacred event is—must be—the *perception* of the event as such.

Remarkably, Eliade's understanding here resembles Karl Barth's doctrine of the *post facto* interpretations of the partial traces left by the actual event of revelation. That is to say, the actual event being beyond our *trăire*, we can only interpret the interpretations. The reality of the event becomes totally dependent on later interpretation, the sacrality of the event is dependent on belief. To that extent Eliade's ideas are remarkably consistent with Protestant Christian thought. However, insofar as Barthians would seek to *restrict* revelation to echoes of the Christ event, to deny the actual manifestation of the sacred in other worldly occurrences, Eliade cannot agree. It is fundamental to his whole vision of the world that *all* mundane manifestations are manifestations of the sacred—potential hierophanies—capable of being perceived as sacred and of revealing absolute Being if perceived and interpreted ("deciphered") in a certain way. It is a particular feature of Eliade's thought that even the most horrifying of events (for him as for most of his generation, the concentration camps of the Second World War) is capable of revealing the sacred. He insists that

> the strangest, the most aberrant behavior must be considered as a human fact; if considered as a zoological phenomenon or monstrosity it is not understood. (*The Two and the One*, 12)

He evidently considers that *everything* people do and everything we have done in the past is valid, if not indispensable, evidence of the meaning of our existential situation. One manifestation of this feature of his thought has been pointed out by Mac Ricketts; evil as such is entirely absent from Eliade's fictional work. Even the inspectors of the secret police who appear in *The Old Man and the Bureaucrats* and in *Les Trois Grâces* are not characterized as evil people. In keeping with this Eliade is insistent that even the most aberrant phenomena of religious history must be recognized as genuine manifestations of the religious life of mankind. The resultant *amoral* nature of Eliade's writings has caused some concern. Surely a commentator on the religions of the world cannot simply *ignore* the entire question of ethics? My comments on this question must await a fuller exposition of other aspects of Eliade's thought.

Finally, a definition of hierophany may be established as "any element of the experiential world of humanity which is perceived in such a way as to constitute a revelation of the sacred."[6] However, by virtue of the fact that it is an element of human experience, the hierophany is simultaneously mundane, which is to say profane. Having delineated the experiential and the paradoxical nature of the

---

6. As such it is comparable with R. M. Hare's notorious "blik." However, it is a "blik" with a specific external and given form. (See "Theology and Falsification," in *New Essays in Philosophical Theology*.)

concept of hierophany, it is obviously necessary to pass immediately on to a consideration of precisely what the hierophany reveals, that is to say, on to a consideration of the sacred.

CHAPTER 2

The Sacred

One of the most fundamental and, as we shall see, one of the most problematic of Eliade's categories for understanding and explicating the phenomena and the history of religion is that of the sacred. It is in terms of and in relation to the sacred that almost all of his other categories are described. And it is in relation to the sacred that secondary scholars can most often be seen to be criticizing their own interpretations rather than the writings of Mircea Eliade.

It is simplest to begin with one of Eliade's best-known and earliest work, *Patterns in Comparative Religion*, first published in French in 1949 as *Traité d'Histoire des Religions*. In section 74, "Stones as Manifesting Power," he states that,

> the hardness, ruggedness, and permanence of matter was in itself a hierophany *in the religious consciousness of the primitive*. And nothing was more direct and autonomous in the completeness of its strength, nothing more noble or awe inspiring than a majestic rock, or a boldly standing block of granite. Above all, stone *is*. It always remains itself, and exists of itself. . . . Rock shows him something that transcends the precariousness of his humanity: an absolute mode of being. Its strength, its motionlessness, its size, and its strange outlines are none of them human; they indicate the presence of something that fascinates, terrifies, attracts and threatens, all at once. In its grandeur, its hardness, its shape and its color man is faced with a reality and a force that belong to some world other than the profane world of which he is himself a part. (216, first emphasis added)

Already we begin to suffer from the lack of transparency of the text, and the uncertainty of interpretation. Is the permanence of matter a hierophany *in fact*, or only "in the consciousness of the primitive?" Is it the rock which is the hierophany, or "something that fascinates?" Does Eliade's final pronoun refer to "the primitive," or to humanity in general? Eliade *was* talking about the primitive. However, we all share this "precariousness of humanity," so is he now indicating humanity in general?

Worse, Eliade immediately goes on to say that,

> the devotion of the primitive was in every case fastened on something beyond itself which the stone incorporated and expressed. A rock or pebble would be the object of reverent devotion because it represented or imitated *something*, because it came from somewhere. Its sacred value is always due to that something or that somewhere, never to its own actual existence. Men have always adored stones simply in as much as they represent something other than themselves.

Is it the self-existence and autonomy of stone which effects the hierophany, its fundamental characteristics of strength, hardness, size, and shape, or is it *something other* than the stone's inherent character? If this is not to be an unresolved ambiguity, then Eliade must mean that what is *beyond* the actual existence of stone, what is *other*, is the *quality* of strength of hardness, the *concept* of absoluteness, the *implications* of motionlessness, the *otherness* of inhumanity. All abstract, notional, conceptual ideas. Although Eliade has frequently been criticized for making *a priori* assumptions of the ontological autonomy of the sacred, it is rather the case that he is investigating an intentional object (to use the language of Husserlian phenomenology) without raising the question as to its proper or pure intentionality. It is an early assumption of *Patterns* that "we shall see each [manifestation of the sacred] as the manifestation *in the mental world* of those who believe in it" (10, emphasis added). That this is not merely my rather forced interpretation is further borne out by his insistence that the structure of the primitive or archaic world was fundamentally Platonic (*Myth of the Eternal Return*, 35, 54). Of course, he has been attacked for ascribing such abstractions outside of the culture and language to which they properly belong, but I tend to agree with his statement that "for our purpose, it is not the vocabulary which matters, it is the demeanor" (*Symbolism, the Sacred and the Arts*, 107). The very fact that humanity, even in its earliest stages and least literate of manifestations, is capable of entering into as complex a relationship as religious reverence with as simple an object as a rock would seem to be a persuasive argument for the operation of powerful abstractions and notional attitudes.

In the somewhat later work, *The Sacred and the Profane*, Eliade attempts clarification.

> The sacred always manifests itself as a reality of a wholly different order from "natural" realities. It is true that language naively expresses the *tremendum*, or the *majestas*, or the *mysterium fascinans* by terms borrowed from the world of nature or from man's secular mental life. But we know that this analogical terminology is due precisely to human

inability to express the *ganz andere*; all that goes beyond man's natural experience, language is reduced to suggesting by terms taken from that experience. (10)

This still leaves us in a possible quandary as to whether this equivocal *ganz andere* is an autonomous entity, an inherent property of the sacred object, or an inherent property of the perception of sacrality. Nor does his continued effort to clarify his definition bring any real solution: "the first possible definition of the *sacred* is that it is *the opposite of the profane*" (10). Yet he presses on, "man becomes aware of the sacred because it manifests itself, shows itself, as something wholly different from the profane" (11). It must be pointed out here that Willard Trask, the translator of *The Sacred and the Profane* from French into English, seems to have been rather insensitive to the common French (and Romanian) usage of the reflexive to avoid the passive which Eliade would have learned in the formal French of the twenties. An acceptable alternative translation of the original "le sacré se manifeste," is *"the sacred is manifested,"* rather than "the sacred manifests itself." The former permits an implication of the sacred as the object of the phrase, rather than as the active subject. This reading is borne out by the agreement of the wording of the later *Encyclopedia of Religions* already quoted (see above, p. 8f.). The perils of translation are many, and in the complex arena of religious belief small inaccuracies such as this can develop into major misunderstandings. I would suggest that there is a greater emphasis on the human *awareness* of the sacred, and the sacred as the object of that awareness than the English translation allows.

> By manifesting the sacred, any object becomes *something else*, yet it continues to remain *itself*, for it continues to participate in its surrounding cosmic milieu. A sacred stone remains a *stone*; apparently (or, more precisely, from the profane point of view), nothing distinguishes it from all other stones. But for those to whom a stone reveals itself as sacred, its immediate reality is transmuted into a supernatural reality. (12)

Thus the *object* is not actually changed; from the profane point of view nothing distinguishes it. Rather it must be the *awareness* of its sacrality, the *perception* of the sacred as manifest in that particular object which has wrought the transformation. For the historian of religions, "our documents—be they myths or theologies [etc. the documents of the historian of religion are always manifestations of the sacred by definition]—constitute . . . creations of the human mind" (*The Quest*, introduction).

Furthermore, the revelation occurring in a hierophany is not irresistible; it can be perceived by some and simultaneously unrecognized by others.

> Awareness of a miracle is only straightforward for those who are prepared by their personal experience and their religious background to recognize it as such. To others the "miracle" is not evident, it does not exist. (*Mademoiselle Christina*, 7, my translation.)

Thus it is unquestionably the perception of the sacred which constitutes it as it is for those who perceive it. What, then, is it that is perceived as sacred? Eliade is quite clear and consistent about this: "the sacred is pre-eminently the *real*, at once power, efficacy, the source of life and fecundity" (28). This is not to say that the sacred is necessarily something independent of this experience, rather "it is this experience of the sacred, that generates the idea of something which *really* exists and, in consequence the notion that there are absolute intangible values which confer a meaning upon human existence" ("Structure and Changes in the History of Religion," 366).

The "sacred" certainly does not "necessarily imply belief in God or gods or spirits . . . it is the experience of a reality and the source of an awareness of existing in the world" (*Ordeal by Labyrinth*, 154). Eliade does appear to be discussing notional, rather than independent realities: to use once again the language of Husserlian phenomenology (which Eliade himself did not do), purely, rather than properly intentional objects.

In "Structure and Changes in the History of Religion," Eliade tells us that "the sacred is manifest in an infinity of forms" (353). It is noteworthy that Eliade uses "infinity" not merely "great variety" of forms. As we have seen, he is clearly arguing that any and every historical/phenomenal object and event can manifest the sacred. Thus the only property necessary to permit the manifestation of the sacred is *existence*.

Eliade repeatedly defines the sacred as the real. Readers must be very careful here not to ascribe any unwarranted assumptions to this real, not to read *their own* real into Eliade's general interpretative category. Like the sacred, the real is an intentional object, the object of belief. As Eliade says, the believer "always believes that there is an absolute reality, the sacred, which transcends this world but manifests itself in this world, thereby sanctifying it and making it real" (*Myths, Dreams and Mysteries*, 202).

The equation of the sacred and the real is consistent throughout Eliade's work since "Cosmical Homology and Yoga" in 1937. However, many scholars have either disregarded this equation or mistakenly assumed it to refer to a deity or a necessarily independent ontology. On the contrary, Eliade also repeatedly states that "the sacred is an element in the structure of (human) consciousness" (*Quest*, i; *No Souvenirs*, 1; and *The History of Religious Ideas*, vol. 1, xiii). In other words, Eliade is not discussing an ontological substratum, like Aristotle's *hyle* or Kant's noumenal, but the psycho-phenomenological real—that which is *apprehended* as real by the consciousness of the aware, experiencing subject. It is all too possible to be misled by Eliade's language. For example, he states,

> through the experience of the sacred, the human mind grasped the difference between that which reveals itself as real, powerful, rich and meaningful and that which does not. (*Quest*, i)

This could be read as granting external, independent ontology to the sacred as the object of experience. However, it is more consistent with Eliade's thought to read the *experience* of the sacred to be the *experience* of the real. In context, Eliade has made it plain that he does not, as Robert Baird suggests, "assume that there is something out there that corresponds to the term 'religion' or 'the sacred'" (*Phenomenological Understanding*, 74). Rather he identifies something in the structure of human consciousness and concomitant phenomena in human history. This is not to say that Eliade ever *denies* the ontological independence of the sacred; he does not. However, this is a question for theology or metaphysics, not for the history and phenomenology of religions.

This, then, is Eliade's view of the sacred. *It is the intentional object of human experience which is apprehended as the real.* His use of the term "sacred" in this way has led to all sorts of criticisms of prejudgment, theological bias, and meta-physical assumptions. However, J. Z. Smith noted occasional similarities between Eliade's and Durkheim's sacred/profane pair. He points out that Eliade may have substituted Rudolf Otto's *language* of the Holy for "Durkheim's more neutral and positional sacred while maintaining the dynamics of Durkheim's dualism" (*Map is not Territory*, 91). William Paden has demonstrated in more detail that the Eliadean category is "under some debt to the French school" of Emile Durkheim. Here the sacred is "an index of a system of behavior and representation which follows its own rules" rather than "the name for the transcendent reality to which religious experience points and to which it responds." This second usage, which Paden attributes to R. R. Marrett, Nathan Soderblom, and Eduard Lehmann has constituted "the predominant model of the sacred" ("Before the Sacred became Theological," 199). But this is *not* Eliade's usage. Eliade's emphasis on the ubiquity of sacred potentiality concurs with Paden's analysis of Durkheim's expression in that "the *nature* of the objects that are sacred is completely incidental to the fact *that* they are sacred *to* some group" (202). Yet it is *not* the case that "the sacred is simply whatever is *deemed* sacred by any group" (203) if "simply" implies an arbitrary choice. Eliade's sacred is not either "a value placed on objects" or "a power that shines *through* objects" but a complex reciprocation of *both*. It is not a disjunction but a conjunction.

As "that which is venerated" or "that which is considered worthy of worship," the sacred unquestionably *does* exist. It exists as the object *par excellence* of the study of religion. To assume an ontological category existing *independently* of human involvement, however, is unnecessary and unhelpful to the study, and Eliade does not necessarily make this assumption. His focus is on humanity, not on the debated independent existence of a Divine Being.[1]

---

1. Indeed, this dispute is unnecessary, and is little more than a resurrection of Anselm's ontological argument: Must God exist in order to be "that than which nothing greater can be thought?" Must the sacred exist (that is, possess independent ontology) in order to be worthy or worship?

That "reality" of which the sacred is an experience can only be whatever one construes to be real. Contemporary thought usually ascribes that reality to "the outside world," that which exists independent of human creation or construal, but that is an ascription which has an historical source and far-reaching implications, as I will discuss later.

On close investigation it appears that Eliade's sacred is a systematic rather than an ontological proposition. The sacred is, by definition, that which underlies all religious experience, possibly all human experience. It is not necessarily an object independent of that experience (see *Ordeal by Labyrinth*, 122; *Myths, Dreams and Mysteries*, 15, 123).

Robert Baird's response to Eliade's sacred in his *Category Formation and the History of Religion* is typical of many assessments of Eliade. He points out that, since Eliade accords ontological status to the sacred without clear definition, he thus "proceeds under the essential-intuitional approach." He "assumed that there is something out there that corresponds to the term 'religion' or 'the sacred,' and also that the historian of religion can identify it intuitively" (74). However, if this alternative assessment is correct, then that is precisely what Eliade did *not* assume. Rather he accepted that there is some meaningful coherence to the category of "religious," and proceeded to analyze the human behavior so designated. This will be considered in greater detail later.

Although Eliade did not give formal and dogmatic expression to his working definitions, they are clearly present to the attentive reader, as Baird himself came close to recognizing when he equates "religion, the sacred, [and] man's response to the sacred" (74). Religion is already defined as man's response to the sacred. Of course, that is only meaningful if one has some notion of the meaning of the sacred. One of the institutional difficulties which militated against Eliade giving clear formal definitions in these terms was precisely the fact that many of the academic scholars of religion, especially between the 1940s and 1960s when he produced his major works, already had clear and distinct ideas of the meaning of the sacred and the real. However, for those of us who are less complacent in our own knowledge, Eliade's work can provide an indication of what the sacred has been *considered* to be throughout the religious history of humanity.

The wary reader might note at this point that Eliade's procedure is somewhat circular: by assuming religion to be the human response to the sacred, he identifies the nature of the sacred as it is encountered in religious history. He is identifying the sacred as that which is involved in religious phenomena and identifying as religious those phenomena which involve the sacred. Only close attention to internal coherence can avoid a vicious circularity. Such "enabling prejudices" have been very credibly argued to be involved in all our understanding: one must recognize that a word has meaning before one can proceed to refine and develop that meaning. It is the "prejudice against prejudice which denies tradition its power" (Gadamer, *Truth and Method*, 270).

The circularity of Eliade's description (for it is a description rather than an argument, although all descriptions are in part persuasive and supportive of the *Weltanschauung* for which they are true) ensures that it is more attractive to the reader with some predisposition to accept it. Accordingly, Baird concluded that Eliade's understanding "will appear useful to all those who share his ontological stance" (91). However, the reader whose predisposed notion of the sacred is of an exclusively Christian deity might equally find it difficult to accept the amorphousness of Eliade's sacred and the ubiquity of its manifestations. In other words Eliade's understanding is *not* appealing simply to those who have a predisposition toward the acceptance of traditional formulations of the sacred as the real. On the other hand, the reader whose predisposition is to resist any ascription of reality to traditional, ideal entities might find it difficult to enter into the play of meaning, to begin the process of refinement and development of the meaning of the sacred. For such a reader the only options are to deny any meaning to such a term, or attempt to apprehend its significance through a different field, such as psychology or sociology, which has previously been apprehended as possessed of real significance.

The major question here is what benefits might be gained in the endeavor to understand religious phenomena and *homo religiosus* by an acceptance of the meaning of religion as the response to this sacred. Does this help make sense of religion? If we cannot invest the word "religion" and its fundamental category, "sacredness," with some meaning then it seems utterly fruitless to attempt to understand religion per se or humanity in its "religious" aspect.

In his study *Homo Religiosus in the Works of Mircea Eliade*, John Saliba has distinguished between anthropologists and historians of religions specifically on the grounds that

> the historian of religions [as opposed to the anthropologist] *assumes the existence of the sacred independent of man*, and takes religious experience as the effect of the sacred on man. History of religions, in Wach's words, "is the story of man's understanding and appreciation of the fact that God has revealed himself to man." The presence of the sacred and its manifestations are among the main assumptions of historians of religions. (40, quoting Wach, *The Comparative Study of Religions*, 135, emphasis added)

If Eliade can be shown to have expressed a coherent understanding of religion which allows for the identification of reality and the sacred, *without involving this assumption*, he has surely made a contribution to both fields.

Douglas Allen, who is certainly one of the more sympathetic of Eliade's critics and one who discovers more benefit than most in Eliade's work, has pointed out that

> Eliade must not be confused with the numerous scholars who hold metaphysical positions concerning transcendence. He is not claiming that

"the value of religious phenomena can be understood only if we keep in mind that religion is ultimately a realization of a transcendent truth." ("Structure and Creativity," 122, quoting C. J. Bleeker, "The Future Task of the History of Religions," 227)

Allen is also aware that Eliade "appears to have given us a 'definition' of religion which is supposedly dependent on the nature of the religious documents he has investigated, but" he is forced to conclude, one "which is not in fact open to change" ("Structure and Creativity," 123). This is obviously a problem; if the "definition" is not open to change, if it is set for all time in its own interdependent, systematic sub-definitions and categories, can it be of any real use in the changing world of human culture?

Allen sees Eliade as one who

has attempted to understand religion as a way that the human being is in the world; religion arises from existential crises and is understood as a mode of existence in the world. For *homo religiosus* the sacred "is the category of *meaning* in the world. The *Sacred* is what is valid in the world, authentic, substantial, real, true, eternal." . . .

Eliade, when he describes the profane as meaningless or nonbeing, is using a religious scale, is describing the profane *qua* profane [Allen footnotes: "we have written 'profane *qua* profane' because the profane does have meaning and value for *homo religiosus*, but only in so far as it reveals the sacred"], and is presenting the view of *homo religiosus* only after he or she has evaluated and chosen the sacred, after one has resolved his or her existential crisis. (131, quoting Ira Progoff, "Culture and Being," 53; and 133 n. 55).

This clarifies further Eliade's appropriation of the religious language of the believer. In granting meaning to such language, that language also becomes meaningful to Eliade, and thus usable by him. It is this utilization of the presuppositional language of religious believers which, I believe, has opened Eliade to such hostile criticism. And yet, is not all language presuppositional in this sense? Must not meaning be granted *before* understanding can be furthered? Allowing the meaning of the term as suggested here at least allows its utilization without immediate accusations of apriorism and obfuscation. The term can be granted meaning *without* necessarily acquiescing to any specific traditions of revelation, "without implying anything about 'The Sacred' as a metaphysical referent," as Paden puts it (208).

This discussion of Eliade's notion of the sacred is already overlong. I cannot immediately settle the problem of the importance which Eliade accords to the word sacred. This is finally a matter of personal experience and predisposition. However, I hope that I have achieved my aim of clarifying what it is that Eliade indicates by the word "sacred." This is still a difficult term and one without which I do not believe one can clearly comprehend Eliade's thought. Thus it will be worth further exposition of the term in its specific dialectical relation to its binary partner, the profane.

CHAPTER 3

The Dialectic of the Sacred and the Profane

Eliade's well-known work *The Sacred and the Profane*, was first published in German as *Das Heilige und Das Profane* (1957), and is very much a response to and in many ways a progression from Rudolf Otto's *Das Heilige* (*The Idea of the Holy*). Thus it is rather fruitless to point out that Eliade identifies the "sacred" with the "holy" since these are simply alternative translations of the German *Heilige*. There is no doubt that Eliade accepts as his starting point Otto's concept of the sacred as *ganz andere*, the *mysterium tremendum et fascinans*, which is seen as the source of numinous experience. Yet Eliade was seeking to go further than Otto in defining the sacred/holy in his specific dialectic of the sacred and the profane. This is, among other things, a heuristic device which Eliade utilizes in order to explicate his conception of the sacred. The specific divergence which he makes from Otto's expression of the sacred is to try to clarify further this numinous concept in its particular opposition to that which it is not; a sort of *via negativa*. This dialectic was taken up by Thomas J. J. Altizer in the first book-length study of the thought of Eliade, *Mircea Eliade and the Dialectics of the Sacred*, written in 1963.

Altizer was considerably ahead of other scholars in this respect; Kitagawa and Long's edition, *Myths and Symbols: Studies in Honor of Mircea Eliade*, was not published until 1969, and the next full-length treatment, John Saliba's *Homo Religiosus in the Works of Mircea Eliade*, not until 1976. This very hiatus in major secondary scholarship may indicate the lack of solid, self-confident interpretations of Eliade's thought, although the articles of Penner and Leach, Radaza, Hamilton, Hudson, Rasmusen, Ricketts, and Welbon (the first two critical, the remainder broadly favorable) indicate that there was a core of assertive critical reaction to Eliade during the sixties.

It will be beneficial at this point to have a detailed consideration of Altizer's description of Eliade's dialectic of the sacred because, given its priority in the field, it has had considerable influence. While Altizer was on familiar terms with Eliade and by no means a severe critic, he has nonetheless misunderstood that dialectic. His enlistment of Eliade's thought to further his own "death-of-God" theology remained the only full-length exposition of Eliade's thought during a twenty-year period after the latter's arrival in Chicago. As such it has set the scene for much of the ensuing understanding of Eliade's thought in the English-speaking world. An inspection of Altizer's analysis provides a convenient forum in which to debate this dialectic and, hopefully, to clarify its nature.

It is in agreement with Ricketts' assessment and with Eliade's own comments[1] that I conclude that Altizer's analysis is rather wide of the mark. Yet Altizer's clear statement of intent brushes aside many potential criticisms. "This book," he states,

> is not a scholarly interpretation of Eliade's work. It is true that the first half of the book attempts to elucidate Eliade's understanding of the sacred, and in doing so, it explores various theological and philosophical implications of his thought about which he himself has chosen to be silent. (18)

Thus Altizer's work is confessedly speculative, and yet he "nevertheless profess[es] to be in a large measure [Eliade's] disciple" (20), and so the reader might expect a fundamental consonance with his "master's" thought. From the outset Altizer states that "Eliade posits a sacred that is the opposite of the profane: it is this very dialectical opposition of the sacred and the profane that makes the sacred meaningful to the profane consciousness (18). Certainly Eliade has said that "the first possible definition of the *sacred* is that it is *the opposite of the profane*" (*The Sacred and the Profane*, 10) and that "all definitions up till now of the religious phenomenon have one thing in common: each has its own way of showing that the sacred and the religious life are the opposite of the profane and the secular life" (*Patterns*, 1), but *in both of these cases he has gone on immediately to indicate that this opposition is problematic and in need of clarification*. In both of these cases, the obvious, primary opposition of the sacred and the profane is a starting point from which Eliade progresses to expound his own, more complex view.

In *The Sacred and the Profane*, the source of the first of the two quotations given above and the major location of Eliade's thought on this topic, he goes on to differentiate the sacred and the profane specifically through the human reaction to these radically different "modes of being," by the differentiation between "historical" and "sacred" being. Altizer explains,

> by purely "historical" being Eliade means a radically profane mode of existence, a mode of existence which has withdrawn itself from an

---

1. Ricketts, "Eliade and Altizer: Very Different Outlooks," and "Mircea Eliade and the Death of God." Eliade, "Notes for a Dialogue," in *The Theology of T. J. J. Altizer*, ed. John B. Cobb.

awareness of the transcendent, and immersed itself in the immediate temporal moment. (23)

There is, no doubt, some truth in this. But is it as simple as Altizer seems to imply? His "death-of-God" theology is interesting and meaningful in its own right, and it is not my intention to criticize that here. Rather I must question whether the analysis he gives of Eliade's conception of the dialectic of the sacred and the profane accurately reflects Eliade's thought. One must consider the identification of the sacred and the real, which I believe I have established adequately enough in the preceding section to now take for granted. Can "historical" being accurately be said to have "withdrawn itself from an awareness of the transcendent" (in this context that is identified with the sacred, the real)? While there remains *any* awareness of "reality," how can "historical" humanity have achieved a "radically profane mode of existence?"

Altizer continues that this "immersion is totally isolated from any meaning or reality that might lie beyond it," (23) and herein, perhaps, lies the misapprehension. Meaning and reality are not sought *beyond* actual, empirical, historical experience, granted; they are sought *in* these "profane" categories. Thus the sacred does not *transcend* the profane in that it "lies beyond" it. Rather, for modern, historical humanity the sacred *is* the profane; empirical actuality *is* reality. This is Eliade's notorious "identification of the sacred and the profane" (*History of Religious Ideas*, vol. 1, xvi) and I will return to it later.

The question here is: Does modern humanity's choice to live exclusively in the "profane" world automatically and necessarily close us off from the realm of the sacred? An analysis of Eliade's thought would indicate quite clearly otherwise. It does however close us off from the realm of the *traditionally* sacred, and it should be noted that Eliade has differentiated modern from traditional humanity in precisely this way.[2] Thus Altizer's perception of "a yawning void in even the most powerful expressions of contemporary religious life" because "theology has lost all contact with the sacred" (14), goes too far to have a real basis in Eliade's thought.

It is rather the contemporary identification of the real with the historical/empirical which opens this void between the traditionally sacred and that which is contemporarily perceived as the real. Altizer's contention that theology

must be prepared for the possibility that the most radical expression of profane existence will coincide with the highest expressions of the sacred, (17)

---

2. Eliade explains that "by this term [traditional cultures] we mean any culture, whether ethnographic ('primitive') or literate, which is governed in its entirety by norms whose religious or cosmological (metaphysical) validity is not doubted by any members of the community." *Barabadur, the Symbolic Temple*, first published in 1937. V. Diane Apostolos-Cappadona, ed. *Symbolism, the Sacred and the Arts*, 131, n. 1.

would no doubt have elicited Eliade's agreement, but to continue that "only the Christian can greet the radical profane with faith" is exclusivist, contradicting Eliade's valorization of Asian and "primitive" religions. The insistence that the Christian can greet the profane with faith because "the Christian believes in both Creation and Incarnation . . . in a Christ who is in some sense Creator and Redeemer at once" (17–18), may be true, but that this is *exclusively* true of the Christian is not supported by anything Eliade has written. In fact, the ability to recognize the sacred in the radically profane is precisely the central feature of *all* religion according to Eliade's analysis of the sacred as the real.

It would appear that Altizer has been misled by a superficial resemblance of Eliade's thought to his own. Reading such statements as "the non-religious man refuses transcendence," or "modern man cannot be content until he has killed the last god" (*The Sacred and the Profane*, 202, 203), Altizer has either assumed a deeper consonance with the death-of-God theology than is actually the case, or he has deliberately made a one-sided presentation of Eliade's thought in order to clarify his own position. Altizer's protestations that his book is "not a scholarly interpretation of Eliade's thought" would seem to support the latter conclusion.

Certainly Eliade's reaction was one of disappointment. In his direct response, the "Notes for a Dialogue" mentioned above, published in 1970, Eliade expresses a desire to

> express publicly my friendship for the man and my admiration for the author. The issue of agreeing or disagreeing with his theological innovations is, at least in my case, irrelevant. I am interested in Altizer's writings for their own sake; I consider them original and important spiritual adventures. (234)

However, that he *did* disagree is the inevitable conclusion, especially considering his 1968 denunciation of the "Death-of-God" theology as part of "the provincialism of the latest crisis, fashion, or cliché of Western religious language and traditions" (preface to *Reflective Theology* by T. N. Munson, vii).

As I have already mentioned, Eliade's main complaint is that Altizer relied entirely on Eliade's scholarly production to the exclusion of his complementary fictional writings. The very fact that Eliade makes such a complaint is alone sufficient to indicate that he considered Altizer's understanding of his (Eliade's) thought to be incomplete. As he says, he does not "recognize [his] thinking" in much of Altizer's description ("Notes for a Dialogue," 240 n. 6).

Altizer clearly saw "an essential foundation of Eliade's understanding of the sacred: the sacred and the profane are human phenomena, they are created by man's existential choice" (24). Yet he could not, apparently, follow this through to its logical conclusion that the opposition of the sacred and the profane lie within the human existential condition and not outside it in some ontological dichotomy. We cannot be completely closed to the sacred, we can only fail to recognize the sacred in some particular form—in the case of modern humanity, in the traditional-mythic form.

Modern humanity "accepts no model for humanity outside the human condition as it can be seen in the various historical situations" (*Sacred and the Profane*, 203). That is we consciously reject traditional culture and its myths and the contemporary speculative imagination as valid sources of paradigmatic models for humanity. However intriguing traditional, mythic, and imaginary conceptions might be, they do not reveal an exemplary model to modern humanity. They do not reveal what humanity might be, what we ought to be, or what we could be. They reveal only curious speculations within unreal imaginary realms. They are no longer sacred, but profane, to the majority of modern minds.

A major disagreement of Altizer's perception of the dialectic of the sacred and the profane from that expressed by Eliade is that "neither can become fully itself apart from a total negation of the other; it is precisely the profane which is negated by the sacred" (26). On the contrary, Eliade states several times that a sacred tree, for example, remains precisely a tree. The revelation of the sacred is always in and through the specifically profane (*Mademoiselle Christina*, introduction, 7; *Patterns*, 29; *Sacred and the Profane*, 12, 14). The sacred does not abolish the profane object in and through which it is manifested,

> in fact hierophanies could not abolish the profane world, *for it is the very manifestation of the sacred that establishes the world*, i.e., transforms a formless, unintelligible and terrifying chaos into a cosmos. . . . In short hierophany is ontophany—the experience of the sacred gives reality, shape, and meaning to the world. ("Notes for a Dialogue," 238f.)

Although the starting point for an understanding of Eliade's sacred is its dialectical opposition to the profane, it becomes apparent that the conclusion is not one of simple opposition but one of complex interdependence. Having pointed out that "anything man has ever handled, felt, come into contact with or loved *can* become a hierophany" (*Patterns*, 10f.), Eliade is quite aware of the difficulty this raises. If anything at all can reveal the sacred, can the sacred/profane dichotomy stand? The answer is affirmative because while all things *can* reveal the sacred, not all things *do*. Not only is there no culture which recognizes all the manifestations of sacrality which have been detected in various times and locations, but also "while a certain class of things may be found fitting vehicles of the sacred, there always remain some things in the class which are not given this honor" (13). Thus there is still a real and meaningful distinction here. The sacred is still *perceived* as distinct from the profane.

The sacred, the significant, is perceived to be manifested *in* the profane, the mere. While the object, symbol, narrative, act, or person which is seen to manifest this surplus of reality, meaning, or significance, is thus itself sacred, it simultaneously, and paradoxically, remains profane. The revelation of the sacred to humanity in our embodied condition *requires* the involvement of the profane. Eliade was most insistent that all such revelations must occur in and through historical time and material occurrence (2f.). Thus despite the fundamental opposition of the sacred and the profane, the one being what the other is not, they are inextricably interconnected, they *are* each other in a very real way. They are radically different modes of being, but they are both modes of being. Eliade's fictional form and style reflect and embody in many ways his understanding of this paradoxical relationship. I will content myself here with the general observation that central to his style is the revelation of the mysterious or fantastic concealed or camouflaged in the quotidian. Eliade has admitted that

> this technique to some extent reflects the dialectics of the sacred: it is characteristic of what I have called "hierophany" that the sacred is thereby both revealed and concealed in the profane. . . . The same dialectic: profane-sacred-profane, explains what I have called "the unrecognizable aspect of miracle." (*Mademoiselle Christina*, 1978 introduction, 6–7, my translation)

Finally the dialectic of the sacred and the profane is the ultimate example of the *coincidentia oppositorum*, the coincidence of opposites, the unity of apparently polar oppositions. The sacred/profane dichotomy is quoted as the religious dichotomy *par excellence* "which, as a matter of fact, signifies a total dichotomy, relating concurrently to cosmos, life, and human society" (*Quest*, 174). This very notion of the coincidence of opposites is one of Eliade's best-loved and most used symbols of the nature of the sacred, the real, and merits independent inspection.

CHAPTER 4

The *Coincidentia Oppositorum*

In his Ph.D. thesis on yoga, translated into French, revised, and published as *Yoga: Essai sur les origines de la mystique Indienne* in 1936, Eliade expounded yoga mainly through two pairs of opposites: magical/mystical and abstract/concrete.[1] However, he did not at that time consider (or at least not publicly) the *coincidence* of opposites to be an important problem. I use the word "problem" advisedly here since Eliade refers to the "problem of the *coincidentia oppositorum*" which "will fascinate me till the end of my life" (*Journal*, IV, 2, a note made in 1979). Evidently he did not consider the *coincidentia* a solution to the mystery of life, but itself a problem to be studied. He again referred to it as a "problem" which still engrosses him in *Autobiography* II (194), written toward the end of his life.

The relationship of apparently polar oppositions obviously concerned Eliade when he was writing *Yoga* and he referred to its conceptual power in a radio talk given on Good Friday of 1935:

> Jesus penetrates into Death and conquers it. The light splits the darkness and scatters it. From this simple confrontation of contraries, the whole greatness of Christianity derives. (*Romanian Roots*, 814)

In the same year as his thesis was published, Eliade wrote "Cosmical Homology and Yoga," an important article and his first published in English. Here he asserts as an extrapolation from his thesis on yoga that the yogin causes Being to coincide with Non–being (202). As I already mentioned it is in this article that Eliade first makes the explicit equation of the "sacred" with the "real" (Being) and

---

1. The polarity "magical/mystical" from the thesis on Yoga is carried on in *Images and Symbols* in the form "magic/religion." Unfortunately, this is hardly any more clear and one must rely heavily on Mac Rickett's interpretation in *Romanian Roots*, 502–4.

the "profane" with the "unreal" (Non–being) (188). It is here also that he first definitively states that the realization of the coincidence of these two apparent opposites is a form of the absolute, a transcendence, an "abolition" of the human condition (203). These insights were incorporated into the later revised text of *Yoga, Immortality, and Freedom* (95–100).

The actual term *coincidentia oppositorum* is not used, as the researches of Mac Ricketts reveal (*Romanian Roots*, 821 n. 54), until an article of 1938, although Eliade was well aware of it, having taught a seminar on Nicholas of Cusa's *De Docta Ignorantia* at the University of Bucharest in 1934–35. In the period 1938–39 he wrote several articles directly on this problem, some of which were published in *Mitul Reintegrarii* and others used in *Patterns in Comparative Religions* and *The Two and the One* (*Autobiography*, II, 82). By the time of the publication of *Patterns* in 1949, the term had assumed major importance. Although Thomas Altizer remarked, and Douglas Allen concurred, that "the *coincidentia oppositorum* is Eliade's favorite symbolism" (*Structure and Creativity*, 221; *Mircea Eliade and the Dialectic of the Sacred*, 17), Eliade's critics and commentators do not have so much to say on this important concept as they do on, say, *homo religiosus*. John Saliba in his book *Homo Religiosus*, affirms that "Eliade is . . . correct in highlighting the concept of *coincidentia oppositorum* and in seeing it as a necessary element in religion. . . . Some of the key concepts in religion unite apparently incompatible ideas" (172.). Saliba refers to Evans–Pritchard, who has agreed that "it is in the nature of the subject [i.e. religion] that there should be ambiguity and paradox" (172, Evans–Pritchard, *Nuer Religion*, 123f.). Yet despite his realization of the importance of the *coincidentia*, Saliba criticizes Eliade for overemphasizing the "withdrawn" (i.e., otiose) nature of God. Given this stress on the complementarity of opposites, it should be emphasized that in Eliade's thought the "transcendence" of the divine being is always complementary to its immanence, as Saliba approvingly quotes John Mbiti as saying (173; *African Religions and Philosophy*, 33).

For Guilford Dudley, Eliade's *coincidentia* is a way in which "mythic language can also reconcile diametrically opposed motifs" and can, for example, "present a God who is simultaneously gentle and terrible in a way that defies rational explanation." This Dudley attributes to Eliade's belief that "mythic language possesses the autonomous power of *coincidentia oppositorum*" (*Religion on Trial*, 150). Altizer considers that the principle of unity behind the sacred rests on a "pretemporal and pre–cosmic Totality" to which the *coincidentia oppositorum* points "in its Hindu and specifically Tantric form" (17). Evidently these critics have recognized the importance of the concept for understanding Eliade's thought, but they have made no great effort to clarify precisely what it is that Eliade means by it. To do this one must turn to a detailed examination of what Eliade himself has to say on the matter.

The earliest prolonged exposition on the *coincidentia oppositorum* occurs in *Patterns*, first published in French in 1949, where Eliade gives credence to

Dudley's analysis by saying that "myth reveals more profoundly than any rational experience ever could, the actual structure of the divinity, which transcends all attributes and reconciles all contraries" (419). The *coincidentia* is here seen as a fundamental "mythic pattern," which "enters into almost all the religious experience of mankind," and is "one of the most primitive ways of expressing the paradox of divine reality" (419). Part of the paradox of divine reality, as we have seen in the chapter on "Hierophany" above, is that the sacred, the really real, is always and necessarily detected in the profane, the conditioned, the unreal. It is paradoxical not only that the profane should have the ability to manifest that which exceeds it in significance and power, but also that the sacred should be limited through its manifestation in the lesser, the quotidian. That is not all, however:

> this conception, in which all contraries are reconciled (or rather transcended), constitutes what is, in fact, the most basic definition of divinity, and shows how utterly different it is from humanity, the *coincidentia oppositorum* becomes nevertheless an archetypal model for certain types of religious men, or for certain of the forms religious experience takes. The *coincidentia oppositorum* or transcending of all attributes can be achieved by man in all sorts of ways. . . . [T]he orgy: for it symbolizes a return to the amorphous and indistinct where all attributes disappear and contraries are merged. . . . The ascetic, the sage, the Indian and Chinese "mystic" tries to wipe out of his experience and consciousness every sort of "extreme," to attain to a state of perfect indifference and neutrality. . . . This transcending of extremes through asceticism and contemplation also results in the "coinciding of opposites"; [the ascetic, sage etc.] remakes within himself and for himself the primeval unity which was before the world was made; a unity which signifies not the chaos that existed before any forms were created but the undifferentiated *being* in which all forms are merged. (419f.)

Eliade cites the further examples of divine androgyny familiar from Greek, Egyptian, and Indian myths and even in some versions of the Adamic myth and also the importance of *maithuna*, the pair, or sexual coupling, to Tantrism, all of whose "real point . . . is to express—in biological terms—the coexistence of contraries." He also refers to a series of rituals which he interprets as "directed towards a *periodic returning* to this original condition which is thought to be the perfect expression of humanity" (421–24). Elsewhere he has referred to the Chinese concept of *yin* and *yang* as an example of the *coincidentia* and to Nagarjuna's *śūnyatāvāda* as being an outstanding original ontological creation in that "one cannot say of *śūnyatā* that it exists or that it does not exist or that it exists and at the same time does not exist." This "carried to the extreme limit the innate tendency of the Indian spirit towards the *coincidentia oppositorum*" (*History of Religious Ideas*, vol. II, 17, 225f.). Eliade also cites the thirteenth century Bonaventure and the fifteenth century Nicholas of Cusa as exemplars of this thought. Toward the end of volume II of *The History of Religious Ideas*, in describing Tibetan Lamaist groups, Eliade baldly states that "as in India, it is above all the various Tantric schools which apply, and transmit in the strictest secrecy, the techniques of meditation and the rituals aiming at the realization of the *coincidentia oppositorum* at all levels of existence" (275).

This is certainly the type of progression which has earned Eliade the opprobrium of his critical commentators. He presents myths widely separated in time and geography and then presents his own interpretation with the same force as the source material, and finally applies the conclusions of his interpretation to describe the primary material. Who is to say that the subjects of his original documentary evidence had any intention of returning to an original perfected expression of humanity? Or that their androgynous myths sought to express in biological terms the coexistence of contraries? Or that there is an innate tendency in "the Indian spirit" toward the *coincidentia*? And if his interpretation should be partial or inaccurate, can he fairly describe Tantric sects as seeking to realize the *coincidentia* if they do not so describe themselves?

However, it should be accepted that, although Eliade's progression from data to interpretation and back to data certainly does not provide us with apodictic logical proof that his interpretation is correct, his evidence does indicate a temporally and geographically widespread phenomenon of the transmission and performance of myths and rituals concerning the unification of a binary pair. It is thus not unreasonable to posit an interpretation of this fact suggesting a human (widespread if not actually universal) fascination with the *coincidentia oppositorum* as somehow representative of the sacrality which Eliade equates with that which is apprehended as the real, the significant, the true. The fact that the *coincidentia* can be detected in such disparate religious systems and in such a variety of forms indicates a lasting human recognition of the reality, significance, and truth of this mythic structure. One of the suggestions which Eliade bases upon this recognition is explicitly revealed in *Images and Symbols*, published in 1952, about three years after *Patterns*. Here Eliade refers to the myth of Narada and Viṣṇu (70ff.), which he takes as indicating "that in the final reckoning *the great cosmic Illusion is a hierophany*" (91). That is to say, this fascination with the *coincidentia oppositorum* develops from an inherent recognition that the profane world in its entirety and in its diversity is itself revelatory of genuine ontology, real being, the sacred. Existence, as it presents itself to us, is itself a coincidence of opposites, it is both sacred and profane, both real and unreal. It is both a concealment and a revelation of the real. This, in its positive form of the profane as inherently embodying the sacred, leads directly and definitively to a concept of general revelation which I believe to be crucial to an understanding of Eliade's thought.

While Eliade was unquestionably challenging the inability of modern thought to provide a meaningful escape from the terror of history, to invest modern life with significance, and to escape the *anomie* of the existentialists, he could still, in perfect keeping with the concept of the *coincidentia oppositorum* as indicative of the nature of the real, recognize that the modern identification of the profane, the material, with the sacred, the truly real, was in fact accurate. Since the *"great cosmic Illusion is a hierophany,"* what is revealed to modern man in his fascination with the material and the empirically manifest is still itself real. What Eliade objected to, I believe, was the arrogance which considered the empirical and/or the rational as the *only* contact with reality; to the evident inability of empiricism to provide meaningful interpretations to those who suffer at history's brutal hands; to the internal inconsistencies of a concomitant historicism; and to the *amnesia* which this total camouflage of the sacred within the profane brings about as regards traditionally transmitted truths. All of which I will return to later.

One such traditionally transmitted truth devalued by empiricism and historicism is, of course, the *coincidentia oppositorum* itself, and one of the traditions which has transmitted it is the Indian, which

> has distinguished *two* aspects of Brahman: *apara* and *para*, "inferior" and "superior," visible and invisible, manifest and nonmanifest. In other words, it is always the mystery of a polarity, all at once a biunity and a rhythmic alteration, that can be deciphered in the different mythological, religious, and philosophical "illustrations": Mitra and Varuna, the visible and invisible aspects of Brahman, Brahman and *Maya*, *purusa* and *prakrti*, and later on Siva and Sakti, or *samsara* and Nirvana.

> But some of these polarities tend to annul themselves in a *coincidentia oppositorum*, in a paradoxical unity-totality. . . . That it is not only a question of metaphysical speculations but also of formulas with the help of which India tried to circumscribe a particular mode of existence, is proved by the fact that *coincidentia oppositorum* is implied in *jivanmukta*, the "liberated in life," who continues to exist in the world even though he has attained final deliverance; or the "awakened one" for whom Nirvana and *samsara* appear to be one and the same thing. . . . Now, however one may conceive the Absolute, it cannot be conceived except as beyond contraries and polarities. . . . The *summum bonum* is situated beyond polarities. (*Quest*, 169)

Although Eliade derived his conception of the *summum bonum* as being "beyond polarities" from ancient and traditional religious data, it was in fact somewhat "ahead of its time." The whole movement of modern thought, or rather *post*modern thought, beyond polarity has been gathering momentum for some time and is particularly evident in the area of literary criticism and linguistic philosophy. It is not thereby simply validated and concluded. As I said, Eliade regarded this matter as a problem which he never satisfactorily resolved. That some polarities "annul themselves in a *coincidentia oppositorum*" is not clearly comprehensible. Did Eliade simply mean that the *opposition* of polarities was annulled in their coincidence? He had seemed to imply earlier that it was the paradoxical nature of the unity-in-opposition which empowered the *coincidentia*; thus surely their opposition is not *annulled*. In what sense are they annulled, then? The answer is perhaps given in *The History of Religious Ideas*, where Eliade refers to

> a conception, widely attested globally, according to which the cosmos and life, and also the function of the gods and the human condition, are governed by the same cyclic rhythm, a rhythm that is constituted of mutually self-implying, alternating, and complementary polarities which periodically resolve themselves into a union-totality of the *coincidentia oppositorum* type.[2]

Thus the opposition of the polarities is not "annulled" as such, but is resolved, falls into an homogenous totality which nonetheless involves the original opposition.

One further observation needs to be made regarding Eliade's understanding of the thought of Nicholas of Cusa. He states that

> in understanding the principle of the *coincidentia oppositorum*, our "ignorance" becomes "learned." But the *coincidentia oppositorum* must not be interpreted as a synthesis obtained through reason, for it cannot be realized on the plane of finitude but only in a conjectural fashion, on the plane of the infinite.

To which he adds the footnote

> Let us note the difference between this conception—i.e., the *coincidentia oppositorum* effected on the infinite plane—and the archaic and traditional formulas relating to the real unification of opposites (e.g., *samsara* and *nirvana*). (*History of Religious Ideas*, vol. III, 211 n. 80)

Eliade clearly detects a difference between Nicholas' doctrine and the "traditional" *coincidentia*. He sees the one conjecturally positing, "on the plane of the infinite" the coincidence in God of *complicatio* and *explicatio*, in other words, that God envelopes all things but at the same time is in all things. In the other, concrete, archaic "formulas" relate, in fact identify, opposites.

In *The Quest* Eliade distinguishes two types of polarities; "(1) the groups of cosmic polarities and (2) those polarities related directly to the human condition" (173). Yet he states that there is a structural solidarity between them and it should

---

2. *The History of Religious Ideas*, vol. III, 267. This should be compared to Eliade's personal experience as alternating between the "nocturnal and diurnal" sides of his life, his fictional and analytic writings.

be pointed out that the sacred/profane dichotomy is subsumed *under the second group*. Thus the difference here is not one of an infinite, eternal as opposed to a finite, temporal dichotomy. My suggestion is that Eliade considered the *coincidentia* of Nicholas of Cusa, regarded as the first *modern* thinker,[3] to be a coincidence on the cosmic level, whereas the archaic forms "related directly to the human condition."

The true *coincidentia oppositorum* consists in the existential unification of utterly opposed poles which, apart from symbolic expression, could not be assimilated to each other. The importance which Eliade attaches to this form of the *coincidentia* is apparent.

> One of the most important discoveries of the human spirit was naively anticipated when, through certain religious symbols, man guessed that the polarities and antinomies could be articulated as a unity. Since then the negative and sinister aspects of the cosmos and the gods have not only found a justification, but have revealed themselves as an integral part of all reality or sacrality. ("Methodological Remarks," 102)

The power of the *coincidentia oppositorum* lies in its equation with the "reconciliation of all contraries," the "transcending of all attributes" noted above. As such it is a concept of enormous existential significance: the archetype of all solutions, the apprehension that all problems contain their own solutions, that profane human existence may be hell, but it is simultaneously heaven.

It should be noted that in common with most, if not all, of Eliade's interpretative categories, the *coincidentia oppositorum* was more than just a scholarly device.

> My spiritual equilibrium—the condition which is indispensable for any creativity—was assured by this oscillation between researches of a scientific nature and literary imagination. Like many others I live alternatively in a diurnal mode of the spirit and in a nocturnal one. I know, of course, that these two categories of spiritual activity are interdependent and express a profound unity. (*Symbolism, the Sacred, and the Arts*, 173)

It is evident from this, and from the whole question of Eliade's "double approach," that the *coincidentia oppositorum* had an experiential basis in Eliade's life. Eliade's journals reveal an ongoing conflict between his desire to write fictional literature and his desire to produce scholarly works of analysis.[4] He seems to have experienced his

---

3. This description was applied to Cusanus by Ernst Cassirer in *The Individual and the Cosmos in Renaissance Philosophy* (10), for many years considered a classic in the field. It was first published in German in 1927 and must have been used by Eliade.

4. As discussed by, for example, Seymour Cain, "Poetry and Truth," in *Imagination and Meaning*, eds. Girardot and Ricketts, 87–103; and Adriana Berger, "Eliade's Double Approach."

life as itself composed of separate, opposed aims and drives which, *in their reconciliation*, gave his life meaning and brought him his most profound insights. This personal experience of the *coincidentia* could sustain considerably more attention than I have given it here.

The *coincidentia oppositorum* may be the area where Eliade makes a real ontological assumption. The final nature of uninterpreted reality (which must, by definition, be sacred for Eliade), is presented as having a nature in which all attributes coalesce, all oppositions are transcended and all differentiations achieve unity. Here is the only point in Eliade's whole structure of thought where the actual nature of existence, rather than the description of human perceptions, is presented as a datum: this is how reality is, which is both indicated by and explanatory of the constant presence of the *coincidentia* in manifest religious phenomena. Such an interpretation in which the nature of an apprehended reality is simultaneously indicated by and explanatory of a phenomenal occurrence, is itself an example of, or at least made possible by, the type of thought which supports the *coincidentia*. The relationship of the undifferentiated unity which is presented as underlying and transcending all material, historical forms, and those very forms, is not a simple one of cause and effect, or of signifier and signified. It is both/and rather than either/or. Still, the logical validity of such a movement from clue to cause then back to the clue with the putative cause as explanation is quite obviously non-existent. If the widespread occurrence of examples of *coincidentia* in the historical religions is indicative of the actual nature of a non-differentiated ontological substrate, then naturally the existence of such a substratum would explain those phenomena. If illness is seen as indicative of demon possession, then, of course, demon possession will appear to be an excellent explanation of illness. The initial acceptance or rejection of such an interpretative stratagem is based on *a priori*, personal, almost aesthetic criteria, and cannot be itself validly proposed as a rational argument. Of course, the utility of such a stratagem is a secondary phenomenon, as is the number of adherents it finds and the uses to which they put it. All these factors can be seen as criteria of evaluation of the validity of the interpretation and thus of the experience which informs it and thus can be used as a form of persuasion.

Homo religiosus, humanity under our religious aspect, can be recognized precisely as humanity insofar as we adhere to a specific interpretative stratagem inspired and informed by particular hierophanies and the symbols which carry forward those hierophanies. It is to a consideration of *homo religiosus* in the works of Mircea Eliade that I now wish to turn.

CHAPTER 5

Homo Religiosus

It is immediately noticeable on studying the term *homo religiosus*[1] in the writings of Mircea Eliade that the infrequency of its use belies the degree of interest it has generated in secondary scholars. Although he was no doubt aware of the term, Eliade does not use it in such important works as *Yoga* and *Patterns in Comparative Religion*, nor did he use it in *Cosmos and History* or *Images and Symbols*. Its earliest thorough application is in *The Sacred and the Profane*, Eliade's major exposition of his dialectical opposition of the sacred and the profane. Here it occurs only some ten times throughout that work, as compared to twenty occurrences of "religious man." This fact alone supports the analysis of Gregory Alles in *The Encyclopedia of Religion*, that Eliade uses *homo religiosus* generally to indicate "religious humanity" and specifically to contrast humanity in its religious aspect from humanity in its non-religious aspects (*Encyclopedia of Religion*, vol. 6, 442). However easy this clarity may be to achieve in retrospect, there has been some confusion along the way. Douglas Allen, in his study of Eliade, stated simply that

> throughout this study, the terms *homo religiosus, premodern man, traditional, archaic,* and *primitive* will be used interchangeably. By *modern* and *nonreligious*, we refer to a characteristic attitude of contemporary Western society. (*Structure and Creativity*, 5)

The characteristic attitude of contemporary society is the determination to be regarded as a purely historical being, to live in a desacralized cosmos, which Eliade expounds in various works (*Rites and Symbols of Initiation*, ix; *Sacred and the*

---

1. According to Joachim Wach, "it was Marett who suggested that we might change the title *homo sapiens* to *homo religiosus*. (Wach, *The Comparative Study of Religion*, 38; R. R. Marrett, *Sacraments of Simple Folks*, 3)

Profane, 100). I agree wholeheartedly with Allen's recognition of this specific usage of "modern," and therefore with his opposition of *homo religiosus* to "modern." His identification of *homo religiosus* with "traditional," "archaic," and "primitive" needs clarification, however. The people of traditional, archaic, or "primitive" societies are featured in Eliade's thought as exemplary illustrations of homo religiosus, but they are not to be exhaustively *identified* as such since *homo religiosus* (humanity in its religious mode) can certainly exist outside of traditional, archaic, or "primitive" societies. As Eliade says,

> the man of traditional societies is admittedly a *homo religiosus*, but his behavior forms part of the general behavior of mankind and hence is of concern to philosophical anthropology, to phenomenology, to psychology. (*Sacred and the Profane*, 15)

Thus "archaic" must be allowed to be *contemporary* on certain occasions. Allen (122) quotes from *The Sacred and the Profane* where Eliade defines and differentiates religious and non-religious humanity in terms of transcendence: "*homo religiosus* always believes that there is an absolute reality, *the sacred*, which transcends this world but manifests in this world, thereby sanctifying it," and "non-religious man refuses transcendence, . . . In other words, *he accepts no model for humanity outside the human condition*" (202ff.). However, the "transcendence" involved is the relatively simple transcendence of actual, determined, conditioned human existence by some exemplary model. This does not imply any independently ontological transcendent entity; any fictional hero can fulfill these requirements.

The most fundamental distinction between religious and non-religious humanity applied by Eliade throughout *The Sacred and the Profane* is actually that of the homogeneity and the heterogeneity of time, a distinction which Allen almost totally ignores. This concept seems to derive, directly or indirectly, from Henri Bergson's analysis of "two possible conceptions of time, the one free from all alloy, the other surreptitiously bringing in the idea of space" (*Time and Free Will*, 100). In this latter, time is "conceived under the form of an unbounded and homogenous medium" (99) and is contrasted to "the heterogenous duration of the ego, without moments external to one another" (108). When the human conciousness

> refrains from separating its present state from its former states . . . it is enough that, in recalling these states, it does not set them alongside its actual state . . . but forms both the past and present states into an organic whole. (100)

Eliade held the latter concept of time to be characteristic of *homo religiosus* and the former characteristic of "modern" or "non-religious" humanity.

The concept of time will be discussed in some detail later. Suffice it to mention for the moment that conceptions of time are highly susceptible to social construction, as even Bergson was aware (94, 98, 99). In emphasising this distinction as fundamental to religious humanity Eliade answers the questions which Allen raises as to the "givenness" of the hierophany or the "creativity" of the believer (181–90) quite positively on the side of creativity.

Barbosa da Silva also makes the equation of *homo religiosus* and archaic man, although in a more qualified form.

> Eliade uses the term "homo religiosus" in at least two major senses. It occurs in Eliade's works in (1) an ideal sense, and (2) a concrete sense. In the sense (1), it designates *archaic man* who is regarded by Eliade as essentially religious and who, in Eliade's view, had the genuine or purest form of experience of the Sacred. In the sense (2), it designates religious individuals who, in different historico-cultural contexts, have actualized their religious capacities and experienced the Sacred. (*Phenomenology*, 196)

In the ideal sense which da Silva detects, *homo religiosus* actually applies to all of humanity. As he realizes, the actual individuals who have "experienced the sacred" are to be found in all "historico-cultural contexts" and thus, even in its ideal sense, *homo religiosus* must be capable of referring to all of humanity, but humanity *qua* religious; the human being in so far as we apprehend and thirst for the real.

John Cave in *Mircea Eliade's Vision for a New Humanism* comes closest to Eliade's meaning;

> Eliade uses the term *homo religiosus* to refer to all humans. It is not meant for only the charismatic individual, such as a mystic, as it does for Schleiermacher, Max Scheler, and also Joachim Wach. For Eliade, *Homo Religiosus* designates a quality of the human condition. The phenomenologist of religion Gerardus van der Leeuw uses it in this way. (92)

Robert Baird assumes *homo religiosus* to be an abstraction: "It is true that Eliade's goal is to understand *homo religiosus*. But *homo religiosus* is not a historical but an archetypal religious man. Historical persons participate in this archetype to varying degrees" (86). Although I agree that this is an archetypal rather than historical category, I am led to ask whether historical persons also participate in the archetype of *Homo sapiens* to "varying degrees?"

Homo religiosus can, perhaps, best be seen as a systematic postulate, dependent on the acceptance of other parts of the system. If it be accepted that the religious person is the person in specific relation to the sacred, and that the sacred is equated with the real, then *homo religiosus* must be seen as humanity insofar as we apprehend the real, and apprehend ourselves as standing in some specific relationship to reality. How then can this be contrasted to some form of "non-religious man?" Is this not so broad as to encompass all of humanity? Certainly "Eliade is hospitable . . . to including atheistic worldviews in the range of phenomena which the historian of religions ought to consider" (Smart, review of *Ordeal by Labyrinth*, 153).

Alles adequately describes Eliade's conception of religious humanity but his description of non-religious humanity is somewhat weaker. That *"homo religiosus* is driven by the desire for being; modern man lives under the dominion of becoming" (*Encyclopedia of Religion*, vol. 6, 442), is too simplistic and uninformative a conclusion. The mode of being of modern humanity is a complex and confusing one in which "the sacred" has become almost completely camouflaged and concealed within and identified with the profane. *Matter*, once the profane *par excellence*, mere, dead material stuff, is now seen as the ultimately real. For example, subatomic physics, the exhaustive study of the nature of the physical world, is often felt to hold the key to human salvation on the scientific level.[2] Alles does recognize that, unlike *homo religiosus*, modern man thus experiences no discontinuity between the sacred and the profane. Finally, "the break between the two cannot be complete. . . . Determined by history, modern man is thus determined by his unrenouncable precursor, *homo religiosus*" (*Encyclopedia of Religion*, vol. 6, 442).

This diffusion of the concept of *homo religiosus* until it is so general as to seek to involve the entire human race is quite deliberate. Only those people who specifically and deliberately insist on their own determination in time by history, are temporarily allowed to escape this classification, and they too are eventually subsumed by the logical argument here given concise form by Alles, and by the acknowledgment that their insistence is itself religious in structure, still claiming access to the ultimately real, but equating that real with precisely that which was formerly regarded as profane—and therefore unreal—material phenomena.

> Nonreligious man *in the pure state* is a comparatively rare phenomenon, even in the most desacralized of societies. The majority of the "irreligious" still behave religiously, even though they are not aware of the fact. (*Sacred and the Profane*, 204)

In "Homo Faber and Homo Religiosus," an article published in 1985, only a year before his death, Eliade made this identification of religious and "nonreligious" humanity in somewhat clearer terms. His analysis involves rock music from Bob Dylan to Blue Oyster Cult, films, science fiction, Newton's involvement in alchemy, and Raymond Ruyer's book on *The Princeton Gnosis*. He concludes that

> in the last analysis, we discover that the latest activities and conclusions of scientists and technologists—the direct descendants of *homo faber*— reactualize, on different levels and perspectives, the same fears, hopes and convictions that have dominated *homo religiosus* from the very beginning. ("Homo Faber and Homo Religiosus," 11)

---

2. On this "confusion of the planes" of science and salvation, see Mary Midgeley's *Science and Salvation*, and Eliade's "Homo Faber and Homo Religiosus."

It is particularly the apocalyptic trend exhibited by these subjects which Eliade takes to be parallel to religious conviction. This takes two forms, the pessimistic—nuclear holocaust, environmental or genetic exhaustion—and the optimistic—technological or political conquest of all human problems.

> Of course, [he continues] the representatives of these two opposite trends are not aware of the religious implications of their despair or their hopes. What is significant is that all of them relate the inevitability and the immanence of our world's end to the fantastic realizations of human workmanship. (5)

That is to say, it is the specific restriction of the termination of history to human agency which distinguishes these moderns from traditional *homo religiosus*. And it is the artificial restriction of humanity to the historical factors that condition our nature which generates the illusion of a discontinuity from traditionally religious humanity.

> Everyone agrees that a spiritual fact, being a *human* fact, is necessarily conditioned by everything that works together to make a man, from his anatomy and physiology to language itself. In other words, a spiritual fact presupposes the whole human being—that is, the social man, the economic man, and so forth. But all these conditioning factors do not, of themselves, add up to the life of the spirit. (*Images and Symbols*, 32)

As a historian of religions, Eliade has thus made a move to bring all of humanity within the purview of his methodical perspective, just as, for example, psychologists who began with the specific study of mentally ill patients expanded their perspective to all of humanity. It can be argued that as long as some people are allowed to avoid classification within an understanding of human religiousness then that understanding will never be complete. Just as, if certain (especially self-identified) people were allowed to be independent of the findings of psychology or sociology, then psychology and sociology could never have achieved coherence as academic disciplines. If it be suggested to, say, sociologists, that a certain group of people simply are *not involved* in sociological realities, their scorn would be guaranteed. However, scholars of religion are all too willing to concede that certain people are not involved in religious realities, usually because they have a prior self-perception as either "religious" or "non-religious." From this predisposed perspective the differences between "religious" and "non-religious" appear all too obvious and essential. They could, however, be accidental, secondary, and partisan. The expansion of the classification of *homo religiosus* to cover all of humanity might appear quite unwarranted. Yet it can equally be argued that the contemporary insistence that a certain group of people, self-styled non-religious people, simply steps out of an otherwise ubiquitous human condition is equally unwarranted. Other scholars, notably Wilhelm Dupré in his *Religion in Primitive Cultures*, have also argued for the inevitability of human religiosity. It does seem possible that Eliade was not aware of the radical importance for the academic study of religion of this conclusion, or perhaps he was not willing to take the considerable risk of making such a claim openly. However, it is apparent throughout *The Sacred and the Profane* that almost every time he mentions "non-religious" man Eliade immediately proceeds to indicate the superficiality of the concept (24, 186, 201–13).

Of course, this is not to say that the distinction religious/non-religious is utterly devoid of meaning. It is precisely the meaning of that distinction which Eliade strives to clarify throughout *The Sacred and the Profane*. The most fundamental distinction is that of time and history: religious man "refuses to live solely in what, in modern terms, is called the historical present" (*Sacred and the Profane*, 70). Humanity in its specifically religious aspect, rather, lives in a time which is

> neither homogeneous nor continuous. On the one hand there are intervals of a sacred time, the time of festivals (by far the greater part of which are periodical); on the other there is profane time, ordinary temporal duration, in which acts without religious meaning have their setting. . . . This attitude in regard to time suffices to distinguish religious from non-religious man.[3]

Thus the distinction between religious and non-religious, radically blurred in other ways, is re-established on a meaningful level. Yet, as I hope to make plain, this is not finally a distinction *between* religious and non-religious humanity, rather, since it is essentially a religious distinction, it is a distinction *among* religious humanity. In the last analysis, modern humanity's self-imposed restriction to and final identification with historical time is itself an identification with the real. As such it is religious and therefore cannot constitute a distinctive characteristic of "non-religious" humanity.

---

3. 68, 70. Once again it is apparent that in order to fully understand one aspect of Eliade's thought, it is necessary to consider another. Obviously, if this is the lynchpin of the distinction of religious from non-religious humanity, then in order to understand *homo religiosus* we must also consider Eliade's conception of time.

CHAPTER 6

Symbols and Symbolism

One element of the study of religion which particularly supports and is clarified by the preceding analysis of *homo religiosus* as ubiquitous is that of symbol. Although symbols are themselves ubiquitous in the human world and play a role even in the life of the most secular of people, they are often interpreted as having some specifically religious connotations. This tension between "religious" and "secular" symbolism has, I would contend, contributed significantly to the difficulty and complexity of the debate over the nature of symbolism. It is specifically "religious" symbolism which I will discuss here, rather than the concept of representation in general, although given the proposed ubiquity of religious thought I realize that such a discontinuity cannot be finally justified.

In order to get a clear idea as to the etymology and history of the word "symbol" and of the history of the study of symbolism, one would be well advised to consult the entry on "Symbolism" in the *Encyclopedia of Religion*, vol. 14, 198–208, by James W. Heisig. It is worth mentioning, however, that as a probable influence on Eliade Goethe is notable by his absence from this entry.[1] René Welleck has asserted that the concept of symbol as we know it derives from the German Romantics.[2] The Belgian-American scholar, Gustaaf Van Cromphout, cites Gadamer, Todorov, and Cassirer among those who have attributed the modern

---

1. Although Eliade does not make many references to Goethe in his scholarly work, the influence of the German author is clearly revealed in the *Journals*. A succinct statement of that influence is made by Norman Girardot in the introduction to *Imagination and Meaning* (eds. Girardot and Ricketts, 3–6). An important reference to Goethe as an exemplary figure is made in *Myths, Dreams and Mysteries*, 33. See also Ricketts, *Romanian Roots*, 19, 101, 170, 640f., 1211f. J. Z. Smith suggests that Goethe's influence on Eliade is apparent, for example, in the latter's concept of morphology, *Map is not Territory*, 225.

2. "Coleridge [for example] picked it up from Goethe, the Schlegels, and Schelling." *Discriminations: Further Concepts in Criticism*, 139.

concept of symbolism to Goethe. Goethe's idea of the symbol was that it was not only representative, but was also a "living, instantaneous (*lebendig-augenblickliche*) revelation of the inscrutable" (69). This is certainly similar to Eliade's conception of the symbol as hierophany and, given his lifelong dedication to Goethe, was doubtless influential in shaping that conception.

Despite this lacuna it is significant that Heisig describes Novalis (Freidrich von Hardenberg, 1772–1801, a younger contemporary of Goethe, 1749–1832) as one who

> defended the primacy of imagination and poetry as means to produce the symbolism of a higher reality, and drew special attention to the "magical" power of words. (199)

In a comment made in 1969 Eliade said of Novalis that he

> rediscovered "the dialectic of the sacred," to wit, that nature, such as it shows itself to us, does not represent absolute reality but is only a cipher. His extraordinary intuition: that it is not necessary to die, to become "spirit," in order to be able to communicate with higher worlds, and that, beginning here below, one can know beatific experience. Someday someone must point out how ancient, even archaic, were the ideas of Novalis: one must also try to explain due to what circumstances these ideas were so long forgotten or voluntarily ignored. (*No Souvenirs*, 326)

This not only indicates the Romantic heritage of Eliade's thought but also gives an insight into the way in which he conceived of the function of symbols.

It is not my intention in this section to enter into a debate about symbolism and Romanticism, or to attempt to disclose Eliade's precise sources (an almost impossible task given the vast scope of his reading). Rather I hope to give a clear exposition of Eliade's conception of the symbol. Although some serious objections have been raised against Eliade's theory of symbolism, I will inspect these later in a section specifically devoted to such objections.

As was remarked earlier, there is an evident connection between Eliade's conception of symbol and that of hierophany. They are both phenomena of the empirical world which are held to communicate or reveal something other than their own physical being. Francisco Demetrio y Radaza, S.J., in his work on religious symbols and the Georgics, gives an extensive (and broadly favorable) critique of Eliade in whose thought he recognizes three dialectics at work: the dialectic of the sacred, the dialectic of hierophany, and the dialectic of symbol. Evidently Demetrio y Radaza detects here a progressive descent of the sacred into the profane world through its own *dialectical opposition* to profane reality, through its *revelation* in hierophany, and through its *representation* in symbol. However, he is not unaware of the difficulties of such an hierarchical organization, since "some symbols are themselves hierophanies" (26).

The actual relationship of hierophany and symbol does present some difficulty to reaching an understanding of Eliade's work. In *Patterns in Comparative Religion*, Eliade says, "the symbol is carrying further the dialectic of the hierophany," and "the majority of hierophanies are capable of becoming symbols" (446). This implies that an hierophany is not *automatically* a symbol. The relationship of these three dialectics may be simply one of increasing dilution of the sacred in the profane since Eliade contends that

> the term "symbol" ought to be reserved for the symbols which either carry a hierophany further or themselves constitute a "revelation." (448)

If this reservation be adhered to, while all hierophanies are not symbols, all symbols are hierophanies or at least "carry forward" the hierophanic revelation of the real. However, a certain *dependence* of the hierophany on the symbol seems to be implied by Eliade's statements that "the symbolism of the moon makes clear the actual structure of lunar hierophanies." And that "I have tried . . . to interpret a given hierophany in the light of its proper symbolism" (449). As he later states,

> a symbolism does not depend on being understood. . . . [Symbolic meanings] make up a symbolic system which in a sense pre–existed them all. We are therefore . . . justified in speaking of a "logic of symbols," of a logic borne out not only by magico–religious symbolism, but also in the symbolism expressed in the subconscious and transconscious activity of man. (450)

Whereas the symbol or "symbolism" (which is used in such a way as to indicate an interrelated "system" of symbols) does not depend on understanding, the hierophany, as we have seen, *is* dependent on recognition to be constituted as a hierophany (24; see above, p. 19f.). A closer look at Eliade's understanding of symbol is required before the systematic implications of this differentiation will become clear.

The best-known source for Eliade's analysis of symbol is his contribution to the volume of 1959 edited with Joseph Kitagawa, *The History of Religions: Essays in Methodology*. This article was reprinted in Eliade's own work *The Two and the One* in 1962. I have drawn from both editions in reproducing this analysis and, although the discrepancies between the two are slight, I have placed alternative renderings from the later publication in [square] brackets, and given the page numbering for both.

> 1. Religious symbols are capable of revealing a modality of the real or a structure of the world that is not evident on the level [plane] of immediate experience. . . . a modality of the real which is inaccessible to human experience.

The example Eliade gives is that of water,

which is capable of expressing the pre–formal, the virtual [potential], and the chaotic. This is not a matter of rational knowledge [cognition]; rather does the living [active] consciousness grasp reality through the symbol, anterior to reflection.

2. *Symbols are always religious* because they point to something *real* or to a *structure of the world* [*World–pattern*].

3. An essential characteristic of religious symbolism is its *multivalence*, its ability to express simultaneously a number of meanings whose continuity is not evident on the plane of immediate experience.

The multitude of meanings thus disclosed are

structurally coherent, although that coherence is neither constituted nor appreciated by a rational process or act of reason. It is disclosed by another order of knowledge [cognition].

4. The symbol is thus able to reveal a perspective in which heterogenous realities are susceptible of articulation into a whole [diverse realities can be fitted together], or even of integration into a "system." In other words the religious symbol allows man to discover a certain unity of the World and, at the same time, to disclose to himself his proper destiny as an integrating [integral] part of the World. . . . Owing to the symbolism of the moon, the world no longer appears as an arbitrary assemblage of heterogenous and divergent realities.

This is but one example, which integrates lunar rhythms, temporal becoming, plant growth, the female principle, death and resurrection. Symbols also have

5. a capacity for expressing paradoxical situations, or certain structures of ultimate reality, otherwise quite inexpressible.

Lastly,

6. a symbol always aims at a *reality or a situation in which human existence is engaged* [concerning human existence]. Symbols have a necessary existential dimension and existential value. (98–101/201–5)

These six points, although quite clearly stated, are evidently not alone sufficient to clarify Eliade's theory. An inspection of his earlier work, *Images and Symbols: Studies in Religious Symbolism* (1952) casts a great deal of light upon the more difficult implications of his thought.

The capacity of the symbol to reveal something not evident to immediate experience (#1 above) is connected with the creative processes of human thought.

Symbols cannot be reflections of cosmic rhythms *as natural phenomena*, for a symbol always reveals something more than the aspect of cosmic life it is thought to represent. The solar symbolisms and myths, for example, reveal to one also a "nocturnal," "evil" and "funerary" aspect of the sun, something that is not at first evident in the solar phenomenon as such. (*Images and Symbols*, 177)

He goes on to say that since this side is not perceived in the phenomenon but is "constitutive in" the symbolism it is proven that the symbolism is a "creation of the psyche." The coincidence of opposites (#5), likewise, is not *given* anywhere in the cosmos, it is not accessible to immediate experience, but it is expressed by symbols, and *simply* expressed. It is this way, as an expression of the creative imagination, that the symbol expresses an otherwise non-sensory modality of the real.

To "have imagination" is to enjoy a richness of interior life, an uninterrupted and spontaneous flow of images. But spontaneity does not mean arbitrary invention. Etymologically, "imagination" is related to both *imago*—a representation or imitation—and *imitor*, to imitate or reproduce. . . . The imagination *imitates* the exemplary models—the Images—reproduces, reactualizes and repeats them without end. To have imagination is to be able to see the world in its totality, for the power and the mission of the Images is to *show* all that remains refractory to the concept. (20)

In this same connection, the ability of the symbol system to express a structural solidarity of meaning (#4) is directly linked with its ability to express something not immediate to perception.

One of the principal functions of the myth is to unify planes of reality which, to immediate consciousness and even to reflection, seem to be multiple and heterogenous. (99)

In certain cases it is precisely that solidarity of meaning, that potential homologization,[3] which was not itself previously perceptible, which, through symbolism, becomes susceptible to the human imagination. The solidarity between the lunar rhythms, temporal becoming, the female principle, and human mortality, for example, is not immediately accessible to human experience. But once grasped, once revealed by lunar symbolism, it then becomes an accessible and communicable reality.

---

3. The word "homology" has been previously encountered in the title of Eliade's first article to be published in English, "Cosmical Homology and Yoga" and largely overlooked. It has the sense of being "of the same rational structure." Thus, "homologization" or "to homologize" will have the sense of assimilation or integration, or to recognize as having similar logical structure.

The implication that such coherent "systems" are "creations of the psyche" or the imagination in no way lessens their potential impact on human life. The valorization of the material and the independently extant, and the accompanying devalorization of the abstract and dependent (i.e., the creations of the human imagination, or *poesis*), is a specific and religious perspective of modern humanity, intimately instrumental in what Eliade calls the concealment or camouflage of the sacred in the profane. I will discuss this later at some length.

Once one begins to combine the various points of Eliade's analysis in various ways, as I have combined points 1, 4, and 5 above, certain deeper implications begin to appear. For example, point 2 states that symbols are religious because they "always point to something real or to a structure of the world," and point 6 that "a symbol always aims at a *reality or a situation in which human existence is engaged.*" In an article of 1968 Eliade has said,

> contrary to what may be called "cosmic symbols"—stars, waters, the seasons, vegetation, etc.—which reveal both the structures of the universe and the human mode of being in the world, the symbolism of tools and weapons discloses specific existential situations. ("Notes on the Symbolism of the Arrow," 465)

Since (#2) symbols always point to something real or to a structure of the world, and since (#6) symbols always aim at a real existential situation, then the something real at which they always aim *must be* an existential situation. Cosmic symbols indicate both (existential situation and structure of universe); tool symbols (for example) indicate only, but necessarily, an aspect or element of the human existential situation. Thus it would seem that the reality of the human existential situation is finally indispensable to symbolism. It is the very *reality* of the situational element thus revealed which sacralizes a particular symbol. The Christian crucifix, for example, can be seen as indicative of the immediate helplessness of the human existential situation, pinned down by the brutal realities of physical existence, but also of the hopefulness of our situation—redeemed by the ultimate sacrifice, the involvement of the deity itself—and thus capable of escaping the doom determined by pure physicality, of "escaping from history." (And here the *cosmic* function of the cross as cosmic tree, ensuring the connection of earth and heaven, of profane and sacred, of conditioned and free, comes into play.) However, the reality and therefore the sacrality of this symbolic significance is determined by the individual reaction to the cross as *hierophany*. Should this apprehension of the human condition strike one as revelatory of the real, then the symbolism of the cross will be self-evident. However, to a mind constrained to the physical determinatives of the human condition; a mind which does not perceive that condition as essentially hopeful, connected with sacred realities which surpass it, and possessed of real freedom, the symbolic reference of the crucifix is lost, and with it its sacrality.

However, it must also be considered that in an article first published in 1960, Eliade states that the symbol translates a human situation into cosmological terms; and reciprocally, more precisely, it discloses the interdependence between the structures of human existence and cosmic structures. (*Symbolism, the Sacred, and the Arts*, 13)

So cosmic structures are not finally dispensable to symbolism, nor is the human situation alone finally sufficient to it. Rather it is specifically the relationship of the two which is at issue here. In fact, in order to be a real existential situation of humanity a given structure must also be a structure of the world or cosmic structure. It is a further function of the symbol that it unifies the human and the cosmic levels of reality.

Symbolic thought makes it possible for man to move freely from one level of reality to another. Indeed, "to move freely" is an understatement: symbols, as we have seen, identify, assimilate, and unify diverse levels and realities that are to all appearances incompatible. (*Patterns*, 455)

And he concludes *Patterns in Comparative Religion* with the observation that

thanks chiefly to his symbols, the real existence of primitive man was not the broken and alienated existence lived by civilized man today. (456)

This has constituted something of a difficulty in the appreciation of Eliade's thought. Not only does it appear to be a polemical valorization of the archaic over the modern, it also appears to be finally incoherent in the light of Eliade's repeated claims that

symbols never disappear from the *reality* of the psyche. The aspect of them may change, but their function remains the same; one has only to look behind their latest masks. (*Images and Symbols*, 16)

Or again that

symbols and myths come from such depths: they are part and parcel of the human being, and it is impossible that they should not be found again in any and every existential situation of man in the Cosmos. (25)

If this is indeed the case, then how can modern humanity suffer so much from the "broken and alienated existence" caused by the *lack* of symbols?

I believe that the only possible coherent explanation of this difficulty lies with Eliade's repeated emphasis on the radical concealment of the sacred within the profane in the modern mentality. For the modern, empirical reality and historical actuality have become exhaustive of the real, the sacred. As remarked above, this involves a simultaneous devalorization of the abstract and the imaginary. However,

although it is true that man is always found "in situation," his situation is not, for all that, always a historical one in the sense of being conditioned solely by the contemporaneous historical moment. The man in his totality is aware of other situations over and above his historical condition; for example, he knows the state of dreaming, or of the waking dream, or of melancholy, or of detachment, or of aesthetic bliss, or of escape, etc.—and none of these states is historical, although they are as authentic and as important for human existence as man's historical existence is. (33)

The alienation in the modern mind is not directly caused by a *lack* of symbolic material, but by an inability to perceive the authentic *reality* of that material, to perceive it as hierophany and thus actually to appreciate it as symbolic. That is to say, in tending to restrict our existence to the plane of the spatio-temporal, modern humanity has lost the ability to apprehend the meanings of other planes of existence as true expressions of our existential situation.

It can be suggested that symbolism has become opaque to us because we have refused, or become unable, to make the fundamental prerational assumptions which empower it as a *language*. It is, finally, as a sort of preverbal language that Eliade conceives of symbolism:

the symbol reveals a pre–systematic ontology to us, which is to say an expression of thought from a period when conceptual vocabularies had not yet been constituted. To give only one example, the terms designated "becoming" appear fairly late in history, and only in some languages of high culture: Sanskrit, Greek, Chinese. But the symbolism of "becoming," the images and the myths which place it in motion are already evidenced in the archaic strata of culture. All the images of the spiral, of weaving, of the emergence of light from shadow, of the phases of the moon, of the wave, etc. . . . [are] symbols and myths of "becoming." (*Symbolism, the Sacred, and the Arts*, 3f.)

Thus symbols are a type of language capable of expressing, to those who use that language, complex relationships and concealed truths which have not received verbal expression.

I must point out that Eliade does not directly use these words. However, that he constantly emphasizes the coherent nature of symbols is consistent with its status as a language.

Certain groups of symbols, at least, prove to be coherent, logically connected with one another; in a word, they can be systematically formulated, translated into rational terms. (*Images and Symbols*, 37)

Furthermore, speaking of Freud (whose originality and contribution to the thought of the twentieth century Eliade respects, despite his frequent statements concerning the scientific inadequacy of *Totem and Taboo*), Eliade states that

Freud substantiated the gnoseological values of the products of fantasy, which, until then, were considered meaningless or opaque. Once the expressions of the Unconscious became articulated in a meaning–system comparable to a non–verbal language, the immense number of imaginary universes reflected in literary creations disclosed a deeper, and secret significance. (*Occultism, Witchcraft and Cultural Fashions*, 54)

Certainly the imaginary universes of symbolism, since they can in fact be reflected by quotidian experiences such as "any immersion in darkness, any irruption of light . . . any experience of mountaineering, flying, swimming underwater, or any long journey," etc. (43f.) are precisely those imaginary universes reflected in literary creations and so are themselves "comparable to a non–verbal language."

It is in terms of linguistic analysis that I would finally like to suggest an applicable differentiation between the concepts of symbol and hierophany. Part of the difficulty, as we saw above, is that Eliade finally wants to identify hierophany and symbol. The effective distinction is between symbol (with which the hierophany *can* be equated) and symbol*ism* (with which it cannot). This is, I think, best seen as the distinction between *parole* and *langue* made by Saussure in his *Course in General Linguistics*.[4] The hierophany and the symbol are words— singular but not self-contained units of meaning—in the language of symbolism.

Eliade states that for symbolic thought "the Universe is not closed, no object is isolated in its own existentialness; everything holds together in a closed system of correspondences and assimilations" (*The Sacred, Symbolism, and the Arts*, 6). The applicability of the image of language, in which all the linguistic elements similarly hold together, to a universe conceived in this way is self–evident. Meaning is thus not the "fundamental" to which all possible significations are reduced, but is itself profoundly symbolic of the relations of elements in a coherent existential reality.

The hierophany, then, is the specific spatio–temporal phenomenon which effectively mediates an otherwise imperceptible modality of the real. If it is not recognized as such, then an hierophany has not occurred. However, the *potential* is still present if the language of symbolism constitutes that phenomenon as symbolic. The best example which occurs to me, although perhaps rather trite and simplistic, is that of a joke. A joke remains a joke, at least *in potentia*, even if the audience does not "get" it. And a symbol remains a symbol, even if an hierophany has not occurred.

The hierophany is the paradoxically limited revelation of the real in history, the symbol is the (possibly non–verbal) linguistic element in an extended and coherent system of such elements (symbolism) which makes such a revelation comprehensible, which dictates its meaning.

---

4. I am aware of Gregory Alles' criticism that "the preoccupation with meaning—with parole and with langue—projects upon all religions the goal for which so many Western theologians, philosophers, scholars, and litterateurs have taught us to yearn . . . : the recovery of meaning." "Wach, Eliade and the Critique from Totality." I respond to it below.

The notion of the coherence of symbolic structures is fundamental to Eliade's interpretations. As well as the system of lunar symbolism and all it entails, he expounds the coherence of the symbolisms of the center; of time and eternity; of shells; of knots; of shadows; of ascension and flight; of death; light; bodily fluids; of the cosmos/city/temple/dwelling/body; and of water and the flood (which is assimilated to lunar symbolism).

At one point Eliade says that,

> in the present state of our knowledge, it is difficult to specify whether their uniformity proceeds from imitation—from "historic" borrowings, in the sense given to this term by the historico–cultural school—or whether it is to be explained by the fact that they all follow *from the very situation of man in the world*—so that they are all variants of one and the same archetype realizing itself on many planes and in different cultural areas. (*Images and Symbols*, 118)

This passage is of considerable significance. First, it calls into question the contention that Eliade insists on the universality of all symbols. In her article on the gnostic symbolism of the trees of life and death, for example, Ingvild Gilhus remarks on two extremes in the analysis of myth in the history of religion. The first insists on the examination of a symbol "as a part of one cultural system of symbols." The second "as a part of a universal system of symbols."

> In the first case, the religious symbol is seen as meaningful only in relation to other symbols in the cultural system. In the second case, the meaning of the symbol is clarified only by comparison with similar symbols in a universal system of symbols. The second approach is especially advocated by Mircea Eliade. (346)

Obviously Eliade is aware of *both* possibilities in his treatment of symbolism and does not restrict his examination to only a single universal system, although his contention that the symbol can develop from the actual physical situation of humanity does allow for the possibility of symbolism as a human universal. Furthermore, although Eliade argues for the universality of certain symbols, one of which is that of the experience of light whose existential basis is only too evident (light is a symbol because human beings can see). He none the less accepts that

> certainly, we do not find universally a well–articulated theology or metaphysics of the divine light, comparable, for instance, with the Indian, Iranian, or Gnostic systems. But one cannot doubt the "experiential" character of the majority of mythologies, theologies and gnoses based on the equivalence: light–divinity–spirit–life. (*Occultism*, 95)

Secondly, Eliade can be seen to connect the concept of symbol to that of archetype and gives us a conception of "archetype" reminiscent of the passage from

The History of Religious Ideas (vol. I, 3), which describes the paradigmatic nature of the *orientatio* in three dimensions as based on the human upright, bipedal form. It is based solidly in the actual embodied nature of the human existential condition and *not* on any conceptual *a priori* or uncritical assumption. This clarifies his continuing contention in *Images and Symbols* that it is the

> tendency of every "historical form" to approximate as nearly as possible to its archetype, even when it has been realized at a secondary or insignificant level: this can be verified everywhere in the religious history of humanity. Any local goddess tends to become the Great Goddess; any village anywhere *is* the "Center of the World," and any wizard whatever pretends, at the height of his ritual, to be the Universal Sovereign. It is this same tendency towards the archetype, towards the restoration of the *perfect form*—of which any myth or rite or divinity is only a variant, and often a rather pale one—that makes the history of religions possible. Without this, magico–religious experience would be continually creating transitory or evanescent forms of gods, myths, dogmas, etc.; and the student would be faced by a proliferation of ever new types impossible to set in order. But when once it is "realized"— "historicized"—the religious form tends to disengage itself from its conditions in time and space and to become universal, to return to the archetype. (*Images and Symbols*, 120f.)

There is an inherent twofold justification here: (1) the *archetype*, which can be seen as the existential basis of each symbol, is based in the "*very situation of man in the world*" and is thus a genuine universal, although every communicable form of that situation is "historicized" or socially conditioned; (2) unless some such archetype be assumed for the purposes of classification, the study of religion, indeed any study, falls foul of what Ibn al-Arabi called the "sea of names" and cannot hope to deal with the phenomenal proliferation of specifics.

Despite the morphological connection of symbols to an archetypal event or situation of humanity upon which he wants to insist, Eliade accepts that

> this is not to say that . . . one cannot distinguish certain groups that are *historically interconnected*, or that we have no right to regard them as dependent upon one another, or as derived from a common source. (121)

He recognizes full well that certain symbols

> are not, as such, spontaneous discoveries of archaic man, but creations of a well-defined cultural complex, elaborated and carried on in certain human societies: such creations have been diffused very far from their original home and have been assimilated by peoples who would not otherwise have known them. (34)

However, this category is by no means exhaustive of the stock of symbols. To give but one example:

> the symbolism of climbing up stairs recurs often enough in psychoanalytic literature, an indication that it belongs to the archaic content of the human psyche and is not a "historical" creation, not an innovation dating from a certain historical moment (say, from ancient Egypt or Vedic India, etc.). (50)

Evidently, if Eliade considers the symbolism of ascending a staircase to be sufficiently widespread and automatically recurrent to be basically autonomous of historically conditioned sources, he must consider the vast bulk of symbols to be independent of this historical "diffusionist" origin. Certainly the references he makes to the *kulturkreis* school associated with Schmidt and Koppers are often dismissive, although he otherwise respects their scholarship (121 n. 74; *Patterns*, 38; *Australian Religion*, 17, 19f.).

Yet the symbol is not simply a reflection of the natural world as we saw in connection with cosmic rhythms; symbols are also reflective of human creativity and imagination. As he says in *Patterns* on the symbolism of the pearl,

> what constitutes the manifold significance of the pearl is primarily the framework of symbolism surrounding it. . . . The "origins" of the symbolism of the pearl, then, were not empirical but theoretical. (*Patterns*, 440)

In this instance Eliade clearly puts theory before fact in the development of a symbol, once again it is the creative human agency which is emphasized rather than any external power, even the existential situation.

There is a confusing shift in emphasis between the statement from *Patterns* immediately above stressing the theoretical origins, and the statements from *Images and Symbols* stressing the existential origins of symbol. Eliade's point seems to be that our power to theorize, "what man thought of his specific mode of being in the world" ("Notes on the Symbolism of the Arrow," 474), is itself an immeasurably significant element of our existential situation, and one which is both conditioned and yet free (through the power of creative imagination). This is itself symbolic, assimilable to all the symbolism of the *coincidentia oppositorum* discussed above. It is possibly this symbolic aspect of human nature which prompted Eliade to suggest that

> by envisioning the study of man not only inasmuch as he is a historic being, but also as a living symbol, the history of religions could become a *metapsychoanalysis*. (*Images and Symbols*, 35)

Certainly, when symbolism is seen as a pre-reflective system of communication of the most complex and the truest elements of the human existential situation, the notion of the study of the history of religions as a "metapsychoanalysis" makes more sense. It should be recalled that, as Kim pointed out, Rudolf Otto

> insists that the cognition or rather the re–cognition of the Holy cannot be derived from "experience" or "history." As he argues throughout the book, the Holy as an *a priori* category must be assumed in order for anything religious to appear "in history" and for us to recognize it as such. ("Hierophany and History" 339; Otto, *The Idea of the Holy*, 175)

It is Eliade's contrary contention that the sacred imposes itself on us in the form of fundamental hierophanies which are apprehensions of existential situations and thereafter it is the creatively constructed symbolic systems which continue the revelation of the real to what extent they can. The innate human desire which he detects to live in proximity and constant contact with the real produces symbolisms which extend the hierophanies throughout otherwise profane human existence. Paradoxically this has eventually led to a complete identification of the profane with the sacred and a concomitant difficulty in recognizing the real even in the primordial hierophanies. This, I hope, has gradually become clear as the primary characteristic of modern secular humanity.

The study of religions, through the study of symbol and myth, can then be seen as the total analysis (the "total hermeneutics") of the creative spirit ("creative hermeneutics") of humanity in our embodied existential situation in the world.

CHAPTER 7

Myths and Mythology

It is not only in the writings of Mircea Eliade that myth appears one of the most tangled of concepts. In the broader arena of academic study, involving the classics, comparative mythology, regional studies, literary criticism, and the study of religion, the situation is no better. To paraphrase a notorious quip on the phenomenology of religion, there are as many interpretations of myth as there are students of myth. Eliade himself said,

> it is not without fear and trembling that a historian of religion approaches the problem of myth. This is not only because of that preliminary embarrassing question: what is intended by myth? It is also because the answers given depend for the most part on the documents selected. (*Quest*, 72)

My purpose is not to validate Eliade's understanding of myth in competition with others—that would be a major work in its own right—but to clarify *what Eliade's understanding was*, and how it has been misunderstood. The "innumerable definitions of myth" which preceded Eliade, he claims, "have one thing in common: they are based on the analysis of Greek mythology." This may be less true today, but in 1966 when Eliade first delivered the lecture which later became this chapter of *The Quest* it was unquestionably the case. In this light I have elected to explicate Eliade's understanding of myth and the mythic through a specific consideration of the work of G. S. Kirk, a well-known classicist and contemporary of Eliade's. Kirk provides not only a broad-based analysis of then current theoretical approaches to myth but also a specific critique of the unique elements of Eliade's endeavors in this area.

Myth has been generally under attack at least since Xenophanes (565–470 B.C.E.) criticized the activities of the gods as related by the Homeric tradition and Hesiod (*Myth and Reality*, 148). More recently, Ivan Strenski has argued that myth is, in fact, non-existent and that the only real products of the academic "myth factory" are theories and "applied writings" about this otherwise non-existent category (*Four Theories of Myth*, 2). Somewhat more conservatively but in much the same vein, Kirk said of books about myth that "if they add anything at all in the way of interpretation it tends to be arbitrary and intuitive—in other words, valueless" (*The Nature of Greek Myths*, 13). This is the sort of charge frequently levelled against Eliade: that, like Frazer and other "armchair anthropologists,"[1] he merely adduces examples to support his original intuitive insight. The fact is that examples are so many and various that support can be found for almost any number of conflicting insights. However, Kirk's statement is typical of those who reject the intuitive as worthless, immediately identifying intuition with the arbitrary, and I believe this attitude to be instrumental in the continuing inability to appreciate fully both Eliade's assessment and myth itself.

Intuition can be seen as the invaluable basis of all research—a combination of insight and intention, based on personal experience, which provides both direction and meaning to our inquiries. Alone and unsupported, one person's intuition has no more weight or sway than any other opinion, but the conclusion that intuition per se is valueless is not entailed. Even in the hard sciences, intuition (as guesswork or hunches) is seen to be a necessary part of the whole process of setting up a program of research and experimentation to produce valid conclusions in our inquiry into the nature of reality. In the humanities, where the very complexity and individuality of our objects of inquiry (humanity) renders experimentation problematic on many levels and often unrepeatable, the role of intuition is of primary importance. Intuition is also involved in the Kantian sense of actual sensory perception. As we have seen, several of the key elements of Eliade's perspective are grounded in experiential perceptions. The task of increasing our familiarity with actual examples drawn ultimately from sensory perception in order to render our insights increasingly accurate involves both senses of intuition. Unfortunately, this task is practically infinite; not only does complete familiarity with the actual data of a field as extensive as mythology exceed the capabilities of any individual; not only are all data increasingly recognized as "theory-laden";[2] but it is almost universally accepted (since the work of Karl Popper) that an infinitude of data is needed to validate any general hypothesis. This not only necessitates the move from validation to falsification; it also implies that any given hypothesis must be in some degree intuitively derived—any chain of induction leading to a conclusion must be

---

1. I should point out that I do not consider Eliade to be an "armchair" anthropologist. Not only does his three-year stay in India constitute valuable fieldwork, but also his position in a theological faculty was a prime location for ongoing practical research. In fact, to one who considers religion a human universal, all rigorous observation of one's fellows could be argued to represent fieldwork.
2. As Goethe pointed out, *Maximen und Reflexionen*, no. 575, in *Gedenkausgabe der Werke, Briefe un Gespräche*, ed. Ernst Beutler, (Zurich: Artemis Verlag), no. 9, 574.

incomplete, every hypothesis remain only *thus far* unfalsified. This is not the place for a detailed digression into the role of intuition in theory formation. Suffice it to say at the moment that intuition is not simply arbitrary but is conditioned by prior experience in a way which is (thus far) supra-rational. Certainly, both intuition and reason are necessary elements of human thought, and it is the utility, applicability, and credibility of any given intuition which best validates it. That is to say, the degree to which it commends itself to and is in correspondence with the intuitions of others, rather than the degree to which it is held to correspond to or derive from "facts."

In accordance with his conceptions regarding authenticity and hierophany, Eliade certainly has made his personal intuitions the basis of his understanding of myth. This cannot be made an *a priori* criticism but must be considered in the light of the significance which that understanding can assume in our confrontation with myth.

We cannot know apodictically and exhaustively the significance of a myth (or any other religious manifestation) to any single individual, certainly not of all myths to all individuals at all times. We can only generate speculative (that is, based on observations, *speculari*, as Eliade points out, *No Souvenirs*, 261) generalizations and attempt specific understandings. It will clarify Eliade's understanding of myth at this point to compare it in more detail with Kirk's analysis. Kirk considers that

> "myth" is such a general term, and its etymology and early applications are so unspecific, that one is compelled to take some notice of contemporary usage. . . . "Most people" assume that myths are a special *kind* of traditional tale, and that the qualities that make them special are those that distinguish them as profound, imaginative, other-worldly, universal or larger-than-life. (*Greek Myths*, 25)

By Eliade's lights, these qualities are truth and reality, in the sense that, as we will see, fables can exceed historical reality in truth value. Through its "truth," myth becomes hierophany and reveals the real, the sacred, to the listener. The cosmogonic myth "narrates a sacred history" (*Myth and Reality*, 5); it "tells only of that which *really* happened" (6); it relates the

> breakthrough of the sacred that really establishes the World and makes it what it is today. . . . The Myth is regarded as a sacred story, and hence a "true history," because it always deals with realities. (6)

Association with the primordial period of creation is an archetypal persuasive argument. "The cosmogony is true because the world is there to prove it."[3]

---

3. It seems likely that Eliade shared this opinion with Raffaele Pettazzoni, see "Mythology and the History of Religions," 101: "as Prof. Pettazzoni remarks, a myth is always a true story because it is a sacred story."

Kirk admits that "on the whole I feel that the attempt to isolate some central specific quality of myths is misdirected. There are too many obvious exceptions" (*Greek Myths*, 27). However, he goes on to say that the distinguishing features of myth must be "not just one such characteristic like sacredness in some sense, but a whole range of possibilities" (27). Among the phrases Kirk uses to describe the possible distinguishing features of myth are:

1. Narrative force, power or charm.
2. Offering an explanation for some important phenomenon or custom.
3. Palliating in some way a recurring social dilemma.
4. Recording and establishing a useful institution.
5. Expressing an emotion in some way that satisfies some need in the individual.
6. Reinforcing a religious feeling.
7. Acting as a powerful support or precedent for an established ritual or cult practice.

Eliade's attitude seems to generally agree with Kirk's analysis thus far: First, the force or charm of the narrative can be assimilated to Eliade's concept of the "truth" of the narrative. Secondly, he positively insists on the etiological aspect of myth. Explanation, recording, and support flow together in the positive valorization of the etiological myth.

> To tell how things came into existence is to explain them and at the same time indirectly to answer another question: *Why* did they come into existence? (*Sacred and Profane*, 97)

Thus, transmitting the mythic origins of an institution or phenomenon performs all three functions.

The third of Kirk's features can be assimilated to Eliade's notion of a consolation from the terror of history and will be discussed elsewhere. Kirk concludes his introductory section on "Problems of Definition" with the declaration that

> the position at which we have arrived is that myths are on the one hand good stories, on the other hand bearers of important messages about life in general and life within society in particular. (*Greek Myths*, 28–29)

The whole question of aesthetics is raised here; what is the exact relationship of the "important message" to the "good story"? In retrospect the two are obviously connected, but is that connection teleological (those messages considered important being deliberately associated with powerful vehicles of transmission to ensure their propagation and preservation), or causal (the importance of the message naturally generating a successful vehicle), or the reverse (the aesthetic power of the vehicle ensuring that its message is perceived and transmitted as important). An answer to this question might help to explain the perennial association of religious themes and (at least pre-Renaissance) art, but it is not my immediate concern.

A revealing statement of Kirk's analysis is that myths must "possess both exceptional narrative power and clear functional relevance to some important aspect of life beyond mere entertainment" (28). In order to "possess exceptional narrative power" must not a story have some *a priori* relevance to some important aspect of life, and can that relevance be anything but functional? That is to say the myth will explain, establish, support, reinforce, or express that to which it has relevance. It should be noticed in this connection that the types of relevance listed by Kirk are always *positive*. He, too, sees myth as a positive rhetorical device, whose function is supportive, establishing, and so on rather than destructive or hostile. The analytic method of philosophy gradually established since the Socratics serves a negative role more readily. Positive valorizations are made by more mythic means. Kirk points out that myth in pre-Socratic Greece, as powerful narrative pieces, was used as supportive material for philosophic standpoints. Even Plato, although reviling this *poesis* of myth as the enemy of philosophy, falls back on this tradition. In the post-Socratic tradition, the reliance on "rational" rather than "mythic" forms of persuasion can be seen as developing from an increased valorization of the empirical/historical as the "real." This provides a convenient touchstone to determine the "reality" of an argument: that which actually historically occurred would be seen as more "real" (i.e., sacred; more powerful, meaningful, significant, and finally authoritative) than that which was a human fabrication. Thus rational discourse upon elements of common human experience would become more esteemed than mythic persuasion which does "not set out to give philosophical proofs, rather to effect an altered emotional response to an aspect of our experience" (83). This is entirely consistent with Eliade's insistence that myth is the true story *par excellence*.

In developing his own theory of myth Kirk gives a résumé of the most influential alternative theories, isolating "five monolithic theories of myth." The first of these theories is that made famous by Max Müller: "all myths are *nature myths*, that is they refer to meteorological and cosmological phenomena" (43). This theory was exploded largely by Andrew Lang. For his own part Kirk states that

> exactly how and why the earliest myth makers thought about the world as they did, and what particular kind of anthropocentric and symbolic motives persuaded them to imagine the gods in the form of the sky, or the sky as behaving in some respects like a man, must remain unknown. (49)

However, the idea that myths are allegories of nature or meteorological events must have corresponded to the intuitions of the nineteenth-century Europeans who so readily accepted it. To Kirk it may now seem "incredible that many of the best minds in 19th century Europe could envisage myths as encoded descriptions of clouds passing over the sun etc." (17). Yet this "strange exaggeration" evidently *was* acceptable at that time, in that place; it accorded with the prevalent view of human nature. In his journal Eliade commented similarly on the acceptance of

Freud's theories on myth despite the paucity of supportive evidence. However, Eliade at least has a partial explanation:

> the interpretations of Freud are more and more successful because they are among the myths accessible to modern man. The myth of the murdered father, among others, reconstituted and interpreted in *Totem and Taboo*. It would be impossible to ferret out a single example of slaying the father in primitive religions or mythologies. This *myth* was created by Freud. And what is more interesting: the intellectual élite accept it (is it because they understand it? Or because it is "true" for modern man?) (*No Souvenirs*, 117)

The implication of Eliade's thought here is that the nineteenth century, naturalistic explanation of myths was, like Freud's primordial parricide, a myth itself. Eliade's usage of the term can be seen to be diametrically opposed to one aspect of the "contemporary usage" of the term which Kirk commended to our notice (*Greek Myths* 25). It is not in the sense of "falsehood" or "fable" that Eliade uses the word "myth." This he considers a "semantic inheritance from the Christian polemic against the pagan world."[4] Myth is seen rather as a narrative "considered to reveal the truth *par excellence*" (*Quest*, 73; see *Myths, Dreams and Mysteries*, 23 on his opposition to myth as "untrue").

Evidently, the type of truth intended in Eliade's description of myth is quite distinct from historical actuality. This is quite consistent with the common alternative usages of "true" given in any sizeable dictionary. The sense of true as being in accordance with an actual, historical state of affairs is a rather recent and specialized usage. To give an example: even the most hard-line of Christian fundamentalists who argue for the absolute historical veracity of the Bible would not insist that it necessarily occurred on some historical occasion that a certain traveller was robbed and beaten by specific thieves, neglected by an actual Levite priest, and rescued by a historical Samaritan for the parable of the Good Samaritan to be a story revelatory of the truth. Once again, truth is not identified with historical actuality. This usage of the concept of truth is further clarified in Eliade's journals. For example, he states that "the Bucharest of my novella *Pe Strada Mantuleasa*, although legendary, is truer than the city I went through for the last time in August 1942" (*No Souvenirs*, 51). And in his narration of the story of Savonarola and Lorenzo de Medici from the same source, one can read more clearly Eliade's dissociation of truth from history. Popular legend had it that Savonarola eventually denied extreme unction to Lorenzo de Medici when the

---

4. *Myths, Dreams and Mysteries*, 23, although elsewhere he says, "if in every European language the word 'myth' denotes a 'fiction,' it is because the Greeks proclaimed it to be such twenty-five centuries ago." (*Quest*, 72)

latter would not restore liberty to Florence, and, apparently, learned critics accepted the historicity of this version. This Eliade takes to be because the

archetypal image—Savonarola the prophet of civil liberties, Lorenzo the absolute tyrant—was too "true," too suggestive, to be invalidated by documents and specific testimony. It was "truer" in legend than in history. In history Savonarola conducted himself as any Christian monk and absolved the repentant sinner. (*No Souvenirs*, 57)

Thus mythic truth is seen as independent of, but certainly not in opposition to, historical actuality. As we saw in the preceding exposition on hierophany, Eliade considers the experience of historical actualities to be the perennial source and auditor of the truth which is expressed in creative interpretation.

The next theory which Kirk inspects is the etiological theory, attributed particularly to Andrew Lang—"all myths offer a cause or explanation of something in the real world" (*Greek Myths*, 53). It is remarkable that Kirk does not consider Eliade in the context of etiological myth. In one of his most widely read books, Eliade states his opinion clearly that

every myth shows how a reality came into existence, whether it be the total reality, the cosmos, or only a fragment—an island, a species of plant, a human institution. (*Sacred and the Profane*, 97)

It is one of the central tenets of the Eliade's understanding of myth that the cosmogonic myth is the pattern of all myths because it is the exemplar of all genesis stories. It is a fundamental characteristic of a myth that it is

always related to a "creation," it tells how something came into existence, or how a pattern of behavior, an institution, a manner of working were established; this is why myths constitute the paradigms for all significant human acts. (*Myth and Reality*, 18)

And again:

In general, one can say that any myth tells how something came into being, the world, or man, or an animal species, or a social institution, and so on. But by the very fact that the creation of the world precedes everything else, the cosmogony enjoys a special prestige. In fact, as I have tried to show elsewhere [Eliade footnotes *The Myth of the Eternal Return* and *Myth and Reality*], the cosmogonic myth furnishes the model for all myths of origin. (*Quest*, 75)

Perhaps Kirk's reading of Eliade is not extensive, though this is not meant as a criticism of Kirk: it is a perennial problem in this field that one cannot cover all available sources, and it is a difficulty with Eliade that one should need to read him so extensively in order to appreciate his thought. Kirk's objection to Lang stands just as well for Eliade. "Myths," he says, "are obviously not concerned just with that [etiology]; they plainly encompass such things as the emotional valuation of many aspects of personal life" (*Greek Myths*, 53). The only possible reply here is that it would seem that, by Eliade's definition, stories which do not encompass these etiological concerns are excluded from the category of myth. Yet stories which "encompass the emotional valuation" of phenomena can be interpreted as giving the origin of that emotional valuation and will thus not be excluded.

Kirk then considers a third theory, that myths are "charters" for customs, institutions, or beliefs. This was the theory forwarded by Bronislav Malinowski, whose

> idea that the "serious" uses of myth are neither emotional nor reflective, but rather are connected with the mechanical functioning of social life, became the core of the exaggerated theory known as "functionalism" that developed into an orthodoxy in the circle of A. R. Radcliffe-Brown. (*Greek Myths*, 32)

Although he evidently opposes this "orthodoxy," Kirk is more favorably disposed to Malinowski's understanding, conceding that Malinowski was right in requiring more observations of myth "in action" rather than theoretical speculation. It will soon become clear in what ways Eliade's understanding of myth encourages a broader observation of myth "in action" in the contemporary world. Also, Eliade quotes from Malinowski's *Myth in Primitive Psychology* (101, 108) at some length to the effect that myth is "a narrative resurrection of a primeval reality," and "supplies man with the motive for ritual and moral actions." Eliade finds support here for the concepts of the internal coherence and exemplary status of myth (*Myth and Reality*, 20). Robert Baird has pointed out that Eliade and Malinowski are in agreement that "men in archaic cultures justify their actions in terms of the prior acts of the gods," although the significance of this differs for the two scholars (*Category Formation*, 79).

To a certain extent the etiological and the "charter" concepts of myth overlap. As we have seen, Eliade points out that insofar as a myth describes the origin of a given institution or phenomenon it thereby supports it. The "accidents" of one's personal life experience are orientated within a given extended matrix of significations and thus "justified." As with any language, from the most natural to the most formal, each element is defined in terms of other elements in the whole structure of meaning. Thus the act of description in the mythic framework simultaneously operates as justification. The significance of a number, for example, is not fixed, not essential, but is given by its relationship to other elements of the mathematical system.[5] Similarly, the significance of one's own existence is not

---

5. For example, 10 can = 8 x 2, as it does in the hexadecimal mathematics used for computers, where the base number is sixteen, or 1 + 1, as it does in the binary system. Usually 10 = 5 x 2, because

given *a priori* by its form; it lacks essential significance. Only by orienting the various experiential elements of one's own existence (mortality, sexuality, social duty, alimentation, in short, one's existential situation, as Eliade often refers to it), in an extended matrix of interrelated significant entities, can one appreciate its significance and escape the dreadful social and psychological consequences of an otherwise utterly insignificant existence. In this aspect of myth, Kirk's concept of "palliating a recurring social dilemma" and Eliade's concept of countering the terror of history combine. To escape further from the implication that this extended matrix is itself insignificant, no more than a palliative or placebo, it must be grounded as frequently and firmly as possible in reality, in the sacred. However, as I have argued, reality itself is a conceptual element in the existential situation of the individual, direct experience of which is necessarily beyond our empirical senses. It, too, is given significance by its relationship to the various elements of our experience. Our concept of the real is grounded in those experiences which we hold to reveal most clearly that which is real, in hierophanies and archetypal intuitions, yet our experience of certain phenomena as hierophanic or ontophanic is determined by our "personal experience and religious background" (*Mistress Christina*, 7). Thus our very apprehension of the significance of the elements of our personal experience takes shape within a hermeneutical cycle of object-observation-subjectobservation-object. This type of constructivist attitude, which ultimately makes humanity instrumental in its perceptions of reality, is implicit in both the Italian humanist insistence on the coherence of "primitive thought" (e.g., Vico) and in Goethe's observation that all facts are theory-laden, both of which certainly influenced Eliade's thought.

The fourth of the "monolithic" theories of myth presented by Kirk is the one which he attributes specifically to Eliade: that "the purpose of all myths is to evoke or actually re-establish in some sense, the *creative era*" (*Greek Myths*, 63). Certainly, this is an important and original element of Eliade's thought, but as we have already seen, it does not exhaust his understanding of myth. Eliade also subscribes to the etiological theory, and to some extent to the charter theory, and even allows some truth to the "primordial physics" concept. Yet it is the "Myth of the Eternal Return" which is unique and original to Eliade's interpretation, and it is that which Kirk critiques.[6]

---

suffixing the zero to any number indicates that that number is thus multiplied by the base number. It is a fundamental assumption of Saussurean linguistics that words are likewise defined, their meaning being given and justified by their relationships to other elements of the language.

6.   The fifth theory which Kirk considers "proclaims that all myths are closely associated with rituals." He recognizes that this "is one of the most long-lived and important," (66) but points out that "it is simply not true that myths are always associated with rituals" (67). This is not immediately pertinent to my analysis and so I have omitted my response to it.

"Many myths of many societies are not of this kind and do not respond to any such interpretation," Kirk states (64). Yet even the Amerindian myth which he offers as a specific exception takes place in "a mythical epoch that was, admittedly, the time when things were put in order" (65). It is Eliade's point that myths refer to such an "other time" in which the cosmos was either created *or ordered*. "Such works constitute properly speaking a cosmogony; the ancestors did not create the earth, but they gave form to a pre-existent *materia prima*" (*Quest*, 85, referring to Australian aboriginal myths). Furthermore, in establishing his own distinctions between myth and folklore, Kirk accepted that myth takes place "in the timeless past," rather than a remote chronological era or an anonymous period (*Greek Myths*, 34). Since the action of myths "take place" in such a timeless, eternal period, it seems pointless to deny that the telling of these myths "evokes" that period, and Eliade's numerous examples must stand as their own evidence that this is seen as the creative period *par excellence*. Whether or not the myths actually seek to re-establish that timeless period here and now is a more complex argument and will be considered later. When Kirk turns to the area of his own expertise, the Greek myths, to cast doubt on Eliade's theory, he occasionally adduces examples which actually support it.

> Greek myths, too, utterly fail to support Eliade's universal theory. The whole range of Greek heroic myths lies outside any true "creative" era. (65)

Yet later in his exposition Kirk states that for Pindar

> the "excellence" . . . that he celebrates in his victors seems to him to owe its value precisely to its heroic and divine connections, to its roots in a radiant mythical past of which the Olympic Games, above all other occasions, are seen as a rare surviving relic. . . . For Pindar, at least, the myths represented a past that was of higher value than the present. . . . In this use of myths as an active force for conserving a semi-divine past Pindar returns to a function that is more than merely literary, and reproduces in a way the evocative function of certain myths that was discussed on page 63ff. [That is, Eliade's theory of the evocation of the creative era.] (101, 102, 103)

This certainly does not "utterly fail to support Eliade's universal theory," even when the aspect of the reinstatement of the primordial, creative period is artificially separated from its properly accompanying elements. As a highly valorized timeless time which is the object of nostalgia and of periodic re-establishment, Pindar's attitude to the Olympic Games is a clear example of Eliade's mythic nostalgia for paradise and eternal return to the primordial sacred time.

It is apparently Kirk's desire to isolate and criticize some "monolithic" and "universal" theory of myth and his resultant restriction of Eliade's theory to the notion of a re–establishment of a creative era which makes his criticism appear credible. The point is that Eliade's "definition" of myth is systematic and taxonomic. It is a deliberate attempt to classify so as to render comprehensible an extremely complex phenomenon. As Kirk says,

> myths are not uniform, logical and internally consistent, they are multiform, imaginative and loose in their details. Moreover their emphases can change from one year, or generation to the next. (29)

Thus, accepting the complexity and polyvalence of myth (which is always and unavoidably a human classification of the broader category of narrative, itself a subset of human communication), Eliade's failure to cover *all* myths is hardly a serious flaw. Eliade makes an attempt to restrict the classification to a particular group of narratives having the characteristics which he highlights. Certainly, he thus cannot cover all tales, stories, records, and so forth which stake a claim to the title of "myth." In order to make one's analytic category of any value in this area, one must necessarily exclude some candidates from the field of mythology. Simply accepting the complexity of myth will always result in some broad and unusable definition. Eliade, though, in his desire to establish the coherence and the exemplary status of myth, has perhaps been too willing to impose upon that category a description which would not be immediately meaningful to those for whom a given myth is current. However, as I said earlier, the value of his intuitions concerning myth should be assessed in the light of the significance they reveal to his readers in their own confrontation with the mythic.

If Eliade's concept of myth appears more restrictive than Kirk's, we must look further to ascertain what it is that qualifies the myth beyond its narrative charm and functional relevance. The clearest expositions of Eliade's thought in this area are in *Myth and Reality* (chapter 9, "Survivals and Camouflages of Myth") and in *Myths, Dreams and Mysteries* (chapter 1, "The Myths of the Modern World"). In the former, Eliade discusses first the continuation of mythic thought in Christianity and then he outlines specifically mythic elements in "secular" thought. The obsession with "the return to the origins" in modern society is related to the etiological function of myth. The "eschatological and millennialist structures" of Marxism are described as mythic. Perhaps more surprising is the perception of mythic structures in the mass media, comic art, modern art, the obsession with success, the exodus to the suburbs, the "automobile cult," the "myth of the élite," and in the novel. These are seen as the surviving, if camouflaged, myths of the modern world. This is where modern man finds his true reality, the meaningful, the powerful.

Despite the chapter heading of "Survivals and Camouflages of Myths," Eliade warns that these mythic elements do not

> represent "survivals" of an archaic mentality . . . [rather] certain aspects and functions of mythic thought are constituents of the human being. (*Myth and Reality*, 181f.)

This pronouncement might at first sound enigmatic and unclear, however, its implications were clarified in a work of six years earlier. There, although he warns of the enormous scope of myths in the modern world, he seeks to trace the general operation of myth. He writes,

> of what is essential in mythic behavior—the exemplary pattern, the repetition, the break with profane duration and integration into primordial time—the first two at least are consubstantial with every human condition. (*Myths, Dreams and Mysteries*, 31)

What is seen as essential to myth beyond its narrative power and relevance is the specific recognition of and response to exemplary patterns. Eliade considers that "the foremost function of myth is to reveal the exemplary models for all human rites and all significant human activities" (*Myth and Reality*, 8). The response to, the repetition of, these exemplary patterns constitutes a repetition of a segment of the primordial time and thus a break with profane, historical time. This is, in fact, integral to the "truth" of the myth. It is the exemplary, imitable elements of the narrative which give a story mythic status. (Allow me to emphasize once again that Eliade is using "true" in a sense which has more in common to the Classical Greek *arete*, virtue or excellence, and less in common with the notion of propositional truth or historical accuracy. This is, of course, consistent with the whole body of his thought.) It is the perception that the myth is exemplary that gives rise to the concept of the "re-actualization" of the primordial, creative era. Insofar as a mythic act is open to imitation, insofar as we can narrate or reenact the events of the mythic era, *illud tempus* is open to re-establishment, we can rediscover and thus re-actualize its meaning and its power.

The greatest suspicion of myth which Kirk expresses in his study is of myth "as a collective term" because this, and other forms such as "mythology,"

> misleadingly imply that what one should be defining is some absolute essence of all myths, some Platonic Idea of "that which is truly mythic." (*Greek Myths*, 20)

However, "myths are a vague and uncertain category, and one man's myth is another man's legend, or folktale, or oral tradition" (21). This sort of suspicion is given free rein in Strenski's complete rejection of myth as a reality. However, it can readily be seen that, in Eliade's understanding, myth is determined by the prevalent attitude to a popular narrative. Myth is the popular narrative which is (either uncritically or with reference to other myths) held to be true, to represent the real, and thus to be exemplary—in Eliadean terms, to be sacred. No doubt, the hostile attitude to myth from Xenophanes to Strenski is grounded in a justifiable rejection of the *a priori*, uncritically positive valorization characteristic of myth. It is a typical and admirable characteristic of science and the "scientific" approach that everything, *especially* traditionally established values, should be open to rigorous criticism. It is this specific characteristic of criticism of tradition which Eliade has cited as definitive of "modern man." The problem here resides in the concomitant claim or belief that for the scientific or critical modern *nothing* is received from tradition without prior critical analysis; that "modern man" "does not believe in myths," that is, has no myths of his own—an assertion with which Eliade is in fundamental disagreement. The implication of his thought is that myth is functional as much when the myth is concealed in the message as when the message is concealed in the myth. The reliance upon pre-reflective, narrative, "emotive forms of persuasion" will always draw upon mythic sources of power. Thus, for example, it could be said that when a specious statistical argument is utilized, one which strictly speaking is not rational, an appeal is being made to the myth of mathematics, that is to the popular and uncritical association of number and truth.

Only if all of one's persuasions are formed on the basis of fully rational support can one be said to have transcended all myth. One of the specific gains made by such an acceptance of our own mythic influences is that the problem of a "Platonic Idea" of the truly mythic repudiated by Kirk is completely avoided. It is the intentional attitude of the believer which makes a myth a myth, not some necessary participation in an ideal form. In terms of Eliade's sacred it is the *perceived* participation in or revelation of the real which makes a particular narrative mythic for a particular believer. However, it is not necessary that the student of myth be party to that participation or revelation to recognize the mythic status of that narrative. It can thus be accepted that "one man's myth is another man's legend," as Kirk puts it (21), while simultaneously recognizing the truly mythic status of the narrative *in its relationship to its hearers.*

Given the preceding observations the foundationalism characteristic of much of modern thought since Descartes can itself be seen as a form of "nostalgia for paradise." The prevalent mythology of premodern society was not seriously challenged, one's firm location within a particular culture would ensure a certitude, a reality, a sacrality, to the mores of that culture. Nowadays, however, with the entry of the Orient into History and the propagation of the mass media, the "sacred" standards of the traditional religion of the West are challenged. That is to say, not simply the doctrines of Christianity, but *all* the heirs of our culture's positive valorizations. As Eliade states in his conclusion to "Cosmogonic Myth and 'Sacred History,'" "it is with such *myths of sacred history*—still alive in many traditional societies—that the Judaeo-Christian idea of history has to vie" (*Quest*, 87).

Secular modern Westerners are no more justified in their complacent acceptance of their idea of history than are Christians in their acceptance of the Atonement. Both are traditionally transmitted and in their apprehension as powerful, relevant and exemplary, with its self-referentially positive valorization, both can be seen as mythic.

It is only through the discovery of History—more precisely by the awakening of the historical consciousness in Judaeo-Christianity and its propagation by Hegel and his successors—it is only through the radical assimilation of the new mode of being represented by human existence in the world that myth could be left behind. But we hesitate to say that mythical thought has been abolished. As we shall soon see, it managed to survive, though radically changed (if not perfectly camouflaged). And the astonishing fact is that, more than anywhere else it survives in historiography! (*Myth and Reality*, 113)

Paradoxically, myth tends to re-establish itself as a fable, an illusion. As in the story of Viṣṇu and Narada (*Images and Symbols*, 70f.), what is the ultimately seductive fault is accepting one's own myths as real, and yet in order to reach this conclusion, we had to begin with the recognition that the myth is the true story *par excellence*. Perhaps the paradox can be resolved in the recognition that the myth is a true representation of reality in the sense that it is honest and has integrity and excellence but *it is not a reiteration of reality itself.*

The hearer of myth, regardless of his level of culture, when he is listening to a myth, forgets, as it were, his particular situation and is projected into another world, into another universe which is no longer his poor little universe of every day. . . . The myths are *true* because they are *sacred*, because they tell him about sacred beings and events. Consequently, in reciting or listening to a myth, one resumes contact with the sacred and with reality, and in so doing one transcends the profane condition, the "historical situation." In other words one goes beyond the temporal condition and the dull self-sufficiency which is the lot of every human being simply because every human being is "ignorant"—in the sense that he is identifying himself, and Reality, with his own particular situation. And ignorance is, first of all, this false identification of Reality with what each one of us *appears to be or to possess.* (*Images and Symbols*, 59)

As he makes clear later on, this does not deny the relevance of the historical situation, or the reality of personal experience. In Indian terms he points out that

the great cosmic illusion is a hierophany. . . . One is devoured by Time, not because one lives in Time, but because one believes in its *reality*, and therefore forgets or despises eternity. (90–91)

In other words, the primary fault is not in perception itself, but in mistakenly assuming perception to be itself the Real rather than a secondary manifestation, a representation or imitation of the real, to mistake the perception for the perceived.

The emphases of myth have changed drastically, as has so much else of human life since the Industrial Revolution. So radical is the change that it is often difficult to recognize the connection of modern myths with archaic ones. The mythic importance of the narrative form has been much reduced; stories are now in enormously greater supply. This has resulted in a general demythologization of narrative and the occasional sundering of myth from its familiar narrative setting. Thus ideology, cosmology, ontology, and other, strictly metaphysical, assumptions might bear no trace of the "good story," but nevertheless be of degraded mythic status because of their perception as self-evident truths, their highly effective emotional persuasiveness, and their etiological character. Although superficially distinct, popular forms of media such as films and comic books[7] still share the common characteristics of myth of etiology, entertainment value, positive valorization but above all, exemplary status. If it is at first difficult to accept popular media as myth, it should be borne in mind that both Franz Boas and E. E. Evans-Pritchard refused to make any absolute distinction between myth and folktale, and that Kirk agrees that "the data show a continual flow of material from mythology to folktale and vice versa, and that neither group can claim priority" (*Greek Myths*, 31). Also of interest in this context is the widespread belief that the violence in children's cartoons is responsible for the violence in society—that the directly exemplary status of these tales is still effective.

One possible weakness of Kirk's analysis, common to many commentators, is the insistence that "it cannot be repeated too often" that myths are traditional tales (38), thus underplaying this concept of contemporary myths, and disabling any attempts to observe "myth in action" in our own society. This would imply that our modern society is in this respect radically different from all others in that it would be the only society ever known to exist without myths. It is a conceit typical of "modern" thought that we in the contemporary West are somehow essentially different from all other societies. Against this, Eliade has said,

> a restriction of the inquiry to "primitive" mythologies risks giving the impression that there is no continuity between archaic thought and the thought of the peoples who played an important role in ancient history. Now, such a solution of continuity does not exist. (Quest, 73)

I would argue that Eliade's universal humanism is one of the elements which makes him a precursor of the "postmodern" rather than himself a typical modern. In defence of Kirk, however, it must be said that the cultural matrix which empowers a myth as a form of persuasion independently of its rationality is necessarily traditional—that is to say, the positive emotional response to a myth is received rather than innate. It is intuitive in the sense mentioned above. Unfortunately, with the devalorization of the "reality" of such a form of persuasion and such uninspected "truths" (that is, with the association of myth and the unreal and the concomitant devaluation of non-rational, intuitive insights), these received persuasions have

---

7. Certainly, fantastic creations such as strip cartoon superheroes cannot be excluded from this later category. Note Eliade's photograph with Jack Kirby's comic art Asgardians, *Waiting for the Dawn*, 66–67, and see *Myth and Reality*, 185 on the "myth of Superman."

largely become concealed and the traditions which support them largely unrecognized. One major cause of this unwarranted association is the longstanding tendency to study as myths exactly those narratives which *are* held by other peoples to be revelatory of the real, but *are not so* held by ourselves. The concept of "myth" was thus formed as "other peoples' myths" rather than as "myths" *tout court* (see Wendy Doniger O'Flaherty's *Other Peoples' Myths*), and it is in correcting this misapprehension that Eliade's consideration of myths has diverged from the conventional understanding of the word.

CHAPTER 8

Illud Tempus—Time by Any Other Name

INTRODUCTION

The terms of the preceding analyses (hierophany, symbols, etc.) are either neologisms of Eliade's own or specialist terms of the study of religio-cultural phenomena. History and time are of much more broad and common usage and yet many elements of the preceding analyses have pivoted on the concepts of time or history without further explanation. In this chapter I hope to rectify that shortcoming.

Eliade's characteristic use of the Latin *illud tempus* clearly indicates an idiosyncratic application of the concept of time and it is, I believe, the tension between this idiosyncrasy and the deeply ingrained common applications of the reader which generates many of the difficulties of comprehension of this aspect of Eliade's thought. As anyone who has tangled with Heidegger's *Sein und Zeit* knows only too well, it is the common and fundamental terms of our conceptual vocabulary which generate the most crucial and labyrinthine problems, time no less than being. Heidegger's influence on Eliade is worthy of consideration (see *The Myth of the Eternal Return*, 150, 152; *Occultism, Witchcraft and Cultural Fashions*, 45f.). Its exact manifestations in his work remain to be explored, however, and Daniel Dubuisson's brief attempt (291–303) is of little help being seriously flawed by his polemical intent (see below, chapter 13).

The notions of time and history as they are applied by Eliade himself, as they are manifest in the documents of the study of religion, and as they are commonly applied in the West today, are of fundamental importance to this study in every respect. As Eliade applies them, they condition the meaning of his entire oeuvre; as they are manifest in the documents of the study of religion (as Eliade conceived it), they represent an expression of the existential situation of humanity other than our own; and as they are commonly applied in the West today, they represent the realities of our own existential situation as it differs from but is conditioned by our cultural precedents. As sacred or sacralizable, as hierophanies, the documents of religious studies are by definition expressions of that which was apprehended as the real. Thus the attitude to time expressed in the sacred traditions of humanity past and present represent the actual apprehensions of those alternative modes of (human) being. Eliade's interpretations of time and history simultaneously condition and are the products of his implicit system and its concomitant methodology.

THE ARCHAIC AND THE MODERN CONCEPTIONS OF TIME

As we have seen, the attitudes to time and to history of modern and of religious humanity in their continuity and diversity are major factors in their discrimination. Although Eliade admits the difficulty of describing concisely the nature of time for modern humanity (*Sacred and the Profane*, 70), he characterizes clearly the conception of time which he has abstracted from religious documents. For humanity in its religious aspect,

> profane temporal duration can be periodically arrested; for certain rituals have the power to interrupt it by periods of a sacred time that is non-historical (in the sense that it does not belong to the historical present). (71f.)

Thus,

> religious man lives in two kinds of time, of which the most important, sacred time, appears under the paradoxical aspect of a circular time, reversible and recoverable, a sort of eternal mythical present that is periodically regenerated by means of rites. (70)

This, as we saw, was Eliade's main means of distinguishing religious, archaic humanity from modern, non-religious humanity, and finally reflects the thesis of *The Myth of the Eternal Return*. As I mentioned earlier, this is no doubt influenced by Bergson's analysis of time and it is helpful to bear this in mind. Eliade felt that *The Myth of the Eternal Return* was "the most significant of my books; and when I am asked in what order they should be read, I always recommend beginning with the present work" (*Myth of the Eternal Return*, preface to the English edition, November 1958, xv). First published as *Le Mythe de l'éternel retour: archétypes et répétition* by Gallimard in 1949, this work was translated into English as *Cosmos and History* (Harper Torchbooks, 1959) and reprinted as *The Myth of the Eternal Return or Cosmos and History* from 1965 onward. It contains the most detailed exposition of Eliade's interpretation of time and history. However, before I attempt to clarify Eliade's position by close reference to that work, let me immediately emphasize one point which he makes in *The Sacred and the Profane*. Sacred time "is a mythical time, that is a primordial time, *not to be found in the historical past*"

(*Sacred and the Profane*, 72, emphasis added). Obviously this "primordial time" is not located in any long-gone historical era of our known world, but is notional, conceptual or imaginary. Eliade is certain that

> the nostalgia for the lost paradise excludes any desire to restore the "paradise of animality." Everything that we know about the mythic memories of "paradise" confronts us, on the contrary, with the image of an ideal humanity enjoying a beatitude and spiritual plenitude forever unrealizable in the present state of "fallen man." (*Myth of the Eternal Return*, 91)

That is to say, the nostalgia is not for a chronological past, an actual or historical condition, rather it is for an imaginary ideal which none the less functions as an exemplar. Once again, as in my interpretation of Eliade's sacred, the ontological status of Eliade's analysis should not be assumed. In the very opening words to *The Myth of the Eternal Return* he states that

> this book undertakes to study certain aspects of archaic ontology—more precisely, the *conceptions* of being and reality that can be read off from the behavior of the man of premodern societies. (3, emphasis added)

Thus it can be seen that at no point is he necessarily discussing archaic ontology; how things were in premodern societies, but rather archaic *conceptions* of ontology; how things were *thought to be*, or, to be more factually accurate; how things were *said* to be.

Eliade's thesis is that the "archaic" mentality, seen as typically representative of humanity in its religious mode, apprehended sacred time (as "a primordial mythical time made present," *Sacred and the Profane*, 68) as the locus of real significance, of the sacred, of the real. Thus it was felt that

> neither the objects of the external world nor human acts, properly speaking, have any autonomous intrinsic value. Objects or acts acquire a value, and in so doing become real, because they participate, after one fashion or another, in a reality that transcends them. (*Myth of the Eternal Return*, 3f.)

Time is one of the primary categories of humanity's knowledge of the world which is subject to the sociologization. Bergson said that

> we may . . . surmise that time, conceived under the form of a homogenous medium, is some spurious concept, due to the trespassing of the idea of space upon the field of pure consciousness . . . nothing but a ghost of space haunting the reflective consciousness. (98)

Lévy-Bruhl, in his *Primitive Mentality*, pointed out that the linear and unrepeatable nature of time was a feature of the modern, "civilized" time-consciousness. Despite the fact that he was forced to retract his postulate of a "primitive mentality," Lévy-Bruhl's recognition of the recent nature of the specific apprehension of time as "dimensional" is still borne out by an overwhelming number of sources and theories. All known religious traditions posit a realm or mode of being which is infinitely more significant than the world of everyday personal experience. George Stirrat has agreed that

> Eliade's formulation of the sacred as existing outside of time . . . is a fair characterization of much that is claimed within the religious discourses of most, if not all, the world religions. Thus, in Hinduism, Buddhism, and Catholicism, it can be argued that what is most sacred, that which is concerned with salvation, is that which is outside time. ("Sacred Models," 202)

The religious person can gain access to this alternative time through performance of ritual, narration of myth, and in "archaic" and "primitive" societies, by the performance of sacralized human functions, such as hunting, fishing, construction, and the more obvious sacraments (to the modern Westerner) of birth, marriage, and death. Eliade suggests that what all of these observances have in common is that they constitute, and are sacralized by, repetitions of a sacred model. This includes, but is not exhausted by, the *imitatio dei* familiar to the Christian West. The implications of the concept that *imitation* can confer ontic substance upon the activities of humanity implies a certain understanding of time:

> insofar as an act (or an object) acquires a certain reality through the repetition of certain paradigmatic gestures, and acquires it through that alone, there is an implicit abolition of profane time, of duration, of "history"; and he who reproduces the exemplary gesture thus finds himself transported into the mythical epoch in which its revelation took place. (*Myth of the Eternal Return*, 35)

The concept of the specific imitation or repetition of divine mythical models is not the only indicator of this alternative attitude to time, "the traditional societies (that is, all societies down to those which make up the modern world) knew and applied still other methods to bring about the regeneration of time" (76). Nor is this attitude utterly foreign to contemporary humanity. It can be most easily recognized in New Year scenarios which feature a return to primordial chaos and a repetition of the creation and in

> the Christian liturgical year [which] is based upon a periodic and real repetition of the Nativity, Passion, death, and Resurrection of Jesus, . . . that is, personal and cosmic regeneration through reactualization *in concreto* of the birth, death, and resurrection of the Savior. (130)

This is of no small significance and emphasizes Eliade's frequent insistence that there is no "solution of continuity" between archaic and modern. However, the present point is that "for traditional man, the imitation of an archetypal model is a reactualization of the mythical moment when the archetype was revealed for the first time" (76). These sacred models Eliade refers to as "archetypal" and as "archetypes," although he expresses regret at this choice of words, which has led to a common equation of his thought with that of C. G. Jung (see p. 7 n. 2 above). As we have seen, the sacred models do not belong to the profane, historical realm, no more do they belong to the un- or sub-conscious mind. They issue from the alternative realm, considered to be the locus of the real and the true and the significant. This realm is *illud tempus*, the continuum of a different, sacred time, which is repeated and re-actualized by repetition of the sacred model, be it an act, bodily function, or narrative structure.[1] Hence this alternative time is repeatable as well as intensely real.

As has already been mentioned, the concomitant of this attitude to *illud tempus* was an inability to perceive ordinary events and objects as inherently possessed of any real value. Since the objects and events of much of one's everyday experience do not have mythical models, do not re-actualize the continuum of real time, they are not in and of themselves of any significance. Since they are not specifically orientated in an extended matrix of familiar, interconnected structures and events of predetermined value, they themselves lack value, they lack a determined response, and hence they lack meaning.

ELIADE'S EVALUATION OF ARCHAIC AND MODERN CONCEPTIONS OF TIME

Although Eliade has been criticized for being a "champion" of the archaic attitude and he is certainly ready to recognize the values of this alternative to the modern view of time, he is not totally uncritical of it.

> The need these [archaic] societies also feel for a periodic regeneration is a proof that they too cannot perpetually maintain their position in what we have just called the paradise of archetypes, and that their memory is capable (though doubtless far less intensely than that of a modern man) of revealing the irreversibility of events, that is, of recording history. (75)

This stands against the contention that Eliade valorized the archaic over the modern, *a priori*. Both visions ultimately fail to "maintain their position" independently of some concept of regeneration. Furthermore,

---

1. For readers unfamiliar with Latin, it is worthwhile to point out that *illud tempus* simply means "that time." It occurs in Jerome's Vulgate where it usually indicates the *heilsgeschichte* in which God's actions were seen as unquestionably decisive for humanity. The alternative, *in illo tempore*, is simply the locative case of the same phrase, *in* that time. In many ways it is a narrative device comparable with "once upon a time," although indicative of far greater sacrality.

> in the last analysis, modern man, who accepts history or claims to accept
> it, can reproach archaic man, imprisoned within the mythical horizon of
> archetypes and repetition, with his creative impotence, or, what amounts
> to the same thing, his inability to accept the risks entailed by every
> creative act. (155f.)

It is true, however, that in the final "dialogue between archaic man and modern
man" (155–59) Eliade gives more credence and more space to the archaic point of
view. It could, however, credibly be argued that he was simply supporting the
underdog, since he does finally indicate strengths and weaknesses in both points of
view and seems ultimately to support a synthesis.

> All that is needed is a modern man with a sensibility less closed to the
> miracle of life; and the experience of renewal would revive for him when
> he built a house or entered it for the first time (just as, in the modern
> world, the New Year still preserves the prestige of the end of a past and
> the fresh beginning of a new life). (77)

One thing that Eliade is certain of is that

> the life of archaic man (a life reduced to the repetition of archetypal acts,
> that is, to categories and not to events, to the unceasing rehearsal of the
> same primordial myths), although it takes place in time, does not bear the
> burden of time, does not record time's irreversibility; in other words,
> completely ignores what is especially characteristic and decisive in a
> consciousness of time. Like the mystic, like the religious man in general,
> the primitive lives in a continual present. (86)

This in itself constitutes a cushion between such a mindset and the impact of brute
historical event. This superiority in enabling a toleration of history is perceived as
the major virtue of the archaic attitude. The major vice of the modern is perceived
to be its self-deceptive nature. "Modern man's boasted freedom to make history is
illusory for nearly the whole of the human race" (156). This is because it is in truth
a small minority of people drawn from a small minority of nations who have any
real effect in the "making of history," that is to say, a very small effect on the
creation of those events which predate and condition the present. However, on the
events which are anyone else's experience, on history as Eliade uses the word,
every one of us has an effect. Since we cannot live in isolation we all do have a
contribution to make to the history whose conception underlies the whole of
Eliade's theoretical edifice. It is Eliade's innate élitism, his refusal to recognize the
contribution of the masses to the creation of history which conditions this flaw in
his thinking. If history is taken on this personal, experiential level, which I believe
it clearly must be in order to render the main body of Eliade's thought coherent,
then humanity is unavoidably free to make history since we are all intimately

(albeit not totally, deliberately, or in a fully controlled manner) responsible for the personal experiences of others.

THE LINEARITY OF THE MODERN CONCEPTION OF TIME

In "Homo Faber and Homo Religiosus," Eliade once again makes important reference to time in his analysis of the religious aspect of human life. He reiterates and emphasizes the point he first made in *The Forge and the Crucible* that the labor of *homo faber* "replaces the work of time." For *homo faber*, who in the contemporary Western world has become "modern man," the identification with historical time has become complete and humanity takes the place of time. Not only is humanity the product solely of history, created and determined purely in historical time, but humanity is now seen as the final judge and arbiter of our destiny; (racial) death or (technological) glory. This identification with historical time, which alone is real and thus sacred, is from this perspective a religious act or awareness. Once again "modern man" is not the antithesis of religious man but a very specific (and possibly rather aberrant) example.

In this same edition Paul Ricoeur presents a paper in which he describes how Steven Toulmin and Judith Goodfield in *The Discovery of Time* "tell the story of [the] progressive expansion of a uniform timescale from human history to geology, to thermodynamics, and finally to the gigantic changes among galaxies." Ricoeur concludes that "cyclical time appears paradoxically as a particular case of, and not an alternative term for linear time" ("The History of Religions and the Phenomenology of Time Consciousness," 14). However, he had already pointed out that linear time seems to have begun from the Judaeo-Christian notion of time as a 6,000-year period which was then extended to make room for the large-scale phenomena that together constitute the history of mankind, of the earth, of the universe, and even of matter itself (14).

Although teleologically a straight-line progression from Creation to Eschaton, this 6,000-year period was a manifestation of *cyclical* time since it proceeded from and returned to the eternal *illud tempus*. We are all familiar with the phenomena whereby an arc of a circle, if sufficiently short in relation to the radius of curvature, or viewed from a sufficiently close range or small scale, is perceived to be a straight line. Rather than cyclical time being a particular case of linear time, the converse would appear to be more credible. Linear time is a particular case of cyclical time viewed from the limited perspective of human history. Not only does the narrow localism of the original Judaeo-Christian viewpoint explain the perception of (microcosmic) time as linear, but the speculations of astrophysics concerning a "big bang" leading, via the expansion and contraction of the universe, to a "big crunch," re-establishes the view of (macrocosmic) time as cyclical. Thus "repetition of some pattern" is not merely "a complexity superimposed on the linear character of chronological time" (15); linearity is rather a perceptual phenomenon, generated by the scale of embodied human existence, which is then expanded into the abstract notion of linear time as Ricoeur describes it.

Once again the perception of modern man as a specific example of the pan-human *homo religiosus* is justified by such a consideration of time-consciousness. It is only the intensely focused self-consciousness (which is admirably utilitarian in certain ways) of modern humanity which has contracted the scale of time consciousness to make our historical time appear linear. Even Eliade's distinction of modern from religious humanity through their alternative perceptions of time begins to blur.

THE DEVELOPMENT OF CONCEPTIONS OF TIME

Eliade does not simply posit this archaic or religious attitude to time and support it with examples, he also attempts a detailed explanation of its development from the universal existential situation of humanity in the world. For example,

> if the moon in fact serves to "measure" time, if the moon's phases—long before the solar year and far more concretely—reveal a unit of time (the month), the moon at the same time reveals the "eternal return." (86)

As this "eternal return" is experienced in human life it is evidently cyclical as opposed to circular. That is to say, it is nowhere claimed that every actual physical being recommences with the new moon. Obviously, each individual still ages and the solar year still progresses. To think otherwise is to equate personal experience with time, an identification which Eliade does not make, and which he claims that archaic humanity repudiated. An analysis of his thought in this area reveals that this identification is part of the characteristic matrix of "modern" thought. For archaic man, on the other hand, the assimilation of temporal duration and human life to the lunar cycle

> is important not only because it shows us the "lunar" structure of universal becoming but also because of its optimistic consequences: for, just as the disappearance of the moon is never final, since it is necessarily followed by a new moon, the disappearance of man is not final either; in particular the disappearance of an entire humanity (deluge, flood, [sic] submersion of a continent, and so on) is never total, for a new humanity is born from a pair of survivors. (87)

Being cyclical, time is not irreversible. Everything begins over again at its commencement every instant (89). Yet the insignificance and the arbitrary nature of much of personal experience cannot be annulled.

The process or development which Eliade seems to envision leading to the modern "historical" view of time is that archaic, cyclically repeated time gives way to a single time-cycle from Genesis to Apocalypse, from *illud tempus* to *illud tempus*, in which every event is seen as of hierophanic value since it is under the direct control of the one true God. This conception is permitted by the novel religious attitude of *faith*, which emphasizes that "for God everything is possible" (160, see 108–10 on the novelty of faith).

> For the first time, the prophets placed a value on history, succeeded in transcending the traditional vision of the cycle (the conception that ensures all things will be repeated forever), and discovered a one-way time. . . . [F]or the first time we find affirmed, and increasingly accepted, the idea that historical events have a value in themselves, insofar as they are determined by the will of God. . . . Historical facts thus become "situations" of man in respect to God, and as such they acquire a religious value that nothing had previously been able to confer on them. . . . [T]he Hebrews were the first to discover the meaning of history as the epiphany of God. (104)[2]

Thus the Judaeo-Christian tradition, for Eliade, provides a bridge between the two types of, or attitudes to, time.

> Christianity radically changed the experience and the concept of liturgical time, and this is due to the fact that Christianity affirms the historicity of the person of Christ. The Christian liturgy unfolds in *a historical time sanctified by the incarnation of the son of God*. (72)

This valorization of time continues the trend which Eliade argues to have begun "among the Hebrews" for whom, "every new historical calamity was regarded as a punishment from Yahweh." In this way there first occurred "History regarded as Theophany" (102), and this eventually leads to the situation of modern man who insists that he is "constituted only by human history" (*Sacred and the Profane*, 100), and in that very insistence is distinguished from traditional *homo religiosus*. It is not my purpose at the moment to perform a detailed analysis of Eliade's argument, rather to inspect and clarify his conclusions. George Weckman has pointed out that other scholars do not agree with Eliade's restriction of the source of this valorization of the historical to the Jewish tradition. For example, Helmer Ringgren "does not want to get caught in asserting that Israel was unique in regarding historical events as acts of God" (13). Also Ninian Smart has remarked that "historical events were considered important by the Chinese" ("Eliade and the History of Religious Ideas," 70). However, as Weckman continues,

---

2. It is interesting to note that Eliade repeats this section almost verbatim in his *History of Religious Ideas* (356) some thirty years later. Although he omits the references to cyclical time and archetypes these are mentioned elsewhere in that volume and so do appear to still have currency in his thought.

it remains distinctive and consequential that ancient Israel first developed
a style of religion on the basis of a special comprehension of historical
events. (13)

While Weckman's unease is perfectly understandable at this point—Eliade does
make strong claims for the priority of the Hebrew valorization of history—it should
be pointed out that Eliade does accept a broader base than the purely Jewish for its
source. "Those with whom history, properly speaking, begins," he writes, "—that is
the Babylonians, Egyptians, Hebrews, Iranians" (*Myth of the Eternal Return*, 74).
Eliade's recognition of the phenomena of the sacralization of the previously profane
in the valorization of historical time is undoubtedly valid whatever its source.

This valorization of the historical event has several implications. First, it leads
to the concomitant de-valorization of the traditionally valorized, religious real,
"emptied of every religious value or meaning nature could become the 'object' *par
excellence* of scientific investigation" (*Symbolism, the Sacred, and the Arts*, 83).
Although this is not an explicit doctrine, Eliade takes it to be an unavoidable
implication of the structure of the Hebrew revelation:

> we may even ask ourselves if monotheism, based on the direct and
> personal revelation of the divinity, does not necessarily entail the
> "salvation" of time, its value within the frame of history. Doubtless the
> idea of revelation is found . . . in all religions . . . but these revelations
> occurred in *mythical* time. . . . The situation is altogether different in the
> case of the monotheistic revelation. This takes place in time, in historical
> duration. (*Myth of the Eternal Return*, 104–5)

The implications of this are borne out by the development of the secular, "post-
Christian" West. The concept of "general revelation" implied by the valorization of
historical time eventually comes to confront that of the "special revelation" of the
biblical text (e.g.. Copernicus and biblical criticism).

Secondly, "history as the epiphany of God" leads to a linear notion of time as
once-and-for-all. This crystallizes in Christianity with the belief in the Incarnation
as the ultimate hierophany—*hapax, ephapax,* (Hebrews 9:12, Eliade also refers to 1
Peter 3:18). Not only is the singular unrepeatable notion of historical event emphasized, it is sacralized, and with it the whole of historical time is "redeemed." Also
the teleological linearity of time leads irresistibly to the notion of evolution whose
"mythical" aspect, that of continual *improvement*, has proved more tenacious than
its scientific aspect of the chance viability of random mutations (see Midgeley,
Evolution as a Religion). Time is increasingly perceived as a linear progression, a
direction, a single continuum outside of eternity (*illud tempus*), rather than an
oscillation *in* eternity. With the concomitant increasing de-valorization of the
traditional concepts of the sacred this time was even extended *ad infinitum*. Rather
than a closed cycle returning to *illud tempus*, the cosmos was for a while seen as

infinite in extent and duration. However, this extension has itself fallen prey to the hierophanization of the manifest. *Observation* has indicated that the universe is not infinite either in time or space. The consensus of scientific opinion is that our universe had a temporal commencement, it is finite, and it may well have a temporal end. This scientific return to a theory of temporal cycles was not lost on Eliade.

> In connection with this rehabilitation of cyclical conceptions, Sorokin rightly observes that present theories concerning the death of the universe do not exclude the hypothesis of the creation of a new universe, somewhat after the fashion of the Great Year in Greco-Oriental speculation or of the yuga cycle in the thought of India. (*Myth of the Eternal Return*, 146)

The Big Bang/Big Crunch concept of time as a closed cycle has certainly gained in scientific support since Sorokin published his observations in 1928,[3] however, the possibility of a re-creation is still an open question.

Weckman concludes that "because Eliade thinks of history as contemporary event he has ignored the important role of history as stories about the human past which can function like myth" (17). But this fails to grasp the point. History which "functions like myth" is by that very definition sacred history. Eliade's contention is that it is by virtue of a spiritual development of the most far-reaching implications that modern humanity has been able to see historical events as themselves exemplary, revelatory, possessed of real meaning. It is in any event *historiography* and not actual history which so functions, and so is not actually a temporal reality. Thus it is that Eliade recognizes the survival of mythology "more than anywhere else" in historiography (*Myth and Reality*, 113). This is the specific characteristic by which Eliade distinguishes "modern" humanity. We have "sacralized" *history*; that is, that we have specifically assumed that the real-time, historical actualities which constitute human experience can function as exemplary, that is sacred, history, and in so doing have "camouflaged" the sacred or "confused" it with the profane.

---

3. *Contemporary Sociological Theories*. For a modern conception of the closed cycle of time, see Stephen Hawkins, *A Brief History of Time*, 138.

CHAPTER 9

History and the Historical

It is obvious that the understanding of and attitude toward history are instrumental in the understanding of and attitude toward time constitutive of *homo religiosus*. In the preface to *The Myth of the Eternal Return*, Eliade, commented that "had we not feared to appear overambitious, we should have given this book a subtitle: *Introduction to a Philosophy of History*" (ix). The need to clarify that philosophy now presses for our attention. Although Eliade refers to history as "a succession of events that are irreversible, unforeseeable, possessed of autonomous value" (95), this is in the context of a claim that history "regarded as" such is *refused* by archaic humanity. So "history" must be more basic than this particular perspective upon it. As Eliade describes it, "'historical' memory . . . is the recollection of events that derive from no archetype, the recollection of personal events" (*Myth of the Eternal Return*, 75). He is more inclined to equate history with personal event, *Erlebnis*, actually lived experience. "Man is ineluctably conditioned," he says, "not only by his physiology and his heredity, but also by History and above all his personal history" (*Myths, Dreams and Mysteries*, 238). This is directly contiguous with his early interest in *trăirism*, authentic, lived experience already mentioned in chapter 1. As Eliade says,

> the expressions "history" and "historic" can occasion much confusion; they indicate, on the one hand, all that is *concrete* and *authentic* in a given human existence. (*Images and Symbols*, 171f. n. 13)

It is this lived experience—rather than history as a record of past events which are perhaps not within the orbit of personal experience—to which Eliade commonly refers as "history." This is the history we must tolerate. Yet history is also "the totality of the human experiences provoked by inevitable geographical conditions, social structures, political conjunctures, and so on" (*Myth of the Eternal Return*, 119). Of course, the totality of that experience is not actually accessible to us, it cannot become part of our own experience, it cannot become our own personal history. We are restricted to the study of the documents, activities, and relics which express that experience—the texts (in the broadest sense of the word) of the student of religion. And so, as Seymour Cain has pointed out,

> the term "history" for Eliade stands for the concrete actuality with which the religico-historical scholar must deal, for which he must account in his interpretations, and to which he has access through the historical documents. But historical data by themselves are not enough for the historian of religions. The facts . . . do not tell us what they mean. ("Mircea Eliade: Attitudes towards History," 14)

This locates Eliade's understanding of history neatly within his overall thought, dovetailing as it does with his concepts of hierophany and the dialectic of the sacred. The real (the sacred) is revealed (and concealed) within the actual historical documentary evidence which confronts the scholar (or anyone else in so far as they seek to discover truth). These documents, in becoming part of our personal experience, part of our history, are potentially hierophanic, depending on our background and personal religious experience to recognize the real which is revealed in and through them.

Yet another sense of history appears in Eliade's writing, however. "Archaic man also knows a history, although it is a primordial history, placed in a mythical time" (155). Here Eliade evidently does not use "history" in the sense of personal experience but of antecedent events considered to lead to and condition the present, without any overt attempt to distinguish the two. This history as antecedent event is what we might call historiography; the *interpretation and narration* of conditioning antecedents. This becomes *sacred history* when perceived as the true account of and for the human condition, it provides the exemplary archetypes for human behavior. Thus we have a reflexively propagating series of interpenetrating "histories" which change on each reflection. History as personal experience, the things which "enter into the lot of each individual and collectivity" ↔ History as the totality of human experiences ↔ History as the (abstract concept of) the chronological succession of unique and irreversible events in the external world ↔ History as the accurate description of all that has come to pass in the course of time ↔ History as (the record of) those events which are held to be the effective determinant antecedents of ↔ History as personal experience. I do not mean to suggest that this is a fixed or closed series, it is rather an unbounded proliferation in which any and every element is contained in any and every element with differing emphasis. "History" is not a simple term, but refers to the real. Human conceptions and constructions of "history" reflect the real with an infinite capacity for nuance and flavor. A growing understanding of the complexity of our involvement with history is one of the primary characteristics of recent thought.

Modern European historiography, on the other hand, sought "to know and describe, as accurately as possible, all that has come to pass in the course of time" (234).

> This interest in history is manifested in contemporary Western philosophy, in the tendency to define man as above all a historical being conditioned, and in the end created, by History. What is called historicism, *Historismus*, *storicismo*, as well as Marxism and certain existentialist schools . . . ascribe fundamental importance to history and to the historical moment. (*Myths, Dreams and Mysteries*, 233–234)

This is not history as Herodotus, Livy, or the Chinese knew it, however—the function of "traditional historiography . . . is always to provide exemplary models" (234).

Given this emphasis on history as the personally experienced time of the individual, what does Eliade understand by the archaic and modern abilities to "tolerate" that time?

THE TOLERATION OF HISTORY

In *The Myth of the Eternal Return* Eliade focuses his examination on "the solutions offered by the historicistic view to enable man to tolerate the increasingly powerful pressure of contemporary history" (141). This examination takes the form of a comparison of the way in which these two attitudes offer resistance to "the terror of history." For the modern mind, "history could be tolerated, not only because it had a meaning but also because it was, in the last analysis, necessary" (132). Although this might at first appear to say very little, our very reaction that of course history is "necessary," that is to us a self-evident truth, indicates our acquiescence to this view that history is tolerable because it is necessary. For the alternative mindset

> historical events could be given value by the expedient of . . . myths. . . . Adapted to a particular myth theory . . . catastrophes could not only be tolerated by their contemporaries but also *positively* accorded a value immediately after their appearance. (136)

Those events which could be so adapted gained ontology and significance by their assimilation to the sacred time of mythic origins and, as such, were no longer seen as history in the strict sense of irreversible events of autonomous significance. Against this history, traditional civilizations "defended themselves,"

> either by periodically abolishing it through repetition of the cosmogony and a periodic regeneration of time or by giving historical events a metahistorical meaning, a meaning that was not only consoling but was above all coherent, that is, capable of being fitted into a well-consolidated

system in which the cosmos and man's existence each had its *raison d'être.* (147)[1]

This periodic repetition of the cosmogony is the major characteristic of Eliade's "eternal return" along with the whole concept of a time which was not linear but cyclic and thus accessible to re-actualization.

The stated point of chapter 3 of *The Myth of the Eternal Return,* "Misfortune and History," is

> to learn how this "history" was tolerated by archaic man; that is, how he endured the calamities, the mishaps, and the "sufferings" that entered into the lot of each individual and each collectivity. (95)

His initial observation is that "suffering had a meaning; it corresponded, if not always to a prototype, at least to an order whose value was not contested" (96), that is, to a mythic order as we have described myth.

Thus "archaic man also knows a history, although it is a primordial history, placed in a mythical time" (155). Again Eliade uses "history" in the sense of antecedent events which have led to and condition the present, without any overt attempt to distinguish this usage from his more idiosyncratic usage of history as personally experienced actuality. It is a matter of pure conjecture whether this equivocation is deliberate stylistic policy, reproducing the conditions of an archaic text in need of decipherment, or an unfortunate oversight due to the lack of methodological rigor in an area of complex speculation. The effects in general have, I believe, been negative, resulting in the suspicion and opposition of those thinkers of a more rigorous disposition and the frequent failure of even those who agreed with Eliade's thought to fully appreciate its ramifications.

Whatever the case may be, it is Eliade's contention that "suffering becomes intelligible and hence tolerable" (98) through mythic and non-historical treatment. It is specifically by explaining hardships, by accounting for adversities, that humanity manages to tolerate them. This, too, is a claim which the critical modern mind might find hard to accept without support or clarification. Is it implied that without explanation suffering cannot be tolerated? That unless the ailment is made intelligible there is no hope of recovery? Obviously, this goes too far. Such an unconditional reading simply does not find accord with our intuitions of the real, our experience of history. Yet we are all familiar with the phenomenon of the increase of human tolerance with the increase of understanding; anguished children seek understanding of stomachache just as terminally ill patients seek understanding of their disease, and both seem to find in the proffered explanations the

---

1. Of particular interest here is this emphasis on meaning as "coherent," which in turn is defined as being fitted into a system. As we saw above, orientation within a system is precisely what the ordinary historical event lacked for premodern humanity.

strength to regain control of their actions, to stem the tears and continue to live in the face of present mortality. It is an undeniable fact of modern medical practice that placebos *work*. A clear strategy is often effective in what is now referred to as "pain management" even if the causal processes are dubious. Arguably, knowing what response to make in the face of hardship is as important as what the response actually is. The "will" is just as important as the "free" in "free will." That is to say, the fact that we will something, and that we have a clear vision of the desired end, and that we believe that we can attain that end,[2] is just as important to the "integral man" as the "freedom" to attain that end.

It is certainly a common enough apprehension of religion to see it as a diagnosis and therapy for the ailment which is the incarnate human condition. William James' *Varieties of Religious Experience* (393), is a clear example.

Eliade sees popular refusals of the hierophanization of history, of historicism, as having occurred because

> it was more consoling and easier, in misfortunes and times of trial, to go on accusing an "accident" (e.g., a spell) or a "negligence" (e.g., a ritual fault) that could be easily made good by a sacrifice. (*Myth of the Eternal Return* 108)

Obviously, the ills that flesh is heir to cannot be "made good" by a simple sacrifice, but the implication is that the archaic conception that these ills were caused by specific archetypal acts (or their negligence) provided a more easily accessible explanation *and one which prompted a clearer response*. This is why

> the great majority of so-called Christian populations continue, down to our day, to preserve themselves from history by ignoring it and by tolerating it rather than by giving it the meaning of a negative or positive theophany. (111)

Alternative means of preserving oneself from history or "abolishing" the significance of its effects are:

1. consciousness of living in an eternal present (coincidence with the atemporal instant of the revelation of archetypes)
2. periodically repeated ritual (for example, the rites for the beginning of the year), and
3. the future abolition of time, as in eschatology. (111)

---

2.   Which, if one accepts Wilfred Cantwell Smith's analysis of belief (*Belief and History*, chapter 2), simply means that we really want to attain that end and to remain loyal to that desire. The effectiveness of an ability to conceptualize and to believe in an end has been pointed out by psychological studies such as Martin Seligman's *Helplessness*.

These are present even in those "historical" religions which do recognize the value of the unique, experienced and irreversible event and, in common with the "pre-historicist" religions they do not "abolish" the event in any ontological sense, but re-establish the importance of a non-temporal, idealized moment, located and orientated within the extended matrix of mythical meanings. They do not "do away with" history as experience; rather they give another significance to those events which can be assimilated to archetypal models and drastically, if not totally, reduce the significance of those events which do not. To use a metaphor from radio reception, they filter out the noise of personal experience in favor of the signal, the message, of the impersonal, non-experiential, and mythological.

The unquestionable implication is that traditional humanity had been unable to adequately valorize their actual lived experience without specific reference to some *non*-historical reality. That reality is *illud tempus*, the non-temporal time, the primordial creative epoch. Since this "time" does not partake of historical actuality, the modern would say it was *merely* imaginary as it is accessible only through the imagination or, so it is said, through rare and difficult religious experience. However, in *The Myth of the Eternal Return*, Eliade collected certain facts for the specific purpose of revealing the "reality" of *illud tempus*:

1. Facts which show us that, for archaic man, reality is a function of the imitation of a celestial archetype.
2. Facts which show us how reality is conferred through participation in the "symbolism of the Center." (5)

It would have been simpler, more accessible to his readers, given Eliade's equation of reality and the sacred, if he had said "sacrality is a function. . . sacrality is conferred." He does stress this equation shortly after: "the outstanding reality is the sacred; for only the sacred *is* in an absolute fashion, acts effectively, creates things and makes them endure" (11). It seems likely that Eliade's insistence that it is *reality* which is in question here is a deliberate attempt to alert the reader to the fact that, for the archaic and religious mind under consideration, the actual perceptions of the real differ from those of the modern mind for whom the actual experience of everyday life, that is to say for whom *history*, has been evaluated as the real.

> It matters little if the formulas and images through which the primitive expresses "reality" seem childish and even absurd to us. It is the pro-found meaning of primitive behavior that is revelatory; this behavior is governed by belief in an absolute reality opposed to the profane world of "unrealities"; in the last analysis, the latter does not constitute a "world" properly speaking; it is the "unreal" *par excellence*, the uncreated, the nonexistent: the void.
>
> Hence we are justified in speaking of an archaic ontology, and it is only by taking this ontology into consideration that we can succeed in

understanding—and hence in not scornfully dismissing—even the most extravagant behavior on the part of the primitive world; in fact, this behavior corresponds to a desperate effort not to lose contact with *being*. (92)

Once again it is emphasized that the archaic ontology is not posited as an independent, autonomous reality, but as the Being within which certain people are, the *conceptions* (cf. Eliade's caveat quoted above, p. 78f.) of reality which condition the perceptions, the belief which governs the behavior.

Opposed to the archaic, traditional, and religious humanity is "historical man" who is equated with the modern "who consciously and voluntarily creates history" (141).

> The crucial difference between the man of the archaic civilizations and modern, historical man lies in the increasing value the latter gives to historical events, that is, to the "novelties" that, for traditional man, represented either meaningless conjunctures or infractions of norms (hence "faults," "sins," and so on) and that, as such, required to be expelled (abolished) periodically. The man who adopts the historical viewpoint would be justified in regarding the traditional conception of archetypes and repetition as an aberrant reidentification of history (that is, of "freedom" and "novelty") with nature (in which everything repeats itself). (154)

However, the modern world is

> not entirely converted to historicism; we are even witnessing a conflict between the two views: the archaic conception, which we should designate as archetypal and anhistorical; and the modern, post-Hegelian conception, which seeks to be historical. (141)[3]

Modern humanity differs from archaic cultures mainly in that the latter quite deliberately derive their valuation of human life from entities and events of non-empirical, non-historical status, whereas the former refuses to attribute any effective ontology to "imaginary" entities. This "ontology of the imaginary" is obviously important and I will return to it.

Whatever else may be implied by this discussion of the archaic and modern attitudes to history, Eliade's explicit conclusion is that "none of the historicistic philosophies is able to defend him [historical man] from the terror of history" (159). In context this implies that historicism leaves the details of personal experience as

---

3. What Eliade specifically denotes as "historicism" is indicated elsewhere. "In the various historicist and existentialist currents of thought, 'history' and 'historic' seems to imply that human existence is authentic only insofar as it is reduced to the *awakened consciousness of its historic moment*. It is to the latter 'totalitarian' meaning of history that I am referring when I take issue against 'historicisms'" (*Images and Symbols*, 172).

unique, unrepeatable, individual events, accidents in the stream of time. They are thus incapable of location in a coherent, consolidated system capable of explaining the *raison d'être* of man and the cosmos. Because of this they are meaningless, insignificant, and thus "intolerable." Eliade does

> imagine a final attempt: to save history and establish an ontology of history, events would be regarded as a series of "situations" by virtue of which the human spirit should attain knowledge of levels of reality otherwise inaccessible to it. (159)

In a footnote he continues that

> it is only through some such reasoning that it would be possible to found a sociology of knowledge that should not lead to relativism and skepticism. . . . But it goes without saying that a sociology of knowledge, that is, the study of the social conditioning of ideologies, could avoid relativism only by affirming the autonomy of the spirit—which, if we understand him aright, Karl Mannheim did not dare to affirm. (159 n. 15)

In light of these considerations, and from the point of view of modern historicism, it would seem that Eliade can be seen to propose a sociology of knowledge conditioned by the creativity and autonomy of the human spirit—a sociology of knowledge in which the spirit as the product of the confluence of conditioning factors (culture and tradition and belief which is the individual response to tradition) is yet seen as autonomous, capable of altering and partially controlling the factors which condition it.

Such a suggestion sees Eliade as moving forward, attempting to add newly created modes of thought, if not being, to contemporary humanity. He is thus not simply attempting to re-actualize the archaic ontology.

SOME PROBLEMS IN ELIADE'S USAGE OF THE WORD HISTORY

It is not only in direct confrontation with religious dogma, nor in scientific theories that this developing conception of time manifests itself. It is especially active and effective in philosophy. As Eliade states,

> Hegel affirmed that in nature things repeat themselves for ever and that there is "nothing new under the sun." All that we have so far demonstrated confirms the existence of a similar conception in the man of archaic societies:[4] for these things repeat themselves for ever and nothing

---

4.   I feel it necessary to point out that for Hegel it is nature, for the archaic, it is *Time* which repeats. It seems likely that, rather then not having detached himself from nature, archaic man had simply not detached his concept of time from nature.

new happens under the sun. But this repetition has a meaning, . . . events repeat themselves because they imitate an archetype—the exemplary event. Furthermore, through this repetition, time is suspended, or at least its virulence is diminished. But Hegel's observation is significant for another reason: Hegel endeavors to establish a philosophy of history in which the historical event, although irreversible and autonomous, can nevertheless be placed in a dialectic which remains open. For Hegel, history is "free" and always "new," it does not repeat itself; nevertheless, it conforms to the plans of providence; hence it has a model (ideal but none the less a model) in the dialectic of the spirit itself. To this history which does not repeat itself, Hegel opposes nature, in which things are reproduced *ad infinitum*. But we have seen that, during a considerable period, humanity opposed history by all possible means. (*Myth of the Eternal Return*, 90)

This is confusing because Eliade has not clearly established an unequivocal concept of history for his reader, he has not distinguished his working definition of "history" from the archaic concept of "history," or from the common sense of antecedent events. How can archaic humanity "oppose history" if they lack the concept? How can the "unreal," "uncreated" elements of the profane world be detected, let alone opposed and refused? His terminology is unclear and confusing. A few pages later he states that

archaic man, as has been shown, tends to set himself in opposition, by every means in his power, to history, regarded as a succession of events that are irreversible, unforeseeable, possessed of autonomous value. He refuses to accept it and grant it value as such, as *history*. (95)

This clarifies "history" as such a succession of events but it also clarifies the problem. How can archaic man, how can anyone, set themselves in opposition to history, regarded as something which they refuse to regard as history? In one sentence the reader must accept *both* Eliade's conception of history as profane personal experience *and* the concept of history as the proper conditioning antecedents, before the meaning becomes clearer. What is opposed in this proposed archaic mentality is personal experience which cannot be assimilated to an archetypal model or exemplary pattern, events which cannot be located in a system and are thus without sacred significance or real meaning. They can be *detected*, as can any meaningless combination of consonants and vowels. Human memory alone would reveal the irreversibility of historical events. But once inspected for meaning—that is, for correspondence to an exemplary model, for a positive orientation in the mythical world which is the source of meaning, for a graspable significance and a clearly required response—events might be "refused," rejected or opposed as mere experiential "noise," and thus would not be apprehended as real causal antecedents.[5] Archaic and religious humanity does have history, but it is "sacred history." It consists of myths regarding *illud tempus* rather than records of temporal antecedents. This sacred history seeks to give an authoritative explanation of phenomena and their origins, but does not seek for that authority in what "modern" humanity recognizes as the "real world."

Weckman considers this another flaw in Eliade's thought since it

> confuses us by using the term "sacred history" to refer to myths about *illo tempore*, the time before time, and not as a translation of *Heilsgeschichte* as it is commonly used to refer restrictively to Israel's perception of God's role in human events. (11)

However, as we have seen, Eliade's concept is broader. "Sacred history" refers to *that which is perceived as the real conditioning antecedent*, thus myths about *illud tempus*, the Hebrew *Heilsgeschichte*, and finally the "plenary" history of the historicists, are all "sacred history."

THE SOURCES OF ELIADE'S "HISTORY"

In the opening section of the final chapter of *The Myth of the Eternal Return*, "The Terror of History," Eliade's Romanian roots show quite clearly. It is still, he states, the traditional defence against history which

> continues to console the agricultural (= traditional) societies of Europe, which obstinately adhere to an ahistorical position and are, by that fact, exposed to the violent attacks of all revolutionary ideologies. The Christianity of the popular European strata never succeeded in abolishing either the theory of the archetype (which transformed a historical personage into an exemplary hero and a historical event into a mythical category) or the cyclical and astral theories (according to which history was justified and the sufferings provoked by it assumed an eschatological meaning). (*Myth of the Eternal Return*, 142)

Virgil Nemoianu has noted that Eliade and Vladimir Nabokov

---

5. Interestingly enough, this idea has received some possible support from recent cognitive psychology. "The most distinct property of the human brain is simply its extraordinary increase in relative size, which translates into increased numbers, and complexity, of memories" (Merlin Donald, Origins of the Modern Mind 8). Although the timescales are very different—Donald suggests 50,000–100,000 years since the advent of language made possible by this increase in size—vestigial traits and the slowness of cultural development could account for the delay in the effective expression of this increased time-consciousness in our effective environment.

were both lifelong emigrés; both are East Europeans. In consequence, the literary work of both is marked by an obsession with the injustice and destructiveness of historical Time which has wreaked havoc in their lives and in that of their family, class, or nation. Their work can be seen as an attempt at a historical retaliation. [And thus that] in the struggle between normal time and mythical time the first is usually the villain and more often than not the loser. ("Wrestling with Time: Some Tendencies in Nabokov's and Eliade's Later Works," 82)

Nemoianu is no doubt right that Eliade's life experience had a decisive effect upon his later apprehensions. It was surely the senseless and unstoppable events of his life as a citizen, and a very proud one, of a "secondary" culture which was frequently victim to the irresistible currents of history, which gave him the perspective of experiential history, the "existential situation" of the majority of humanity, as inherently without meaning. It is only through the "sacred histories," the mythological narratives and religious beliefs, that meaning can be invested in the otherwise vacuously horrible and horribly vacuous events of life itself. This in no way lessens the importance or validity of that viewpoint. History (both sacred and profane) is too often written by the victorious, the triumphant, the conquerors; founders of empires and inheritors of a powerful culture. For such people, their own historiography *is* sufficient to invest the motions of "real-time" history with coherent meaning. Certainly on the social and cultural level and also, to a lesser extent on the personal level. However, it is very much time that we listened to the point of view of the other, those from the "lesser" cultures; the victims of empire, whose cultures are constantly under threat from some "superpower" or other. These are, after all, the great majority of humanity. How do we invest our lives with meaning? It is not always the history of some successful, vigorous culture with which the individual can identify, which lends form and significance to human life. Eliade points out the ubiquitous human tendency to defer to the sacred history, the mythological time (and also, by extension, to the socially constructed historiography) by means of which human life (both individual and collective) can be interpreted as meaningful and coherent. It may be true that Eliade is, as Nemoianu suggests, "devoted to Language as opposed to Time" (89), but in a society in which time can only be grasped either directly through personal experience or indirectly through language, should not a great deal of attention go to that language through which impersonal Time is expressed, rather than to lionize that which we can never really know?

This is not a simple retreat into fantasy. As Charles Long has pointed out,

Eliade accepts the fact that historical reality defines reality *par excellence* for many in the modern world, but he is unwilling to accept the imperialism of the historicistic and rationalistic modes of interpretation as the only valid approaches to the real. ("The Significance for Modern Man of Mircea Eliade's Work," 136)

In other words, the meaning conferred upon historical time by mythic interpretations is also real. By way of explanation Long continues that

> a materialistic approach to history can explain the progress of man's technology and account for the abundance of material goods in our life, but it cannot tell us why we cannot truly enjoy our life; it cannot tell us why we have lost our sense of meaning. (142)

This obviously comes from a modern Western man for whom the historiography of his own culture manifestly fails to invest life with sufficient meaning, hence his "loss of a sense of meaning." It is Eliade's contention that modern humanity's only possible reply to this loss of meaning, orientated as we are to the historical as the real, is hermeneutics, the increase of significance through the interpretation of historical data.

This is precisely what Eliade does in interpreting the historical background of his native country and it is also worthy of note at this point that Eliade had an even more personal experiential basis for his notion of re-actualizable, alternative, and significant time. At the very beginning of his *Autobiography* he quite candidly tells of an event when he was four or five years old, walking with his grandfather on the Strada Mare in Tecuci, when his eyes met those of a fellow toddler, also walking with her grandfather.

> For several seconds we stared at each other before our grandfathers pulled us on down the street. I didn't know what had happened to me; I felt only that something extraordinary and decisive had occurred. In fact, that very evening I discovered that it was enough for me to visualize the image from Strada Mare in order to feel myself slipping into a state of bliss I had never known. . . . For years the image of the girl on Strada Mare was a kind of secret talisman for me, because it allowed me to take refuge instantly in that fragment of incomparable time. (*Autobiography*, vol. I, 4)

Shortly thereafter, although the occasion seems to be chronologically earlier, Eliade relates another incident in which he entered a room into which he was not normally allowed to go:

> the next moment I was transfixed with emotion. It was as if I had entered a fairy-tale palace. The roller-blinds and the heavy curtains of green velvet were drawn. The room was pervaded by an eerie iridescent light. . . . As was true also of the image of the little girl from Strada Mare, I could later evoke at will that green fairyland. . . . I practiced for many years this exercise of recapturing the epiphanic moment, and would always find again the same plenitude. I would slip into it as into a fragment of time devoid of duration—without beginning and without end. (7)

The very phrases are obviously meant to recall his theory of *eternal return*; the "fragment of incomparable time," the "epiphanic moment," "devoid of duration," which he can later "evoke at will" is evidently an echo of *illud tempus* which later animates his apprehension of religious life. This is not to say that Eliade's theories are based on mere subjective experience, grotesquely expanded to subsume all of the spiritual experiences of humanity. Eliade did not begin writing his memoirs until the 1960s, and these events were supposed to have taken place in 1910 or 1911.[6] It is rather the vocabulary of his theories which shapes his later descriptions. Nor would Eliade, after a lifetime of academic involvement, be ignorant of the accusations such a description could evoke. I believe that he is quite deliberately revealing that he considered this subjective experience of re-actualizable, non-chronological time to be an elementary human experience, and furthermore that subjective experience is not "mere" but is in fact the source of hierophany. In Judaeo-Christian terms it is a "terrifying dialogue with Yahweh" (*Myth of the Eternal Return*, 108).

ELIADE AS ANTI-HISTORIAN

When history as personal experience is seen as the source of all hierophany the question of Eliade's "anti-historicism" takes on a wholly different aspect. In a recent discussion of this criticism Douglas Allen has said,

> while demonstrating the primacy of the nonhistorical in Eliade's history and phenomenology of religion, even showing that this approach does indeed have an antihistorical normative basis, I shall argue that simply to dismiss or praise Eliade as antihistorical is to neglect what is essentially historical in his method and theory of religion. I shall argue, in other words, for the need to recognize a complex, dynamic, historical-nonhistorical, dialectical interaction if one is to do justice to Eliade's hermeneutical approach. ("Eliade and History," 547)

Allen's discussion of the critical appraisal of Eliade as "antihistorical" points out Wallace, Lord Raglan, Lessa, Leach, and Saliba as anthropologists who support this contention and Strenski and Baird as scholars of religion who do likewise (547). Allen accurately traces much of this reaction to the response to *Patterns*, in which

> critics noted that this synchronic, morphological study was not historical; religious structures were detached from their historical and cultural contexts. (563)

---

6.   Although Eliade did utilize the description of his experience in the iridescent room in his *Noaptea de Sanziene* (*The Forbidden Forest*), written between 1949 and 1954.

He would insist that

> Eliade affirms that one must do justice to both the historical particular and the universal structure, there can be little doubt that his approach emphasizes the nonhistorical universal structure rather than the concrete historical particular and that he conceives of his primary task as the interpretation of transhistorical religious meanings. (559f.)

Allen even goes on to say that

> without a recognition of the historical dimension of the data, there would be no appreciation of the contrary historicising movement; there would be no understanding of the structurally necessary dialectical tension existing between the contrary but interacting dialectical movements. In short, without the dynamic historical-nonhistorical interaction, there would be no process of sacralization as the universal structure of religious experience. (561)

I think this could be even more directly phrased: Without an incarnate existence involving the physical experience of the external world (history), we could not perceive those structures and relationships which we recognize as real (the morphology of the sacred). But without the sacred, which is abstract, hence nontemporal, non-empirical, and unmanifest, we could not react coherently with that world. That is to say, we could not survive, could not *be*.

Still, Allen concludes that "Eliade's approach does indeed have an antihistorical normative basis" (564), which, I think goes too far. Eliade is unquestionably *anti-historicist*, in that he repudiates that restriction of humanity to a purely historico-temporal, physical reality (see above, n. 3).

> It seems to me, indeed, that the authenticity of an existence cannot be limited to the consciousness of its own historicity; one cannot regard as "evasive" or "unauthentic," the fundamental experiences of love, anxiety, joy, melancholy, etc. Each one of these makes use of a temporal rhythm proper to itself, and all combine to constitute what might be called the *integral man*, who neither denies himself to his historic moment, nor consents to be identified with it. (*Images and Symbols*, 171f. n. 13)

The motivations, the reasons, the justifications, for any action ultimately lie on an ideal or abstract plane. Very few human actions can be satisfactorily or fully explained by physical determinatives. The reasons why we act in a certain way are almost always grounded in ideal structures of good and bad, right and wrong, normative notions which form archetypal, exemplary structures which, in their ideality, exist quite independently of the actuality of human experience which for Eliade constitutes history, and which are thus eternal. Although we cannot be said to be actually repeating an archetypal *act*, we can still be said to be following an archetypal model or *morphology*. As Eliade pointed out in connection with Hegel, the use of the ideal as model still follows the exemplary morphology of the sacred (see above p. 97). It is an important "methodological presupposition" of Eliade's that

> human creativity and, ultimately, the history of human culture is more directly related to what man has dreamt, believed and thought of his specific mode of being in the world than to the works which he has undertaken in order to promote and validate this mode of being. ("Notes on the Symbolism of the Arrow," 474)

Thus the alternative to a reality restricted to physical space and historical time, while allowing for the reality of the religious, while insisting, in fact, on the reality of God, the Dharma, the Tao, Allah, and so on, could none the less be explained in terms of the autonomy and creativity of the human spirit. Hence Eliade's terminology of hermeneutics as a "metapsychoanalysis" and his drive toward a "new humanism." Eliade cannot accurately be called "antihistorical" since the human condition still admits of the possibility of having its plenary existence in historical time and since he undoubtedly takes history to be the source of hierophany, the actual revelation of the real. Eliade certainly conducts a polemic against the valorization of history as the only real as provincial, Western, divisive, crypto-religious, spawned as a "decomposition product of Christianity,"[7] and capable of fulfilling a soteriological function only through an omniscient and omnipotent deity ("God for whom everything is possible"—*Myth of the Eternal Return*, 160; *History of Religious Ideas*, vol. I, 176), yet incapable of supporting *belief* in such a deity.

Seymour Cain echoes Charles Long's insistence on Eliade's historical basis.

> There is a firm commitment on Eliade's part to starting with the scholarly sources, directly or secondarily, through the work—translation, textual and historical criticism, etc.—of other scholars. "To the historical sources" would seem to be his motto. ("Attitudes toward History," 13)

ELIADE'S CRITIQUE OF HISTORICISM

Whether the historical sources to which Eliade returns are personal experience in Romania, or the learned observations of his fellow intellectuals (e.g., the story of the mythicization of an accidental death in the mountains, *Myth of the Eternal Return*, 44–46), in fact, whether his other particular observations are right or wrong,

---

7. *Sacred and the Profane*, 112. See also *Images and Symbols*, 170: "Historicism as such is a product of the decomposition of Christianity: It could only come about insofar as we had lost faith in the transhistorical reality of the historical event."

the principle still stands. Humanity observably inhabits a cosmos in which those elements which fit into a well-consolidated system capable of describing and explaining the existence of humanity, the cosmos, and humanity in the cosmos, are emphasized and those which do not so fit are repressed. The manipulation of our perception of time and history is a particularly influential factor in our overall conception of the cosmos and construction of such systems of meaning. The substitution of a linear and singular structure of time for a cyclical and repetitive one has far-reaching implications in any attempt to decipher the meanings of any religious reality.

In the section on "The Difficulties of Historicism" (*Myth of the Eternal Return*, 147–54), Eliade does, perhaps, overstep the bounds of his philosophical bailiwick in depreciating historicism and appreciating the archaic outlook on time. His proposed examination, as we have seen, is of the ability of the two conflicting attitudes to "enable man to tolerate the increasingly powerful pressure of contemporary history" (141), and there can be no doubt that he considers the archaic approach to be superior in this respect. As we have seen, the ability to enable toleration is equated with the ability to explain or describe meaningfully, which in turn is equated with an appropriate orientation or coherent fit into a consolidated system. Thus inconsistencies or self-contradictions are reductive of meaning and therefore of the ability to tolerate history as so defined. Eliade's major criticism is of the historicism of Hegel which emphasizes the unalterability and thus the *necessity* of historical events. Hegel had long been a fascination of Eliade's. In the *Journal* he writes, "I return to Hegel. This has been happening for the past five or six years, since I've been wrestling with the meaning of 'history'" (*Journal* I, 174, entry for September 1952). His conclusion was that in order to know what was "necessary" in history,

> Hegel believed that he knew what the Universal Spirit wanted. We shall not insist on the audacity of this thesis, which, after all, abolishes precisely what Hegel wanted to save in history—human freedom. But there is an aspect of Hegel's philosophy of history that interests us because it still preserves something of the Judaeo-Christian conception: for Hegel, the historical event was the manifestation of the Universal Spirit. Now it is possible to discern a parallel between Hegel's philosophy of history and the Hebrew prophets: for the latter, as for Hegel, an event is irreversible and valid in itself inasmuch as it is a new manifestation of the will of God—a proposition really revolutionary . . . from the viewpoint of traditional societies dominated by the eternal repetition of archetypes. (*Myth of the Eternal Return*, 148)

Although Eliade's major point seems to be to emphasize the dependence of Hegelian philosophy of history on the spiritual insights of the Hebrew prophets, he also points out the contradiction in this philosophy of its own declared end, that of retaining human freedom. This poses a serious challenge to the adequacy of such a philosophy to the task of increasing the ability to tolerate history. Of course, Eliade was aware that Hegel's was not the only philosophy of history, not the only "historicism," and he also crams mentions of Rickert, Troeltsch, Dilthey, Simmel, Croce, Karl Mannheim, Ortega y Gasset, Meinecke, Heidegger, Gentile, and Karl Löwith onto one page (150). He states that

> this essay does not require us to discuss either the philosophical value of historicism as such or the possibility of establishing a "philosophy of history" that should definitely transcend relativism.

And he repeats,

> again, there is no question of judging the validity of a historicistic philosophy, but only of establishing to what extent such a philosophy can exorcise the terror of history. (150, 160)

However, it would seem that in the last analysis that is precisely what *is* required. As he repeatedly says, "only one question concerns us: How can the 'terror of history' be tolerated from the viewpoint of historicism" (150)? Since the ability to tolerate history is intimately connected with internal coherence and the uncovering of *raisons d'être* (142), this question cannot be answered independently of an assessment of the philosophical validity and transcendence of apparent internal difficulties. Despite his manifest philosophical timidity here, Eliade does, in fact, attempt a concise attack on the philosophy of the historicist position; the substance of this attack is that Dilthey and Meinecke failed to surpass the problems of relativism and that Heidegger showed that the historicity of human existence forbids all hope of transcending time and history. Furthermore,

> justification of a historical event by the simple fact that it is a historical event, in other words, by the simple fact that "it happened that way," will not go far toward freeing humanity from the terror that the event inspires. (150)

Eliade immediately goes on to explain that this is because beyond the historical event per se the suffering man

> can see no sign, no transhistorical meaning. . . . In the past, humanity has been able to endure the sufferings we have enumerated: they were regarded as a punishment inflicted by God, the syndrome of the decline of the "age," and so on. And it was possible to accept them precisely because, for the greater part of mankind, still clinging to the traditional viewpoint, history did not have, and could not have, value in itself. Every hero repeated the archetypal gesture, every war rehearsed the struggle

between good and evil, every fresh social injustice was identified with the sufferings of the savior, etc. (151)

This is to say, historicism fails to answer this need in the endurance of the human condition because it does not orientate the historical event in an extended system of recognizable evaluations, a mythic matrix of meanings. Accurate *description* of the event does not fully suffice to this end, it merely represents the event rather than revealing its significance, it reforms it rather than transforms it. Of course, if you say that an event has no significance, then it has no significance; this mythic significance *must be* a construct of socialized knowledge and as such is always open to refusal.

While fulfilling the requirements of coherence a purely factual description neglects the question of the *raison d'être*. The modern, historicist attitude states finally, "that is how it is because that is how it is," which is no account at all. The archaic attitude is, "that's how it is because that's how the Gods made it, or because when Śiva passed this way with the dead Satī a drop of her blood fell here." This is an account which appeals to mythic structures to reveal the correct evaluative response and thus to provide a specific relation to the phenomena in question and a means of dealing with, "enduring" or "tolerating" it. While the historicist might reply that such an explanation induces complacency and unnecessary languishing in a situation which might be improved, Eliade's counter is that

> by virtue of this view, tens of millions of men were able, century after century, to endure great historical pressures without despairing, without committing suicide or falling into that spiritual aridity that always brings with it the relativistic or nihilistic view of history. (152)

CONCLUSIONS

This is an argument which will not be easily settled. The fact is that much of humanity, both in the past and in the present, *has* survived without the benefits of a "modern" civilization. It is also a fact that "modern" humanity is not committing suicide in droves, although given the material benefits of contemporary Western civilization, suicide and other acts of palpable despair do seem troublingly common. It is Eliade's contention that the despair of modern humanity

> is a despair provoked not by his own human existentiality, but by his presence in a historical universe in which almost the whole of mankind lives prey to a continual terror (even if not always conscious of it). (162)

I cannot hope to deal with the question of the relative adequacy of the historicist as opposed to the mythic attitudes to explanation of the harsh realities of life any more than Eliade could. I take my lead from the footnote which he adds to his discussion in which he points out that "historicism" was created and professed above all by thinkers belonging to nations for which history has never been a continuous terror. These thinkers would perhaps have adopted another viewpoint had they belonged to nations marked by the "fatality of history." (152 n. 11)

It seems likely that historicistic positivism is a philosophy which is adequate for those societies and individuals who can "afford" it, that is, who are not suffering from the continuous vicissitudes and turmoils of political, social, economic, or geographical crises. If this were the case, then those societies which are so troubled would not only be marked by the mythic attitude of return to the "horizon of archetypes and repetition," they would, in fact, be sustained by it. The twin difficulty which arises is then, how does a crisis-ridden "traditional" society escape the complacent acceptance of historical event as divinely ordained which ensures the continuation of its condition, and how do the members of a modern secular society endure the personal existential crises for which historicism and positivism fail to adequately account? The only answer would seem to lie in a struggle for equilibrium between the two; whenever one attitude becomes prevalent or achieves a monopoly, society is dependent for its health and improvement on the reassertion of the alternative. Such an account would not only recognize the value of both attitudes to history but would also account for Eliade's staunch defence of the traditional attitude in a world (the Europe of 1948) where the modern historicist-positivist attitude seemed to be in danger of sweeping all before it and burying all spiritual values completely beneath an adamantine crust of empirically assured and materially manifestable dicta. His conclusion, that humanity must have "faith or despair," stems from these considerations.

> Faith, in this context, as in many others, means absolute emancipation from any kind of natural "law" and hence the highest freedom that man can imagine: freedom to intervene even in the ontological constitution of the universe. (161)

It should be recalled that "archaic man takes part in the repetition of the cosmogony, the creative act *par excellence*" (158), and is thus also involved in the ontological constitution of the universe.

As a propaedeutic to a sociology of knowledge which posits the autonomy of the human spirit, Eliade's thought can be seen to reveal a potentially valid dynamic which conditions and produces positive evaluations of history as experience. In so doing Eliade could attempt a restitution of "faith" without the total abandonment of the critical attitude. In order to have such faith in one's religious tradition, one need not relinquish all criteria of recognition of the historically real, but must see these apparently conflicting and mutually exclusive attitudes as rather different planes of reality. They are different paradigms which apply independently, different models which both partially and incompletely represent the totality which language, as a closed system is inadequate to express. (Both Gödel's theorem and deconstruction support this contention.)

It is my hope that this prolonged discussion of Eliade's treatment of time and history has served not only to clarify his meaning but also his implicit method. As we have seen it is crucial at certain points that one accept his definitions, even though they remain only implicit, in order to grasp his meaning. The given relationships of the elements of his analysis must be accepted as given before the meaning of the whole becomes transparent. *Credo ut intelligam* becomes a methodological device relating at least to the temporary suspension of one's disbelief if not the active engagement of one's acceptance. The interrelations of the elements of a mythic matrix must be accepted as they are before they can be understood for what they imply. This does not mean that I must become a Buddhist with all that that entails in order to understand Buddhism, any more than that I must become French in order to understand French. It does mean that I must accept that *lapin* means rabbit and that *sauvage* means undomesticated rather than vicious, before I will understand the meaning of *un lapin sauvage*. (And it could be argued that in so doing I do become that little bit more *français*, but that's another story.) The point is that in order to come to an understanding of the religious meanings of other peoples' beliefs scholars of religion must not "isolate themselves in their own beliefs" (*No Souvenirs*, 233). We cannot commence by insisting on our own intuitions of the real and thus denying others' hierophanies any reference to reality, any more than we could arrive at an understanding of Eliade's meaning here if we commenced by insisting on the accepted usage of the word history and denying his alternative usages of the word as personally experienced events or as determinative antecedents. If we insist on our own usual interpretations of *sauvage*, then *un lapin sauvage* becomes quite ridiculous. Similarly, if we insist on our own intuitions of the real, conditioned by our own personal experience of our own culture, then the expressions of different modes of human being, be they exotic or merely alternative, will remain opaque to our interpretation.

CHAPTER 10

Some Initial Conclusions

The possibilities of a conceptual schema which permits both the committed believer and the skeptical researcher to express mutually comprehensible ideas concerning the nature of the real and the human relation to it, should be obvious. The tendency of the field of religious studies to polarize into entrenched and opposed camps of belief/non-belief could be reversed. Mutually incomprehensible expressions concerning the revelation of the sacred, or human apprehension of the nature of the real, can become the common ground for debate rather than the frontline of battle. There is a possible objection that all that has been increased is the lack of clarity, that what one person (a Christian believer, for example) understands by "the sacred" is radically different from what another (a secular rationalist, for example) understands. Thus it is misunderstanding rather than understanding which has been increased. However, I would argue that a recognition has been made of the true polysemic nature of the speculative language of human confrontation with our environment. The desire to simplify language, to strip it of all ambiguity and reduce its significations to a single, technical, and unmistakable meaning is admirable in its place and eminently useful when it succeeds. However, in the vocabulary of ultimate meanings, the real, the sacred, the true have never been reduced to singular meanings and to insist otherwise is simply inaccurate.

Religion is the total structure of values held, traditionally transmitted through a cultural matrix of symbol, oral and written narrative, scripture and ritual, and reinforced by mythical rather than by rational means. This structure is dependent upon self-authenticating intuitions of the real, hierophanies or revelations apprehended in individual experience, human cognitive interaction with our environment. Theology is a combination of reinforcement of a pre-existent value-structure and the delicate adjustment required of that structure to ensure its successfully continuing existence. The study of religion is the scrutiny of those values and their derivation. Both are necessary to the existence of value in human society. As an opinion this is not entirely new but was anticipated to some extent by Joachim Wach:

> If it is the task of theology to investigate, buttress, and teach the faith of a religious community to which it is committed, as well as to kindle zeal and fervor for the defense and spread of this faith, it is the responsibility of a comparative study to guide and to purify it. (*The Comparative Study of Religion*, 9)

Without the honest search for and questioning of "orthodoxies," the theologians would have no instruments to measure their success, no critical tools with which to perform their self-appointed task. Without the positive commitment characteristic of theologians, there would be no value systems to question. The final truth is that we are all compounds of both; we all apply some values to test others. Having found what was sought, men of even the greatest faith were not inclined to leave it unchanged (Aquinas and Augustine, for example). Scholarship tends to emphasize scrutiny of old and development of new values, while theology emphasizes the preservation and transmission of pre-existing values. Often the enthusiasm of the latter seems to stem from a recognition of the frailty of human cultural values, of the traditionally encoded significations that they have recognized. This can all too easily be seen as a lack of faith in their own tradition, but is based in a real recognition of the frailty of specific vehicles and the absolute importance of their contents. (Their importance is absolute in the sense that without them there would be no hierarchy of values, no discrimination, and finally no value.) While it is denied that any specific concept is exclusively absolute or fundamental, it is allowed that all self-consistent systems are descriptions of reality—albeit partial and incomplete—and as such do have importance and are, in some wise, true. For this to be acceptable it must be recognized that any self-consistent system is based in genuine intuitions (used consistently in the sense of a self-authenticating apprehension, be it sensory or rational) of the real. The specific conclusion which renders this acceptance consistent in the writings of Mircea Eliade is that everything, all apprehensions, all phenomena, are potential hierophanies.

ELIADE'S HISTORY OF RELIGIONS

I have argued that Eliade had a specific, and rather idiosyncratic, understanding of history which did not prevent him from also using the word in its common sense of temporal antecedents. In this light his "history of religions" is the study of the historical antecedents of the human phenomenon referred to as "religion," but it is also the interpretation of the data which present themselves to the individual scholar and thus become part of his or her actual lived experience (history in his personal sense).

Insofar as the scholar recognizes the real revealed by these data, they constitute hierophanies for him or her. That this makes the history of religions itself a religious exercise is no adverse criticism since it is held that *"living as a human being* is in itself a *religious act"* (*Quest*, preface). The historian of religions can thus realize the meanings of archaic, exotic, or contemporary religious phenomena, that is to say, can realize both the significance of that religious phenomenon for the actual life of the believer and the significance of that particular phenomenon for the general existential situation of humanity in our confrontation with our environment. In order to do this, it would seem that a certain commitment is necessary to the acceptance that those data *are* (or were) actually and realistically meaningful to the believer and that this meaning is capable of reactualization. Given this commitment, an extensive exposure to the actual historical data is absolutely necessary in order to "ground," as it were, one's interpretations with the external realities implied in one's texts, as opposed to the internal realities of one's own personal experience. This corresponds to *both* Eliade's much criticized principle of the non-reduction of religious experience *and* his insistence on the dependence of the scholar on accurate historical information. The religious phenomena must be understood in their own terms in order for their meaning, both for the believer and for the present scholar, to be realized. It is precisely this principle of understanding one's object of study in its own terms that I am seeking to apply in understanding Eliade in his own terms as he used those terms.

It should be borne in mind that Eliade's master's thesis at the University of Bucharest was written on Italian Renaissance philosophers from Ficino to Bruno, and that Italian Renaissance humanism was one of the major influences on the young Eliade before he set off for India in order to "universalize" the "provincial" philosophy he had inherited from his European education.[1] Isaiah Berlin, in his book *Vico and Herder*, indicates seven theses thought to be Vico's main creations; the fifth of these is that

> the creations of man—laws, institutions, religions, rituals, works of art, language, song, rules of conduct, and the like—are not artificial products created to please, or to exalt, or teach wisdom, nor weapons deliberately invented to manipulate or dominate men, or promote social stability or security, but are natural forms of self-expression, of communication with other human beings or with God. The myths and fables, the ceremonies and monuments of early man, according to the view prevalent in Vico's day, were absurd fantasies of helpless primitives, or deliberate inventions designed to delude the masses and secure their obedience to cunning and unscrupulous masters. This he regarded as a fundamental fallacy. Like

---

1. On Eliade's master's thesis, see Ricketts, *Romanian Roots*, 319–24. On his motivations for visiting India, see Al-George, "India in the Cultural Destiny of Mircea Eliade," 124f.

anthropic metaphors of early speech, myth and ritual are for Vico so
many natural ways of conveying a coherent view of the world as it was
seen and interpreted by primitive men. (xviii)

This explains as clearly as any words could Eliade's attitude of "nonreduction."
Berlin sees this principle of Vico as leading directly to a nonreductive type of
aesthetics in which

> works of art must be understood, interpreted, evaluated, not in terms of
> timeless principles and standards valid for all men everywhere, but by
> correct grasp of the purpose and therefore the peculiar use of symbols,
> especially of language, which belonged uniquely to their own time and
> place. (xix)

This was the same banner which Eliade carried forward in his attempt to understand religion "in its own terms."

A further thrust of Eliade's thought on the history of religions is clearly
evident in his criticism of van der Leeuw, who

> thought, wrongly, that he could reduce the totality of all religious
> structure to three *Grundstructuren*: Dynamism, Animism, and Deism.
> However, he was not interested in the history of religious structures. Here
> lies the most serious inadequacy of his approach; for even the most
> elevated religious expression (a mystical ecstasy, for example,) presents
> itself through specific structures and cultural expressions, which are
> historically conditioned. (*Quest*, 35)

Thus Eliade strongly affirms the significance of history (that is, both *erlebte Zeit*
and recorded history) as established, as he would have it, by the Abrahamic
traditions. He is in no way denying the importance of the "desacralized cosmos,"
but seems to be saying that it is one among many loci of significance, and that, in
accordance with his dialectic of the sacred, significance is in everything in which it
is apprehended. Only our failure to appreciate it as sacred makes a thing profane.

Eliade's writings are so profuse on one hand, and unsystematized on the other,
that there is an almost irresistible tendency to read into them things he may not
have intended. However, it is also quite possible to miss in the huge haystack of his
oeuvre some very significant needles, and his insistence on the importance of
historically accurate data has been one of the most critical.

Eliade's conclusions are in favor of an integral study of religion:

> if the "phenomenologists" are interested in the meanings of religious data,
> the "historians" on their side attempt to show how these meanings have
> been experienced and lived in the various cultures and historical moments.

This can provoke a tension by means of which *Religionswissenschaft* escapes
dogmatism and stagnation. Unfortunately, as is so often the case, his concluding

sentence of this section of *The Quest* (9) imparts an almost mystical tone: "the history of religious meanings must always be regarded as forming part of the history of the human spirit." This is a vague caveat whose meaning remains unclear to me. It may be that Eliade merely seeks to remind us that, on the one hand, the history of religions is a process of self-understanding for humanity rather than an attempt to reveal any transcendent ontology. On the other hand, such terms as "spirit" are not without significance to the latter process.

He repeatedly states that the ultimate aim of his research is to discover the *meaning* of religious facts and particularly of the change and development of religious facts through history. Rather than seeking an accurate "archeological" reconstruction or phenomenological description of religious data, Eliade is attempting to discover the meanings of these data. It is typical of a hermeneutical approach to assume there to be a "meaning" in a certain datum. In literary theory, "positive" hermeneutics assumes a singular meaning to have been deliberately and consciously embedded in a text by an author. The aim of interpretation is to recover that meaning unchanged. "Negative" hermeneutics, on the other hand, assumes that the meaning is derived from the text but is also dependent on the act of inter-pretation.[2] Eliade certainly agrees with the latter, but his "creative hermeneutics" of religious data reflects a development in which the response of the interpreter, conditioned by historical influences but liberated from determinism by the creativity of human imagination, is recognized as crucial to the interpretation of all lived experience, not purely of the literary text.

Possibly a major source of this conviction is the Romanian folk ballad, the *Miorița*, discussed by Eliade in his *Zalmoxis, the Vanishing God* (226–56). To relate briefly and simplistically the salient point, a shepherd is warned of his own impending murder at the hands of rival shepherds by a clairvoyant ewe-lamb. Rather than bemoaning his fate, the shepherd imaginatively valorizes his death as a celestial marriage. (This is a grossly oversimplified reading of a complex issue and Eliade's discussion should be consulted for an introduction to the themes involved.) This theme of an imaginative reappraisal of an unavoidable death is repeated in Eliade's play *Iphigenia*, based on Euripides' play *Iphigenia in Aulis*. Iphigenia, daughter of Agamemnon, is sacrificed to pacify the gods whose winds held the ships of the Achaeans and their allies pinned on the shore at Aulis, unable to depart for Troy. Once again the victim, to the complete incomprehension of the other characters, manages to see her fate as positive if not glorious. Once again the point seems to be (or, rather, one of a complex of points seems to be) that the exercise of the creative imagination can render meaningful (which is to say, can provide an adequate and satisfactory personal response to) the most grossly determined of historical events.

---

2. This division of hermeneutics can be attributed to Wolfgang Iser; see for example "The Reading Process: A Phenomenological Approach," *New Literary History* 3 (1972): 279–99.

Another factor of Eliade's history of religions is indicated by his statement that

> the contribution made by the historian of religions seems to me crucial. It lays bare the unity of the human condition, and it does so in our modern world, which is becoming a "planetary" one. (*Ordeal by Labyrinth*, 122)

This is to say that, although specific individual experience and personal history condition (and are reciprocally conditioned by) the individual creative imagination, Eliade recognizes a basic unity of the human race revealed in universal religious structures even though the capability to apprehend certain meanings in certain events is itself culturally conditioned. Not only the common anthropological biology, but the location of that biology in a common world and the possession by that biology of a creative faculty of imagination, ensures a human unity to the history of religion.

This fundamental unity of religion ensures that the understanding of religious phenomena is finally a self-understanding. Eliade speaks of "profound changes in religious concepts and behavior," and recognizes that "religious structures are susceptible to radical changes" ("Structures and Changes in the History of Religion," 353). Such a change

> indicates modifications in man's existential situation. It is part and parcel of the discoveries which man has been led to make about himself and his world. These discoveries are of a religious nature. The task of the historian of religions is to show how they are articulated in the total process of history. (354–55)

Thus he sees the task of the historian of religions to be to show how humanity's progressive discoveries about ourselves in the world lead to changes in our existential condition, expressed as changes in the history of religion. Finally, Eliade sees this process as a way to increase our awareness of our contemporary existential situation (*Two and the One*, 13), a task some might consider more suited to philosophy. But it must be remembered that Eliade considered the history of religions to be an essentially philosophical task (see the 1952 foreword to *The Myth of the Eternal Return*).

THE ETHICAL QUESTION

In this context I would like to suggest a possible explanation of Eliade's failure to address the question of ethics. The existential philosophy so active in Eliade's cultural background challenges any and all moral codes or systems. The emphasis upon human freedom implies that no amount of *reason* can validate or ensure compliance with any particular moral standard. Hume's assault on the naturalistic fallacy in the eighteenth century had already emphasized our formal, logical inability to derive moral standards from factual claims. Eliade's whole pattern of thought, based as it is in empirical but interpreted sense data, accepts this formal inability even though it indicates the mechanisms by which in fact moral systems are supported by empirical experience. The difficulty which remains is cultural relativism—very much a live problem in Eliade's time. Ruth Benedict's *Patterns of Cultures*, often cited as exemplary of the position, was published in 1935, for example. Any attempt to recognize the roots of any conceptual schema (moral, mythical, doctrinal, or political) in physical experience runs directly into the problem of the relativism of that experience. Different life-experience produces and is produced by different moral standards. There is no single monolithic or mono-logical basis or validation of any ethics (except perhaps in retrospect). Our freedom to interpret our experience both renders the notion of any basis for moral abso-lutism vacuous and at the same time provides a response to the Humean dictum of "no 'is' implies an 'ought.'" No element of practical experience can logically, formally, and apodictically imply an ought, but, in fact that is exactly what happens. Through the reciprocal reinforcement of cultural experience and interpretation our experiences do imply a binding moral system, as pleasure and pain are produced in some kind of response to our actions and apprehended as reward or punishment— the approval or disapproval of Yahweh, the operations of eternal *karma*, and so on. Of course, these interpretations can allow different moral values to be implied by the same physical manifestations as they are experienced by differently prepared individuals—and the thicket of cultural relativism looms.

In some ways it could be thought that Eliade was constantly talking about ethics, despite his non-use of the standard vocabulary of moral philosophy. Like the untellable secrets of *Le Macranthrop* and *Uniformes de Général*, the data was expressed in forms his audience were not as yet equipped to appreciate.

Merely formal rejections of cultural relativism valorize the interpretative forms of our own culture over the empirical fact that different life experiences *do* produce different moral standards. The history of religions could embrace that factual relativism and proceed from there rather than attempting to impose an interpretative framework *a priori* upon the data. It might be suggested that Eliade's apparent avoidance of ethical issues is an indication of his avoidance of *apriorism*, for ethics can be authorized in no other way. And yet the implied ethics of his thought would be worth pursuing since it does assume an *a priori* evaluation of the human ability to interpret events as hierophanies (or not) as constitutive of humanity and as universal, and it seems possible that it could lead to a type of relativism without skepticism.

MORE POSSIBLE PROGRESS?

The positive connotations of this analysis need to be considered. First, one of the greatest barriers to an adequate understanding of religion could thus be removed.

The belief that certain people, specifically positivists, empiricists, historicists, are not religious has necessarily entailed the rejection of all definitions broad enough to include, say, early Buddhism or Marxism. Such definitions are also broad enough to include positivists and historicists, and their categorical denial of religiousness appears to invalidate their inclusion. In fact, it is typically religious behavior for the newly emerged sect to attempt to divorce itself radically from previous religious forms. Even Karl Barth's early rejection of all religion as idolatry, compared with the true divine revelation of Christianity, is a typical attempt to claim as essential differences which are finally incidental. Observable fact seems to concur with Eliade that humanity everywhere throughout history has been classifiable as "religious" in some, possibly unrecognized, way and that contemporary humanity is no different, despite a unique existential situation and an unshakable conviction in the meaning and significance of manifest event. One must wonder whether psychology could have ever coherently constituted itself if some people were allowed to have no psyche, or sociology if some people had no society. Of course, the converse claim of neo-orthodox theology, the Roman Church, or any religious institution, to be in possession of the *only* revelation must likewise be surrendered.

Secondly, another positive implication of Eliade's thought is that truth, reality, power, significance, in short his "sacred," are freed from historical actuality and ontological independence. The occasionally frantic attempts to establish the historical veracity of religious texts, encountered in varying degrees from fundamentalism to religiously motivated archaeology, must be called into question. They would seem to be attempts to reconcile two different traditions, that of modern historicism and that of an earlier traditional belief. As Eliade pointed out in one of his fictional works, theological or mythological systems of thought can be utilized in "integrating the presuppositions and conclusions" of one's experiences of reality, *regardless of the historical accuracy of their contents* (*Tales of the Sacred and Supernatural*, 44), and "one of the fascinating aspects of the 'cultural fashion' is that it does not matter whether the facts in question and their interpretation are true or not" (*Occultism, Witchcraft, and Cultural Fashions*, 19).

Thirdly, such an understanding would serve to stand against all sweeping rejections of religion per se as meaningless reference to a non-existent realm. The insistence upon empirical, manifest, "reality" as the ultimate locus of meaning is itself a recent belief of a religious nature. It has no more inherent authority than any traditional religious system. Its powerful compulsion resides, in fact, in its breadth of acceptance, its spread as a faith. Quite contrary to this insistence is the ease with which we accept the intangible and mysterious trappings of modern science, from black holes to quantum interconnectedness. We now inhabit a world more densely stocked with accepted invisible entities than the most superstitious of medievals ever did. As I have said, Eliade insists that the sacred (and therefore the real) is present and active in the imaginary universes of contemporary humanity. Yet our imagination is often exercised in realms which are so radically divorced from that of human experience that meaning, in the sense of exemplary structures requiring a human response, is increasingly difficult to find, and the meanings of traditional religious expressions have tended to be increasingly occluded. Traditional religions are not thus meaningless but their impact has been considerably reduced by this "identification of the sacred and the profane." However, as with any structured narrative, the meaning of a religion, the point of a parable, like the wit of a joke, or the meaning of a myth, can be re-actualized, re-realized, by scholarship which involves the creative imagination, informed by experience with a coherent sense of the reality or sacrality originally apprehended in that narrative. It is the exhaustive identification of a specific historical situation with the real, the simultaneous denial of the imaginary worlds of others and the affirmation of the unique and independent reality of one's own "historical situation," which constitutes a novel and dangerous departure from the traditional operations of the religious mind.

PART TWO

Previous and Potential Criticisms

INTRODUCTION

In the first part of this work I have expounded a particular interpretation of the academic writings of Mircea Eliade on religion and in that light undertaken an analysis of his various neologisms, specialist terms, and idiosyncratic uses of language. In this second part I intend to inspect some of the implications of this interpretation, in respect of our understanding both of Eliade and of religion. Previous scholarly interpretations and analyses of Eliade's thought will be inspected in the light of the present interpretation. Possible objections will be considered, and some implications for a revised understanding of religion will be examined. Finally, I will make some observations regarding the application of this interpretation to recent critical theory including the rather vexed contemporary issue of postmodernism.

It is not my purpose to orient the thought of Mircea Eliade in the historical development of the academic study of religion. This has been admirably and clearly done by others, for example, Douglas Allen, in *Structure and Creativity*. Instead, I wish to consider in some detail the criticisms that other scholars of religion have made of Eliade's approach.

CHAPTER 11

Relativism

One major problem which emerges from the foregoing analysis is that of relativism. Is it not the case that my interpretation of Eliade, by deferring the question of the ontology of the sacred, by reducing the questions of religion from reality to being and meaning, by making truth dependent on belief, and particularly by relativizing "reality" itself, opens Eliade's thought to accusations of relativism? Previous critics have stopped short of accusing Eliade of relativism precisely because of his apparent insistence on the sacred as real. Robert Segal, for example, has said that

> Eliade declares that a believer's belief in the transcendent is true because it corresponds to external reality, Wittgensteinian fideists would declare that belief is true only because it is as coherent as a non-believer's. ("In Defense of Reductionism," 106)

Thus if the external reality of "the transcendent" be held in abeyance as the preceding arguments contend, Eliade is left in the same relativist trap as the fideists with no criteria of judgment other than pure subjectivity. Certainly, *subjectivism* has been prominent in the charges levelled against the Romanian historian of religions, and as Roger Trigg has pointed out

> the term "relativism" is often used without any great precision, and it sometimes appears to be no more than a synonym for "subjectivism." The subjectivist thinks that what I think is true for me and what you think is true for you. He is making truth relative to individuals rather than to groups of people. (*Reason and Commitment*, 3)

Furthermore, it is noticeable that Mac Ricketts had appealed to precisely this subjectivist aspect of Eliade's thought in his article, "In Defense of Eliade."

> Eliade has misled some readers by his definition of the sacred as the "real." Some have thought that this means that Eliade himself regards the

sacred as Reality: that is that he is making a theological statement. Eliade would deny this. All he means here is that *for the believer*, that which is sacred *for him* is the Real, the True, the meaningful in an absolute sense. (28)

In order to clarify and adjudicate in this issue, I would first like to consider the nature of "relativism" before attempting to decide whether or not this appellation is applicable to Eliade.

WHAT IS RELATIVISM?

Keith Yandell has described "simple relativism" as the contention that "a proposition P is true if and only if it is true for me" ("Some Varieties of Relativism," 62). "Complex relativism" Yandell sees as the same contention but concerning truth "for" a society rather than "for" an individual. These two forms of relativism can, although not exactly, be assimilated to conceptual relativism and cultural relativism respectively. Finally, Yandell describes "a more sophisticated relativism" in which it is held that

> if both of radically different worldviews can be immune to external rational assessment and are internally coherent and not observationally disqualified, according to whatever their possibly quite different internal standards (if any) require, then each, the suggestion goes, passes what muster one can rationally ask a worldview to pass and if one person accepts one and another accepts the other, neither is more rational in so doing than the other. A person who must choose between one such worldview and another had best hope that *tossing a coin* is included in his present perspective (so he can make a choice) and in both worldviews he is choosing between (so that once he has chosen he can still understand how it was he, conceptually speaking, came to be where he is). (65)

Roger Trigg clearly points out one of the conclusions of both conceptual and cultural relativism: "truth is then made to depend on what groups of people happen to believe. The possibility of false beliefs is ruled out" (*Reason and Commitment*, 2). This would agree with William Paden's characterization of the sacred as inherited from Durkheim being "simply whatever is *deemed* sacred by any group" ("Before the Sacred," 203). Yandell drives home the point with, "one simply cannot be wrong, if relativism is right," and indicates one of the further "alleged benefits" of relativism, which is that "the enterprise of trying to rationally assess religious, ethical, philosophical, etc. traditions and claims, insofar as these deal with basic issues at any rate, is no longer necessary" (70). Both Trigg and Yandell are agreed that once one defers to the relativism of truth and belief one relinquishes all appeal to rational criteria of judgment and to truth as corresponding to an external, objective reality. As W. W. Bartley has said, "if relativism is inescapable then a consistent rationalism becomes intellectually impossible" (*The Retreat to Commitment*, xxv).

William C. Sheperd refers to another consequence of the relativist tendency. In Berger and Luckmann's *Social Construction of Reality*, he detects an "extreme form" of "anthropological circumspection" which argues that, "there is no such thing as human nature, only the manifold varieties of human natures, culturally relative artifacts ("Cultural Relativism, Physical Anthropology, and Religion," 159). Such extreme forms of relativism which categorically repudiate the possibility of a universally valid conception of human nature have been more or less critically devastated. As Yandell says of cultural determinism, "that horse is dead, and it need not be beaten more—one need only put up a memorable gravestone" (74). However, it is an unavoidable consequence of extreme conceptual relativism that the denial of an objective reality leads to the denial of a universal human nature. As Trigg insists, "relativism does not lead to the denial of objectivity since that is itself the very essence of the relativist position," and "the denial of objectivity is the denial of any kind of independent reality" ("Religion and the Threat of Relativism," 299f.). Thus it would seem that if cultural determinism is an unavoidable consequence of relativism, and cultural determinism has been critically devastated, then relativism cannot be an acceptable stance. In this light it must be determined whether or not Eliade can be said to be a relativist.

ELIADE'S RELATIVISM

As I have already mentioned, Mac Ricketts in "In Defense of Eliade," makes reference to what can be seen as a relativist aspect of Eliade's thought, the truth for the believer is what is apprehended as the sacred. Reality for the believer is what is revealed in hierophany, it is what symbols and myths refer to, by definition. This certainly appears to make truth and reality dependent on personal or communal belief rather than upon an external, objective reality. The fact that the capacity to perceive the sacred in certain specific hierophanic objects or events is conditioned by prior personal religious experience further smacks of cultural determinism. Also, Eliade has asked,

> which is the true meaning of Durga and Śiva—what is deciphered by the initiates, or what is taken up by the mass of the faithful? In this book I am trying to show that both are equally valuable. (*Patterns*, 7)

Likewise, he has stated,

> idolatry and its condemnation are thus attitudes that come naturally to a mind faced with the phenomenon of the hierophany; there is justification

for both positions. To anyone who has received a new revelation . . . the earlier hierophanies have not only lost their original meaning . . . but they have now become obstacles to the development of religious experience. (25)

These simultaneous avowals of competing positions as equally true, valuable, or justifiable seem to be characteristic of relativism's inability to recognize any belief as false. So does Eliade's insistence that

for the historian of religions, every manifestation of the sacred is important: every rite, every myth, every belief or divine figure reflects the experience of the sacred and hence implies the notion of *being*, of *meaning*, and of *truth*. (*History of Religious Ideas*, vol. I, xiii)

If all manifestations of religion imply the notions of being, meaning, and especially truth, has Eliade not fallen into the relativist trap of relinquishing all access to rational, objective criteria of truth by making applicable criteria internal to each religious system?

Certainly, Eliade himself did not openly espouse the relativist stance; in fact, he seems to attack it. In *The Sacred and the Profane* he describes

man's desire to take up his abode in the objective reality, not to let himself be paralysed by the never-ceasing relativity of purely subjective experiences, to live in a real and effective world, and not in an illusion. (28)

In *The Myth of the Eternal Return*, he seeks to avoid the discussion of a philosophy of history that "should definitely transcend relativism" (150). But he points out that

in vain did [Wm. Dilthey] proclaim an *allgemeine Lebenserfahrung* as the final means of transcending this relativity. . . . In vain did Meinecke invoke "examination of conscience" . . . Heidegger had gone to the trouble of showing that the historicity of human existence forbids all hope of transcending time and history. (150)

He considers the relativity of purely subjective experience "paralyzing" and indicates the inability of historicism and sociology of knowledge to avoid relativism to be failures (see above, p. 105), but he does not explicitly describe how he himself might escape from it.

The implication, however, is that the historical situation of humanity, that is to say, the exhaustive identification of reality with history (in this case both actual temporal antecedents and personal physical experience), is what gives relativism its cutting edge. As long as historicism is accepted, as Eliade argues Heidegger to have demonstrated, relativism cannot be transcended. The question must be, how does positing the autonomy of the human spirit, as Eliade certainly does, through creativity and imagination, achieve the escape from relativism which he seems to desire?

One indication of an answer can be found in Yandell's discussion of "simple relativism" mentioned above. He considers that this "simple relativism"

> carries the power of positive thinking to the final degree, since if I can only persuade myself that I am an indestructible and wise billionaire, I am one, and in order to have the perfect marriage I need only believe that I have one. (62)

It must be seen that the two examples given differ enormously. In one the external state of affairs is necessarily involved: one's physical reaction to being struck by a falling safe, one's ability to give sound advice to others, the amount of money stored in one's bank. Whereas in the other the mental state of the experiencing subject could be sufficient—the external, physical world is not necessarily involved. It may, indeed, be the case that it is the necessary and sufficient condition of perfect marriage that one believes one's marriage to be perfect (even if one's spouse does not). Similarly, the conditions of religion do not necessarily involve the external, physical/temporal world, as has been consistently argued. Belief can be the necessary and sufficient condition for salvation (or *mokṣa, nirvāṇa*, etc.). In these non-physical (spiritual), non-temporal (eternal) worlds, the human spirit is autonomous and effective.

It should also be noted that Yandell operates with exactly the modern view of "belief" which Wilfred Cantwell Smith critiques as spurious or at least a recent and culturally specific development: that belief = acceptance of a propositional truth (*Belief and History*, chapter 2). Yandell is aware of the problem this engenders for relativism: if relativism is the contention that a proposition is true if and only if someone believes it, then, if "believes" means "accepts as true," the word "true" appears in both *definiens* and *definiendum*, rendering the definition, and relativism, meaningless. However, he does not consider the alternative: if belief is held to mean "to hold dear, to prize, to give allegiance, to value highly" (*Meaning and End of Religion*, 41), then a meaningful definition is made. It is one in which "truth" is seen as a function of the human will, which restores the older sense of the word "true," as "true love," a "true humanitarian," and so on. That is to say a mode in which the actual conforms to the ideal. Along with the restoration of the older concept of truth goes the older concept of belief as "I believe in non-violence," or "I believe in marital fidelity," and so forth. That is to say, not a propositional affirmation, but a commitment to an ideal state of affairs.

The gradual shift of the words "believe" and "true" toward propositional accuracy and correspondence to external data can be seen to reflect exactly Eliade's apprehension of the gradual camouflage of the sacred in the profane. That in which we believe has been increasingly identified with that which we cannot propositionally deny, that is, material existence. The real has been increasingly identified with the physical and manifest, valorizing what *is* over what *ought to be*, so that "true" human existence is now equated with the profane, mundane, and gross, whereas previously the "true" nature of humanity was apprehended as a desired ideal of nobility, responsibility, humaneness, and so on. It is this "myth" of objective reality, that is, the uncritical valorization of the actual over the ideal, and the concomitant exhaustive equation of truth with actuality, which renders relativism, the understanding of "truth" as dependent on "belief," unacceptable. As Yandell has it, "for realism belief is truth's prisoner; for relativism, truth is properly the product of belief" (68). From this alternative viewpoint both these statements would be acceptable, each depending on the systematic definition of belief and truth operative in the (pre-reflective) system of the realist or the relativist.

However, this seems to raise exactly the problematic position of two conflicting and mutually exclusive worldviews and a hapless subject with no way other than arbitrary random selection to choose between them. But surely this is a radical fiction designed specifically to increase the attractiveness of the proffered criteria of assessment, the "rational." None of us starts from nowhere and chooses between total and preformed worldviews. The process of acquisition is gradual and recursive. Elements and expressions of worldviews are assessed, based on prior experience, and interpreted and incorporated into our pre-existent worldview. Yandell evinces one of the basic positions of those who oppose relativism. He accepts as a "necessary truth" that "if P is true, then P is *either true or false*" (67). To make the truth characteristic of universal categorical propositions in formal logic exhaustive of human truth is hardly adequate. In normal circumstances that P is true implies only that P is true for certain people. This allows the possibility that it is not true for certain others, that is, that P is both true and false, certainly not either true or false.

Another answer can be given in relation to Trigg's statement that the "seeds of relativism" are sown when "the emphasis is moved from a question about reality to one about our response to that reality" ("Religion and the Threat of Relativism," 301). This, too, can be seen to apply to Eliade; he certainly shifts the emphasis from the sacred per se to the human reaction to the sacred. In fact he seems to consider this a procedural necessity for a discipline which would study the human response to reality—those expressions and activities of humanity which are classified as religious (the history of religions), as opposed to a discipline which would study the nature of ultimate reality (theology, the philosophy of religion, or philosophy *tout court*). Trigg insists that this leads to the conclusion that

> only a participant can properly understand a society, which can never be judged by external standards. Each society has its own conceptual scheme, and reality for that society is what the scheme says it is. This is conceptual relativism. (302)

However, Eliade's insistence on archetypal intuitions, or fundamental, transhuman experiences, or the universal basis of the human existential situation, allows a common ground from which all societies can be (begun to be) understood. That is not to say by *external* standards, however; the point is that we, as humans, are not totally external to other human societies, and that all human conceptual schemes overlap precisely because they are human. External standards are not required to understand an exotic society; internal standards, given by our similar human biology, and our occupation of a singular planet, will suffice. William Sheperd points out the human constant of birth, which "quite simply orders that paradisal intrauterine omnipotence be suddenly and dramatically left behind in favor of a world far less happy" (170). This constant is evidently comparable to Eliade's constant of nostalgia for paradise or the religious constant of the "fallen" world. As well as this human constant there is the subsequent process which we all undergo of language acquisition and the dependent period of culturally specific learning. This is possibly sufficient to account for the ubiquity of the symbolic. All humans have experienced a period in which they were not adept verbal language users, in which they were dependent upon preverbal understanding. We have all undergone a period of prelogical (or at least preverbal) mentality in which symbolic signification would have been our only way of understanding the world at large. Each society may have its own conceptual scheme but no such human conceptual scheme, will be utterly opaque to another human being because we are human. As Eliade indicated to Claude-Henri Roquet in the conversations published as *Ordeal by Labyrinth*,

> that is why I am so very proud of being a human being, not because I am a descendant of that prodigious Mediterranean culture, but because I can recognize myself, as a human being, in the existence taken upon himself by an Australian Aborigine. And that is why his culture interests me, and his religion, his mythology. (137)

CONCLUSIONS

Although Eliade manifests the primary characteristics of the relativist in seeing alternative worldviews as each true, and of making truth a function of meaning and meaning a function of belief, and although he might accept that there are truths relative to systems, his understanding of the ultimately common basis of human nature reduces the implications of relativism from complete incommensurability to partial and temporary unintelligibility, and thus evades the thrust of the major arguments against total relativism. As Trigg says, "total relativism is incoherent" ("Religion and the Threat of Relativism," 305). This is precisely the point. Total, or absolute, relativism *is* incoherent almost by definition. It is a contradiction in terms. What is critiqued by Trigg and others who would warn us of the dangers of absolute relativism, is not an actual position held by actual people, but a logical extension of the trend of relativism, a sort of monopolar relativism which is held to exist without reference to its other pole of absolute realism. In such a form relativism is absurd, but in such a form relativism does not seriously make any claims to our attention. Such relativism might claim that "people can believe what they like [and] there is no point believing one thing rather than another" (305). Eliade certainly does not make such a claim, for example, "I oppose with all my strength Hegel's 'historic' vision" (*Journal*, I, 54). Rather it is fundamental to his understanding that one is prepared by one's religious experience and cultural background to apprehend the real in certain modalities. Thus there is no "choice" in one's apprehension. The real appears to impose itself upon one's perceptions as a self-authenticating experience. However, this does not issue in total cultural relativism since humanity is universal in human culture and thus we all have a similar preparation and inhabit a similar reality. Thus Trigg goes too far when he claims that

> once it is stressed that different cultures have different concepts, and that their members see the world differently, it is no very great step to saying that there is no right way of seeing the world and that it is pure arrogance to assume that one's own society's understanding of things is the correct one. It thus becomes impossible to judge other cultures at all. (*Reason and Commitment*, 6)

This type of criticism, typically accompanied by "it is then a very small step" or some such phrase, is common throughout Trigg's analysis.[1] My point is that it does not matter how small a step it is if it is not made. This kind of logic could state that it is a small step from open-heart surgery to murder. The step from culturally conditioned difficulties in communication to absolute conceptual incommensurability is one which Eliade's whole life was dedicated to refusing.

The extremes of conceptual relativism ensuing from interpretations of Wittgenstein are resolved in this interpretation of Eliade. Trigg has said that

> according to Wittgenstein, our basic religious or moral commitments can make no claim to truth. The only way to adjudicate between them is for us to adopt one and reject the others. We can never tell someone who does not share our commitment that he is wrong. (53)

The understanding that all people are already religious emphasized by Eliade's work resolves the problem of such a statement; we do adjudicate between religious and moral commitments precisely by virtue of the fact that we have already made a "religious" commitment to our present worldview. The view that rational people are not religious and have made no such commitment is itself the cause of the basic

---

1. See also Trigg, *Reason and Commitment*, 32, "it is only a short step from this to saying that the meaning is the commitment," and 146, "there is only a short step from this admission to the view that the rational man does himself make a non-rational commitment."

problem here; if we have no such commitment we cannot adjudicate between commitments and we will never know what commitment to make. Once again the linguistic metaphor is applicable: if we do not assume that words are meaningful we will never be able to begin the process of language acquisition. Likewise, without some prior commitment to some conceptual system (which, it must be recalled, Eliade held actually to precede rational reflection), we will not be able to adjudicate between competing concepts. However, the point is that we do utilize pre-reflective modes of coming to a decision, and the commitment to rationalism can itself be seen as such a commitment. At this point it becomes apparent that the word *commitment* could be rather misleading. It could be seen as implying a conscious and reasoned decision, whereas it is crucial to the understanding of this theory that the deference to a given conceptual schema is pre-critical. The fact that rationalists would hold that their commitment to reason is wholly rational and conscious in no way lessens the possibility that that commitment occurred prior to its rational analysis and justification.

Finally, it must be said that we can, of course, tell someone who does not share our commitment that they are wrong. We cannot, however, persuade them to change or somehow force them to accept that they are wrong. No doubt if everyone were absolutely reasonable we could, by applying the rules of reason, persuade any dissenters that they were simply mistaken in their application of those rules. Trigg states that

> the presence of reason does not force us to adopt any particular position. No reason can have any influence until it is recognized by someone to be a reason. . . . Men would still be free to assess such reasons as they wish and to ignore or reject what are in fact perfectly good reasons. (134)

However, do their decisions to ignore good reasons themselves have (good) reasons? The point is that our reasons are compelling or they are not finally reasonable. Absolute rationality removes the human freedom which is part of our experience of life and is thus finally as absurd as the absolute relativism against which Trigg argues. The empirical fact is that certain people (in fact, the vast majority) find themselves emotionally committed to a conceptual schema which does not clearly and entirely correspond to the dictates of rationalism. They are not so committed to rationalism that this failing persuades them to alter their commitment. The further empirical fact is that these people can lead entirely well-adjusted lives, some of them even managing to be productive and beneficial to society in a purely practical manner, some of them even being successful scientists. Trigg points out that the extreme relativist position on the "incommensurability" of different conceptual systems results in the religious scientist suffering from a "totally crazy compartmentalization of understanding" (120)—he can provide no more acceptable description. His ongoing argument seems to be that science and religion are fundamentally incommensurable, which does not account for the empirical facts. Any rationalist claim to exclusive viability finds no empirical support, but is itself only supported by the internal criterion of coherence within its own dictates.

This is not to say that the rationalists' commitment to reason is itself unreasonable. No such claim is being made; it is absolutely reasonable. The point is that reason is not experienced by the majority of humanity as fully adequate for the management of their lives, certainly not to the fundamental adjudication of their basic conceptual systems. Reason is not experienced as hierophanic to the majority of humanity; it is not an exemplary revelation of the real. This could quite conceivably be because most people do not have any really clear grasp of what "reason" is and so do not know exactly how to apply it to the formulation or adaptation of their conceptual systems. Alternatively, it could be because many people accept that the formulation of belief systems occurs on a subconscious level where reason is not entirely dominant. My purpose here cannot be to adjudicate between absolute reason and relative reason but to point out that the criticisms of relativism operative here amount to little more than the statement that relativism is not absolutely rational and thus fails to permit the reasonable adjudication of all decisions. Of course, absolute relativism is not absolutely rational. The point is that truth is capable of more than a singular interpretation. There is truth which refers to the actual states of external reality, but there are also truths which refer to the internal worlds of human creativity and imagination. There are truths which can be determined by the rational criteria of the Western tradition and there are truths which can only be assessed through criteria of meaning internal to their own traditions.

This plurality of truths is fundamental to the de-provincializing of Western attitudes and to authentic religious dialogue. Both Trigg and Yandell can be seen to argue from an unyielding position of unequivocality as regards the meaning of truth, but a more fluid, polysemic, or plural concept of truth admits of a far more fertile understanding. While the attack on extreme relativism reopens the possibility of a universally viable conception of human nature and of religion closed by radical relativism, that same attack has reduced the likelihood of such a conception by discouraging the deference to relational concepts of meaning and truth. Eliade's concept of human nature, humanity as *homo religiosus*, in proposing a universally valid schema for humanity does so precisely via the relationality of meaning and truth: the subjective and self-validating experience of the Real through the hierophany. The potential to detect, to apprehend, the real, the sacred, in a particular profane object or event is culturally conditioned, but it is also affected by, and effected through, the creativity of the human imagination, and thus it is not culturally *determined*. Meaning, truth, reality, sacrality are defined inter-referentially and culturally relationally, however, this is done in the context of a unified vision of human nature based in our physical existential situation with this particular biology in this particular environment. The truth of this vision is maintained through the insistence upon the external world as the locus of hierophany; only what *is* can reveal the nature of being.

In this context, it is worthwhile to refer to Richard Bernstein's *Beyond Objectivism and Relativism*. It is Bernstein's "central thesis that we are witnessing and participating in a movement beyond objectivism and relativism" and that this can be seen in the works of Gadamer, Habermas, Arendt, and Rorty. Rorty, for example,

> claims that it is a illusion to think that there is a permanent set of ahistorical standards of rationality which the "philosopher" or epistemologist can discover and which will unambiguously tell us who is rational and who is not. (67)

This would be thought to be the worst form of relativism to one entrenched in the "Cartesian persuasion" of the search for an assured foundation for knowledge. In fact, it actually corresponds to a redefinition of rationalism as an effective, but not inescapable, form of persuasion. In Rorty's discussion of the controversy between Galileo and Cardinal Bellarmine he points out that

> much of the 17th century's notion of what it was to be a "philosopher," and much of the Enlightenment's notion of what it was to be "rational," turns on Galileo being absolutely right and the church absolutely wrong. (66, from *Philosophy and the Mirror of Nature*, 328)

"Lurking in the background here," Bernstein points out,

> is a false dichotomy: either permanent standards of rationality (objectivism) or arbitrary acceptance of one set of standards or practices over against its rival (relativism). We need to alter our understanding of how rational argumentation (and the history of forms of argumentation) works, to realize that there are times when there are disagreements that we cannot immediately resolve by appeal to fixed standards. (68)

He further refers to "The Recovery of the Hermeneutical Dimension of Science" as one of "the areas in which there has been a significant movement beyond objectivism and relativism" (30).

I would suggest that Eliade, in attempting to assert the hermeneutical dimension of the history of religion, was likewise attempting a transcendence of the specious dichotomy of objectivism and relativism by rejecting the Cartesian dilemma and asserting this liberation in and through the creativity of human nature. Like Gadamer, Eliade operates with an understanding of truth which "is not exhausted by the achievements of scientific method and which is available to us through hermeneutical understanding" (151). His understanding admits of a pluralism of truths and a pluralism of reasons or rationalities giving rise to those truths. From the objectivist standpoint this comes dangerously close to relativism as the refusal of all categorical truth. It seems that Eliade was never able to explicitly resolve these difficulties, particularly concerning moral relativism.

CHAPTER 12

The Retreat to Commitment

THE PROBLEM

Another criticism which arises in part out of the preceding considerations is the inherent attitude to commitment implied by my interpretation of the thought of Mircea Eliade. Not only do I follow the lead of Eliade's thought in claiming the finally religious nature of all human apprehension of reality, but I also explicitly argue for the prior commitment involved in all coherent thought, specifically in the recognition of phenomena or events as meaningful. I have argued that "only if all of one's persuasions are formed on the basis of fully rational support can one be said to have transcended all myths" (73), and that "without some prior commitment to some conceptual system we will not be able to adjudicate between competing concepts" (129). This will undoubtedly be apprehended by rationalist and realist critics as a restatement of the neo-orthodox theological argument that everyone, all human thought, is eventually dependent upon a commitment to an ultimately non-rational, intuitive, or emotional stance—arguments put forward ostensibly to support a position are in fact *ex post facto* attempts to justify, or to persuade others to adopt, that position, which is actually held independently of its "supporting" arguments. All positions are positions of faith, including the rationalist, and, finally, justification is by faith alone. Thus Christian faith is as acceptable as rationalism.

William Warren Bartley III has traced the development, implications, and criticisms of this argument in great detail in his *The Retreat to Commitment*, although he says nothing of Eliade's potential contribution. In the context of a consideration of this book, I would like to assess Eliade's relevance to this argument.

As Bartley has incisively pointed out, this argument concerns the problem of the limits of rationality. It is the argument relied upon by both Karl Barth and Søren Kierkegaard. "The argument provides a rational excuse for irrational commitment," as Bartley says, calling it the *tu quoque* (you also) argument, since it claims that all people are in the same final position of irrational commitment. The expression *tu quoque* is conventionally used to indicate the circumstantial *ad hominem* fallacy of irrelevance. That is, challenging opponents' conclusions as dictated by their special circumstances rather than inferred by reason or evidence. Neo-orthodox Christians attempt to reject as irrelevant and fallacious the rationalist critique of their faith since that critique comes from uncommitted critics and is simply an indication of the lack of reason sufficient to convince those specific critics. Such a lack of reason is inherent in *any* position which fails to convince all possible critics. Bartley states it like this:

> (1) for certain logical reasons, rationality is so limited that *everyone* must make a dogmatic irrational commitment; (2) therefore, the Christian has a right to make whatever commitment he pleases; and (3) therefore, no-one has a right to criticize him (or anyone else) for making such a commitment. The theologian can reply *"tu quoque"* to his critic, and remind him that people whose own rationality is limited should not admonish others for admitting that the limitation exists. (72, 78)

The relation to Eliade's position is this: if Bartley is right and this argument proves to be finally specious, then the position which Bartley describes as "pancritical rationalism" does not rely upon prior irrational (or non-rational) commitment to the nature of reality as it is apprehended in "archetypal" (or any other type of) intuitions. That is to say, it is not dependent upon the real as mediated through hierophany, symbol, and myth and is thus not religious, even in the broad sense implied by Eliade's terms. The fully rational person need have no recourse to prerational, precritical, or prereflective judgment. Pancritical humanity is not *homo religiosus*, and Eliade's claim to a universally valid comprehension of human nature is overthrown. It is this, or some substantially similar, objection which is most often raised counter to any claim that religion is a human universal. It is not possible to deal with all possible individual rejections of this claim since they are made on individual grounds. This, however, provides one example of such a rejection which is clearly and strongly made.

THE *TU QUOQUE* ARGUMENT

I cannot do justice to all the issues discussed in Barley's book, but I hope to assess fairly the specific points of argument relevant to my interpretation of Eliade. Bartley indicates the historical harmony of Protestant and rationalist thought; it has only been during the twentieth century that the relationship between the two has broken down. Since that schism, he would claim, the only "rational" excuse available to the religiously minded for their commitment to an "independent starting ground" in faith, is the problem of ultimate commitment and the limits of rationality. He sees the real schism as having resulted from the "Quest for the

Historical Jesus." Schweitzer's study revealed that Jesus could not be the practical and moral leader conceived of in Protestant liberal thought but rather was a radical, mystical apocalyptist. The real problem then is that

> a truly Christian identity, it was plausibly argued, demanded assent to the person of the historical Jesus—as he actually had been, not as one might have liked him to be. To the extent that honest identification with the rationalist tradition required that one withhold assent to the newly discovered historical Jesus, it became impossible for a man to be, in good conscience, both a Protestant Christian and a rationalist. (*Retreat to Commitment*, 35)

This brings us to the position that Protestant liberal Christians have refused to relinquish their belief, even when their supportive argument was removed. They are thus not rational.

> When a person sees no reason to abandon a position when an argument put forward to support it is refuted, that indicates that his position, far from *depending* on the argument, was held independently of it. (71)

As Bartley then goes on to say,

> the "truth" of one's beliefs is then ultimately rooted not in their self-evidence or in their universality but in one's whim, or in the belief, say, that God has commanded one to accept these standards. (74)

Like the criticism of relativism this criticism targets the final inability to adjudicate between conflicting truth-claims and the incapacitation of criteria of rational judgment and contributes to the problem of pluralism. As Bartley concisely states the case:

> in sum, the belief that rationality is ultimately limited, by providing an excuse for irrational commitment, enables a Protestant, or any other irrationalist, to make an irrational commitment without losing intellectual integrity. But, at the same time, anyone who makes use of this excuse pays a high price for it. For anyone who uses it may no longer, in integrity, *criticize* the holder of a different commitment. One gains immunity from criticism for one's own commitment by making any criticism of commitments impossible. (82)

Bartley, as representative of the whole rationalism-as-opposed-to-religion school of thought, considers a (if not *the*) crucial problem of contemporary philosophy to be

> showing that it is possible to choose in a non-arbitrary way among competing, mutually exclusive theories, and—more broadly speaking—among competing "ways of life" (83),

and thus of defeating the *tu quoque* defense. In the hope of achieving this, Bartley rejects *panrationalism*, which he characterizes by two rules,

> (1) A rationalist accepts any position that can be justified or established by appeal to the rational criteria or authorities; and (2) he accepts only those positions that can be so justified. (87)

The "rational criteria" are either intellectualist or empiricist, but Bartley can accept neither because the Kantian antinomies indicate that clear and distinct ideas can lead to competing theories and Hume argued convincingly that neither belief in natural law, memory, nor other people could be inferred from purely empirical premises (89). Bartley is aware that for post-Humean empiricists, submission to the rational authority of sense experience became "an irrational procedure" (93). He further attacks this species of rationalism on the grounds that the first rule is not, itself, "justifiable by sense experience, by intellectual intuition of clear and distinct ideas, or by any other rational authority." Furthermore, such justification, even if possible, would carry no weight except "to those persons who had *already adopted* the belief that arguments should count." These arguments militate toward a compromised form of rationalism whose integrity Bartley would rescue by his appeal to "pancritical" rationalism (93–94).

This "pancritical rationalism" would provide a clear exception to the Eliadean analysis of the universality of human religiousness. It is a development from Karl Popper's critical rationalism and is also referred to as "fallibilism" since it holds that even its own basic tenets are open to error and revision.

> By dropping the comprehensive claim that all legitimate positions must be rationally justifiable and by candidly admitting his supposed limitations the critical rationalist saves himself . . . from a crisis of integrity. (97)

Bartley will not accept any position which, like A. J. Ayer's, claims to evade the requirement of proof. Ayer's discussion begs the question and is itself a variety of fideism. (98) Fideism is any position which *assumes* that its basic tenets are correct or that its particular standards of rationality are true.

> If some particular standards of rationality *are* correct, then there can exist no other standards which are also correct but which can nevertheless invalidate the former as irrational . . . *this is precisely what is at issue.* (99)

He concludes that "the rationalist position, unable to be rationally based or justified, is finally based on irrational moral commitment" (100). In fact, he goes further to state that

> the position of arch rationalists and anti-theologians like Ayer and [Morton] White are closely parallel not only, as might be expected, to

fideistic positions like contemporary Oxford theology, but also to that of the arch theologian and belligerently fideistic irrationalist, Karl Barth. (101)

The question, of course, must be whether Bartley's pancritical rationalist escapes this structural similarity and establishes his own logical starting point critically. Bartley even regards Popper as "fideistic." Popper has said,

> the fundamental rationalist attitude is based upon an irrational decision, or upon faith in reason. Accordingly our choice is open. We are free to chose some form of irrationalism, even some radical or comprehensive form. But we are also free to choose a critical form of rationalism, one which frankly admits its limitations, and its basis in an irrational decision. (*The Open Society and Its Enemies*, 416–17; *Conjectures and Refutations*, 357)

Bartley is obviously close to Popper and influenced by him; this, however, is a major point of disagreement. Bartley's point here is that

> an unjustifiable commitment to accept the results of argument is not strictly parallel to the unjustifiable commitment that existentialists, Protestant theologians, or Marxists speak about. (106)

This is because any argument on behalf of any position presupposes a precommitment to accept the results of argument. Bartley proposes a "new framework" which

> permits a rationalist to be characterized as one who is willing to entertain any position and holds *all* his positions, including his most fundamental standards, goals, and decisions, and his basic philosophical position itself, open to criticism; one who protects nothing from criticism by justifying it irrationally; one who never cuts off an argument by resorting to faith or irrational commitment. (118)

This is "pancritical rationalism." It is an integral part of Bartley's argument that positions cannot finally be justified at all, since justification is an archaic remnant of a bygone authoritarianism (89). So final justification is not an element of his new framework but rather critical assessment. As he puts it:

> if all justification—rational as well as irrational—is really abandoned, there is indeed no need to justify irrationally a position that is rationally unjustifiable. The position may be held rationally without needing any justification at all—*provided that it can be and is held open to criticism and survives severe examination.* The question of how well a position is justified differs utterly from the question of how criticizable it is, and how well it is criticized. (119)

By rationalism Bartley does not mean the seventeenth-century sense of the opposition to empiricism, but rather "the tradition whose members are dedicated to the task of trying to learn more about the world through the practice of critical argument". (xxvi n. 3) Also he states that rationalists are "eager to make all their decisions—moral, scientific or otherwise—rationally, on rational grounds, or with good reasons" (76). This is not necessarily exclusive of religious conviction, both by empirical and logical derivation, unless the irrational commitment to doctrine be an *a priori* condition of being "religious." A belief of the "general revelation" kind could easily square the two. There are good and sufficient reasons for one's commitment, involved in one's interpretation of one's experience of life, though they may be too subtle, complex and personal to communicate. In the light of the suggested interpretation of Eliade, it could it be said that one is not aware of the full range and extent of the "reasons" which persuade one to a specific conclusion. One is aware of many supportive arguments, none of which are necessary or sufficient. The fact that committed believers can and do lose faith indicates that their commitment is supported by something frangible, it is dependent on *something* but not on conscious reason alone. If there are such grounds for belief, despite their existential and incommunicable nature, then the "irrationalist" is *not* "free" as Bartley suggests, but is just as constrained by environmental factors as the "rationalist." There are, in fact, no grounds for accepting that commitments are "necessarily arbitrary" rather than based on subtle, complex, and personal data. Such a view is, in fact, suggested by the fact that "Protestant existentialists often deny that this is a matter of picking and choosing, stressing that *we are chosen*," as Bartley recognizes (77 n. 9). This can be likened to asking whether we are actually "free to choose" our aesthetic preferences, for example.

Rejecting "self-evidence" or "universality" as grounds for religious conviction, and having *assumed* a rejection of reason, Bartley can only conceive "whim" as the foundation of belief. Although this is not actually an argument but a simple premise ("any belief which is not rooted in reason, self-evidence, or universality is mere whim"), it must be considered. Is religious conviction based on some support other than mere whimsy? If so, what? Are self-evidence and universality the only arbiters of reason? Do rationalists hold only those opinions rooted in self-evidence and universality? This restores the *tu quoque* in a slightly different form. Not that all opinions are finally irrational, but in experiential fact people do accept profound convictions which are not based on the conscious application of a reasoned process. The reasons for one's convictions transcend argumentative logic only in the holistic sense that the commitment is greater than the sum of the supportive reasons since one cannot adequately, consciously, consider all reasons simultaneously in detail and in all their complex relations. A committed religious believer assumes that there are good and sufficient reasons for their belief; Bartley assumes that there are not. The difference may be mainly that the former has a tendency to accept that the grounds of belief will be mysterious, inaccessible, while the latter insists that they must be accessible. But if rationalists were supported by accessible reason alone, would they not find more consensus among themselves? That they do not stems from both the inability to acceptably define reason and the impossibility of standardizing experience.

Although this is still an argument from the limits of rationality, it is not a formal but an existential limitation. It is rarely adequate to transfer such an existential problem of conflicting truth-beliefs into the forum of pure logic. Although this is still open to accusations of relativism, the issue can be addressed by verbal argument, exposing opponents to the reasons which add to one's own convictions to discover whether those reasons carry more weight than opposing ones. This certainly does not make nonsense of historical development but is integral with it. Even the "pancritical rationalist" still "holds countless unexamined propositions and assumptions, many of which may be false" (121). Assessments of validity are already made, based on non-conscious, complex reasons, "chaotic" in the sense of preformal and unpredictable. This itself lends a new valorization to the symbolic structure of order out of chaos. The fact is that most people do establish their own "ultimate concerns" without conscious rational procedures—thus empirical, logical procedures should lead us to the conclusion that the establishment of ultimate concerns is not consciously rational, that is, not necessarily describable in terms of logical, rational argument. So the establishment qua establishment of ultimate concerns may be beyond criticism, but elements of experience claimed to be constitutive and supportive can be personally assessed and judged, and one's concurrence can be (and is) given or withheld.

In further clarifying his position on rationality, Bartley quotes the *Fontana/ Harper Dictionary of Modern Thought* that rationalism denies "the acceptability of beliefs founded on anything but experience and reasoning, deductive or inductive" (86). My point is that *all* beliefs are so founded, although not necessarily on *direct* experience and *conscious* reasoning. Different life-experience and different styles of reason, deeply conditioned by cultural tradition, will produce different beliefs. These differences need not be justified by appeal to *ir*rational criteria. According to Bartley's reasoning, they cannot be justified at all. That the same critique can produce different reactions in different auditors leaves the pluralist position unscathed. Eliade's theory seems to be that the decipherment of the existential situation reveals the relationship of the individual with the sacred (i.e., that which is apprehended as the real, the true), and therefore conditions what one apprehends to be the rules of reason. The existential situation is one's own personal experience, and the means of decipherment are the rules of reason. It is questionable whether the latter have ever been successfully universalized, and even if they were, since the former cannot be universalized, the resulting relationship revealed thereby will always be relative to the individual. Of course, standardizing the rules of reason would be desirable if only for the increase in effective communication, but we cannot standardize experience, and so we cannot hope for complete consensus of the beliefs "founded upon experience and reason."

CONCLUSIONS

As we have seen, Bartley's argument is forced to consign most thinkers who would wish to be considered rational to the same fate as the "irrationalists," even Ayer and Popper. Yet, he has shown committed "irrationalists" like Barth to be dependent on rational forms of argument and attempted "justification." It would seem that as irrationalism is "infected" with rationalism, so rationalism is infected with irrationalism. A schema such as underlies Eliade's work, recognizing a presystematic rationale, a coherence which precedes methodic thought, and the importance of the *coincidentia oppositorum*, would account for this. Rationality is suffused with irrationality and vice versa, since both are based on a perceived coherence which preceded rational reflection, yet which was itself possessed of a system, and thus was in some way rational. Because of this, any attempt to distinguish absolutely between reason and unreason will inevitably run into difficulty.

Bartley's answer to the question of the establishment of rational authority is constant criticism. But since more than one position on the same point evidently can survive severe examination and constant criticism, pluralism becomes an unavoidable outcome of "pancritical rationalism." Apparently Bartley and Eliade are finally in agreement that the real problem of rationalism, or of any form of human thought, is to assume one's own absolute, unquestionable, and complete correctness. Bartley takes fideism to be any position which assumes that its basic tenets are correct or that its particular standards of rationality are true (99). Similarly, although more in the style of a historian of religions than a philosopher, Eliade states:

> if Time, seen as Maya, is itself a manifestation of the Divinity, to believe in Time is not itself a "bad action": "bad action" is *to believe that nothing else exists, nothing outside of time. (Images and Symbols, 91)*

Thus, commitment—in the sense of insisting that I am absolutely and exhaustively and exclusively correct in my apprehension of the real, and thus cannot be criticized and need never alter my beliefs even if I am—is a position repugnant to both scholars. However, commitment, in the sense of having recourse to a prior apprehension of the real (a hierophany in Eliade's terms; for Bartley, the apprehension that constant criticism provides rational authority), is also basic to both scholars. Bartley accepts, along with "countless unexamined propositions and assumptions," that "pancritical rationalism" is desirable. He believes in it and to that extent he is committed to it and one must say, "*tu quoque*, Professor Bartley." His insistence that his commitment is not absolute, unquestionable, or unchangeable is wholly admirable. However, his claim that "pancritical rationalism" is the only fully rational position, that it *exclusively* makes full use of the exercise of reason, which is our *only* guarantee of the truth and hence "reality" of our beliefs, smacks of the very exclusivism which he seems to attack.

Certainly, these arguments do not finally convince me that Bartley himself, or any "pancritical rationalist," escapes religious commitment in the sense which it has been interpreted here, and hence they do not disprove any of the contentions made concerning the ubiquity of religious belief and behavior, or compromise the integrity of Eliade's thought. That that commitment is *ir*-rational and thus not open to criticism is not a necessary concomitant of that thought. Rather it is prerational and not open to conscious inspection as it happens. It can certainly, and I agree with Bartley that it should, be open to later consideration and criticism. I am forced to speculate as to what precisely "uncriticizable" or "accepted as uncriticizable" means? It would appear to mean not open or susceptible to rejection despite severe criticism. As long as one person holds a position (despite the critical argument which have swayed others away from it), then that position could be said to be uncriticizable. Contrariwise, if a million people hold a position (despite the critical arguments that have swayed one other away), then that position could still be said to be uncriticizable. No argument is guaranteed to achieve the rejection or acceptance of a position, so acceptance of any position which is rejected by any other can be seen as "cutting off an argument by resorting to faith" (118). The conclusion of any and all arguments is a position of faith since no argument is the source of apodictic knowledge. Since apostasy does occur—even amongst Barthians—it can be argued that despite their protestations to the contrary they do not accept uncritically their own faith. The question is: at what point does criticism become conviction? Granted that the neo-orthodox argument loses its impact against one who insists that all his convictions are open to revision or rejection, does not the very possibility of a lapse of faith indicate that even a committed Barthian, for example, is also open to revision and rejection in fact?

The fact that the pancritical rationalist (claims) to hold all convictions open does not and cannot philosophically elevate his position above all others. How many would accept the title "pancritical rationalist" in this sense but still disagree with each other? Are we not all pancritical rationalists in fact, despite an occasionally expressed desire to be other? What does it mean, apart from the admittedly honest methodology of admitting that one could always "change one's mind?" And what, then, is commitment apart from the equally honest admission that one does not wish to change one's mind?

The reasoned criticism that specific conclusions rising out of faith commitment are irrational cannot be said to commit the circumstantial *ad hominem* fallacy of irrelevance. However, the blanket rejection of all religious commitment as unacceptable and fundamentally irrational, as opposed to the position of the rationalist critic which is held to be acceptably rational, must remain open to the *tu quoque* defense or else grant an *a priori* privilege to any soi-disant "rationalist." This may appeal to those who would preserve the imperial sovreignty of the Western rational tradition, but to those who would recognize the autheticity of alternative traditions, it is anathema.

CHAPTER 13

Eliade's Political Involvement

In recent years Eliade has come under some attack in connection with his politics in the thirties and forties. The *ad hominem* fallacy could all too easily be invoked when criticism of this type arises—what has this to do with his academic work? Yet I tend to agree that such criticisms are not irrelevant. Political beliefs and scholarship are not hermetically sealed off one from the other, nor should scholarship be held to be somehow above and beyond moral judgment. That said, however, when a critic sets out to investigate the political activities of an earlier author, care must be taken to ensure that historical details are accurately assessed and conclusions validly drawn before allegations and recriminations are published. Even hypothetical statements and tentative insinuations might themselves be uncritically accepted and thus become the presuppositions of further scholarship. In this chapter I will consider Eliade's political history, as far as it has been possible to research such a question in an analysis of this kind. I will, however, concentrate more upon published criticisms of Eliade's involvement with a view to assessing their accuracy and validity.

Throughout the thirties Eliade was prolific in his contributions to newspapers and other periodicals in Bucharest such as *Vremea*, *Cuvântul*, and *Credinţa*. He was fiercely nationalist in his politics and roundly denounced the ceding of any Romanian autonomy to any "non-Romanian" group or element, particularly Hungarians, Bulgarians, and Jews. He gave support to a movement known as the Legion of the Archangel Michael, also called the Iron Guard, a movement of the extreme right whose members were guilty of violence, murder, and antisemitic atrocities. In 1938 Eliade was imprisoned for four months in connection with his Iron Guard sympathies but was released without charge. In 1940 he was appointed to the Romanian Legation under a fascist-royalist dictatorship and served for nine months in London and thereafter in Portugal, where he was briefly press attaché in the department of press and propaganda and later cultural attaché under General

Antonescu's military dictatorship. At that time he wrote a small book, *Salazar şi revoluţia în Portugalia*, which was supportive of the Portuguese dictator Salazar (see Mac Linscott Ricketts' *Romanian Roots* 1106–16).

When Romania was delivered into Russian hands at the end of the Second World War and a communist regime was established, Eliade's connection with the right-wing government of the late thirties and early forties precluded his safe return home and he began his exile in Paris. It is this connection with the right, particularly with the evils of the Iron Guard, which has cast doubt on Eliade's political beliefs. A more extensive and detailed consideration of the historical context must be undertaken, however, before the implications can be judged.

Greater Romania had crystallized out of the surrounding empires toward the end of the nineteenth century. The waning influence of the Ottoman Sublime Porte allowed the "Old Kingdom" or United Principalities of Wallachia and Moldavia to be recognized by the European powers in 1859. The coastal Dobrogea was wrested from the Bulgarians in the Second Balkan War of 1907. Transylvania was added following Austro-Hungarian defeat in the First World War. At that time Bucovina and Bessarabia were also incorporated on the grounds of Romanian national identity but also from their fear of Russian Bolshevism. The whole was governed as a monarchy, originally under the Romanian Alexandru Ion Cuza, but soon under the Hapsburg Carol of Hohenzollern.

In the turmoil of interwar Europe, dominated by the rise of German and Italian fascism to the West and Russian communism to the East, Romanian nationalism had given birth to the Legion of the Archangel Michael,[1] founded by Corneliu Zelea Codreanu and his father in 1927. Although explicitly committed to a religious and spiritual renovation of the Romanian people, this movement was quite capable of violence. In 1933 three of its members were responsible for the assassination of the Romanian prime minister, I. G. Duca. They immediately gave themselves up to the authorities and claimed to have acted independently. Codreanu was arrested at the time but was cleared of complicity in that crime. The Legion spawned a paramilitary organization, popularly called the "Iron Guard."

Threatened from all sides, the monarchy under King Carol II imposed a fascist-inspired dictatorship in February of 1938, with Patriarch Miron as president and Armand Calinescu as minister of the interior. Together they set out to crush their popular rival, the Iron Guard. On the grounds of slander against the Romanian scholar, Nicolae Iorga, Codreanu was arrested and imprisoned for six months. This was soon increased to ten years at hard labor. Other Legionary leaders, and their

---

1. The Archangel Michael was, ironically enough, regarded as Israel's guardian angel extraordinary. His martial aspect led to his appropriation by Christian cultures as their angelic warrior. He seems to have been connected in popular Romanian imagination with Michael the Brave, the sixteenth-century Wallachian prince who temporarily "united" Wallachia, Moldavia, and Transylvania. The Archangel Michael is still widely regarded as the patron of policemen.

intellectual supporter, Eliade's philosophy professor, friend, and mentor Nae Ionescu, were arrested in April.

Ricketts has made a thorough study of Eliade's Romanian journalism of this period (*Romanian Roots*) and his chapters 18 and 19 should be consulted for more details. As he describes it,

> between January 1937 and the imposition of the royal dictatorship in February 1938, Eliade gave open and enthusiastic support, through his periodical writings, to the Legionary movement. Because of the eight or ten explicitly pro-Legionary articles he wrote in this period of slightly more than a year, and because of the close association with Nae Ionescu who had been a Legionary supporter (though he was never a member) since late 1933, Eliade became suspect in the eyes of the government. (882)

In mid-June of 1938 Eliade's house was searched and papers were taken away, mainly correspondence in languages other than Romanian from scholars such as Ananda Coomaraswamy and Raffaele Pettazzoni who were contributing to Eliade's journal of Comparative Religion, *Zalmoxis*. Eliade himself managed to evade arrest by retiring to the country after an anonymous telephone call warned him of the impending search. General M. M. Condeescu, the president of the Society of Romanian Writers, and related to Eliade through his first wife, Nina, contacted Calinescu, who assured him that there were no accusations against Eliade, who accordingly returned to Bucharest. However, on 14 July his house was raided by the Siguranţa and Eliade was taken to their headquarters for questioning. He was held there for three weeks and told that he could leave as soon as he signed a "declaration of dissociation" from the Iron Guard. Eliade refused to do so.[2]

In the first week of August he was transferred to the internment camp at Miercurea Ciucului where many other Legionary supporters were being held. Eliade was treated relatively well. Despite having had to sleep on the floor of a permanently lighted cell at the Siguranţa H.Q. for three weeks, he was not actually tortured. It seems likely that Calinescu's regime was primarily interested in him as a spokesman of the Romanian youth. He was 31 at the time and his popularity had been well established by the publication of his best-selling novel *Maitreyi* four years earlier. Thus his dissociation from the Legion would have been a useful propaganda coup for the royal dictatorship, of which Eliade did not fully approve, mainly because of its acceptance of Western (fascist) ideology.

---

2. Why? Dissociation from the popular Legion would mean dissocation from his whole generation. Also there was a danger of later accusations that he *had been* so associated or would not have needed to sign. These are motives attributed to Eliade's quasi-autobiographical Stefan Viziru in *Forbidden Forest*. There is, however, the further possibility that the Legion might succeed in coming to power—as in fact it did—which would place anyone having signed such a declaration in real danger of their lives.

When Eliade began coughing blood in October of that year, it seems that the government again acted from similar reasons. The death of a popular young writer in their custody would be anything but useful propaganda. Fearing tuberculosis they had him transferred to a clinic at Moroeni. As it transpired, the blood was from a ruptured vein in his throat, a relatively minor condition brought on by excessive coughing, in turn caused by incipient pleurisy. He was given a clean bill of health and on 12 November, almost four months after his arrest, he was simply released. That same November the king and Calinescu ordered the execution of C. Z. Codreanu. Evidently no entente with his movement had been reached.

Eliade had been employed at Bucharest University as the assistant of Nae Ionescu and was now without work. For some time he worked at the Society of Romanian Writers, but the unexpected death of General Condeescu in the spring of 1939 removed his "protector." He still had friends, however, and Prof. Alexandru Rosetti prevailed upon Constantin Giurescu, the minister for propaganda of the Carol regime, to send Eliade abroad to work for the Romanian legation in the office of press and propaganda.

IVAN STRENSKI

One of the earliest scholars to become aware of Eliade's political past and to draw connections to his scholarship was Ivan Strenski.[3] In his book *Four Theories of Myth in Twentieth-Century History* (1989), Strenski critiques Eliade's theory of myth. He concludes that Eliade disdains history, disregards falsifiability, assumes the *a priori* reality of the activity of the sacred, and makes methodological prescriptions which are disastrous for the study of religion. More to the point for the purposes of this chapter, he argues that the traditionalist and mythico-religious feelings of the Romanian right-wing Iron Guard have produced Eliade's ontological and religious viewpoint. Although the various points of Strenski's critique are worthy of consideration, being presently concerned with Eliade's political involvement I will inspect Strenski's aggressive claims in that specific area. Strenski's conclusions are based on several elements, some of which are actually "textual" and some of which are "contextual." It is the contextual elements which chiefly concern us here, but the textual elements are finally inseparable, as we will see.

Strenski was well aware that

> if "influences" are claimed one needs to show that there are true similarities between the thinkers in question, some sort of awareness of their "influences," and significant dependence on the thought of the "influence" (*Four Theories*, 9)

---

3. I am here referring to writers in the English language. As early as 1955 Zaharia Stancu had reacted to the publication of some of Eliade's journal writings with bitter interrogation—why did Eliade not have more to say about the "odious mass crimes of Sima's Legionaries?" No doubt there were others.

yet he continues as if merely *stating* such an admirable methodological caveat were sufficient. He does not put it into practice regarding Nae Ionescu's influence on the young Eliade nor regarding the influence of the Legion of the Archangel Michael. Strenski was aware of the dubious and speculative nature of his case. "Readers," he says, "should also be cautious in drawing inferences concerning Ionescu's (and especially Eliade's) involvement in legionary politics" (*Four Theories*, 96). No conclusive evidence is given to indicate any "significant dependence" on nor even a "similarity" with the thought of the Iron Guard. However, this does not prevent the boldly stated conclusion that the traditionalism and mythico-religious feelings of the Romanian right "become" Eliade's ontological judgment of the world and the basis of his dominant religious viewpoint (102). In fact, Strenski fails to demonstrate an accurate understanding of what Eliade's judgment and viewpoint might be. His major motivation, evident in "Some Theoretical Problems" of 1973, was to oppose any appeal to intuition or "introspectively-detected information" (49) as utterly removing a stable basis of knowledge. He has wrongly assumed that "Eliade has taken the self-authentication of intuition and introspection as the epistemological grounds for his discipline" (49). If that were the case, Eliade would not have stressed the need for the generalist historian of religion to be constantly aware of the developments in specialized fields and to diligently return to original sources whenever possible.[4] This confusion seems to spring from the fact that Eliade insists that for *homo religiosus* the self-authenticating appearance of intuitions[5] permits the recognition of the sacred/real in the profane/contingent. It is, however, not the case that the historian of religion's own intuitions as regards his data have logical priority and are thus the epistemological foundation of his discipline. The foundation is, and always has been, the original source documents and the researches of specialists, including fieldwork.

Exercising Strenski's own "contextual" approach, it would be interesting to investigate how Strenski came to these conclusions, since this cannot be directly inferred from a reading of Eliade's works. I lack the data to do so decisively and so it is speculation to suggest that he has perhaps encountered supposed "followers" of Eliade who *did* apply this cavalier, authentication-by-intuition approach to the history of religions and has attributed this fault to their supposed "leader."

Whatever may be the case, this fear of "autonomy from historical and cultural data" seems to have had an adverse effect on Strenski's scholarship. He is not in a position to determine accurately what affinities Eliade's thought may or may not have with other ideas since he does not demonstrate an accurate understanding of that thought. Certainly, Eliade was influenced by his existential situation and his

---

4. See, for instance, *The Sacred and the Profane*, 15; *The History of Religious Ideas*, xiii; *Images and Symbols*, 163; and also Seymour Cain, "Mircea Eliade; Attitudes towards History," 13; and Charles Long, "The Significance for Modern Man of Mircea Eliade's Work," 133.
5. Especially "archetypal intuitions." See Ricketts, *Romanian Roots*, 1151.

particular cultural background. His experiences as a citizen of a nation "marked by the fatality of history" (*Myth of the Eternal Return*, 152 n. 11) influenced his attitude to the "terror of history," for example. However, it is a considerable progression from this to the attribution of the basis of Eliade's judgment of the world to a specific political movement. Strenski's conclusions bear the stamp of a polemical attitude. For example, he has stated that the traditional Romanian poem, the *Miorița*, concerns "a nuptial death for the sake of others." It is about "death both as a defiant gesture and as an heroic, selfless act of comradeship" (*Four Theories* 99). Nothing could be further from the truth. The text of the *Miorița* (a prose translation of which can be found in Eliade's *Zalmoxis* 227–28 which Strenski cites, but see above p. 113 for a précis) concerns rather a shepherd's transformation of a meaningless death—which benefits no one, except perhaps his murderers—into a mythical identification with Nature.[6] It is a creative valorization of an otherwise meaningless event. A frequent criticism of this ballad was, in fact, that it valorized a submissive resignation to death. Nor does Eliade at any point in his consideration of the scholarship centered upon this ballad indicate it to be "part of universal human nature" as Strenski states (127). In fact, Eliade concludes,

> the "adherence" of a whole people to this folk masterpiece nevertheless remains significant, and it is impossible to conceive of an adequate history of *Romanian* culture which should fail to analyze and interpret that profound kinship. (*Zalmoxis* 256, emphasis added)

This misreading of the *Miorița*, carried over into Strenski's discussion of the philosopher-poet Lucian Blaga and "*Volkish*" themes, serves further to falsely associate Eliade with some "heroic," violent ideal reminiscent of the "Aryan" ideals of Nazi Germany. That said, it should be recognized that Strenski's consideration of the affinities between Eliade and Blaga is reasonable and justified. I imagine that Eliade would not have objected to such a comparison (see Ricketts, *Romanian Roots*, 857–64).

Despite the accepted importance of context, text, as the deliberate statement of the author's intention, is still of enormous significance and cannot be wholly disregarded on the grounds of an initial suspicion. Not having established the extent of Eliade's connection with the Romanian right, having repeatedly warned against "political labels" and "leaping to conclusions" (*Four Theories*, 96, 213 n. 97), Strenski, with no support other than the assertion that history does not deny his intuition, requires more than a questionable textual understanding of Eliade before leaping to the conclusion that Eliade's own descriptions are valueless. For example, volume one of the *Autobiography*, published in 1981, makes it clear that Eliade did not "detach

---

6.   Considerable light can be thrown on Eliade's conception of the *Miorița* by a reading of his play *Iphigenia*, (see above, p. 000).

himself from the Indian scene of 1932 in order to devote himself to writing" (*Four Theories*, 88). In fact, he was recalled to Romania to fulfil his national service, a duty which he felt himself compelled to discharge (*Autobiography*, vol. I, 208). Nor was his "detachment" from Romania entirely a matter of choice. Strenski actually quotes him as saying, "it was a departure which saved my life." Yet Strenski insists that "we can know little of the real significance of Eliade's choice to leave his own country" (88).

His consideration of Eliade's fictional production also suffers from conflict with recorded history. The claim that "creating fiction seems not only to have been Eliade's first love, but perhaps his truest" (*Four Theories*, 101), is unsubstantiated. While writing in general was compulsive for Eliade, and he considered occasional immersion in fantasy and fiction as necessary for his mental health, both Eliade's own words[7] and the testament of his literary legacy bear out the fact that "scientific" analysis of the human existential situation as recorded by the documents of historical religions was indeed his greatest obsession. In fact, it seems that he almost gave up fiction in 1948, despairing of an audience since he felt capable of producing literature only in Romanian, until his wife Christinel persuaded him otherwise (*Autobiography*, vol. II, 132). Strenski is also aware that Eliade's "longstanding affection for dream and fantasy may have been put aside for a while in the 1930s" (*Four Theories*, 97). Finally, many of his conclusions cannot be justified and the connection of Eliade to the Iron Guard, and of Guardist thought to Eliade's worldview, is nowhere substantiated.

ADRIANA BERGER

These questions, once raised, will not be easily dismissed. "Anti-Judaism and Anti-Historicism in Eliade's Writings," a paper written by Adriana Berger and presented on her behalf at the American Academy of Religion (AAR) Annual Meeting in New Orleans in 1990,[8] continues the attack on Eliade's political and personal history made in an article of 1989, "Fascism and Religion in Romania" (*Annals of Scholarship* 6, no. 4 (1989):455–65).[9] Before the AAR Berger claimed that "official biographies" make "a deliberate effort to conceal" Eliade's "collaboration with the Iron Guard and Romania's Nazi governments" (13). This evidently refers to

---

7. In a letter of 1934, after the publication of the novels *Isabel si apele diavolului*, *Maitreyi*, and *Lumina ce se stinge*, Eliade referred to his work on yoga as "my first book." His other publication he refers to as, "a mere *passe-temps*, a safety valve against overwork." See Ricketts, *Romanian Roots*, vol. I, 745.

8. An article under the same title but bearing more resemblance to the 1989 article was published in Hebrew in *Hadoar: the Jewish Histadrut of America*, 70 no. 25 (June 1991).

9. Berger also gave a particularly damning paper at the colloquium on "Tainted Greatness: Anti-Semitism, Prejudice, and Cultural Heroes" at Boston University, 21 and 22 April, 1991. This paper was later published in *Tainted Greatness: Antisemitism and Cultural Heroes*, edited by Nancy A. Harrowitz. Philadelphia: Temple University Press, 1994, pp. 51–73.

Ricketts' volumes. Her earlier article was a review article focused on the second volume of Eliade's *Autobiography* and on Ricketts' work. Here she made a direct attack on Ricketts' contribution, complaining that he distorts Eliade's articles and quotes them out of context (463). The best example of Berger's disagreement with Ricketts involves their respective citations of an article called "Blind Pilots" from the September 1937 issue of *Vremea*. Ricketts states:

> Eliade lists region after region of Greater Romania where the non-Romanian population has been allowed—by the "blind pilots" who have been at the nation's helm—to increase and become dominant. He is alarmed especially that Slavic types have been permitted to move north from Bulgaria into the Danube Delta, while other Slavs (Ruthenians) from the north were allowed to move south through Bessarabia to meet them. He expresses alarm also over the "invasion" of large numbers of foreign Jews into the Northwestern border provinces of Maramureş, Bucovinia, and Bessarabia—to the extent that they have become a majority in all the cities of the last-named province. "I know very well," he writes, "that the Jews will scream that I'm an antisemite and the democrats that I'm a hooligan or Fascist." These cries do not alarm him, he declares; he can sympathize with the Jews for "defending their economic and political primacy" which they have obtained with great effort. "I understand their struggle and I admire their tenacity and genius." Nevertheless, they constitute a non-Romanian element in the population which weakens the nation as a whole. Democratic leaders have argued that "industrious and intelligent" foreigners, such as the Jews, are beneficial to the country. Eliade finds such a view detrimental to national pride: "A nation in which the leading class thinks this way, which tells you about the *good qualities of foreigners*, no longer has much time to live." (*Romanian Roots*, 911)

Berger, on the other hand, renders the piece more fully. "Eliade," she states, "argued that Romania should no longer be 'colonized' by Jews and other minorities:" She quotes Eliade:

> we stayed passively and watched how the Jewish element became stronger in Transylvanian cities, how Deva became completely Hungarian, . . . how colonies of Jewish ploughmen were established in Maramureş, how the forests of Maramures and Bucovina passed into Jewish and Hungarian hands, etc. etc. . . . instead of cruelly eliminating the Bulgarian element from the entire Dobrogea, we have colonized it with Bulgarian gardeners.
>
> At the same time the blind leaders have opened the gates of Bucovina and Bessarabia. From the [first world] war on, the Jews have

swamped the villages of Maramureş and Bucovina, and obtained absolute majority in all the cities of Bessarabia. . . . I think that we are the
only country in the world that respects minority treaties, encouraging
their advances, promoting their culture and helping them create a State
within a State. I know very well that the Jews will be crying out that I am
anti-Semitic, and the democrats complain that I am a hooligan or a
Fascist. . . . I do not get angry when I hear the Jews cry, "Anti-Semitism,"
"Fascism," "Hitlerism"! These people who are energetic and clear-
sighted, defend their economic and political primacy, obtained through so
much effort, after wasting so much intelligence and spending so many
billions. It would be absurd to expect that the Jews would resign
themselves to be a minority, with some rights and very many obligations,
after having tasted the honey of power and having conquered so many
positions of leadership. The Jews are struggling with all their might to
keep, for the moment, their positions, while awaiting a new offensive,
and, as far as I am concerned, I can only admire their vitality, their
tenacity and their genius. . . . And if you tell [the blind leaders] that in
Maramureş, Bucovina, and Bessarabia, that Yiddish is being spoken, that
Romanian villages are disappearing, that the face of the earth is
changing, they think that you are employed by the Germans. . . .
Forgetting that a nation cannot be regenerated through aspirin, but
through substantial nourishment. . . . Sometimes, when they are in a good
mood, they say that the number of Jews does not matter, because they are
hardworking and intelligent people, and if they become rich, their wealth
still belongs to the country. If this is how things are, I do not see why we
should not colonize the country with English people, since they too are
hardworking and intelligent. But a nation whose leading class think in
this way, and speaks about the qualities of foreigners—does not have
much longer to live. ("Fascism and Religion in Romania," 457f.)

First, Ricketts' rendering does not seem to substantially distort or seek to conceal
what is revealed by Berger's fuller translation. This kind of nationalism is dangerous and disturbing. Yet it is evident from this quotation that Eliade was just as
opposed to Bulgarian and Hungarian usurpation of Romanian autonomy as he was
of Jewish. As this is the worst example Berger cites of Eliade's "anti-Judaism" it is
apparent that she has uncovered nothing substantially more incriminating in the
Romanian materials than did Ricketts.[10]

---

10.   Another quotation from Eliade's journalism of the period which I have located comes from
Norman Manea's article: "in the name of this Romania that began many thousands of years ago and will
not end until the apocalypse, social reforms will be enacted with considerable brutality." Also, "the Hungarians—after the Bulgarians the most imbecilic people ever to have existed—"(33).

Although I am not myself a reader of Romanian and thus cannot check Berger's Romanian references, she refers to certain British Foreign Office material in English as a major historical source for her further criticism. These documents are preserved at the Public Records Office in London and I have been able to inspect them and assess the degree to which they support her conclusions and the picture they give of that period of Eliade's life. What they reveal is this.[11]

Eliade set out for London in early April to begin his posting with the Romanian legation. Unfortunately, there are no records of diplomatic appointments available from the British Foreign Office for the year of 1940. The documents referred to by Berger as revealing that "the inclusion of his name among the names at the Romanian Legation raised objections from the British Foreign Office" ("Anti-Judaism," 9; "Fascism and Religion," 459 n. 9) are not available. The index of records does *list* these files (T7026/318/383), but only as referring to Eliade as "on the staff of the Romanian Legation," with no mention of any objections. The other file to which Berger refers (T6561/1522/378) is, in fact, a later file referring to his visa for Portugal.

From his arrival at the Romanian legation in London on 15 April 1940 onward, Eliade's diplomatic status was not recognized by the British government. Actual reasons for this refusal are not given in any of the documents available in the Public Records Office. There are, however, several possible explanations. His recent incarceration as a sympathizer of the Legion of the Archangel Michael is not the least among these, but there are others. Although Viorel Virgil Tilea was not appointed minister until 1 February 1939, he and other members of the legation under him had been in Britain for some years and their loyalties were assured, or at least known. Tilea himself had been president of the Anglo-Romanian Society in Romania and along with D. Mateescu, for example, was regarded as zealously anglophile. New arrivals, favored by the current fascist-royalist dictatorship, were automatically regarded with suspicion. And yet it was this very dictatorship which had had Eliade incarcerated.

King Carol abdicated in 1940 and General Ion Antonescu and Horia Sima allied themselves with the Iron Guard and declared a "National-Legionary" state. Tilea was recalled from his position as Romanian minister in London but refused to return. Thereafter all Romanians who continued to show allegiance to the legation under the acting chargé d'affaires, Radu Florescu, were seen by some as those who "threw in their lot with the Iron Guard by remaining on the Romanian Legation under M. Florescu."[12] Florescu himself was regarded with suspicion and a Foreign

---

11.   This material has been covered in greater detail in my "The Diplomatic Career of Mircea Eliade: A Response to Adriana Berger," *Religion* 22, no. 4 (1992): 375–92.

12.   FO 371 29993, R1424, 138. Telegram to H. L. d'A. Hopkinson at the Foreign Office, 19 February 1941. The British government often refers to foreign diplomats as *Monsieur* (abbreviated M.).

Office note of 21 September 1940 reads, "we must request his removal as soon as M. Stoica takes up his duties" (FO 371 24989, 14). On the first of September 1940, Eliade's appointment at the legation in London ceased and in mid-September he and his wife and several other Romanians moved to Cambridge to escape the blitz. Shortly thereafter he was appointed *secretaire presse* at the Romanian legation in neutral Portugal (FO 371 24996, R7698/6850/37, 143).

While Eliade's application for an exit permit was under consideration, suspicion of his political sympathies surfaced. When six British subjects were arrested by "Iron Guard Police" in Romania and brutally treated and tortured, the possibility arose of arresting some Romanians in direct retaliation.[13]

Mr. P. J. Dixon of the Foreign Office wrote to Sir Norman Kendal at New Scotland Yard on the 4 October 1940 that

> when we heard of the first arrests of British subjects in Romania last week, M.I.5 were asked to produce a list of suitable Romanians in this country for possible arrest as a retaliatory measure. (FO 371 24989, R 7624, 167)

Eliade was not included on this particular list, which was made up of businessmen and women and excluded all diplomatic staff. Evidently the government was taking the standard *quid pro quo* approach and seeking to arrest only civilians, rather than to expose their own diplomatic staff in Romania to the danger of retaliatory arrest. However, the Romanian legation included several people, like Eliade, whose status was not recognized. Although he was listed as an "official in active service of the Legation" attached to the Press and Propaganda Office by Radu Florescu, when Florescu called on Lord Dunbar on 2 December he was told that it was impossible to place Eliade on the diplomatic list.[14] Florescu continued quite strenuously to try to obtain Eliade's inclusion on the diplomatic list, but to no avail.

Sir Reginald Hoare, head of the British Mission in Bucharest, had telegraphed Dixon on 7 October to say that the "arrest of any six Romanian nationals merely [as] hostage would in no way strengthen my hand." On the bottom of this telegram, which is preserved at the Public Records Office, P. L. Rose, Dixon's immediate junior at the Foreign Office, wrote, "I still think we might arrest perhaps one or two hangers-on at the legation—such as M. Eliade who is known to have Iron Guard sympathies." Dixon, however, adds to this, "I doubt whether . . . it is worth pursuing this question" (175). Yet the very fact that he had been considered for such retaliatory arrest would ensure that Eliade would never be accorded diplomatic status. Berger has made some meat of the application of this term "hanger-on" to

---

13. *The London Times*, 28 September and 7 October 1940; FO 371 24989, 53ff., 184.
14. FO 371 29999, R119/119, 10. Again the actual reasons are not stated in this document.

Eliade ("Anti-Judaism," 9; "Fascism and Religion," 459). However, the Foreign Office used the term even for British citizens attached to their legation in Romania, quite legitimately, but without diplomatic status.

Dixon's recommendation notwithstanding, the question of Eliade's possible arrest was pursued. A note from Commander Croghan of Naval Intelligence Division indicates that this option was being kept open (FO 371 24996, R7624, 122). It is this same Croghan who describes the telegram cited by Berger. In this telegram, which itself is not extant, Eliade reportedly denounces one Dimancescu of the Romanian legation as anglophile, and requests that he (Eliade) be appointed in the latter's stead. He also is said to have "added to his message the Romanian equivalent of 'Heil Hitler'" ("Fascism and Religion," 459; "Anti-Judaism," 10).[15] These events are quite possible, and quite explicable. Several of the members of the legation *were* actively anglophile, as we have seen, and were seeking to continue to be paid by their government for the privilege of remaining in Britain with no intention of serving their government. Some people might consider this "deserving" of denunciation. The government of the royal dictator Carol had actually been overthrown by General Antonescu, with the backing of the Iron Guard and considerable popular support, and recognition of the "*conducator*" was a condition of loyalty to the current government. It seems that Croghan's informant in this matter was Dimancescu himself, who was evidently motivated by fear for his employment and fear of returning to his own country. However, in the same file which refers to this telegram, Dixon said of Eliade: "there is considerable disagreement as to his sympathies and a minute has just reached us from the Police Intelligence Department urging that he is a man who might be useful to us" (127). One Captain Campeanu, who is also mentioned in the Naval Intelligence Department document, left no such doubt in the minds of British Intelligence. He was arrested by Military Intelligence (M.I.5) on 7 November and incarcerated in Pentonville prison (R8543, 204). He was finally released only when his transport out of Britain had been assured on 28 March 1941 (R8410, 197; R8543, 202–7; FO 371 28953; W3656).

Eliade, on the other hand, although clearly thought to be connected to the Iron Guard, was viewed rather differently. Specifically, he was known to be opposed to German influence in Romania and thus potentially useful to the British government (FO 371 24996; R7858/6850, 146). Mr. Philip B. B. Nichols, Dixon's immediate senior at the Foreign Office, wrote concerning a discussion he had had with members of the Romanian legation on 28 September 1940,

---

15.   An article by C. Popescu-Cadem (see bibliography) confirms that "a telegram denouncing Dimancescu (named press counselor to London on 19 March 1940) does not exist in the Ministry of Propaganda file that [he] examined" in Bucharest, either. It also confirms that "the formula with which the telegram [presumably] concludes was *obligatory* in official correspndence."

I asked what was the position of M. Eliade, concerning whom we had a request from Prof. Mitrani that we should facilitate his departure. M. Styrcea said that M. Eliade was an intellectual with Iron Guard leanings. He had written a book on Yogi [sic] in India. He thought it possible that if he returned to Romania he might well become closely identified with Iron Guard activities.

On 1 October 1940 Nichols further asked Tilea about the possible return to Romania of Eliade.

M. Tilea made it plain that he hoped it would be possible for H. M. Government to refuse facilities for the return of any of his Romanian personnel. His reason was that if we facilitated the departure of M. Eliade, the Romanian government would then inquire how it was not possible for e.g. Captain Iliescu and M. Styrcea to return; and he was strongly of the opinion that these two latter would be of more use in this country. (R7698/6850, 133)

In another Naval Intelligence document Eliade is mentioned in a list of Romanian legation personnel who would require passage out of Britain. Everyone listed, it states

with the exception of M. Eliade, are anxious for their departure to be postponed as long as possible. . . . Captain Iliescu . . . is known to be very pro-British; he therefore fears that he will be killed, if he returns to Romania. M. Eliade is an intellectual, to some extent a supporter of the Iron Guard, and is willing to return to Romania. (135)

Professor Mitrani, referred to by Mr. Nichols above, was then at Balliol College, Oxford as a Fellow of the Royal Institute of International Affairs. He has written widely on political theory and the political history of Romania and southeastern Europe. According to a note from Mr. Dixon, he "frequently assured us that Eliade is a friend," but his word alone could not be relied upon in such matters of diplomacy (FO 371 29995; R119/119, 8). Beginning in late September 1940 Mitrani made several polite requests on Eliade's behalf for permission to leave the country, but was equally politely refused by Philip Nichols, initially in deference to Tilea's tacit request.

Although pressure was still being brought to bear from Rose in the Foreign Office, from Mr. White of M.I.5, and particularly from Dimancescu, to detain Eliade, Dixon and Nichols were not convinced. "It will be seen that the suggestion is that to allow Eliade to return to Romania will be dangerous for the loyal Romanians remaining in this country," wrote Mr. Nichols, having considered the others' arguments. However, he continued, "I do not myself believe there is much in this, particularly if Eliade stays in Lisbon" (FO 371 29999; R119/119, 19). It was eventually decided, in response to some pressure from the Romanian government, to allot two seats for Eliade and his wife on the Bristol to Lisbon service on 9 February, at least four months after he had made his first moves to leave the country (FO 371 24996; R7858/6850, 144, 164, 165). At this time Dimancescu wrote to the Foreign Office suggesting that if they wished to delay Eliade's departure further, they could simply make one seat only available to him on the flight. Eliade would not leave his wife behind and so would be prevented from leaving the country, while the British government would be seen to have fulfilled their political obligations (FO 371 2999, R119/119, 19). I believe this speaks for itself as regards Eliade's loyalty to his wife, and as a condemnation of Dimancescu's underhand tactics. The British government did not act on his recommendation.

The members of the British legation to Romania were in the process of withdrawing, a state of war having been declared between the two countries effective from 7 December 1940. Under such conditions the British government was responsive to requests concerning the movements of Romanian Legation members to avoid retaliation impeding the movement of their own diplomats. It is noteworthy that even Tilea joined in the voices speaking out for Eliade's departure and invoking the latter's "tuberculosis" as grounds for granting an exit permit (FO 371 24996, 219). However, the initial suspicions of Military Intelligence, fueled by Dimancesu's protestations, had never been allayed. Thus when Eliade presented himself at the airport in Bristol claiming diplomatic status, carrying a courier's passport stamped "diplomatique" but not signed by the relevant British authorities, and carrying a diplomatic bag, he was treated by the Security Control Officer as something of a fraud. Military Intelligence, whose job it is to act on suspicions, were suspicious that Eliade would leave the country with sensitive documents and had ordered in advance that all his belongings be thoroughly searched. The Romanian legation, in fact the whole Romanian government, were treating Eliade as a bona fide member of the legation and of diplomatic status. It is hardly surprising then that an embarrassing incident ensued.

Eliade, considering himself to be a member of the legation, was incensed at being stripped and searched, and thought the refusal by the Security Control Officer to allow him to carry his diplomatic bag out of the country without search to be a breach of protocol. He evidently complained bitterly to his home government. On 13 February the Foreign Office received a telegram from Sir Reginald Hoare which read:

> it appears that Mr. Eliade who, according to the Ministry of Foreign Affairs, is cultural attaché of the Romanian Legation and bearer of a diplomatic passport was most rigorously searched at Bristol airport a few days ago and [the] diplomatic bag which he was carrying was returned to the Legation. It is obvious that any repetition of this treatment will lead to reprisals here. (FO 371 29993, R1061, 50)

Evidently the Romanian government was consistently insisting on Eliade's diplomatic status at the highest level. The British government was just as consistently refusing to recognize it and immediately replied to Sir Reginald that

the facts are as follows:—

Mr. Eliade was not, as has been claimed, cultural attaché to the Romanian Legation in London and had no diplomatic status, a request by the Romanian Chargé d'Affaires to have him placed on the Diplomatic List having twice been refused. On being questioned at the airport, Mr. Eliade first claimed that he was Press Attaché, but subsequently admitted that this was not so. A place was reserved for him on the aeroplane to Lisbon at the urgent request of the Romanian Government, but no prior notification was received that he was to carry a diplomatic bag. An examination of his courier's passport and of his ordinary passport showed that the Legation had not complied with the regulations regarding temporary couriers with which all Missions in London are fully acquainted. The Security Control Officer accordingly invited him to obtain his Legation's confirmation of his bona fides. Mr. Eliade refused to return to London for this purpose, but stated that he would burn his bag. The S.C.O. refused to allow this, and Mr. Eliade then handed in the bag for return to the Romanian Legation and it was duly returned to them. It will be clear from the above that the diplomatic bag was not taken away from Mr. Eliade and that the incident was due entirely to his not possessing diplomatic status and to the failure of the Legation to obey the regulations regarding temporary couriers. (W3239/2008/49)

Thus the British government justified its actions without breach of protocol, ensuring Eliade's departure from Britain without any possibility of his transporting sensitive information, and forestalling, as far as possible, any direct retaliatory action against British diplomats still in Romania. This was successful and the British legation left Romania without serious incident on 15 February, after which date all diplomatic relations with Romania ceased.

That the suspicions which fell upon Eliade were finally unfounded seems to be indicated by the pattern of events which followed upon his departure from London. There is no evidence that the legation staff who remained in Britain suffered any persecution at his instigation. Eliade only once again visited Romania and there is no evidence that he was particularly highly regarded by or involved with the increasingly fascist regime, or with the Iron Guard. Otherwise he did remain in Portugal until the end of the war as Nichols had hoped, when his break with Romanian politics was final. Radu Florescu was allowed to remain in Britain. Evidently the suspicion with which he was regarded and which had fallen on Eliade by association was eventually dispelled. The antisemitic atrocities of which the Iron

Guard were guilty occurred some time after Eliade had left the country and he cannot be realistically seen to share any culpability in respect of such actions. When the Iron Guard murdered Nicolae Iorga in November 1940 Eliade deemed this an "odious assassination" that nullified the religious meaning of the "sacrifice" made by the Legionaries executed under Carol and irreparably discredited the Iron Guard (*Autobiography* vol. II, 69). After the execution of C. Z. Codreanu in 1938, his father established an alternative Legionary movement in opposition to Horia Sima's Iron Guard. This suggests a change in the nature of the Guardist movement which some of its original leaders, let alone possible sympathizers, could not tolerate.

Although these documents do not give hard evidence either way about Eliade's connection with the Guardist movement, circumstantial evidence and the possible alternative explanations serve to minimize the significance of any such connection. One conclusion which can be drawn from this information is that Berger has been biased in her treatment and presentation. She has referred to Foreign Offices files which, although listed in the index, are no longer extant and which thus cannot provide any real evidence (T6561/1522/378; T7026/318/383). She has quoted several references to Eliade's being "a member of the Iron Guard" without reporting that *the same sources* admit that there was "considerable disagreement as to his sympathies." She has adduced no hard evidence that Eliade ever *was* a member of the Guard. The only actual evidence which Berger can give is that since Eliade wrote "for those Christians who were outside the movement" this "therefore implies that Eliade was writing as someone from within" ("Mircea Eliade: Romanian Fascism," 63). She has made statements which are completely insupportable, such as: "Eliade was detained in England because of his political activities on behalf of the Iron Guard and also of Nazi Germany" ("Fascism and Religion," 459; "Anti-Judaism," 9). This is clearly not the case; Eliade was detained in Britain originally at the request of V. V. Tilea and later because of unconfirmed suspicions of his anti-British propagandizing. She has failed to recognize even the possibility that Eliade's actions could be more easily accounted for by his loyalty to the country of his birth than by any malice against anyone. Finally, she has distorted his Romanian nationalism, which stood against *all* foreign influence, presenting it as specific antisemitism.

While we must guard against the possibility of any scholar being idolized, we must just as zealously guard against personal antipathies being allowed to bias our presentation of the facts. To baldly state that "Eliade was not a Cultural attaché (or Secretary) as he had stated in interviews, diaries, and in his *Autobiography*" ("Anti-Judaism," 9), is to attempt to make a liar out of Eliade by wholly ignoring the fact that he *was* appointed to the Press and Propaganda Office of the Lisbon legation. Berger has failed to indicate any actual activity in which Eliade might have been involved which might justify the slur of "anti-Judaism." Seymour Cain's article on exactly this topic is a level-headed contribution to this debate, and he makes the clear statement that he never saw the slightest sign of anti-Semitism in [Eliade's] works or in his person. He always impressed me as a good man as well as a great creative scholar, and above all, as a treasurable human being. ("Mircea Eliade, the Iron Guard, and Romanian Anti-Semitism," 27)

I should hope that such a personal assessment is actually more weighty evidence than a tendentious rendition of "factual history" such as Berger presents. Regarding the criticism of Ricketts' volumes, there seems to be more evidence in his favor than against him. Norman Manea, for example, a Romanian who has done research into Eliade's material, called *Romanian Roots* "a meticulous monograph," (29) "of extraordinarily thorough documentation," (32) which "provided a large quantity of carefully researched material and he has drawn fair and balanced conclusions" (32).

LEON VOLOVICI

One Romanian writer who does disagree with Ricketts on the specific topic of Eliade's antisemitism is Leon Volovici. In a short but significant monograph on *Nationalist Ideology and Antisemitism: the Case of Romanian Intellectuals in the 1930s*[16] Volovici concludes that Eliade "underwent a strong phase of intellectual adhesion to the fascist and blatantly antisemitic Iron Guard" in the 1930s (ix). Volovici's book provides readers of English with a significant source of translations of Eliade's journalistic output of that period other than Ricketts' and it deserves to be consulted in its own right. It is certainly true that, as Volovici says, "the evolution of Mircea Eliade in relation to nationalism was especially fascinating" (87) and Volovici chronicles that evolution thoroughly and with considerable reference to and quotations from Eliade. Beginning with Eliade's devotion to Nae Ionescu and his increasing Romanianism, Volovici traces Eliade's "spiralling commitment" (90) to the right wing.

From 1936, his opinion for [sic] the extreme right was clear–cut. Instead of abandoning it, "tradition" had to be transposed in its entirety as the basis and justification of the new current. In Eliade's writings, the offensive appellation "hooligan," as applied to right–wing extremists as a pejorative by their adversaries, became a title of honor that he awarded to [his] nineteenth–century forerunners.[17]

---

16. Translated from the Romanian by Charles Kormos.
17. Volovici, 90; Eliade, "Mai multe feluri de naţionalişti . . .," *Vremea*, 444, 15 July, 1936; and "În jurul poeziilor lui Hasdeu," *Vremea*, 507, 3 October, 1937.

Eliade's most explicit statement of support for the Legion came in December 1937 in an article entitled "Why I believe in the Victory of the Legionary Movement."[18] This is quoted extensively by Volovici, for example:

> I believe in this victory because, above all, I believe in the victory of the Christian spirit. A movement originating from and fed by the Christian spirit, a spiritual revolution that fights especially *sin* and *dishonor* is not a political movement. It is a *Christian revolution*. But never before has *an entire people experienced a revolution with all its being*, never before has the word of the Savior been understood as a revolution of the forces of the soul against the sins and weaknesses of the flesh; never before has an entire people chosen monasticism as is ideal in life and death as its bride. . . .
>
> . . . That is why, whilst all revolutions are *political*, the aim of all contemporary revolutions is *the winning of power* by a social class or by a person, the supreme target of the Legionary revolution, is, as the Captain has said, *the salvation of the people*, the reconciliation of the Romanian people with God. That is why the sense of the Legionary movement will lead not only to the restoration of the virtues of our people, to a valorous, dignified and powerful Romania; it will also create a *new man* attuned to a new *type of life* in Europe. (Volovici, 84f.)

Clearly, Eliade was carried away by his enthusiasm for reinterpreting political events in religious terms. Without a doubt, his confidence in the religiously-inspired morality of the Legionary movement was badly misplaced. However, there is here no evidence that Eliade supported in any way the violence, antisemitism, and bigotry of which the Legion was guilty.[19] Thus this adds little to Ricketts' observation that Eliade gave open support to the Legion in 1937–8 (*Romanian Roots*, 882). It seems that Eliade's agenda was to harness the religious elements of these political movements in a vain attempt to coerce the moral, honorable, virtuous, and dignified behavior of its adherents.

While Volovici might be justified in stating that Eliade (and Emil Cioran and Constantin Noica) "'discovered' in the Legionary movement the national and spiritual setting so 'natural' to their philosophy" (74). He assumes the "fundamentally antisemitic orientation of the Iron Guard" (ix, 75) and thus the antisemitism of any supporters, without showing any sensitivity to the increase and development of this bigotry and the distinction, albeit confused, between Codreanu's Legion and Sima's Iron Guard. While it is undoubtedly true that the Legion eventually became

---

18.   "De ce cred în biruinţa Mişcării Legionare," *Buna Vestire*, 244, 17 December, 1937. Eliade denied writing this article, although Volovici points out that there are reasons to doubt this. See Volovici, 126 n. 85 and Ricketts, *Romanian Roots*, 928f.

19.   I have read Ricketts' translation of the whole of this article and have found no more damning evidence in it.

violently antisemitic, antisemitism was not an indispensable part of its early development when Eliade was sympathetic to it. While the antisemitism which later developed certainly could be said to be inherent in the fundamental tenets of the Legionary movement, antisemitism could be said to be fundamental in Christianity in the same way. The gospel accounts of the crucifixion are quite specific in laying blame at the feet of the Jews.[20] My point here is that incipient antisemitism need not necessarily develop into full-blown persecution, and that one who is sympathetic to an *incipiently* or *inherently* antisemitic organization is not thereby proven to be himself antisemitic. Depending on one's own political position, Eliade's rightist leanings may be seen as lamentable, but they have not been proven culpable.

Volovici, however, insists that Eliade was guilty of "extremist xenophobia" (124) and that he "wish[ed] to justify ideological and political antisemitism" (110, 191) and he marshals Eliade's most extreme statements to prove it. From those which have not already been discussed, perhaps the most troubling is Eliade's assertion that "everybody knows from his own experience how sensitive real Jews are, how vain and intransigent." In context, Eliade continues,

(in everyday life, this Jewish intransigence, so productive in spiritual achievements, is an expression of an inferiority complex; a really strong and self–confident person is not intransigent). You know how difficult it is to be objective when dealing with an intelligent Jew. He suffers when any allusion is made or any doubt is expressed. He always thinks that he is faced with an antisemite and is always ready for another persecution. That is how the history of the Jewish people is made, that is how the Jewish defensive spirit functions. we must see things as they are. Jewish inferiority complexes have been produced mostly by the history of the Christian world. . . .

The Jews have the right to act because it is their destiny to demonstrate their existence by making the most tragic human efforts. They may consider themselves persecuted because this helps them to survive.[21]

This, then, is Eliade at his most antisemitic. It must be noted that he is writing about the similar inferiority complex which afflicts his fellow Romanians. His point is that they *share* this "Jewish spirit." Note also that he directly blames Christian history for the inferiority complex of the Jews, *not* the Jews themselves.

Volovici continues,

for quite some time, Mircea Eliade's attitude toward the "Jewish question" in Romania remained ambiguous. Contradictory pronouncements

---

20. See, for example, John Dominic Crossan's *Who Killed Jesus.*
21. Volovici, 110–11; Eliade, "Românismul şi complexele de inferioritate," *Vremea*, 386, 5 May, 1933.

seemed to stem from concern not to resort to stereotypes and clichés and to avoid clear-cut statements. The measure of his antisemitism came to light gradually. There was no detailed theory, but signs of a doctrine that was never presented in a coherent way (120). . . . Eliade avoided declaring his sympathy with Nazism in public (131).[22]

Not only was Eliade's antisemitism "never presented in a coherent way," and never declared in public, Volovici provides some significant evidence that Eliade defended Jews against the growing antisemitism of his fellow Romanian intellectuals. For example:

Mihail Sebastian (1907–1945) was the most important Jewish writer and essayist affiliated in spirit, although not politically, to the "young generation." He had been launched as a publicist by Nae Ionescu in *Cuvântul.* As a close friend of Mircea Eliade, to whom he was linked by strong bonds of spiritual affinity, he lived within the sphere of influence of his professor of logic (101).

When Nae Ionescu expressed a clearly antisemitic theology in the preface to Sebastian's novel *For Two Thousand Years* (see Ricketts *Romanian Roots* pp. 727–41 for a detailed discussion of this issue and pp. 91–126 on Ionescu) Eliade was

drawn into a purely theological exegesis, Eliade reproached his master with having transferred the discussion from the philosophy of history to Christian theology. He contested the validity of a theologically justified antisemitism. The dogmas of the Church, he maintained, did not confirm the eternal damnation of the Jews:

What would the meaning of "antisemitism" be at the level of Christian theology? The impossibility of salvation, the certainty of the Jews' damnation. But this the Church does not say anywhere. . . . because nobody can interfere with God's freedom. God can save as he wishes to, he can save anybody, even if that anybody is outside of the community of Christian love.

From the Christian point of view, said Eliade, the fate of the Jews remained open-ended. God's judgement was not definitive:

But a Christian, a Christian theologian cannot commit the sin of despair, cannot affirm the universality of Israel's destiny of

---

22.   It seems to be solely from the diary of Mihail Sebastian that Volovici finds evidence of Eliade's "private" antisemitism. (See pp. 73 n. 90; 131 n. 109.) I do not mean to cast doubt on Sebastian's veracity, but the fact that Volovici derives this evidence from one man's diary implies that he could *not* derive it from the numerous articles from Eliade's own hand, nor from other sources.

suffering. All he can say as a Christian and an Orthodox [Christian] is that Divine Grace is free to save or not to save the Jews.[23]

In another polemical intervention, Eliade declared that only Judas was damned for all eternity, not the Jewish people:

Does our Church say anywhere that the Jews cannot be saved because they are Jews? No. . . .

And the sin of Judas is and remains the sin of Judas, not the sin of Israel, and not the sin of the Jews.[24]

Furthermore, Volovici elsewhere points out that

Eliade had "pro-semitic" antecedents, which he sometimes mentioned quite proudly, like a man who had suffered because of them. He repeatedly voiced his indignation that three great Jewish scholars, Moses Gaster, H. Tiktin, and Lazăr Şăineanu, had been expelled from Romania.[25]

Volovici often biases his case for Eliade's involvement by making no clear transition between quotations from Emil Cioran, who was explicitly anti-rational, pro-Nazi, and antisemitic, and discussion of Eliade (for example, pp. 78, 110, 120, 131). Yet he finally contrasts Eliade and Cioran because the latter, "unlike Eliade, . . . took the opportunity . . . of repudiating the Iron Guard and of denying that he had belonged to it" (149). It is this failure ever to deny or repudiate his connection with the Iron Guard which finally determines Volovici's conclusion. With reference to Eliade's autobiographical writings, Volovici points out that,

half a century after the events, the Legion is still seen as an essentially ethical and religious—not political—movement, with the aim of creating "the new man." (144)

He sees this as

a determined effort to *rewrite* the past, to wipe out what he may have thought to be a disreputable episode, [which] produced an almost magical selective amnesia. (141)

The circularity of Volovici's thought becomes clear here. If Eliade never was guilty of any reprehensible activities connected with the Legion, he would not need to repudiate them, and since his autobiography was about the perceptions of his youth rather than about contemporary political positions, it would be simply inaccurate to

23. Volovici, 104; Eliade, "Judaism şi antisemitism," *Vremea*, 347, 22 July, 1934.
24. Volovici, 104; Eliade, "Creştinătatea faţă de judaism," *Vremea*, 349, 5 July, 1934.
25. Volovici, 120; Eliade, "Judaism, şi antisemitism," *Vremea*, 347, 22 July, 1934.

represent himself as seeing the Legion in any other light than that light in which he did, unfortunately, see them at the time. However, by beginning with assumptions of guilt, Volovici finds evidence of guilt, and what is not said becomes guilty silence. Of course, this criticism moves both ways, it could as easily be said that beginning with assumptions of innocence will produce evidence of innocence. I find it not only more just, but in this case more coherent, to accept Eliade's innocence. The vicious circularity of Volovici's thought is revealed by its self-contradictory elements: "no thought, no regret, no pang of conscience disturbs a youth retold in almost mythical and saintly terms" (141). If Eliade felt no pang of conscience, then why would he be inclined to rewrite the past? If he did feel some general discomfort from his initial support of the Legion, but had no specific culpability to explain, would that not explain his reluctance to broach the subject in any way other than he did?

Eliade's own opposition to unthinking prejudice is shown by Volovici's quotation: "it is much more difficult, more dramatic and—why not admit it?—practically speaking, much more inefficient to try to think for yourself." As is his opposition to "intransigence and intolerance."[26] The fact that Eliade accused Romania's ruling class of being totally indifferent to and blinded by the expansion of the foreign element to the detriment of the Romanians ("Blind Pilots" Volovici, 123f.), while distastefully nationalistic to liberal twentieth century palates, is hardly sufficient evidence to warrant accusations of extremist xenophobia and antisemitism.

In the end it is true that

Eliade "rediscovered" the myth of regeneration, awareness of historic mission, a "new man" and a new meaning of life in the new Legionary aristocracy . . . (134)

And that

Heidegger at Freiburg and Robert Brasillach in Paris were at the same time voicing essentially the same mystical and nationalist ideas, attributing the same sacred finality to Nazism or fascism. (135)

However, Volovici's interpretation of the evidence is not convincing. His reference to Eliade's "years of decisive and public support for the Iron Guard" (143) seems an unwarranted conclusion. More accurate would be Rickett's statement that "between January 1937 and the imposition of the Royal dictatorship in February 1838 Eliade gave open and enthusiastic support . . . to the Legionary movement" (*Romanian Roots* 882). There seems to be no positive evidence that this support was "decisive," and it was not continued for years. Considering the extremes of the rightist "psychosis" and the "terrifying nightmare" of the development of fascism

---

26.   Volovici, 122; Eliade, "Judaism și antisemitism" and "Românismul și complexele de inferioriatate."

(Mihail Sebastian and Eugene Ionescu, see Volovici, 137) the sum total of Eliade's involvement, while not entirely faultless, is mild, and can be seen as a moderating influence in the prevailing atmosphere. Eliade's case provides an example of how patriotism, manifested as ethnic nationalism combined with religious zeal, all too easily becomes violence, bigotry, xenophobia, and oppression. Eliade himself does not seem to have clearly analyzed the dynamics or implications of his own involvement. Our analysis is not complete, however, unless we take into account the irreducible pluralism of Eliade's later theories about religion in general and the sacred in particular. I would suggest that Eliade's brush with totalitarian ideologies in the 30s influenced his theoretical position as expressed in his later books as a reaction *against* such tendencies; that his perilous attraction to the extreme right in his younger years led to a far more mature position; that, in its own way, his later works were a repudiation of the exclusivism and ethnic superiority of the later Iron Guard. One has to recall Eliade's understanding of the noumenal status of "real" history. We cannot disclaim our own responsibility for the creative "rewriting" of his story any more than could Eliade himself. We do not *know* the exact extent of Eliade's involvement, and I would have little hesitation in affirming that we *cannot* know the exact nature of his inner motivations. Not that we should ever abandon the attempt to extend and authenticate our knowledge. But we must seek never to judge, and certainly never to punish, reject, or refuse on the grounds of our ignorance.

DANIEL DUBUISSON

In a work of 1994 on Dumézil, Lévi-Strauss, and Eliade, Daniel Dubuisson[27] reaches even more damning conclusions regarding, not only Eliade's political involvement in the thirties, but also about the extent to which this involvement manifests itself in his later work. According to Dubuisson, Eliade "played an active part in the legionary movement" (220). He was a "militant fascist" and a "journalist involved in the heart of a fascist, mystical and anti-semitic movement" (221) and "adhered to a virulently anti-semitic fascist movement in the thirties" (18). The argument which is given in support of these conclusions is this:

> Eliade did not condemn Cornelia Codreanu the founder of the sinister Iron Guard (Autobiography, vol. I, 280f.; vol. II, 64–66), and maintained his unrealistic claim "that the legionary movement did not constitute a political phenomenon but was, in its essence, ethical and religious" (vol. II, 65) although it involved a militia which terrorized, tortured, and massacred innumerable Jewish victims. (220)

---

27. The following material is taken from Dubuisson's *Mythologies du XXe Siècle* (see Bibliography). All translations are my own.

Furthermore, Eliade

> compared "the famous *Wandervögel*" (*Occultism*, 88 n. 37) to "contemporary youth movement(s)" simply forgetting to specify that this organization willfully proclaimed itself to be *judenrien* ("pure-of-Jews")! (220)

Therefore Eliade was himself antisemitic.

This makes the model fallacy of drawing positive conclusions from negative premises. No *evidence* is given regarding any of the accusations of militancy, fascist journalistic activity, or antisemitic tendencies. Requiring some actual statement of the antisemitic tendencies of the Iron Guard Dubuisson is forced to quote "one of its partisans . . . cited by Jean-Paul de Longchamp" (219 n. 1) without having established any connection to Eliade at all. Dubuisson does introduce the detail that

> Ernst Jünger was one of the rare writers retained and referred to by Heidegger . . . now it was also with this former Wehrmacht officer that Eliade founded the review *Antaios* in 1961. (292)[28]

This, along with the fact that Eliade admits to having read Heidegger, and the fact that he uses a similar vocabulary (Dubuisson cites *Urgrund*, modes of being, ontic, 291 n. 1) allows Dubuisson to equate Eliade's thought with that of Heidegger. In fact, Eliade specifically stated that

> the expression "being in the world" is not used here in the post-Heideggerian sense. . . . It means that man simply discovers himself in the world. ("The Sacred in the Secular World," 101)

Dubuisson merely dismisses any *discontinuity* between the thought of the two scholars and disregards Eliade's evident disagreements with Heidegger in *The Myth of the Eternal Return* (150, 152). He does the same regarding Plato and refers to all three when he speaks of "the totalitarian regimes of which they dreamed" (293).

It is also pointed out that

> after the war, among the thousands of pages they published, Eliade and Heidegger never attempted to re-examine their political and intellectual involvement and even less to retract them. It is true that such a starting point would without doubt have revealed to them the solid affinities which their own thoughts display with those which finally issued in the monstrous crimes of nazism. (292)

---

27. Jünger was no Nazi, however. See *Dictionary of Literary Biography* for a brief introduction to the complex question of Jünger's position.

In response to Norman Manea's warning that

> to draw a connection between (Eliade's) scholarship and his "fascist" period, to cast an inquisitorial eye on "suspect" details in his many learned studies, would be to provide a perfect example of totalitarian methodology. ("Happy Guilt," 28)

Dubuisson asks,

> why then would it be bad method to examine the memory of a militant fascist of the thirties and to wonder, among other possible hypotheses, whether, and to what degree, his antisemitic opinions have not then contributed to and nourished his thought as a historian of religions? (221)

This, of course, begs the question. *Was* Eliade a militant fascist with antisemitic opinions? Dubuisson simply assumes that he was. *That* is precisely why it is an example of totalitarian methodology. Taking the Anglo-Saxon rather than the classical Roman legal system as axiomatic, Eliade should not be assumed guilty until proven innocent but should be assumed innocent until proven guilty. It seems unlikely that the postwar communist regime which censured Eliade would have failed to uncover information connecting him to the extreme right. If it existed, it would surely have come to light by now. Since the "corroborating evidence" of Eliade's connection with the Iron Guard has been accepted without evidence, Dubuisson's continuing argument for Eliade's "antisemitism" must be treated with serious suspicion.

The substance of his argument is that in Eliade's work Jews always appear as the "prototype of the adversary who stands opposed to the maintenance of this cosmic sacrality" (250). The Hebrews are presented as solely and wholly guilty for

> the disruption of the magic circle of the *eternal return* (by inventing linear history, for example). . . . Considered as active accomplices of non-Being [they thus must accept the] total, irreversible responsibility of which he accuses them. (271)

Thus "the Jews, and their Christian successors, are consequently responsible for the anguish, for the feeling of dereliction, of modern man" (275). Dubuisson inquires

> whether Eliade was motivated by the sole intent of seamlessly uniting the Hebrews with history . . . of making them responsible for a sort of inexpiable metaphysical crime? (271)

His positive response is invalid for various reasons. First, Eliade did not consider the Hebrews solely responsible for the development of history. I have already mentioned, in connection with the development of the concept of historical time (above p. 86) that Eliade accepted that this valorization began among the Babylonians, Hebrews, Egyptians, and Iranians, and that it finally crystallized in the Hellenic Christian tradition. In an interview shortly before his death,[29] Eliade stated that "one of the great *merits* of the Western tradition is that the West takes history seriously" (149, emphasis added) and he attributes that to the Jewish tradition. In the same interview he pointed out that with

> the appearance of the Assyrians and, later on, of Alexander the Great, the Roman Empire—those men who really did make history—. . . people began to live with what I call a terror of history, which was based on historical reality. (151)

Certainly, Eliade argues that what destroyed a fundamental sense of the sacred was the irruption of history into human time as it was introduced by Judeo-Christianity. However, to say that Eliade unvaryingly presents the Hebrew as alone opposed to the maintenance of cosmic sacrality is to discount the *Christian* element of the Judeo-Christian tradition. Origen, Basil, Gregory, Augustine, all reacted against the theory of cyclical time and subscribed to the linear progress of history (*Myth of the Eternal Return*, 145).

In the Western tradition, the manifestations of this valorization are recorded in our traditional mythical texts, the most widespread of which is the Christian Bible, which includes as its oldest component the Hebrew Tanakh. Going back to the oldest sources of our culture results unavoidably in a return to Hebrew tradition. Dubuisson accepts that "Roman Christianity . . . also sanctified history and even surpassed its Jewish model in this" (272), thus the "guilt," if guilt it be, is not solely attached to Judaism.

Yet Dubuisson concludes that the really pernicious aspect of Eliade's understanding is that Eliade can claim that

> the millions of Jews killed or burned in Nazi concentration camps constitute the avant garde of humanity which is waiting to be incinerated by the will of "History." Cosmic cataclysms (floods, earthquakes, fires) are also known in other religions. The cataclysm provoked by man, as a *historical* being, is the contribution of our civilization. The destruction, it is true, will be possible only thanks to the extraordinary development of Western science. But the *cause*, or the *pretext* of the cataclysm is found in man's decision to "make history." Now, one must remember, "history" is the creation of the Judeo-Christian tradition (*No Souvenirs*, 145f.)

Thus the Jews are seen as themselves responsible for their own destruction. Even allowing Dubuisson's argument to stand without challenge (which I am not inclined to do), the conclusion can only be that *some* Jews would have *some* guilt for their own immolation in the Holocaust, not that Jews alone are guilty as Dubuisson

---

29.   *Chicago* magazine, June 1986, with Delia O'Hara, 146–80.

implies, and *not* that the perpetrators of this atrocity were innocent. Can any of us, as humans, be totally innocent of man's inhumanity to man? Certainly not according to the Judeo-Christian tradition.

When Eliade refers to historicism as "a decomposition product of Christianity" (*The Sacred and the Profane*, 112), it is in the midst of a discussion of *Hegel's* debt to the Judeo-Christian ideology of history, and in the *Myth of the Eternal Return* it is *Heidegger* (not a Jew) who is seen as putting the finishing touches to the historicism which the Judeo-Christian religious tradition fostered and which Eliade condemns. It was Heidegger who "took the trouble to show that the historicity of human existence forbids all hope of ever transcending time and history" (150). "All the varieties and shades" of historicism, says Eliade, extend from "Nietzsche's 'destiny' to Heidegger's 'temporality'" (152).

> "Historicism" was created and professed above all by thinkers belonging to nations for which history has never been a continuous terror. These thinkers would perhaps have adopted another viewpoint had they belonged to nations marked by the "fatality of history." (152 n. 11)

The Jews are (or at least were until 1947) the very epitome of the people for whom history has been a continuous terror and are thus not responsible for the creation of historicism. It was the creation of history as we know it—historicism, the concomitant desacralization of the universe, and the development of science—which was responsible for the Holocaust and permits the possibility of the greater global holocaust of which Eliade wrote.

We should also consider the message of the Deuteronomic historian. Is it not through their failure to observe their covenant with their God that the Jews were seen as responsible for their own fate? Does this make the Torah an "antisemitic" work? Certainly not. It does not seek to *justify* the inhumanity of "the nations" toward the Jews, and neither does Eliade.

It might be expected that Dubuisson's argument would be more substantial than this and not so easily discarded. Indeed, this is the case. Although the accusation of an "anti-semitic ontology" is the most damning element of Dubuisson's attack, it is only a part of his overall analysis of Eliade's "neopaganism." Throughout Eliade's thought Dubuisson detects the strains of a valorization of Nature as a cosmic force, a tolerance of violence, irrationality, and bloody sacrifice, and a totalitarian tendency. Dubuisson makes a constant association of rites of regeneration with violence, bloodletting, and orgy. Certainly, Eliade *did* analyze such rituals, and he did attempt to justify his analysis in the face of the conservative distaste of the forties and fifties. Yet it is ludicrous to imply, as Dubuisson does by his constant and relentless association, that this is the *only* type of rite of regeneration or that Eliade sought to valorize violence. Throughout Eliade's work such specific types of religious activity are in the minority and he refers to them as "aberrant" (*The Two and the One*, 12; "Structures and Changes," 357). This does not deter Dubuisson from writing

> now, of all these models, the most essential is that of the eternal return, because it is in this, in the (orgiastic and bloody) rituals that it requires . . . (269)

as if rites of eternal return were necessarily orgiastic and bloody, which Eliade nowhere implies. Every time Dubuisson mentions such rites he refers to them in similar terms (250, 252, 269, 272, 278, 283, 286, 287) and falsely infers that Eliade "seemed to be fascinated above all by bloody sacrifice, orgiastic ceremonies, and cannibalism" (283). This is crucial to his critique of Eliade's "neo-paganism."

Finally, Eliade's

> conception of Being, or of the sacred, expanded into a brutal exaltation of Life, of fertility and of power, could be made to resonate so as to permit the possibility of certain disquieting sophisms which justify the "religious valuation of torture and violent death" (*Myth and Reality*, 144). . . . It is thus against the judeo-christian tradition, against the double principle of faith and the law, against the liberating role of reason and study, and against the imperative to love one's neighbor that Eliade sets this pagan figure [of *homo religiosus*]. (250, 289)[30]

This apprehension of Eliade's thought as itself "justifying" brutality and violence finally leads Dubuisson to read with astonishment Eliade's comparisons of violent "primitive" rituals, cruelty, torture, the massacres of the Mongol hordes, and Aztec human sacrifice with the annihilation of millions in Nazi death camps. Assuming that Eliade justifies and even valorizes the "primitive" rites, Dubuisson can only conclude that Eliade justifies and valorizes the more recent horror. Eliade was discussing the justification and valorization of this aberrant behavior, *not* justifying and valorizing it himself. It is the *perpetrators* of these acts who justify them in the manner referred to. Dubuisson follows the unacceptable path that anyone who can understand the justifications of a rapist must be a rapist, or somehow encourage rape. Eliade was following the path that in order to understand the rapist we must understand how he justified his actions *to himself*. These two paths are indeed parallel—they never converge. Eliade's comments can be seen as an attempt to understand rather than to justify the incredible reality of the inhumanity of the death camps.

With the exception of those comments regarding Jünger and Heidegger already noted, Dubuisson's accusations add no historical detail to the material which has already been covered in the consideration of the arguments of Strenski and Berger. He quite rightly points out that

> to pretend that the thought of Eliade was the result of a sort of intemporal and discorporate meditation is no more than intellectual mystification and fraud. (222)

---

30. Note that the original context speaks of the "tragic conception of life, resulting from the religious valuation," etc.

but we must insist on the *accuracy* of the historical detail and the validity of the argument based upon it. It is neither accurate nor valid to simply make Eliade conform to the model of Heidegger and state that

> both spent the thirties associated with organizations (nazism in one case, the Romanian legionary movement in the other) and currents of thought which, whatever their differences and singularities, agreed in their condemnation of democracy, science and the modern world, of progress (social, technological) and freedom of thought in favor of an elitist, aristocratic anachronism and of an agrarian and archaizing mysticism and a verbose exaltation of *Volk.* (291)

Dubuisson's whole style of criticism is disturbingly unscholarly. He is venomously sarcastic:

> the long eclipse of Being is over. History has found its direction by a recovery of the meaning of its original destiny, and that thanks to the historian of religions, Eliade himself, the inspired hermeneut! (232)

His predisposition to accept Eliade's guilt is evident in his simple, categorical statements about Eliade's past. Before he attempts to detail his case, Dubuisson has repeated ten times that Eliade was a "militant fascist" who "played and active role" in a movement which was "violent, mystical, reactionary, and antisemitic" (18, 220, 221, 222, 261, 262). He dispenses guilt by association, mentioning the political connection of *only* those thinkers who had connections with the extreme right (Julius Evola and, of course, Heidegger) but completely ignoring the politics of any other associates. Many of his "conclusions" are so baldly stated as to appear little more than personal insults: Eliade's "work, however abundant, does not give rise to a single new concept nor does it clarify anything" (237). Eliade writes "'as a historian of religions,' in other words without any scientific rigor" (256). In fact, "the anti-reductionism of the phenomenology of religions, . . . is finally nothing more than the dogmatic refusal to accept the real world for what it is" (258). Several other elements of Dubuisson's argument are equally disturbing. For example, that

> it cannot be said too often that there is, among numerous twentieth century thinkers (and without doubt the first rank of these are those who, like Eliade, stayed freely in Berlin in 1942), an indisputable affinity between certain political themes and a certain germanomania [sic] (which begins with the citation of certain terms "in German in the text": *Urgrund, Meister, Männerbund, Wandervögel*; now it can be easily verified, none of these are innocent). (281)

This smacks of a certain "germanophobia" which is equally suspect.

According to Dubuisson, Eliade seeks "to denigrate all the improvements and all the progress ensuing from the ideals of the eighteenth century (democracy,

social welfare, the right to education etc.)" (266). Also "individual liberty, tolerance, political democracy, social progress, the right to happiness, legal protection,
citizenship (293) . . . the nation, republican legalism, social laws" (302). I am
completely at a loss to see how or where Eliade does this. Dubuisson has simply
implied that Eliade is anti-modern and anti-democratic and thus concluded, with
only the most vague, abstract, and theoretical argument, that he *must* then share
these tendencies. Certainly, no textual evidence is adduced.

Now, Dubuisson asks,

> how, in this muddle, this hodge-podge of superstitions and irrational
> beliefs, in this bizarre metaphysics victim of every whim of facile credulity,
> could anyone detect a scientific work worthy of our times? (261f)

He continues that "finally Eliade, as an inspired prophet, expects an unthinking and
instinctive adherence to his theses, not a solid critical exegesis" (246). Dubuisson
now insults not only Eliade but any reader who might be favorably disposed toward
him: Eliade "doubtless imagines that the reader, spellbound by his erudition,
wouldn't have the time or the courage necessary to patiently review his work in an
attempt to disentangle its confused genealogy" (239). Dubuisson thoroughly
"poisons the well" of discourse, not only by insulting any reader who feels
positively disposed toward Eliade, but by referring to

> the image which Eliade and his disciples have patiently attempted to
> impose after the fact, that of a benevolent *guru* and liberal savant, open to
> all formes of spirituality, (218f. Note that Eliade specifically denied being
> a guru, *Ordeal by Labyrinth* 109–11)

and by referring to

> the chaste (*pudique*) version proposed by Eliade himself: "the impru-
> dence and the faults committed in my youth constitute a series of
> misunderstandings which followed my all my life" (Mem II, 135). (221)

This simply does not permit the possibility that Eliade might be telling the truth
here.

A close inspection of Dubuisson's argument reveals a series of reciprocally
reinforcing assumptions and classic misinterpretations of Eliade's thought which
seriously compromises his whole reading. One of the worst of these assumptions,
and one which is not original to Dubuisson, is that Eliade slavishly followed Rudolf
Otto's concept of the sacred. Dubuisson even attributes Otto's description of the
sacred as the wholly other (*totalement autre*, 245) to Eliade without any quali-
fication. As has been pointed out, Eliade was more influenced by Durkheim than by
Otto in his conception of the sacred. Otto's concept (not Eliade's) encourages an
assumption of the necessary ontological independence of the sacred: "the existence
of an instantiated transcendence (*une instance transcendent*), the sacred, which has

the power to make itself visible to the eyes of man" (223). As we have seen, this is not necessarily the case in Eliade's thought. In fact, it is a specific insistence of the assumption that Eliade uncritically and categorically adopts the believers' belief. Dubuisson consistently attributes to Eliade the attitudes and beliefs which Eliade *describes* as characteristic of religious believers.

> Eliade accepts that "the world is holy" (*Ordeal by Labyrinth*, 92), "that it is sanctified by the presence of God" (*The Two and the One*, 77), that its existence is in response to a providential will. (242)[31]

The original context reveals that this is the belief which Eliade attributes to the religious person, the subject of his study, and not a declaration of his personal belief. This assumption, coupled with the assumptions which Dubuisson makes concerning the nature of the sacred, brings him to the specific fallacy that

> the assumption that Eliade most commonly makes is that the sacred does not resemble that of Durkheim or Cassirer, it is not a particular zone of symbolic thought, it *is*, essentially and intemporally (243)

This is not, in fact, a specific affirmation of Eliade's but an axiom characteristic of *homo religiosus*. It is *for the believer* that "every religious fact *is*, not a simple belief or superstition, but an authentic manifestation of the sacred and thus of Being" (244). Clearly, Eliade cannot accompany each and every description of a religious belief with a disclaimer and thus it is relatively simple to take his statements, especially out of context, to be affirmations of his own rather than descriptions of other people's beliefs. It is a definitive constituent of religious belief that believers *do* so believe; ignore this and we ignore something factual about religion. Dispense with the belief and its implications and we do not see the cosmos which the believer sees. We must see the belief through in order to see through the belief. This is entirely consonant with an analysis of Eliade's sacred as closer to Durkheim's that to Otto's.

Ascribing the attitudes of the believers to Eliade, it is entailed that "the idea is always implied that it [the universe] . . . responds to the intelligent will of a benevolent divine architect" (226). This type of specific monotheism was studiously avoided throughout Eliade's work (and hardly seems consonant with neo-paganism). It is very misleading to assume it. Assumed, it leads to the accusation that Eliade makes an unwarranted methodological move: he insists

---

31. Again note the original contexts: "that made me think of the "Cosmic Christianity" of the Eastern European peasant, for whom the world is 'holy' because it was sanctified by the incarnation" and "each man discovers what he was spiritually and culturally prepared to discover . . . a meeting with the Light produces a break in the subject's existence, revealing to him—or making clearer than before—the world of the Spirit, of holiness and of freedom; in brief, existence as a divine creation, or the world sanctified by the presence of God."

that the field of religion is a- or trans-historical, that it transcends the human world, [which] is to adopt a point of view which places its defender beyond the methodological rules and principles which form the starting point of the historian of religions. (228)

It also leads to the perception of Eliade as a mystic in the sense defined by Bertrand Russell. That is, that he affirms

the belief in the possibility of a mode of knowing which could be called revelation, vision, or intuition, as opposed to sense perception, reason, and analysis. (225)

Eliade's concept of hierophany, however, was not opposed to sense perception or to reason. As we have seen it was always accomplished through the senses and has its own reason and was thus open to analysis.

According to Dubuisson,

Eliade elevates the primitive, the man of archaic or traditional cultures, to an extraordinary status, he is considered the privileged witness of a series of essential experiences. (244)

Furthermore, primitive man is seen as "essentially" religious and even "obsessed with the ontic" (244). This insistence on the elevation of the primitive is frequently repeated and is crucial to Dubuisson's argument. He concludes that the ontology constructed by Eliade is primitive because it accords most interest and value to the most elementary manifestations of the natural world—Eliade incessantly valorizes these vital animating forces of nature. This ignores completely Eliade's emphasis on the imagination, which is not usually considered a vital animating force of nature. Eliade does not consider prehistory to be more "ontic" than the present— rather "primitive" religions have a more immediate (or less mediate) access to their own sources of the real. This is a wholly different concept. Considering the ubiquity of religious experience, it is not "primitive" humanity which is so elevated, but religious experience itself, and the elevation is not made by Eliade but is a status accorded by *homo religiosus* to that experience. To claim that "'ontic' perfection is contemporary with the first moments of humanity" (265) flagrantly ignores Eliade's specific protestations to the contrary (discussed above in the section on "Archaic and Modern Conceptions of Time"). That "it is urgent to restore all primitive religions in order to re-establish contact with the sacred" (244) is an aim which Eliade specifically repudiated in "Notes for a Dialogue," and in the 1964 preface to *Le Sacré et le Profane.*[32]

---

32. "Rereading the text after eight years, we have better understood how such an enterprise invites misunderstanding. To attempt to present, in 200 pages, with understanding and sympathy, the behavior of *homo religiosus*, primarily the situation of the man of traditional and Oriental societies, is not without hazard. This attitude of receptive openness risks being taken for an expression of secret nostalgia for a bygone condition of archaic *homo religiosus* which was foreign to the author" (10, my translation).

Dubuisson's insistence on "the fundamental Eliadean equation (primitive = 'ontic')" (265) is simply incorrect. It is, however, implied by his other assumptions, especially that the sacred/profane dialectic is an unqualified polar opposition or confrontation identical to the Platonic dualism of ideal Forms and the material world (253, 294; cf. my analysis of this dialectic above, chapters 2 and 3). Although he recognizes that "it is impossible to reduce the structure of all ancient, archaic, or primitive religions to such a basic (sacred/profane) opposition" (254), Dubuisson insists that this is precisely what Eliade is intent on doing. Not only does this permit a gross oversimplification of all of Eliade's thought informed by the complexity of this dialectic, it also allows Dubuisson to make the unqualified equivalence of the thought of Eliade and Plato mentioned above. After first insisting that Eliade himself *is* a Platonic thinker, Dubuisson is critical that

> it would be difficult to be a worse Platonist, because Eliade makes Nature, which is at best a distant reflection of the Ideal for Plato . . . the very expression of Being. (254)

This is a very obvious example of the way Dubuisson "discovers" incoherencies in Eliade's thought by imposing his own interpretations on the text rather than finding coherence by deriving his interpretations from the text.

Finally, it is assumed that

> history is synonymous with corruption; it literally empties beings and the world of their 'ontic' substance whose continuance is assured only by the orgiastic and bloody rites of periodic regeneration. (272)

Hence Dubuisson's perception of Eliade as repudiating all the advances and benefits of modern history. While it is true that Eliade does lament the valorization of the historic over and above the ideal, he specifically denies that history itself is negative. It is rather the insistence on the *exhaustive* constitution of humanity by history which he protests. This oversimplification can be traced back to the oversimplification of the sacred/profane dialectic.

My comments have been too brief to conclusively dismiss all of these assumptions. Many will be given more attention in the following chapters. They have, I hope, been shown to require more support before they are assumed *a priori*. More to the point, it has been shown that Dubuisson argues from his own assumptions and prejudgments rather than from an adequate grasp of his subject. Guided by his assumptions, he "arrives" at the numerous accusations which he levels against Eliade. He can be seen to "reach" his conclusions by making them the criteria whereby he simplifies and selects from Eliade's texts. No doubt I have done the same, all interpreters do. The validity of such criteria are borne out by the absence of clear errors and omissions. As well as those errors we have already seen, it is an egregious error to point out that

the Christian perspective is not only linear: the liturgical year which
repeats itself infinitely, the theme of the final resurrection (can there be a
better example of regeneration?) . . . can annul the deleterious effect
which Eliade attributes to history (273)

as a means of discrediting Eliade's understanding of the influence of Judaism on
Christianity. Doing so ignores Eliade's clear awareness of this aspect of Christianity
already mentioned. To state that the antonym of Being

in the fascist movements to which Heidegger and Eliade adhere was
always represented as the wanderer, the exile, the uprooted, the
fatherless, and the homeless (300)

is to ignore the great number of references which Eliade makes to himself as a
wanderer and exile, torn from his roots. To read Eliade's lament over modern
society as a call for a "natural society" guided by a few "exceptional individuals"
(302) and thus radically anti-democratic is to ignore Eliade's concomitant lament
that only a very few individuals actually do "make history." An alternative reading
is that it is the *lack* of individual autonomy which is deplorable, and that is finally
pro-democratic. To conclude that

the quasi-totality of the Eliadean disposition seems to have been
conceived with the goal of opposing science, society, political principle,
humanism [*sic*!], morals, and modern rights with a mystical, antisemitic,
agrarian, and archaic system in which one finds the barely concealed
elitist principles of the old metaphysicians mixed with the ideological
obsessions and the mythologies of the fascist thinkers of the thirties, (303)

is to reveal a gross misinterpretation of Eliade's thought.

One could almost admire the relentless determination with which Dubuisson
prosecutes his case. However, his arguments for guilt-by-association, guilt-by-
inaction, guilt-by-proximity, his *a priori* accusations and question-begging all
smack of sensationalist Nazi-hunting rather than sound scholarship. The most
damning of Dubuisson's argument, sadly, could be turned against him. He himself

by composing this cursory version of history, invents above all a new
indictment against the Jews, that of an ontological crime, consequentially
a major and certainly unforgivable crime. (273)

Certainly, for all my reading of Eliade, it was not until I read Dubuisson that I was
aware of the possibility of this accusation.

CONCLUSION

Undoubtedly, there is more work to be done in this area. Eliade's contribution to the
department of press and propaganda and his work as cultural attaché in Lisbon

between 1940 and 1945 particularly need to be inspected in more detail. His insistent nationalism in the thirties is certainly distasteful, especially to our palate in the nineties. Yet, in conclusion, it has to be said that there is to date no evidence of actual membership, of active services rendered, or of any real involvement with any fascist or totalitarian movements or ideals. Nor is there any evidence of continued support for nationalist separatist ideals after their inherently violent nature was revealed, nor of the imprint of such ideals in Eliade's scholarship. On the other hand, there is clear evidence that those scholars who have published their suspicions of Eliade have pursued their own agendas with little regard for the integrity of their textual sources.

There seems to be a gradually developing interpretation of Eliade as a pernicious force in the academic study of religion which has nurtured suspicions, with the benefit of slight factual evidence, concerning his political position. This opinion, although unsubstantiated, has in turn (hardly surprisingly) further nourished a specific but ultimately incoherent interpretation of his writings. The whole dynamic has been driven by the current of criticism flowing against Eliade in contemporary academic analysis. It is to a general consideration of that analysis that I wish now to turn.

CHAPTER 14

Scholarly Criticism of Eliade

SOME OLD AND NEW CRITICISMS

Much of the foregoing criticism, particularly in the case of Daniel Dubuisson, has relied on established analyses of Eliade which have become almost standard in the academic world. The survey of criticisms given by R. F. Brown in his article "Eliade on Archaic Religions: Some Old and New Criticisms," although he insists it is not exhaustive, is full and informative and makes an excellent basis for a consideration of the criticisms levelled against Eliade.[1] Brown identifies two main areas of criticism. First, a number of ways in which critics find Eliade's general methodology wanting. In this he recognizes seven separate criticisms of Eliade's approach;

1. His use of anthropological *source material* is irresponsible. Specifically: (*a*) He often neglects to evaluate the quality of his sources and therefore uses data which contemporary anthropologists repudiate as inaccurate or outdated by later or more thorough fieldwork. (*b*) He fails to take sufficient account of the interpretative bias of authors, treating secondary sources as if they were usable in the same way as primary data. (*c*) He lumps together the most heterogeneous kinds of data (scriptures, artifacts, ethnographic reports, etc.), deploying them as if they were uniform in meaning and evidential value.

2. Eliade's use of the comparative method is defective.

---

1. I should point out that, although I have made use of some French and German sources, I am specifically referring to the scholarly interpretation of Eliade in the English speaking world, where it seems misapprehension has been the rule rather than the exception.

3. The *procedures of generalization* which Eliade employs are not properly inductive and fail to satisfy scientific criteria.
4. Eliade utilizes *Lévy-Bruhl's discredited theory* that non-literate peoples lack the scientific attitude because their mental structure and logical thought differs fundamentally from that of modern Western people.
5. To construct his profile of the archaic religious mind, Eliade *groups living non-literate peoples together with ancient cultures* no longer extant.
6. Anthropologists are sharply critical of Eliade's *"descending approach"* [a term taken from John Saliba's book, *Homo Religiosus*, 40], which begins with the assumption that in religious phenomena one has to do with a transcendent sacred reality disclosing itself.
7. Many censure Eliade's "science" as *not value free. . . .* His over-riding personal wish to recover and preserve the religious values of the archaic perspective, . . . is itself a religious program of the sort that ought not to be distorting a genuine quest for knowledge.

The second area or type of criticism concerns objections to Eliade's particular theories and explanations, of which Brown highlights a further six arguments.

8. The *sacred/profane contrast is not an all-important category* for non-literate peoples.
9. Non-literate peoples are *not constantly preoccupied with religion*, with *myth*, or with *origins*.
10. Eliade presents a *one-sided portrait of religion* as an effort to escape from the profane sphere. However, in most societies religion involves a variety of rites and techniques employed to cope directly with the challenges of ordinary life, taken on their own terms.
11. His *interpretation of myth* largely *ignores* its *social functions* and consequently treats it in a *one-dimensional* manner as almost exclusively religious in orientation.
12. In his treatment of *symbolism* Eliade is guilty of *ignoring two levels* of investigation and concentrating only on the third. . . . [He ignores the ethnographic and exegetical level in favor of the explanatory level.] His procedure needs to be emended by attending to how the people themselves use these [symbolic] objects, and what they say about the structure and meaning of their own symbols.
13. In particular, Eliade *dwells* far *too much on death/rebirth symbolism.* (432–34)

One of the clearest statements Eliade makes against these criticisms comes from his *Images and Symbols.* Although written in French in 1952 the English translation was published in 1961, and so considerably anticipated these critiques. Here he states,

> we have now gone beyond the "confusionist" position of a Tylor or a Frazer, who, in their anthropological and ethnographical researches, accumulated examples which had no geographical or historical contiguity, and would cite an Australian myth together with one from Siberia, Africa, or North America, persuaded as they were that always and everywhere they were dealing with the same "uniform reaction of the human mind before the phenomena of Nature." Compared with this position, so similar to that of a naturalist of the Darwinian epoch, the historico-cultural school of Graebner-Schmidt and the other historicist schools represent an undeniable progress. It was important, however, not to let ourselves become fixed in the historico-cultural point of view, and to inquire whether, in addition to its own history, a symbol, a myth or a ritual, might not reveal something of the human condition regarded in its own right as a mode of existence in the universe. . . . Thus, when leaving on one side the "history" that divides them, we compare an Oceanian symbol with a symbol from northern Asia, we think we are entitled to do so, not because both the one and the other are products of the same "infantile mentality," but because the symbol in itself expresses an awakening to the knowledge of a "limit situation." (*Images and Symbols*, 175f.)

Elsewhere he explains further that

> it is somewhat as if, in order to gain a better understanding of the poetic phenomenon, we should have recourse to a mass of heterogeneous examples. . . . From the point of view of literary history, such juxtapositions are to be viewed with suspicion; but they are valid if our object is to describe the poetic phenomenon as such, if we propose to show the essential differences between poetic language and the utilitarian language of everyday life. (*Sacred and the Profane*, 16)

Thus Eliade himself replies to points 1c, 4, and 5. The related, and interrelated, points 1a and 1b, are only indirectly countered, however. No scholar can be utterly unaware that the texts we read are written by other scholars and are thus subject to their interpretive bias. Nor can we hope to become exhaustively acquainted with our subject materials. The acceptance of such unrealistic aspirations results in statements such as John Saliba's unreasonable insistence that

> formulation of generalizations can only be reliably reached after many individual studies have been carried out. . . . It is not an easy task to decide when there are enough studies at one's disposal. . . . The task of

the scholar is to take into account *all available literature* and at the same time be aware of its contributions and limitations. (Homo Religiosus *in the Works of Mircea Eliade*, 142, 143, 149, emphasis added)

Obviously, this sets the historian of religions (and most other scholars) a quite impossible task.

That Eliade accepted Lévy-Bruhl's discredited theory is a rather ludicrous suggestion in view of the former's criticisms.[2] Although he does cite Lévy-Bruhl quite extensively in *Patterns* (twenty times, in fact), Eliade was well aware of the untenability of his "prelogical mentality," and takes every opportunity to mention it. For example, in *The Sacred and the Profane*:

Lévy-Bruhl sought to prove that religious behavior could be explained by the prelogical mentality of primitives—a hypothesis that he renounced towards the end of his life. (231)

In *The Two and the One*:

at the end of his life Lévy-Bruhl abandoned the hypothesis of a primitive mentality pre-logical and radically different from the modern mentality, and actually argued against it. (189f.)

Even in *Patterns*, although he refers to Lévy-Bruhl's *L'Expérience mystique et les symboles chez les primitifs* as an "excellent book" (444), Eliade uses this work as a source book for the beliefs of native peoples rather than a source of theoretical understanding. He even suggests a disagreement with Lévy-Bruhl's original restriction of the "primitive mentality" to "primitive" people. Speaking of an example of "infantilized magic" among Romanian peasants, Eliade compared it to an African belief cited by Lévy-Bruhl.

In the minds of the natives, the symbol communicates itself concretely by participation, just as . . . in the infantilized magic just quoted. . . . This, I must repeat, is only one instance of an infantilism of which there are great numbers of examples in the religious experience of every civilized people. (445)

In fact, of "primitive man" in general, Eliade insists

their mind was neither "pre-logical" nor paralysed by a participation mystique. It was a fully human mind. But this also means that every significant act was validated and valorized both on the level of empirical

---

2. Apparently he did accept, at the age of 19, that magic "represents a primitive rudimentary mentality," (Ricketts, *Romanian Roots*, 141). However, this does not indicate that he was unaware of the critical shortcomings of the "prelogical mentality" as we will see.

experience and in a Universe of images, symbols and myths. No conquest of the material world was effected without a corresponding impact on human imagination and behavior.[3]

Not only does Eliade specifically repudiate the prelogical fallacy, he also reveals how he considers the prerational or presystematic to operate in all of us through imagination and behavior.

Eliade's criticism of Lévy-Bruhl seems to be that there is some kind of alternative mentality: an ability to grasp a coherence in a system of symbolism prior to its logical or verbal extrapolation. However, this mentality, this ability, is far from absent in "civilized" peoples. In fact, "every historical man carries on, within himself, a great deal of prehistoric humanity" (*Images and Symbols*, 12). It was precisely the untenable contention that the "prelogical" mentality historically preceded and radically differed from the mentality of modern, logical humanity which finally forced Lévy-Bruhl to abandon the concept. Eliade's recognition of some kind of "preverbal," symbolic mentality in which communication is achieved "concretely by participation," is considerably more critical than Lévy-Bruhl's concept, although it is doubtlessly the cause of this disparaging contention.

Points 1c and 3 above seem to combine to produce the second criticism. That Eliade "lumps together heterogenous material" and uses improper induction in his procedures of generalization is surely the cause of an apprehension of a "defective comparative method" in his work. As we have seen, Eliade makes his own defence against 1c. In support of the procedures of generalization employed by Eliade, Brown discusses the alteration of the conceptions regarding scientific theory formation, the new paradigm becoming that of the creative and imaginative insight rather than the step-by-step linear deduction/induction. New paradigms are not formed from the integration of new data, but rather from a relinquishing of the old paradigm (which necessarily implies an immersion in the chaos of undifferentiated perceptions), in order to come up with a new way of seeing the problem. From such a point of view, Eliade's procedures, idiosyncratic as they may be, are not immediately open to criticism simply because they lack a repeatable linear progression.

Of the criticism of Eliade's "descending approach" (point 6 above), I will simply state here that Eliade's "assumption" concerning the ontological status of the sacred has been the source of some of the harshest criticism marshalled against him and will be considered in detail later. Similarly, the seventh point is integral to the consideration of Robert Baird's criticism of "Normative Elements" and so may be held until later. I would, however, like to point out that Brown passes with remarkable ease from "not value free" to "itself a religious program." While an increasing number of scholars would accept that no investigation, and perhaps even

---

3. "Notes on the Symbolism of the Arrow," 465; and *Quest*, 16, where he refers to the prelogical mentality as "an erroneous hypothesis."

no *perception*, can be value free, few of them would insist on the religious dimensions of that fact. However, in their eagerness to criticize Eliade, several scholars have argued precisely that: that because he is not utterly objective, he is religious (and vice versa). Eliade could not consider this a criticism in the light of his claim that "to be—or, rather, to become—a man means to be 'religious'" (*Quest*, preface). Furthermore, a reading of Eliade's works suggests very strongly to me that his overriding personal concern is not to recover the religious values of the archaic perspective (cf. his denial in "Notes for a Dialogue" that he held the archaic to be exemplary). Rather it is to combat personal and collective despair, to generate individually and socially meaningful optimistic understandings of human existential conditions. He seems to perceive the modern secular values as having left humanity with little more than the common slogan, "the one who dies with the most toys wins."

Against points 8 and 9 Eliade accepts that "the great god of Heaven, the Supreme Being, Creator omnipotent, plays a quite insignificant part in the religious life of the tribe" (*Patterns*, 47). It is not religion or myth as we commonly conceive them, anymore than it is the specific sacred/profane dichotomy as expounded by Eliade, which is held to preoccupy non-literate peoples. Rather it is the common human trait of focusing exclusively upon those elements of our experience which we have been predisposed to recognize as manifesting the real, the meaningful, the significant, and the powerful: that which Eliade classifies as the sacred.

In fact, the difficulties of points 8 to 11 are largely terminological. To say that the sacred/profane dichotomy is not all-important, or that people are not preoccupied with religion, or that Eliade's treatment of myth is inaccurate because exclusively religious, depends very much on the prior understanding of the terms involved. It is quite clear in point 10 that anyone who levels such a criticism has simply failed to grasp Eliade's use of his terms. He obviously equates "tolerating" or "withstanding" the terror of history with "escape" from profane time. His critics do not. It must be remembered that the *jīvanmukta* does remain in historical time, while paradoxically transcending it. Escape does not imply removal from time but avoidance of the causal distress of temporal existence (on the paradoxical state of the *jīvanmukta*, see *Quest*, 169, and *Images and Symbols*, 89). Thus, in fact, "escape" *is* "coping with" time although this might be difficult to appreciate if escape is held to imply *avoiding* dealing with that which one escapes. As Eliade repeatedly states, this state is paradoxical, it partakes of the exemplary structure of the *coincidentia oppositorum*, it is by escaping time that one deals with it.

Similarly, if the inclusive meanings of sacred/profane, myth, and religion are grasped, these points are not problematic. Since both religion and myth lack predetermined and widely accepted definitions, it is part of the task of scholars of religion to establish their own. Eliade's definitions, as we have seen, are mutually supportive and imply a ubiquity of religious orientation. In these terms myth *is* exclusively religious in orientation and the social functions are secondary (although not unimportant) to the religious orientation of the apprehension of the real in the myth. However, the twelfth point immediately becomes involved here. Can Eliade simply pass off his interpretative categories and his implicit definitions despite the conscious refusal of many of his subjects? Must he not defer to what religious people themselves say about themselves? (And what non-religious people say about themselves?) Eliade himself said of Durkheim that he "would have done better had he taken into account the work of his ethnological and anthropological colleagues" (*Images and Symbols*, 23). Brown considers Eliade's own defence against these pointed questions, and he states the latter's case for him.

First, he concurs with depth psychology that often persons grasp symbolism unconsciously while they are simultaneously unaware of it explicitly in the conscious mind. This working assumption probably accounts for his scant interest in the anthropologists' demand that one take as the primary control a people's explicit interpretation of its own symbols. Second, Eliade asserts that religious symbols, even those standing for the most inward human experiences, possess "cosmological values" which correlate closely with the objective features of the natural environment. These environmental features are directly accessible to inspection by the interpreter and are significantly uniform from the experience of one culture to that of another. Therefore, the interpreter can turn directly to them and not be stymied by an inability to occupy the subjective posture of the particular believer, nor predisposed to find only isolated and unique meanings for particular symbols when several diverse cultures are in view. *Finally,* Eliade believes that there is a "spiritual unity" to the human race more fundamental than its accidental historical divisions and differences. This belief demands that the interpreter deliberately stress those elements common to separate instances of a particular type of symbolism and play down their differences. Even if Eliade cannot convince his critics to share them, all three of these assumptions in concert show that he is well aware of how and why he handles the data as he does. (436)

Despite his support in these areas, Professor Brown considers two "systematic issues" as problematic in understanding Eliade. First, Eliade's anti-reductionism, the "problematic assumption that religious phenomena are *sui generis* and not reducible to mere natural events" (435). As I have indicated (especially concerning points 7, 10, 11 above), critics have not grasped Eliade's theories as coherent. His understanding of religion as *sui generis* and of Eliade as anti-reductionist suffer the same lack of a coherent interpretation. It is rather the case that "religion" is not susceptible to one explanation since religion itself is an attempt to construct a total explanation of the human encounter with the real.

The issue of the irreducibility of belief also concerns Brown's consideration of Dudley's argument that Eliade's methodology should be reconceived as a research program. One of the points is of specific interest and can best be made by direct quotation.

> If the interpreter should discount completely the possibility that the sacred (as an object of belief) actually could be a transcendent reality distinct from the believer's own consciousness and distinct from the natural and social environment itself, then his or her naturalistic interpretation would violate the integrity of that very human belief which is to be understood. The limited extent to which Eliade can pass muster as a phenomenologist in any very definite philosophical sense appears in this determination to honor rather than to dissolve the intentional structure of religious consciousness. But wholesale dissolution is just what the reductionistic social scientists demand when they insist *a priori* that the sum and substance of religion comprises merely natural events and human cultural creativity. For them, one captures the true meaning and purpose of each rite and belief by giving an account of its purely natural functions in the life of the group or the individual. Against this naturalistic bias Eliade poses as a defender of the sacred as autonomous, as *sui generis*, as something which must not be banished by a reductionist prestidigitation if one intends to take seriously the structure of belief as it is actually found in human experience. Because of his conviction that the independent reality of the sacred should be accepted as a "given," and also because he regards the sacred as having specific and relatively invariant structures Eliade does not see the historian of religions as bound to the narrow orthodoxies which constrain empirical social scientists. His perspective is broader and therefore presumably superior because it does not overlook the essence of religion as he thinks theirs does. Moreover, he is confident that by examining a sufficient number of examples he can get a handle on the essential structures of the sacred. All these assumptions taken together enable him to feel justified in "reading into" certain anthropological data more or different symbolic meanings than those which the anthropologists themselves find there by operating cautiously within narrowly empirical criteria. (436–37)

First of all, I agree wholeheartedly with the analysis of the value of phenomenology in respect of the intentional structures of religious consciousness. The contentious nature of all descriptions, the theory-laden nature of fact, unavoidably implies the self-assertive nature of description. Even if one intends no more than a completely accurate description of a rite or belief, then one's own intentional apprehension of complete accuracy will condition that description and make its truth dependent upon the "truth" of that apprehension. For the believer a description cannot be complete if it omits the essentially true relation of the creature to the creator, the fundamental dependence on the real, the conditional and imperfect nature of human existence. In order to redeem our descriptions there must be a recognition of, a willingness to defer to, the intentional structure of those beliefs which we would describe. Actually this redemptive willingness is present, albeit muted, in the social sciences (as Brown describes them) in their desire to include "human cultural creativity" along with natural events. The recognition of the creativity of humanity—in Eliade's terms, our imitation of and involvement in the primordial and archetypal creative event, the cosmogony—saves both humanity itself and the social scientific attempt to comprehend it from a total "fall into history." Strict biophysical determinism cannot account for either the human will or the human ability to create (or not yet, at least). Creativity itself is a participation in Eliade's sacred time, a reactualization of the mythic realities, evincing the structures of the emergence of form out of chaos, the re-emergence of life from its own dissolution.

However, caution must be exercised in seeing Eliade as a "defender of the sacred as autonomous." Brown is quite insistent on this phrase, repeating it at intervals throughout the remainder of his analysis: "the autonomous integrity of the sacred" (437). And

> Eliade routinely supposes that uniformities in meaning of separate instances of religious symbolism derive from the nature of the sacred power presenting itself through the symbolic objects. (443)

I think it more consonant with Eliade's actual words to conclude that what he regards as autonomous and *sui generis* is the existential situation which constitutes and conditions the actual perception of this or that religious phenomena as real, as sacred.

The mistake is quite apparent if one pays close attention to Brown's words. He has himself fallen into the trap which he lists as argument 1b: he has interpreted an interpretation rather than the primary source. It is *Dudley's* insistence on the sacred as autonomous and independent which seems to have dictated Brown's vocabulary here rather than Eliade's own words. It is this type of second-order analysis which galvanizes, for example, Dubuisson's analysis. Coming to Eliade's texts with preformed opinions influenced by earlier criticism it is all too easy to confirm those opinions. The fact that Brown interprets Dudley, and in so doing utilizes the vocabulary determined by Dudley determines his own interpretation.[4] Eliade's own

---

4.   This is not to reject Dudley's important work on Eliade. I do not consider it in detail because the issue of the ontology and autonomy of the sacred is discussed with reference to other scholars. Other differences between Dudley's interpretation and mine are not at issue here. However, his important question as to the *goals* of "Eliade's Research Program" should be constantly borne in mind as my interpretation progresses.

vocabulary and terminology must be used to understand his intentionality. There is an important lesson to be learned here about the process of interpretation: one must become engaged with the vocabulary of a religion, on its own grounds, before one will understand the intentionality being represented. Even then one might still not share the intuition of the real intended, but it is a fundamental assumption of Eliade's analysis that it is the real which is intended in any religious expression.

The alternative to Dudley's and to Brown's interpretations, which is closer to the actual words of the original scholar, is that the sacred is eternal supreme reality—*whatever that might be taken to be*—and therefore that which manifests it or partakes of its structures possesses power (rather than "the sacred is an eternally real power").

As it is the reality in which we dwell, the Being by virtue of which we are, we cannot in any way possess the sacred, nor exhaustively describe it. Perhaps we could aspire to an exhaustive description of present spatio-temporal reality. However, the whole point here is that this is not exhaustive of the real; there are also subjective and even imaginary realities which are of enormous significance, and future realities which necessarily surpass our powers to predict because the predictive models we can construct cannot bring about the result any faster than the reality being modelled. So the question

> might not these common features which are purported to be manifestations of a supernatural reality, more appropriately be attributed to uniformities in the biological and psychological constitution of *homo sapiens* as it interacts with relatively constant features of natural objects which make up our environment, (428)

once again misses the implications here. Those concepts which are used to represent the real, that which the real is said to be or thought to be, that which it is believed to be, are, of course, socially, culturally, and historically conditioned, including the biology, psychology, and physics to which Brown would appeal. As such they are not autonomous, not independent. That is to say that while the sacred as absolute reality might be fairly said to be independent, *expressions* of the sacred such as "God," "Jahweh," "Brahma," or "scientific fact" are not. The problem is that "absolute reality" is itself such an expression and so, in the last analysis, is *not* itself autonomous. What is held to be autonomous and independent is the human experience which constitutes the perception of the real and the human creativity which constitutes those expressions of the sacred which are capable of communicating that reality to others correctly predisposed to be able to decipher the communication.

Since religion is based on the total orientation based in turn on these self-authenticating perceptions, religion is *sui generis* in the sense that any claim for the reality of a theory is thus itself religious and only the total study of all such self-authenticating intuitions of the real (the history of religions) can claim to be the unpredisposed interrogation of the real.

This does leave a problem of differentiating possible pseudo-religions. For example, what if L. Ron Hubbard, the founder of Scientology, did not himself perceive any reality to Scientology's main scripture, *Dianetics*, as he wrote it? Whatever he perceived, certain of his followers do perceive the real here and it must be interpreted accordingly. This does concur with Eliade's insistence that *anything* can become a hierophany, which itself implies that the real is the undifferentiated sum total of all possibility. (So Eliade's system may be an "answer" itself, but it is also a method of allowing other answers to become accessible, meaningful, for one's consideration or simply for one's education.)

Eliade's perception of the historian of religions as unconstrained by the narrowness of "orthodoxies which constrain empirical social scientists" is rather due to the insistence of the latter on a specific and *a priori* limitation of the working concept of the real. Of course, in exactly the same way, if historians of religions limit their working definition of reality to the dogmatic expressions of any one tradition, they too are narrowly constrained and, in fact, fail to be historians of religion so conceived.

In these lights, the question, "does Eliade himself believe that the sacred is objectively real?" and even the statement of Ricketts that "as to what the real 'really' is, Eliade never ventures an answer" (438; Ricketts, "In Defense of Eliade," 28) reveal a partial misapprehension of Eliade's systematic thought and its implications. Eliade has made an *a priori* identification of the phenomenally real and the transcendent sacred. Obviously, he cannot but believe then that the sacred is actually real. It is real both on the level of the expressions of the sacred which are (or have been) apprehensions of the truly real and on the level of the final Being which is. Only if it be denied that humanity has believed in contrasting realities and that there is *something* real can these be seen as unwarranted assumptions.

Specific criticisms made by individual scholars must be assessed on their own merits. J. Z. Smith points out that chaos is not just "profane" but rather sacred "in the wrong way" (*Map Is Not Territory*, 97), that mythic first times are not always paradigmatic (99), and that the modern/archaic is not the only or necessarily the best structure for the interpretation of religions. Probably his most incisive criticism is that Eliade's

> focus on the explicit presence of the term "center" leads Eliade at times to employ questionable interpretations of his material. [For example the Babylonian term *Dur-an-ki*] probably does not mean, as Eliade often implies, the place of intersection of the upper world with the earth but rather the scar, the navel, left behind when heaven and earth were forcibly separated in creation—it is the disjunctive rather than the conjunctive which is to the fore. (98, repeated in *To Take Place*, 122 n. 2)

This criticism, however, does not amount to much when one considers the specific affirmations made in Cassirer's analysis of Nicholas of Cusa that disjunction implies conjunction:

> far from excluding each other, separation and participation, χωρισμός and μέθεξις, can only be thought of *through* and *in relation* to each other. . . . the separation itself guarantees the possibility of true participation of the sensible in the ideal. (22, 24)

The navel embodies the pure possibility of creation.

More serious, perhaps, are the flaws in Eliade's understanding of early Buddhism in *Yoga, Immortality, and Freedom* revealed by Richard Gombrich. The connection which Eliade draws with shamanism seems more than dubious ("Eliade on Buddhism," 226) and the emphasis on the importance of the *guru* seems quite wrong (228). Eliade "misquotes and misinterprets the *Brahma-jala-sutta*" (229) and "has given no evidence valid for Buddhism that "one arrives at the beginning of time and finds non-time" (230). There are numerous spelling errors and misreadings of the Pali text in Eliade's chapter on "Yoga Techniques in Buddhism" (225–28) and his "argument for the aboriginal origin of Tantrism seems unsatisfactory" (231). These are factual statements which must simply be accepted. However, that Eliade makes specific errors and misinterpretations and occasionally accepts common misapprehensions as true descriptions reflects the fallible and interdependent nature of the scholarly endeavor and does not seriously compromise the overall coherence of his thought. That these errors are made *uncritically* is simply untrue. Eliade minimizes the risk of being egregiously misled by broadening the scope of his readings as much as possible in a considerable number of languages, thereby avoiding serious misapprehensions contracted through concealed bias. He was, in fact, extremely critical of the majority of Western authors, and of their interpretative biases, even of those who most impressed him.

Russell McCutcheon's consideration of the implications of Eliade's political attitudes raises some valid questions ("The Myth of the Apolitical Scholar"). How can Eliade's emphasis on the ethical and spiritual aspect of the Legionary movement be reconciled with their later atrocities and their antisemitism? Certainly, his youthful nationalism cannot be simply defended as "non-political." Is Eliade, like Heidegger, guilty of

> "abstraction by essentialism," whereby the particularities of historical events are glossed over in favor of some purported ahistorical core meaning? (658)

Were the strategies of essentialization, universalization, and dehistoricization which were used to bolster Romanian nationalism simply rehashed to effect the differentiation of historians of religion from anthropologists and social scientists (662)? If so, is this necessarily a serious flaw?

It is once again the case, however, that McCutcheon, concentrating on the implications of Eliade's autobiographical writings, has missed many of the implications of his scholarly work. For example, he accepts without question that

> unlike the French sociologist Émile Durkheim (1858–1917) who accounted for the sacred as a projection of the group itself, Eliade held that it was the ahistorical sacred—related to the "wholly other" of the German theologian Rudolph Otto (1869–1937)—which, through an intimate relationship with historical conditions, manifested itself within certain previously profane items. (653f.)

Hence "believed that an ahistorical sacred (a term he never adequately defined) was actually manifested in variously profane conditions" (654), and, further, that he was

> reversing the traditional priority through devaluing the technological, secular era in favor of what he described as the exemplary mode of existence found in both archaic and religious persons. (655)

These assumptions are problematic, as we have seen, and contribute to an overall misunderstanding of Eliade's thought. I hope that my analysis has gone some way toward providing a more extended response to criticisms of Eliade's philosophy and method than has previously been available.

ELIADE'S HIDDEN THEOLOGICAL AGENDA

One frequent criticism levelled against Eliade, despite his repeated insistence that he was not a theologian (for example, in the preface to *Reflective Theology* by T. N. Munson and in *Images and Symbols*, 158), has been that of a hidden theological agenda, or more specifically of making an a priori assumption of the ontology of the sacred which disqualifies him from serious academic *Religionswissenschaft*.[5] Paul Tillich has said that

> the "scientific" theologian wants to be more than a philosopher of religion. He wants to interpret the Christian message generally with the help of his method. This puts before him two alternatives. He may subsume the Christian message under his concept of religion. Then Christianity is considered to be one example of religious life besides other examples, certainly the highest religion, but not the final one and not unique. Such a theology does not enter the theological circle. It keeps itself within the religious-philosophical circle and its indefinite

---

5.   Altizer, Hamilton, Penner, and Reno argue Eliade to make "theological assumptions." Baird, Saliba, Strenski, and to a lesser extent Allen argue Eliade to make unwarranted ontological assumptions. (See bibliography.)

horizons—horizons which beckon towards a future which is open for
new and perhaps higher examples of religion. The scientific theologian,
in spite of his desire to be a theologian, remains a philosopher of religion.
(*Systematic Theology*, vol. I, 10)

Obviously, in these terms, Eliade did not even desire to be a theologian, scientific or
otherwise. Even accepting that he could still be a theologian despite himself, one
can see that since he evidently "subsumes the Christian message under his concept
of religion" he thus cannot "enter the theological circle" in Tillich's terms.

It is very doubtful that Eliade accepted the Christian message as "the highest
religion." Douglas Allen has argued, with support from Eliade himself, that Eliade's
evaluation of the "highest" types of spiritual manifestation is at least partially based
on a position much more characteristic of Indian mysticism than Western religious
traditions.[6] It is specifically Eliade's refusal to valorize the Christian religion
unequivocally above all others that simultaneously constitutes his escape from the
theological circle and animates his academic study of religion. Tillich has said that
"Christian theology is the theology in so far as it is based on the tension between
the absolutely concrete and the absolutely universal" (*Systematic Theology*, 19).
This attitude is, no doubt, exactly what Eliade had in mind when he stated that *for
the Christian* the revelation of the Christ event is the highest (*Patterns*, 29, 30 n. 1).
I emphasize "for the Christian," because it seems surprisingly easy for readers to
miss the disclamatory thrust of his phraseology. Throughout *Patterns* Eliade
consistently qualifies his valorizations of the Christian Incarnation with phrases
such as "one might say," "one could attempt to vindicate," and "from this standpoint" (29f.). This fact is often ignored in analyses of Eliade. He is in no way
claiming that Christianity is the absolutely highest form of religion, but rather that it
has characteristics which have allowed it to be convincingly perceived as such by
certain specific people.

Eliade refuses to share with Tillich the focus of his ultimate concern in the
Christian religion. Nonetheless, he manifests undoubted similarities with the
thought and methods of Paul Tillich which have attracted the criticisms of those
would-be scientific scholars of religion to whom the predisposition necessarily
involved in the theological approach is anathema, preventing all possibility of
genuinely creative, free research. I contend that it is mainly because of the detection
of this predisposition to the acceptance of the reality of the sacred that Eliade has
been so widely misread. That such a predisposition is finally incompatible with
genuine research is a conception of both reality and of the sacred which does not
derive from Eliade's work and which is finally incompatible with his whole
understanding of religion.

---

6. "A Phenomenological Evaluation of Religious Mysticism," revised in chapter seven of *Structure
and Creativity*: see 222 and also the foreword by Eliade. This contention is also supported by Sergiu Al-
George.

The similarities which Eliade does have with Tillich—the implications of which I do not believe to have been fully realized or researched—is the systematic nature of the categories of the thought of both scholars. Douglas Allen comes closest to this analysis of Eliade and recognizes its lack in other scholars when he acknowledges that "our analysis is in contrast with most of Eliade's interpreters, who seem to feel that Eliade has never developed a systematic methodology" (*Structure and Creativity*, 106). To this extent I am in agreement with Allen, although I disagree with his strict emphasis on phenomenology and his objection to Eliade's "normative ontological claims."

I would like to consider briefly why it is that so many scholars have been unable to appreciate the coherence of Eliade's thought and have perceived a theological agenda where none is apparent. I have already mentioned factors such as the idiosyncratic and inadequately explained concept of history and the problems of both translation and prejudgment. Added to these, however, is the fact that Eliade did not write with systematic clarity. Unlike Tillich, whose systematic mentality and approach was a source of wonderment and admiration for him (expressed in "Paul Tillich and the History of Religions"), Eliade lacked the neatness and clarity of expression which would render the implicit system of his thought obvious to his readers. It is not only Eliade's complexity of expression which obscures his systematic conceptions. It is also a deliberate policy on his part, partly inherited from his philosophy teacher and mentor Nae Ionescu, to avoid elaborated systematic thought as "the philosophers' tombstone" (on which see Ricketts, *Romanian Roots*, 862). The implication of this is that once any interpretative system becomes perfectly transparent, fully elaborated and clarified, it ceases to have either value or allure. Certainly the fact that Eliade did not systematically codify his thought will ensure that scholars will be debating over his texts for quite a while to come. Of course, this does not necessarily mean that Eliade could have simply made a clear and systematic exposition of his thoughts had he so chosen. I have already mentioned his dismay at the inability to communicate certain secrets (see above, p. 4). It certainly does not mean that internal consistency is completely lacking. Adrian Marino has made an admirable attempt to systematize Eliade's hermeneutics, but I believe that this is yet to be done for the larger system of his thought.

Regarding the contentious ascription of theological prejudgment to Eliade's work, several factors have been instrumental. Eliade himself referred to "the secret message of [*Patterns*], the 'theology' implied in the history of religions as I decipher and interpret it" (*Journal*, vol. II, 74). However, the very fact that he employed 'scare quotes' in this context should alert the reader to an unusual or equivocal use of the word. Far from an uncritical assumption of institutional doctrine, the word 'theology' in this context would apply to *any* discussion of conceptions of the real. In my consideration of Eliade's sacred, it was pointed out that the identification of the sacred and the real will unavoidably generate opposition from those predisposed to deny the reality of any traditionally conceived sacred. Especially to those who conceive the academic integrity of religious studies to have been won only by its radical separation from traditional theology, any such *a priori* ascription of reality to the intentional objects of religious devotion would indicate a complete "failure of nerve" in academic religious studies—a return to theology. (I am, of course, referring to the stimulating and often heated discussions of Robert Segal and Donald Wiebe.)

This alone is enough to ensure that Eliade has been seen as having a concealed theological agenda, or even as a "closet theologian" by many scholars and it has been further compounded by other factors. Eliade's favorable reception among theological academics is one. The consistent translation of the French reflexive by an English active rather than passive is another—the sacred reveals itself, rather than the sacred is revealed. These can both be explained other than by any theological bias on Eliade's part. As for the question of translation, Eliade's first major publication in English, *Patterns in Comparative Religion*, was published by Sheed and Ward, a leading Catholic publisher of the time, and was translated by Rosemary Sheed. It is not surprising that the most theologically acceptable translation was adopted, nor is it surprising that Eliade failed to correct it. Willard Trask, the translator of the majority of Eliade's later works, merely kept to the course already set. Eliade's thought was well received among theologians because it accurately described the religious attitude to those who experienced it. It must be noted that the young Eliade clearly stated that he *"didn't believe in God,"* that he "was a Christian though not a believer in God" (Ricketts, *Romanian Roots*, 123). The general accusation of theological bias has, however, taken much more precise form in accusations of ontological assumptions and normative prejudgments. These, and other specific criticisms, must be considered in more detail.

CHAPTER 15

Some More Specific Criticisms

THE ONTOLOGY OF THE SACRED

In connection with Eliade's putative theological agenda and with several of the general criticisms of chapter 14, a consideration of the assumed ontological status of the sacred was postponed until it could be given full attention. What status does Eliade afford to the sacred and how do his assumptions affect the coherence and credibility of his thought? Antonio Barbosa da Silva analyzed Eliade's sacred as a phenomenological term and an ontological term (175). I am broadly in agreement with da Silva's evaluation of the sacred as a phenomenological term, however, it is his analysis of the sacred as an ontological term with which I take issue.

One must question to what degree the sacred is given a necessary and independent ontology, even when it stands for "the cosmos as a whole" or "the Ur-datum of Eliade's creative hermeneutics." It is undoubtedly true that Eliade regards every element of existence as capable of revealing the sacred, that is, as sacralizable, as potentially and inherently sacred, and thus as "real," simply because it exists. The sacred is disclosed in the manifest realm of historical being, in the existential world of historical time and physical space, it thus has ontological status. To this extent it unquestionably partakes of the characteristic of being.

Similarly with the sacred as the ur-datum, the presuppositional given of Eliade's hermeneutics, this notion of the sacred is adjectival rather than substantial. It should be remembered that only after Durkheim's usage of the term as a noun was it commonly employed in this way. In Eliade's use, it evidently refers to a mode of experience, "a structure of the human consciousness" (*Quest*, i; *No Souvenirs*, 1; *History of Religious Ideas*, vol. 1, xiii), a *relationship* with the real, rather than the real itself. It is the very fact that the sacred as the real is perceived in so many modes, and that we carry our own inner certainty as to what is and is not "real" which permits, in fact positively encourages, so many varied interpretations of Eliade's thought and generates the almost unavoidable impression that he is describing an autonomous, independent ontology. However, detailed analysis without any prior assumption as to the referent of the sacred reveals that the sacred does not occur in Eliade's writings in any context independently of human perception. It is always presented as occurring in and through the act of its perception. It is always presented as an intentional object, without the question of its pure or proper intentionality actually being raised.

Again, this is by no means to deny the autonomy of the sacred, but in the familiar Kantian structure of the noumenal/phenomenal dichotomy, it insists that the sacred is accessible only through its manifestations in historical forms. The function of the historian of religions is presumed to be the study of the historical manifestations of the sacred, which exist exclusively (for the historian of religions qua historian of religions) in those historical manifestations. For the committed religious believer, the sacred might also be held to exist as an element of immediate experience, but that experience per se is the object of mystical theology. The *expression* of that experience as a historical datum is the proper object of the history of religions.

To affirm as a given the independent ontology of the sacred as it is described by any individual, group, or tradition is to step immediately beyond the bounds of the study of religion into the practice of a particular religion. This Eliade does not do. However, the temptation to read Eliade as doing precisely that is enormous because of the language which he employs, identifying the sacred as the real. Yet the fact is that he does not seem to conceive of sacrality independent of the act of its perception, leaving the sacred as a potential of human experience, *possibly* an abstract idea but one which is nevertheless ubiquitous and unimaginably significant throughout human history.

Da Silva asks whether a sacred object "*really* possesses some intrinsic properties which constitute a necessary condition for the sacredness of [that object] or not." He concludes that this must be the case as far as Eliade is concerned. He specifically rejects the interpretation that "'sacred' means the same as that there is a religious person [who] . . . perceives [some object] as sacred" (179), on the grounds that the necessary condition for the perception of any object as sacred is that the object possess some intrinsic property which evokes or causes the numinous experience (180). This leads further to the conviction that Eliade attributes some necessary independence to sacrality as a manifest property of sacred objects. However, both interpretations can be reconciled when it is realized that the only *necessary* inherent property that an object must posses in order to be sacralizable is *existence*, its own objecthood. "All nature is capable of revealing itself as cosmic sacrality" (*The Sacred and the Profane*, 12). Further, there is no inherent property which is a *sufficient* condition to evoke numinous experience to any and all religious people. Thus there need be no identifiable "inherent property" (apart from the fundamental one of existence) in the sacred object which could be equated with an ontologically independent sacrality. The rejection of the former interpretation is not necessitated; the fact that an object exists and is perceived as sacred is the necessary and sufficient condition for its sacrality in Eliade's terms. The perception of the sacred *qua* the real (and the real *qua* the sacred) is the primary characteristic of *homo religiosus*, humanity in the religious mode.

Of course, this does, as da Silva recognizes, leave the problem of

> how to prove that the numinous experience is not an exclusive product of man's mind. If it is so, and if it has only a purely intended object, it can be regarded as a merely subjective experience. (182)

I would suggest that the lack of "proof" of the independent existence of the sacred as the source of numinous experience is first of all itself characteristic of Eliade's self-imposed restriction to the history of religions as eschewing personal theological statements. It is thus evidence that Eliade does not insist on the sacred as a specific autonomous ontological entity, although his methodical openness to that possibility permits the alternative interpretation. Secondly, this lack of proof is completely consistent with his morphology of religious history in which the sacred can only be manifest in historical actualities. Since it cannot otherwise be manifest, that is, since it cannot otherwise be experienced, it is not susceptible of proof either logically or empirically. The direct experience of believers is not itself communicable, and their subsequent expressions are always and necessarily historical and conditioned and thus proof of nothing but an experience whose intentionality cannot be established unless it be shared.

Da Silva has already accepted that

> whether it [religious experience of the Divine Being as meta-cosmic reality] has a proper intentional object is a very controversial question into which we cannot go here. (70)

He has made precisely the same evasion of the theological problem of the pure or proper intentionality of numinous experience as I insist that Eliade does. Yet he accuses Eliade both of assuming the proper intentionality of the sacred and of failing to provide any proof for this assumption. My point is that Eliade does not provide any proof for this assumption because he does not make it.

ELIADE'S ONTOLOGICAL ASSUMPTIONS

The essential criticism put forward by Douglas Allen in his excellent *Structure and Creativity in Religion* is that "Eliade's more-than-historical-explanation claim involves ontological judgements about the nature of the human being and experience" (178). The "non-historical" elements in Eliade's writings are considered to be finally unwarranted ontological "universals." That is to say, if Eliade claims that he has logically induced the existence of universal entities, and that these universal entities are autonomous of humanity, capable of imposing their perceptions on a receptive and essentially passive observer, then he has thus made assumptions which are ontological and unwarranted by the available data, and which take him "far beyond the descriptive and involves highly normative judgements based on an assumed ontological position" (160).

Eliade has said that religion "does not necessarily imply belief in God, gods, or ghosts, but refers to the experience of the sacred" (*Quest*, i). Allen has gone on to inquire as to what precisely the sacred is and to draw his understanding of this element of Eliade's thought not wholly from Eliade's writings, but in part from phenomenologists of religion who are supposed to have ideas in common with Eliade. The sacred may be described as a "Power" (van der Leeuw), as "wholly other" (Otto), as "ultimate reality" (Wach) (120f.). Allen recognizes Eliade's usage of a wide variety of terms related to the sacred, such as "absolute reality, being, eternity, divine, and also metacultural, transhistorical, transhuman, transmundane, and the source of all life and fecundity" (Allen, *Structure and Creativity*, 121; and Eliade, e.g., *Rites and Symbols*, 130; *Yoga*, 165; *The Sacred and the Profane*, 28). Allen concludes that "Eliade seems to be indicating that religion always entails some aspect of *transcendence*" (121). This is in some ways correct. The second group of terms do indicate transcendence—but transcendence of specific, known "modes of being": the cultural, the historical, the human, and the mundane. This is no way necessarily involves an ontological transcendent—*the* transcendent, which goes beyond *everything* and thus has independent, unconditioned existence. While not excluding such a possibility, it does not assume it either. In fact, Eliade's understanding of hierophanies—that we can only conceive of transcendence because the sky is there—militates *for* a dependent, conceptual "transcendence." The simpler interpretation is assume that by transhistorical Eliade meant "not subject to historical conditioning," by transhuman, "not subject to the human condition," and by transmundane, "highly significant."

In terms of such an interpretation, it is no real criticism to comment that "Eliade intends this sense of transcendence to be viewed as a universal structure of religion" (121). The concept of exceeding the merely historical, the mundane, and the biologically human is, by definition, universal in Eliade's understanding of religion. In order to challenge such a contention, one would need to adduce some religious phenomena which had no conceivable reference to the transcendence of human physical and temporal limitations and successfully defend its status as religious.

Allen recognizes that "Eliade must not be confused with the numerous scholars who hold metaphysical positions concerning transcendence" (122). For example, Eliade is distinguished from C. J. Bleeker who held that "the value of the religious phenomena can be understood only if we keep in mind that religion is ultimately a realization of a transcendent truth" ("The Future Task of the History of Religions," 227, quoted by Allen, 122). Eliade put his name to a document, the so-called "Marburg platform" drafted by Zwi Werblowski, which includes a positive and direct refutation of Bleeker's statement as "outside the terms of reference of *Religionswissenschaft.*"[1]

Although he is aware of the possibility of "a purely descriptive and secular sense of transcendence" (121), Allen insists, without actual textual support, on a differentiated "religious" sense of transcendence. "What differentiates the religious sense of transcendence is its special normative basis for *homo religiosus.*" (121) What Allen seems to have done is to have constructed a possible descriptive characteristic of the sacred—its "special normative basis for homo religiosus," but then to introduce another term, "transcendence" (not actually employed by Eliade who talked of transhistorical, transhuman, as we have seen), under the influence of the "other" phenomenologists of religion. In so doing, Allen destroys *his own interpretation* of Eliade as a phenomenologist by insisting upon a necessarily abstract and thus non-phenomenal category, the transcendent, as a universal structure of religion. Eliade himself does not appear to do so in his writings. For example, that the sky gods, whose primary characteristic is transcendence, tend to become *dei otiosi* rather undermines this emphasis on transcendence.

It must be concluded that Allen's insistence on Eliade as a phenomenologist among other phenomenologists has resulted in his overemphasis on the ontology of the transcendent and a concomitant de-emphasis on the active role of humanity in our religious aspect in constituting the hierophany. Daniel Dubuisson made the same unjustified move of crititicizing Eliade via a critique of a phenomenology of religion which Eliade did not embrace. With no more evidence than their mutual disapproval of "reductionism," he assumed a far greater consonance of Eliade, van der Leeuw, and Michel Meslin than I believe is warranted. It is significant that Dubuisson had to harvest Meslin's work for quotations indicative of the assumed ontology of a transcendent reality equivalent to the divine rather than continuing to quote from Eliade (260).

Allen's conclusion is none the less problematic, however. Namely, that Eliade

is making general judgments about the human mode of being in the world and the human condition as such; and on the basis of such judgments, he is claiming that the "historicistic philosophies" of Hegel, Marx, Dilthey, and others cannot defend the modern Western human being from the terror of history.

Now such a procedure clearly involves an ontological stance. On what basis can Mircea Eliade proceed beyond his perspectival limitations? Isn't he guilty of the same *reductionism* he attacked . . .? It would

---

1. *Numen* 7 (1960): 237; see also 215–40 for a discussion of the platform taken by certain scholars at the 10th International Congress of the International Association for the History of Religions in Marburg, 11–17 September 1960.

appear that Eliade *assumes* that the structures of religious experience . . . reveal fundamental structures of the human mode of being generally. (236)

Allen's own defence against these troubling questions is that "*such an ontological move is founded on and informed by the primary symbolic structures*" (237, italics in original). That is to say,

> symbols serve as "ciphers" of reality. We can decipher the meanings of such ciphers in an infinite variety of ways and on many planes of interpretation. (238)

However, he has to add that

> Mircea Eliade, on his levels of greatest generalization, is involved in a reductionist analysis, which, if he upholds his previously elucidated methodological principles, probably pushes his phenomenology of religion beyond the proper domain of the History of Religions. (242)

Allen has uncovered a real difficulty here. There is an inescapable circularity to the fact that Eliade has moved from the "primary symbolic structures" to conclusions about the real nature of human existence and the actual existential condition of humanity. According to Eliade's own thought (or rather, my exposition of it), the symbols of flight, of the moon, of the lost paradise, *actually constitute hierophanies for Eliade.* That is to say, they are apprehended by him as self-authenticating revelations of the real.

Ultimately, I cannot imagine how such a claim can be liable to rational verification. However, it is indicative of Eliade's success that he identifies the real as the source of meaning and meaning as the significant ordering of elements within a cosmos. I believe that Eliade would agree with Charles Long's assessment of revelation as an "ordering principle."

> Man's world is an ordered world of meaning, but the organizing principle is interpreted as a revelation which comes from a source outside his ordinary life. It is the source which is given (revealed) and [it] defines any future possibility of man's existence. (*Alpha: The Myths of Creation*, 10–11, quoted by Allen, 128)

Thus, the fact that what Eliade has apprehended as the real has allowed him to order a massive amount of data into a coherent *oeuvre* militates for the recognition of the accuracy of his vision. Of course, I am aware of the circularity of this defense: if Eliade's *oeuvre* be initially apprehended as incoherent, then he must have failed to have perceived the real in what he apprehended as hierophanies and his whole structure topples. To put it bluntly, just because he wrote a lot about a lot doesn't make him right. However, I hope I have allayed a certain amount of the suspicion often felt against such circularity of argument in my discussion.

If the final ontological status of the sacred be held in abeyance as a problem for theology or the philosophy of religion, then those ontological claims which Eliade does undoubtedly make do not seem excessive. It is a necessary concomitant of this refusal of the indubitable autonomous ontology of the transcendent as it is apprehended by an individual or group, that the active, creative role of humanity in the apprehension of reality will be increasingly emphasized.

NORMATIVE ELEMENTS

Robert Baird's chapter on "The Category of Understanding" in his *Category Formation and the History of Religions*, includes a section on "Phenomenological Understanding: Mircea Eliade." His major criticism of Eliade is that not only does he make an unwarranted assumption of the ontology of the sacred but that this leads him to "normative" statements which are insupportable and unacceptable in a supposedly unbiased academic study. First, Eliade "proceeds under the essential-intuitional approach" (74). That is to say, he employs

> a method in which the historian of religions does not recognize a need to begin his work with a definition of "religion," thereby marking the limits and extent of his study. This method assumes that we all know what is meant by the word, and that, given room for accidental differences, "religion" is essentially unambiguous. This introduces the other aspect of this method: essentialism or realism. It means (by implication and by method) that religion is something out there whose "essence" can be apprehended by the historian of religions. (2)

Eliade proceeds to accord ontological status to religion and to the sacred without clear definition. His assertions concerning the structures formed by symbols are

> based on an implied ontology which is nowhere philosophically defended. This ontological stance is most apparent when clear hiero-phanies are used to clarify the intention of obscure "hierophanies." Such a hermeneutic is possible only if one assumes not only that the sacred has ontological status, but also that its structures (and hence the system of symbolism) also have ontological status.(77)

The final flaw in Eliade's analysis comes, as Baird sees it,

> when it is suggested that modern man is poorer because his cosmos has been desacralized, because the human body or the process of eating is no longer a sacrament, a shift has been effected—a shift made possible only because an ontological basis has already been posited. If not before, then at least here it is clear that Eliade is not dealing with what men have held to be sacred, but with the structures of the sacred. His focal point is not

> only the subjective, but also the objective and hence ontological. Not only are the hierophanies which he describes hierophanies for those involved, but they are *in fact* hierophanies. One would normally expect further argumentation when a shift is made from the apparently descriptive to the normative. Here, however, an ontology has been posited from the start. (87)

Here Eliade has moved, provoked by his assumption of the real ontology of the sacred and of those symbolic structures which reveal that reality, to an assumption that "archaic man is the most authentic," and thus provides the norm of human behavior. He has moved from a description and analysis of historico-religious phenomena to a stance on how things *ought to be* and to an attempt to influence the behavior of his readers. This is not only unacceptable for a detached scholar, but potentially misleading and quite possibly wrong (91).

This apparently strong argument, however, proves specious on close inspection. *Homo religiosus* represents humanity in its religious aspect and is the *connecting*, and not the differentiating characteristic between contemporary and archaic man. Archaic man is certainly not seen as the "norm," although there is a sound reason in the structured thought of Mircea Eliade for suggesting that the traditional and archaic is more authentic, as we shall see.

Also, the suggestion that modern man is the poorer for the desacralization of his cosmos, which Eliade certainly does make, is not a value judgment based on the assumed ontology of the sacred. Rather it is a lamentation for the confusion of sacred and profane, for the concealment of the sacred within the profane, and finally, for the concomitant lack of self-awareness. As Douglas Allen puts it, Eliade

> maintains that our limiting views of the human mode of being in the world and the human condition have not allowed us to understand our own behavior. This has led to self-deception and impoverished sensitivity and creativity. (*Structure and Creativity*, 244)

This may be compared to what Gadamer calls "the tyranny of hidden prejudice" (*Truth and Method*, 270). In the identification of the sacred and the profane, modern man has lost the capacity to recognize clearly the different levels of significance involved, and the processes whereby they are differentiated. Eliade's focus is still on the subjective level; it is a personal impoverishment by a subjective lack of understanding which he is bemoaning.

Thirdly, the hierophanies which he describes he quite positively states do *not* exist for those who are not prepared to recognize them (cf. the quotation from the introduction to *Mistress Christina* given above, p. 19). Again there is no shift from the descriptive to the normative (although all descriptions are persuasive and theory-laden as I have said, and thus *all* description assumes a normative base in presuming to talk about reality at all).

Fourthly, there is no necessary assumption of an independent ontology, as I have consistently argued. Once again Eliade is exposed to the superficially accurate criticism that he fails to support an assumption, when he has not, in fact, made such an assumption. It should be borne in mind that, while Eliade can be accurately described as insisting that hierophanies are not only hierophanies for the believer but are in fact revelations of the real, behind his assertion is the structure which insists that *everything* could be a hierophany. Any object which exists, any event which occurs could be an hierophany. Everything which is, reveals the true nature of being because it is. Of course, the true nature of being is only partially revealed in each event or object; it is simultaneously partially occluded. This is precisely Eliade's dialectic of hierophany. It is based on no more of an ontological assumption than that something exists, that the world we inhabit is real. Only if he were to deny the validity of such an assertion could Baird finally maintain his claim that Eliade's posited ontology is unacceptable.

The question remains as to the "normative" nature of Eliade's judgments as to the benefits or detriments of the recognition or refusal of specific hierophanies as being revelatory of the true nature of the human mode of being. As Baird says,

> once one sees "the sacred" or "religion" as an ontological reality and once one operates as though its structures are also ontologically real, having identified these structures one has discovered reality. It then follows that those whose lives are lived in the sacred as completely as possible are the most authentic since they exist closest to reality. (87)

This is a remarkable example of Eliade's concept that one need not understand the meaning of a revelation to communicate it. From the context it is not unreasonable to assume that Baird intends this statement as a refutation of Eliade's ideas. He intends to reveal the unwarranted arrogance of the "normative" stance which insists that religious believers are in some wise superior to secular humanity. It is true that, according to Eliade's definitions, "those whose lives are lived in the sacred as completely as possible are the most authentic since they exist closest to reality." But, in order to be consonant with those definitions, this should be interpreted as follows: Once one recognizes the reality of the sacred for the believer and once one has identified the structures which transmit and maintain that specific apprehension (*this* sacred = the real) then one has discovered a fact of human existence. It then follows that those who recognize the structures which identify the real in their own lives have the most authentic existence since they exist in the awareness of the facts, that is, more completely in the real, the sacred. It is the mistaken apprehension of an distinction between religious and "non-religious" humanity which implies a normative judgment. Eliade is not insisting that humanity *should be* religious. He is pointing out that, in truth, we *are* religious. To live one's life as fully as possible "in the sacred" is then to be aware of the sources of one's own apprehensions of the real, of one's own hierophanies, one's own religion.

In the end, Baird's striking and oft-repeated accusation that Eliade "assumed that there is something out there that corresponds to the term 'religion' or 'the sacred,' and also that the historian of religion can identify it intuitively" (74) can be seen to be a procedural assumption of Baird's own analysis. It relies entirely on the assumption that Eliade proceeds under the essential-intuitional approach described above, in other words, that he does not attempt to define religion or the sacred. Baird's reasoning is, in fact, tautological—viciously circular. Eliade is accused of assuming the ontology of the sacred because he must assume that he can intuit its essence because he uses the essential-intuitional approach, which is to say that he gives no definition of his object because he assumes its prior ontology. It could equally be argued that Eliade does not need to presume the independent ontology of the sacred because he assumes that the word religion, and also the word sacred, has a meaning and can thus be used meaningfully whether its referent is autonomous or not, and that its meaning will be revealed through its use.

The affirmation or denial of the ontological reality of the sacred as expressed in a specific religious tradition is actually irrelevant to the study of religions. As an *expression* the ontology is open to verification. (Or falsification, if it be preferred.) For example, that some people have considered a voluptuous female with bloodied lips, decorated with a garland of dead infants and human heads, to be the highest expression of divinity can be factually verified. Once verified, its ontology as an expression of the real is no longer open to doubt. Thus the hierophany has ontology as an hierophany, and it has effect as exemplary, but at no point is it necessary to debate the independent ontological existence of the sacred behind the hierophany. In fact, it could be argued that such a debate is not only irresolvable, but is finally impossible, since it is only the *expressions* of the sacred, of the real, which can be brought under scrutiny, never the sacred itself.

THE OBJECT OF RELIGIOUS BELIEF

In defending Eliade's thought against these accusations of ontological assumptions and normative judgments in this way, another problem is generated. If the ontological status of the sacred is not assumed, then what is the "intentional object of the believers' devotion?" What is the referent of religious symbolism? What is the proper object of religion and the phenomenology of religion? This is precisely the point raised by Hans Penner in his assessment of Eliade. He states,[2]

---

2. Hans Penner's critique of Eliade's understanding of symbols was published in German in 1967 as "Bedeutung und Probleme der Religiosen Symbolik bei Tillich und Eliade," *Antaios* 9 (1967): 127–43. I have worked from the German. I am sure that Bridgitte Weitbrecht's translation is quite adequate and so any weaknesses in the retranslation are my own.

both [Tillich's and Eliade's] opinions have the same problem . . . the problem of a phenomenology of religion without a defined object, for the object is, and remains, "wholly other." (127)

He goes on to explain,

a phenomenological enquiry into religion which grounds itself in the sacred, the meta-empirical (the wholly other) cannot, by definition, describe the object which religious symbols characterize or indicate. As we see, it is thus wrong to speak of a religious or sacred object at all as we once again apprehend these expressions symbolically. Such a phenomenology of religion remains pansymbolic and the development of this phenomenology into a metaphysical system, explicit in Tillich, implicit in Eliade, only further reveals this pansymbolism to defer to a very abstract, notionally contrived symbolism. (141)

It would appear that Hans Penner has, to a certain extent, anticipated my defence of Eliade against the ontological accusations of his other critics. It would seem that the only way to avoid these criticisms is to deny—or rather to refuse to affirm—the ontological reality of the sacred, which leaves religion devoid of a proper object, and symbolism with nothing to symbolize.

A response to this criticism consistent with the preceding interpretation of Eliade can take two forms. First, there is an erroneous conflation of the reality that the believer believes with the reality *in which* the believer believes. This can most clearly be seen in Penner's later *Impasse and Resolution*. Here Penner quotes Brede Kristensen as saying,

"we gain a different conception of the 'holy' when we take the reality of the believer's faith as our starting point. . . . This reality proves to be self-subsistent and absolute; it is beyond all our rational criticism. The only difficulty for us is to form an accurate conception of this reality and to understand it from within."

[Penner continues]

Notice that the difficulty is not understanding a certain religion but the "reality" to which religions refer. Just how a historian of religions knows that this reality is "self-subsistent," "absolute," and/or "beyond rational criticism" is never explained. (34)

This reveals an unwarranted shift from "the reality of the believer's faith" to "the reality to which religions refer." It is the former which is the proper object of the study of religion, the latter is the object of religion itself.

Secondly, "reality" is itself an interpretative category which becomes applicable only in interpretation based on personal subjective intuition (that is, all interpretation). The history of religions as conceived by Eliade is founded upon the sacred *qua* the taxonomic assumption of a reality inherent in all religious phenomena. However, the applied taxonomy is based on the actual experience or perception of reality which is itself conditioned by previous experience, by culture, and by "archetypal intuitions."

It should further be said that if conscious reflection is supported by a symbolic foundation, as Penner understands Eliade to suppose, then nothing escapes Penner's critique. Nothing can finally be described other than symbolically. This seems to be in accordance with the deconstructionist critique of the limitations of language (e.g., Jacques Derrida's *Of Grammatology*). Thus Eliade's symbolism is not especially vulnerable to this claim of pansymbolism. The fact that the referent of religious symbols can never be apprehended on the empirical plane as other than the referent of symbolism does not immediately deny it real existence. Objects of experience can be genuine intentional objects even if they are experienced as an element of inward subjective reality (see Berger and Luckmann, *The Social Construction of Reality*, 20). It is central to Eliade's position that to deny reality to subjective experience, or even to hierarchize ontology with "subjective" as lesser than "objective" experience, is a religious perception characteristic of modern Western humanity, and is open to dispute. The exhaustive identification of ontology, of being, with material manifest existence, is what Eliade identifies as the complete concealment of the sacred in the profane.

Penner's insistence on the restriction of the referent of religious symbolism itself to the level of symbol is finally no criticism. Since the true symbol is a hierophany, the symbol *is* a manifestation of the real, the real has initially been restricted to the level of the symbol. The fact that Penner does not himself perceive any true ontology inherent in symbols merely indicates his acquiescence in the mindset of the modern. The contention that both symbols and the phenomenology of religion lack a proper object can be seen as an insistence that God, for example, is "merely" imaginary (or Allah, Brahman, etc. I use the English word "god" as a specific and conditioned concept involved in the religious mythology of my own culture), that symbols have an imaginary reference only, that people only imagine that God exists. In fact, this is another example of reduction, of contending that symbolism is *only* symbolism, "pansymbolism" and nothing else. Eliade would not agree with this, nor does he say that religion is just hierophany or just meaning. In fact,

> the interpretation of symbols by this reductive method, that is to say the reduction of all possible significations to only one proclaimed "fundamental," appears erroneous to us. (*Symbolism, the Sacred, and the Arts*, 6)

To say that it is *just* some (or any) such thing is to attempt to reduce its ontological significance, to limit its becoming to mere mental image. On the contrary, Eliade seeks to increase the ontological impact of religion in general both by his insistence on the sacred as the real and by his stress on the imaginary as effective. For example, he has said,

> no conquest of the material world was effected without a corresponding impact on human imagination and behavior. And I am inclined to add that the reflections of the objective conquests upon such imaginary Universes are perhaps even more important for an understanding of man. ("Notes on the Symbolism of the Arrow," 465)

To Eliade's mind it has been a quite recent, and very positive, development that "we are now beginning to acknowledge the importance of that mysterious *sur-réalité* revealed by any imaginary universe" (*Occultism*, 88). He clarifies this in his *History of Religious Ideas*, where he states that

> the empirical value of [practical] inventions is evident. What is less so is *the importance of the imaginative activity inspired by familiarity with the different modalities of matter*. . . . The imagination discovers hitherto unsuspected analogies among the different levels of the real. (vol. I, 34)

For the history of religions, it is the actual phenomenon of belief which is the proper object of our study, not the putative ontological status of the object of belief. The existence of religious concepts as imaginary objects is not open to doubt, although the significance of such concepts is debatable. Evidently, religious symbolism, religious behavior, and religious concepts are extremely resilient, adaptable, and (especially if Eliade's understanding be accepted) ubiquitous. This empirical fact alone should secure the recognition of their significance.

That imagination is not only of great importance but that it is also considered to be an integral part of *religious* life is indicated by Eliade's statement that

> one can pass through a Symplegades insofar as one is able to act "spiritually," insofar as one possesses imagination and intelligence and, consequently, is capable of detaching oneself from immediate reality." ("Methodological Remarks," 101)[3]

This clearly identifies "spiritual" existence with imagination and intelligence and, specifically, with the ability to "detach oneself from immediate reality." This shows an identification of soul or spirit and mind which might escape the normal English-speaking reader, although it will be familiar enough to German speakers as *Geist*. The concomitant implication is that, for Eliade, it is the specific human imaginative ability to become detached from immediately experienced reality, *Erlebnis*, or "history" as he conceives it, which constitutes "spiritual" existence. This is the "escape from history," nothing more (or less) mystical than the ability to learn from

---

3. The Symplegades were the perilously moving rocks between which the Argonauts sailed.

that which one has not oneself experienced and to avoid via mental (spiritual) discipline the purely physical effects of causal determination. At the extremes this may be sitting naked on a glacier for three days, or simply not allowing the quotidian pressures of life to "get you down." In such an interpretation one "escapes from history" every time one smiles in the face of adversity or performs any act which is not fully determined by historical/empirical preconditions. The study of the phenomena of religions strongly suggests that this has been most effectively accomplished with reference to the object of religious belief—the sacred.

THE TYRANNY OF MEANING

In the earlier consideration of Eliade as a phenomenologist of religion, his recurrent emphasis on meaning was noted. Gregory Alles' critique of Eliade concludes that the latter's analyses are procrustean and inadequate, subordinating the acts which condition both the content and interpretation to the *meaning* of the text ("Critique from Totality," 124). Not only that, but Eliade is seen as representative of those historians of religion who "long for a position at the center of European and American culture, indeed, at the center of an emerging global culture" (132). Not only does Alles challenge Eliade's thought but he further seeks to impugn Eliade's motives as a concealed egoism.

Alles' critique relies on the thought of Rüdiger Bubner, a dialectical theorist:

> if the claim to totality is made, concepts become, despite their differences in content, incompatible with each other . . . one concept stands to the other in the peculiar relation of denying its claim to totality in order to assert the same claim on its own behalf. (119, quoting Bubner, *Modern German Philosophy*, 164–65)

The critique from totality that results Alles considers to have a direct bearing upon the Chicago school's attempt (exemplified by Wach and Eliade) to articulate the totality of religion via hermeneutics. Not only is their claim to have access to the totality of religion insupportable in the first case, but their approach to that supposed totality is inadequate.

> Hermeneutics—the drive to "decipher" "deeper meanings"—over-whelms the impulse to totality. Concerned to do justice to what he sees as the one irreducible element of religion, its intended object, Eliade writes a history of religions capable of doing justice virtually to that element alone. (119)

As Alles goes on to say, "there is always more to religion than just meaning" (123). Evidently, Alles is contributing to the idea that Eliade falls foul of his own critique of reductionism and himself reduces religion to an overly narrow category. Not only that, but hermeneutics in and of itself suffers when it is conjoined with the emphasis on totality that the history of religion requires, for religion is greater than meaning as life is greater than language. The history of religions must be more than a hermeneutical enterprise.[4]

Alles has made this progression from religion being more than just hierophany to religion being more than just meaning by reference to Eliade's statement in *Patterns* (126) that we may summarily define religious life "as the experience of kratophanies, hierophanies and theophanies," and by an identification of Wach's *Religionswissenschaft* as "a vast monument to meaning conceived as the systematic ordering of parts in a whole" (112). He sees Eliade as guilty, not only of reducing the study of religion to the study of meaning ("to count as religious, an activity had somehow to be meaningful," 122f.), but of simultaneously claiming that this constituted the totality of the religious phenomenon and that the religious phenomenon is a totality at all. Regarding the totality, Alles paraphrases Eliade as claiming that

> the irruptions of the Sacred constitute a totality, an integral, coherent system that crosses the bounds of culture and history. . . . every hierophany tends to reveal the Sacred in its totality. As a result, to be understood, every hierophany must be placed in the context of the Sacred as a totality. (115)

Unfortunately this, which is the heart of Alles' identification of a "totality" in Eliade's thought, is an erroneous reading of the text. Alles' source for his paraphrase is *Patterns* (8, 26), where in fact Eliade says that, although hierophanies are heterogeneous in origin and in form, in history and in structure, the historian of religions should

> make use of all these kinds of evidence. . . . In this way we shall get a coherent collection of common traits which, as we shall see later, will *make it possible to formulate a coherent system* of the various modalities of the vegetation cult. We shall see in this way that every hierophany in fact supposes such a system. (*Patterns*, 8, emphasis added)

The fact is that, in the first case, and by implication in all other cases, it is *we* as the interpreters of hierophanies who "formulate" the system. Granted that there is a system presupposed by the recognition of every hierophany, but that system is nonetheless formulated by the human agent in his or her particular embodied

---

4. See also Segal, "In Defense of Reductionism." Eliade's "equation of the actor's point of view with an irreducibly religious one proves entirely arbitrary. Indeed it becomes hard to see why his interpretation of the actor's point of view is any less reductionistic than the interpretations of religion he opposes as reductionistic" (99).

human existential situation. There is, of course, a paradox of the chicken-and-egg type involved here, but that paradox has never prevented chickens from laying eggs. No more does Eliade say that every hierophany tends to reveal the sacred in its totality and can only be understood in the context of that totality. Rather,

> the sacred expresses itself through something other than itself; it appears in things, myths or symbols, but never wholly or directly. . . . in every case the sacred manifests itself limited and incarnate. (26)[5]

The value which Eliade accords this formulation of all hierophanies as being part of a whole is this: "it would preserve the older hierophanies, by according them value on a different religious level, and the performance of a function there" (26). In other words, this recognition of hierophanies as part of a whole system *which we formulate* has the specific function of allowing for the valorization of archaic hierophanies as hierophanies, which the insistence upon only some events as revelatory of the real does not do.

Alles has interpreted Eliade's "system" as necessarily referring to an "autonomous intended object" and to "autonomous" or "disembodied meanings" (119, 124, 130) whose activity constitutes the whole of religion. However, "the history of religions must include the entire interaction of the subject and the object, human activity as well as divine" (119). In the alternative interpretation, the latter is precisely what Eliade does. In fact some would say that this interpretation allows too great a possibility of overemphasizing the human side of the equation and excluding the divine as an independent agent.

In the same way, Alles can be seen to have misinterpreted the one irreducible element to which Eliade seeks to do justice. It is not so much the "intended object" as the recognition of that intentional object by specific individuals. That is, not the intended object, but the act of intention. All religion involves the act of intention of the real, the true, the significant, in some object or event which does not, and cannot, autonomously and automatically communicate that intentionality to all observers. This certainly could be criticized as an aprioristic assumption, for such is what it is. Given the extreme dubiety of ever "bracketing" our critical contentions and other assumptions, it is an eminently practical assumption to make that a religious text which has been cherished for millennia, or a native myth which permeates the life of a tribe, is apprehended as possessed of real meaning. In Alles' case, however, we are presented with no such assumptions and thus we are left with

---

5. It should be pointed out once again that the language of the original French is more ambiguous than the English translation. "La manifestation du sacré à travers quelque chose d'autre que lui-même; il apparaît dans des objects . . . en se manifestant le sacré s'est limité" (*Traité*, 35f.). This allows for a considerably more passive function of the sacred than Rosemary Sheed's translation: "The manifestation of the sacred appears through objects, . . . as it is manifest the sacred is limited," which in turn allows for a more active function of the human subject for whom a given phenomenon is an hierophany.

no apparent means of identifying *what religion is*. Alles' whole critique of totality has, from the outset, refused to allow that if the word religion be given a specific definition, then the group of cases to which that definition refers constitutes a totality. This does not make competing concepts of totality incompatible, as Bubner's quotation suggests, but it does challenge competing definitions which circumscribe a differing totality. The problem arises if, and only if, the concept be mistaken for the object. Eliade's concept of the totality of religious phenomena, being circumscribed by his implicit definition of religion, cannot exclude anyone else's concept and thus cannot exclude anyone else's totality. It can, however, have different, debatably preferable, characteristics.

Alles seems to have likewise misapprehended Eliade's concept of meaning. Eliade's conception of meaning is related to the response to an exemplary pattern. It is a human action, or becomes meaningful in activity. He cannot "idolize meaning" as Alles fears, precisely because he recognizes the manifestation of the real in *all* hierophanies and thus in all "competing" meanings. The fundamental error in Alles' analysis is to react against a concept of "autonomous meaning" where none exists.

Alles calls for an escape from the "preoccupation with meaning" (123), implying that it is a provincial Western concept artificially foisted upon all religions. This might be true of a narrower concept of meaning, such as that ascribed to Dilthey and Wach of the relation of parts to the whole. However, one which is grounded in human activity in such a way escapes this provincialism. (I might add that anyone familiar with Eliade's journals would recognize his horror of such provincialism.)

While Alles' desire to escape provincialism, to allow the Shinto priests to dance, rather than trying to force our theology upon them,[6] is wholly admirable, it is in some ways naïve. One might insist that life is greater than language, but as a colleague responded, "try and convince me of that—without using language." This is no mere quip; it is through language, and through language alone, that we can become *aware* of "life's greatness." It is no mere attempt to elevate humanity to a fallacious "higher" status by a preoccupation with a mere form of communication when we distinguish ourselves from other sentient beings as a language-using animal. In his attempt to install the event as the grounding category of religious studies, Alles fails to recognize that the concepts of space, time, and consciousness of which the event is "a constellation" (125) are themselves socially constructed concepts, and so, it follows, is event. How can we then put the event before the "linguistic code" which determines it?

Alles affirms that he "deliberately correlate[s] [t]his view with a metaphysics that assigns priority to actuality rather than to potentiality and an anthropology that

---

6. The anecdote to which I refer was related by both Eliade and Joseph Campbell; respectively in *Autobiography*, vol. II, 199; and in the introduction to Campbell's videotape of *The Power of Myth*.

sees thought as activity" (125). But in so doing he seems to be unaware that thought is the activity *par excellence* which is governed by exemplary models, by mythic structures, and thus by structures of language and meaning. His desire to escape the inescapable leads him into the finally self-contradictory position of claiming that "the obsession with meaning is yielding to topics that assume greater significance," and to recommending Michael Baxandall's book *Patterns of Intention* as avoiding the notion of meaning (126, 137 n. 32). Only the narrowest possible definition of meaning could escape its restoration as "intention" or "significance," and Eliade's concept of meaning, whatever else may be the case, is not that narrow.

I respect deeply Alles' attack on scientism, analytical economism, technologism, and Western provincialism. I would contend, however, that his insistence on history and event, extraversion, and critical thought does not counter these trends as effectively as does Eliade's emphasis on coherence, original meaning, totality, and hermeneutics. Alles has been less than extravert himself in attributing his own meanings (of history, religion, hermeneutics, and meaning itself) to Eliade rather than seeking to disclose Eliade's meanings. Eliade, in producing his *oeuvre*, attempted to communicate a constellation of thought which was to him coherent, adequate, and tailored to his own experience, both personal and literary. Alles subordinates Eliade's endeavor to the meaning which Alles himself derives from the texts, in this case, *Patterns*, *The Quest*, *Shamanism*, and secondary sources.

CONCLUSIONS

As I have interpreted Eliade's thought, he provides us precisely with all that Gregory Alles seeks in the history of religions. Human activity is the grounding category of the historical study (as we have seen); the history of religion is an extraverted rather than introverted discipline (the *religiosi* do not receive privileged status because all humanity can be seen as religious, and the original meanings of other peoples' myths are sought rather than our own meanings); and it is both critical and self-critical (because Eliade encourages us to inspect the dialectical sources of our own hierophanies as constituted in a similar way to those of exotic and archaic peoples).

Similarly, this interpretation of Eliade raises serious doubts as to the validity of other criticisms, revealing them to be more coherently comprehensible as misunderstandings of Eliade rather than revelations of self-contradictions or unwarranted assumptions. If such a defense of his thought can be sustained, it must be recognized that further consideration of Eliade is a valid project for the study of religion. We may need to go beyond Eliade, but we need to understand him first. Certainly, we should not simply ignore his work as corrupted by egregious flaws.

PART THREE

Beyond Eliade

INTRODUCTION

In an article of 1978 Ninian Smart wrote of the need to go "Beyond Eliade," a need no serious thinker would deny. Of course we cannot rest on the laurels of earlier theorists, we need to proceed beyond them. Yet it is incumbent upon us to understand those theorists before we go beyond them and little grasp has been shown of Eliade's underlying conception of religion. So far I have developed an interpretation of Eliade's academic writings on religion, and have considered its resistance to some of the most carefully considered criticisms levelled against his thought. It remains now to investigate where this interpretation might take us in extrapolating beyond Eliade. One initial area of inquiry concerns Eliade's incomplete analysis of the religiousness of modern humanity. If religion is indeed ubiquitous, then in what ways does it manifest itself in contemporary people who would deny or even repudiate "religiousness?" Can this interpretation be applied to complete Eliade's unfinished observations on the religious creation of the moderns? If so, what might it reveal about even more recent developments, "postmodernism" for example?

CHAPTER 16

The Religious Creativity of Modern Humanity: Some Observations on Eliade's Unfinished Thought[1]

In the preface to the first volume of his *History of Religious Ideas*, Eliade stated that the

> unity of the spiritual history of humanity is a recent discovery, which has not yet been sufficiently assimilated. Its importance for the future of our discipline will become manifest in the last chapter of the third volume. It is also in this in this final chapter, in the course of a discussion of the crises brought on by the masters of reductionism—from Marx and Nietzsche to Freud—and of the contributions made by anthropology, the history of religions, phenomenology, and the new hermeneutics, that the reader will be able to judge the sole but important creation of the modern Western world. I refer to the ultimate stage of desacralization. The process is of considerable interest to the historian of religions, for it illustrates the complete camouflage of the "sacred"—more precisely its identification with the "profane." (xvi)

Unfortunately, things did not go according to this plan. In the preface to the third volume, Eliade invoked his failing health and increasing age to explain the delay of that volume's appearance. He was 76 at that time and suffering from arthritis in his hands (he still wrote longhand) and failing vision. He drew attention to the modifications made to the plan announced in the preface to the second volume and once again said he would "undertake to analyze the religious creativity of modern societies" in the final chapter of the final volume.[2]

---

1. Parts of this chapter originally appeared in *Religious Studies* 31, no. 2 (1995): 221–235, under the same title.
2. In fact, the preface to the second volume contains no such plan, being little more than an announcement of the death of Eliade's translator Willard Trask and an acknowledgment of the services of Lawrence Sullivan. Perhaps the preface to the first volume is intended.

It is a disappointment to me personally, and quite possibly a loss to the history of religions, that this final volume never appeared. Eliade's office in Chicago was damaged by fire in 1984 with the loss of much that was intended for that publication. That misfortune was followed in two years by Eliade's death. The efforts of the late Ioan Culianu resulted in the publication in 1991 of *Geschichte der religiösen Ideen*, Band 3/2, *Vom Zeitalter der Entdeckungen bis zur Gegenwart*, the work of authors other than Eliade. Richard Schaeffler, author of the concluding chapter of that work, also draws attention to Eliade's uncompleted observations on the religious creativity of modern humanity.

Although the recreation of the proposed discussion of "the crises brought on by the masters of reductionism" is an interesting project, it is beyond my scope. In fact, it is with trepidation and caution that I propose to make some suggestions as to the possible content of Eliade's proposed analysis of the "religious creativity of modern societies." Having undertaken a thorough reading of Eliade and given the clue that this process "illustrates the complete camouflage of the sacred—more precisely its identification with the profane," I believe that this attempt is at least feasible. An inspection of Eliade's understanding of the sacred and of references to its camouflage or concealment coupled with his references to "modern man" sheds a great deal of light upon Eliade's understanding of the religious attitudes of the latter.

Eliade said that, "I am trying to write a short history of religious ideas from the Stone Age to the contemporary atheist theologies" ("Sacred in the Secular World," 78). This description of the final topic of the *History* might easily be thought to indicate a projected response to the Death-of-God theology of such as T. J. J. Altizer or even Mark C. Taylor as the specifically religious creation of modernity. Interesting as such an undertaking is, however, it seems most credible that the Death-of God theology is *not* the sole unique creation of modernity. As Carl Olson has rightly pointed out,

> it is evident that the death of God is not a recent phenomenon acknowl-
> edged only in the works of philosophers and theologians, nor is it some
> type of radical innovation. Death-of-God pronouncements are surely an
> unconscious revival of the *deus otiosus* known in the history of religion.
> (52)

What then *was* Eliade's understanding of the sole but important creation of the modern Western world, the ultimate stage of desacralization, and the religious creativity of modern societies?

RELIGION AS RELATION TO A "SACRED"

As an historian of religion rather than a metaphysician or theologian, Eliade's approach to the sacred was to "the *something* intended in ritual actions, in mythical speech, in belief or in mystical feeling" (these are the words of Paul Ricoeur, a close colleague of Eliade, in *Freud and Philosophy*, 29). As that which is worshipped, whatever it might be, the question of the *existence* of the sacred does not occur. In studying religion, one cannot deny that humanity worships. That which is worshipped, the intentional object of reverence, whatever it may be, whatever ontological status it might be afforded, is real and meaningful as a category of study. The sacred exists *qua* the intentional object of worship and *qua* an object of the study of religion. To debate its existence is no more meaningful than to challenge the existence of psychosis, injustice, value, or any other intangible or abstract category. It is worthy of note that the English word "worship" is from *weorthscipe*, Old English for worth or worthiness, its original sense seems to have been to valorize or hold something in high esteem.

Many commentators insist either that Eliade fails to define the sacred or they assume a facile identification with the Judaeo-Christian God or with some indeterminate but autonomous "transcendent" ontology. I have argued, however, that it is the *perception* of the sacred which constitutes it as such for those who perceive it. Eliade insists that "the sacred is pre-eminently the *real*, at once power, efficacy, the source of life and fecundity" (*Sacred and Profane*, 28). Specifically, the sacred is not to be conceived independent of experience, rather sensory perception is the locus in which the sacred is originally perceived, but the sacred is constituted by the mode of perception rather than the contents of perception.[3] Anything, any phenomenal entity, could be perceived as manifesting the sacred (*Patterns*, 11).

THE UNRECOGNIZIBILITY OF MIRACLE—THE CAMOUFLAGE OF THE SACRED

Eliade frequently applied the adjectives "concealed," "camouflaged," "hidden," "unconscious," or "unrecognizable" to religious phenomena. Mac Linscott Ricketts, in *Mircea Eliade: The Romanian Roots*, concluded that the "Unifying Theme" of all Eliade's writings is "the unrecognizibility of miracle" (1209). The Romanian literary critic Matei Calinescu has likewise said that "the problem of miracle and the disguises through which it renders itself unrecognizable is central" to some of Eliade's fiction (561). Since the sacred, the mediated perception of true power, ultimate worth, the source of significance, *could* be experienced in any phenomenal entity, the fact that it is not so perceived becomes highly significant. The fact that the sacred fails to be manifested in certain experiences to certain people is as characteristic of their religious culture as are those entities and events

---

3.   J. Z. Smith's statement that "sacred and profane are transitive categories; they serve as maps and labels, not substances; they are distinctions of office, indices of difference," would find full agreement with my analysis of the sacred as a mode rather than a content of perception. (*To Take Place*, 105)

which they recognize as hierophanies. A central question here must then become—how and in what ways did Eliade consider the sacred to be concealed or camouflaged from "modern humanity?"

WHAT IS "MODERN?"

It is imperative to provide some clarification of the identity of "modern humanity." Although the dubious accuracy of the term "primitive" has been recognized and it is now usually placed in quotation marks, the parallel has not been recognized that "modern" is possibly even more problematic. From the Latin *modo*, "just now," its literal meaning is one of recent occurrence. It has, however, received a plethora of alternative applications (see, for example, Matei Calinescu's *Five Faces of Modernity*).

As we have seen, Eliade views the sacred as the intentional object of human experience which is apprehended as the real. It is, then, not surprising that he states that

> modern man, radically secularized, believes himself, or styles himself, atheist, areligious, or, at least, indifferent. But he is wrong. He has not yet succeeded in abolishing the *homo religiosus* that is in him: he has only done away with (if he ever was) the *christianus*. That means that he is left with being "pagan" without knowing it (*No Souvenirs*, 164).

In "Sacred Tradition and Modern Man," on the other hand, Eliade opposes "modern man" to *homo religiosus* by making the attitude to tradition definitive in his understanding of modernity: "by definition *traditional* ideas cannot play a role in *modern* societies" (78). Yet again, in a paper originally given to the Eranos conference in 1955, Eliade contrasted the contemporary "popular soul" with the man of the modern society ("La Vertu Créatrice Du Mythe," 76). So it would appear that "modern" is used in three distinguishable ways: first, as recent or contemporary but not substantially distinct from religious humanity; secondly, as recent or contemporary but distinct from traditional *homo religiosus* because of the attitude to tradition; and finally, and most specifically, as an element of secular society which is distinct from both religious humanity and from the contemporary "popular soul." In a passage cited earlier, Eliade seems to use the word in both the first and last senses:

> the modern world is, at the present moment, not entirely converted to historicism; we are even witnessing a conflict between the two views: the archaic conception, which we should designate as archetypal and ahistorical; and the modern, post-Hegelian conception, which seeks to be historical. (*Myth of the Eternal Return*, 141)

Clearly, in its most distinctive application "modern" is closely related to "historical."

In order to clarify this application, it is necessary to investigate Eliade's understanding of secularism and the operation of religious thought in the contemporary era. Eliade is not particularly explicit about the survival of "religion" in secular thought *by that name*. He is more forthcoming about the survival of myth. In Eliade's thought the two categories are inseparable. Where there is religion, there is myth; where there is myth, there is religion. Recall that it is not in the sense of falsehood or fable that he uses the word myth but, on the contrary, as a narrative which he describes as considered to reveal the truth *par excellence*. Myth narrates a sacred history; it "tells only of that which *really* happened"; it relates the "breakthrough of the sacred that really *establishes* the World and makes it what it is today" (*Reality*, 1, 5, 6; *Dreams*, 23; *Quest*, 72f.). Myths are inseparable from that which is apprehended as the real, from the sacred, and from religion. Where myths survive in the secular milieu, there we have concealed religion.

To say that "real" is equivalent to materially and/or historically actual is, in Eliade's terms, to grant sacred significance to the historical situation and to the empirically manifest. These are the religious valorizations of a large portion of contemporary humanity. It is, however, crucial to recognize that Eliade did not simply equate valorizations of the empirical and valorizations of the historical. He had far more sympathy for "the elevation of physical nature to the rank of the one all-embracing reality" than he did with "continual talk about history, the historical condition, the historical moment." The article from which these quotations are taken, "Cultural Fashions and the History of Religions" (*Occultism, Witchcraft, and Popular Fashions*, chapter 1), portrays empiricism as "a reabsorption of man into nature," whereas historicism is merely the tired remnant of French existentialism.

> For many years the French intellectual was forced to live almost exclusively in his "historical moment," as Sartre had taught that any responsible individual should do. (24)

Eliade saw this "gloomy, tedious, and somehow provincial atmosphere" as infertile and unsatisfactory and easily replaced by the "*mythology of matter*," which was to be found, for example, in the popular French magazine *Planète*, in the theology of Teilhard de Chardin, and in the sociology of Claude Lévi-Strauss, all of which expressed

> the importance of "things," of material objects—ultimately the primacy of space and of nature—and the indifference to history and to historical time. (28)

Finally, Eliade seems to depict existentialism and historicism as idolatrous—the fallacious overvaluation of products of human creation—whereas empiricism and positivism ("neopositivism" in the case of Lévi-Strauss) are accepted as valid religious forms—the recognition of genuine hierophanies, sources of revelation.

THE SACRED AND THE MODERN

Modern Western people find it almost impossible not to accord automatically the greatest significance to, for example, that speculative reconstruction which is deemed to conform to the actual historical event. This, we think, is the real, the true, the powerful. But is this necessarily the case? Newtonian mechanics was once considered to conform to the actual but has been superseded by relativity, which itself has been challenged by quantum theory, yet classical Newtonian mathematics was enough to put men on the moon,[4] enough to alter radically the situation of humanity in the world. Historical studies frequently refer to the impossibility of an unbiased account, an objective reconstruction, of history. Chaos theory stresses the superiority of the simple, manipulable, theoretical model rather than the complex model which attempts to faithfully correspond to external reality (Gleick, *Chaos*, 278). The advances of technology have proved as threatening as they have benevolent. Theory does not need to be understood or even accurate to be practically applicable (Gribbin, *Schrödinger's Cat*, 123). Yet modern humanity still clings to the conviction that the real, the true, the powerful, is the historically accurate, the independently extant, the empirical. Whether or not this attitude is finally justified is not at issue here; the point is that this constitutes a belief of a basically religious nature characteristic of "modern" humanity. This, I would contend, underlies the "sole but important creation of the modern Western world . . . the ultimate stage of desacralization." It certainly "illustrates the complete camouflage of the sacred—more precisely its identification with the profane." Whereas "archaic" humanity considers sacred myths to recount the real, "modern" humanity considers the observable to be the real. It is in the discoveries of contemporary physics that modern humanity seeks for meaning. The works of such writers as John Gribbin, Fred Alan Wolf, Gary Zukav, Carl Sagan, Fritjof Capra, Paul Davies, and other popularizers of science are increasingly read by the ordinary seekers after truth. As Stephen Toulmin pointed out, "the popular scientist has won over the audience of the popular preacher" (21).

If the sacred is seen simply as that which is worshipped, that which is considered worthy of respect, that which reveals real being and has real meaning, then modern humanity's sacred is largely the material. The actual events of the external world are considered to be more worthy of attention, to reveal greater truth, to be more meaningful than traditional cultural forms. This is not a generic shift from religion to non-religion as is usually thought to be the case in a consideration of secularization. Rather, it is the triumph of a particular, concealed religious attitude of valorization of the empirical as the major manifestation of the

---

4.   Although quantum mechanics was necessary to produce the computers used in the space program, the actual programs which they ran were Newtonian. As Ilya Prigogine puts it, "space trip experiments . . . confirm Newton's equations to a high degree." *Order Out of Chaos*, 251.

real. However, when the events are valorized as the real in and of themselves, then we have a conflation of the independent and the creative, a virtual reality in which modern humanity contrives to live. When "every effort is directed toward saving and conferring value on the historical event as such, the event in itself and for itself" (*Myth of the Eternal Return*, 147), then the events of the external world are thought to be exhaustive of the truth, to constitute the real rather than to reveal the real, and the sacred is confused with the contents of perception rather than the mode of perception. It is the exhaustive identification of a specific historical situation with the real, the simultaneous denial of the reality of the imaginary worlds of others, and the affirmation of the unique and independent reality of one's own "historical situation," which constitutes a novel and dangerous departure from the traditional operations of the religious mind. It is the refusal to countenance our creative involvement in the construction of reality, our "freedom to intervene even in the ontological constitution of the universe" (160f.) which Eliade labels "modern" and "historical."

Eliade even grants some responsibility for this misapprehension to historians of religion:

> To some extent, it is we the historians of religions, who are responsible for this. We wanted at all cost to present an *objective* history of religions, but we failed to bear in mind that what we were christening *objectivity* followed the fashion of thinking in our times. (*Images and Symbols*, 28)

Concomitant with the emphasis on the significance of the materially extant is an emphasis on its independence. Human creation is not independently extant and so is considered "less real," less significant than independent empirical phenomena. In other words, the valorization of the empirical/historical is accompanied by an unavoidable devaluation of the imaginative. This devaluation is neither rational nor coherent. Imaginative constructs, the quantum theory of physics, the American Constitution, religious beliefs, or ideologies, may have no independent ontology or empirical manifestation. They nonetheless exist and are arguably our most effective constructs. In the case of historicism, the incoherence becomes even more marked. One cannot deny human responsibility in shaping human history; the history of the human race is a product of the human race. I do not mean the "historiography" here but the actual events of the past. If human history is seen as significant, then other creations of human activity cannot be denied significance (and vice versa). As Eliade clearly states, human creativity is more directly related to concept and imagination than to event and action. It is not so much that Eliade depreciates history; rather, he insists on the *appreciation* of the non-historical, the imaginative. In fact, Eliade insists that in the modern world "the 'sacred' is present and active mainly in the imaginary universes" (*Quest*, 128). In the final analysis, then, even historiography could not be denied relevance as a vehicle of revelation of the real, a locus of hierophanies, especially if it is regarded as more imaginary than actual. It is the perception of Eliade as depreciating the historical which to some extent explains the antipathy of many of his critics. J. Z. Smith accuses Eliade of ignoring the categories of space and time and excluding historical data. Ninian Smart also makes this accusation of ahistoricism and the devaluation of historical consciousness. Robert Baird criticizes the ahistorical nature of Eliade's search for structures. Guilford Dudley considered Eliade's interpretation of archetypes to be so insulated from history as to be closed to empirical verification. Yet the less disparaging of Eliade's critics have insisted on his *dependence* upon history.[5]

I would venture to suggest that Eliade's objection to historicism and existentialism was twofold. First, the marked tendency to deny the operation of human creativity in the construction of historiography leads to a confusion of history and historiography, to a lack of clear discrimination between the creative and the independent. Secondly, the acceptance of the historical situation as independent, as a datum rather than a fiction, as "sacred," unavoidably leads to an entrenched historical determinism in which humanity can never escape from "the all-embracing reality" of history. History is seen as making humanity rather than humanity as making history.

This analysis might, at first glance, appear to be directly contradicted by one of Eliade's clearest expositions of the modern/archaic dichotomy—the final chapter of *The Myth of the Eternal Return*. Here Eliade describes "historical man" (modern man), who consciously and voluntarily creates history" (141—the parenthetical insertion is in the original). However, he goes on,

> the modern man can be creative only insofar as he is historical; in other words, all creation is forbidden him except that which has its source in his own freedom; and, consequently, everything is denied him except the freedom to make history by making himself. . . . It is becoming more and more doubtful . . . if modern man can make history. On the contrary, the more modern[6] he becomes—that is, without defenses against the terror of history—the less chances he has of making history. For history either makes itself . . . or it tends to be made by an increasingly smaller number of men. . . . Modern man's boasted freedom to make history is illusory for nearly the whole of the human race. . . . [F]or traditional man, modern man affords the type neither of a free being nor of a creator of history, . . .

---

5. J. Z. Smith (*Map is not Territory*, 259; *Imagining Religion*, 22–23; *To Take Place*, 14), Smart, ("Beyond Eliade," 182), Baird (*Category Formation*, 152) Dudley (*Religion on Trial*, 36). Among the more appreciative critics are Charles Long ("The Significance for Modern Man of Mircea Eliade's Work," 136) and Seymour Cain, ("Mircea Eliade: Attitudes towards History," 14).

6. [Eliade's footnote:] It is well to make clear that, in this context, "modern man" is such in his insistence upon being exclusively historical; i.e. that he is, above all, the "man" of historicism, of Marxism, and of existentialism. It is superfluous to add that not all of our contemporaries recognize themselves in such a man.

history—which, for the modern, is not only irreversible but constitutes human existence. (156–57)

This failure of the "modern" is strongly manifested by the neo-deconstructionist "followers" of Jacques Derrida, whose concept of meaning is restricted to the play of signs, the interrelationship of signifier and signified, and finally to the denial of any transcendental signified and to the infinite deferral of meaning. Colin Falck has pointed out

> that the much-mentioned "aporias," and the "abyss," along with the rest of the transcendence free vocabulary of post-Saussurean literary theory represent only post-Saussurean theory's uncomprehending encounter with the inherent mystery of all life and all experience. (25)

Such uncomprehending encounters are by definition the failure of the understanding of the critic and are identical with the inability to detect a "transhistorical meaning" (*Return*, 151). They usually lead to an insistence of non-ontology (what Falck refers to as the "abolition of reality"). That is, an insistence that there is nothing there to understand, hence the lack of meaning (like the linguistic philosophers' rejection of "God-talk" as "meaningless"), because the "signified" is claimed to have a merely assumed or imaginary, *a priori* existence. However, Falck also draws attention to the fact that

> the Derridean notion of *différance* takes us beyond both Kant and Saussure in its recognition of the essential inseparability of the *a priori* and the empirical. (21)

Such a notion would be quite familiar to a student of Goethe such as Eliade, from Goethe's insistence on the theory-laden nature of the fact. Here the inseparability of the imaginary and the empirical, the theory and the fact, the thought and the perceived, the felt and the seen, is emphasized. The assumed, the imaginary, is anything but mere.

THE ONTOLOGICAL IMAGINATION

Our ability to "escape history" as discussed above (chapter 10) is directly dependent on our relationship to imaginative narrative. An example can be taken from Martin Seligman's book *Helplessness*. "Helplessness" is the condition in which a subject no longer attempts to avoid "powerful negative stimuli" (pain), acquiescing in suffering, rather than making an effort to avoid it. This condition is induced considerably more easily in subjects which have no way to control the suffering. Given some measure of control the subject will not simply tolerate its condition (this applies to a large range of animals as well as people), but will continue to strive for an improvement of its condition, no matter how elusive the control may be. In an empirically controlled experiment, Seligman reported that "merely telling a human subject about controllability duplicates the effects of actual controllability" (48). In other words, a story which one is told, a narrative structure to which one is exposed (and Seligman is quite clear that it does not have to be "true" in the sense that it does not have to correspond to the actual state of affairs in the world of experience), can have the same effect as if it were a part of the world of real experience. By dint of imagination the human spirit can be seen to "escape history," to be "detached from the immediate reality." In other words, and to this degree, the human spirit is "autonomous" in that it is not wholly determined by its physical environment but contributes, through the imaginative generation of narrative, to the construction of its own determining environment. In terms of archaic mythology, humanity participates in the cosmogony.

Even as a concept, an imaginative fiction in the sense indicated here, God is an infinitely creative entity, a being of unbounded imaginative fertility, capable of supporting a wealth of imaginary universes. Once the idea of God has been conceived, it is eminently possible to conceive, for example, the idea of heaven, paradise, and so forth, that is to say, a mode of being in which humanity is not conditioned or limited by our actual, physical state. It can quite credibly be suggested that if one cannot imagine an eternal and flawless state of human existence then one cannot have really imagined, or imaginatively realized, the idea of God. Yet it seems to be precisely those people who cannot imaginatively realize the possibility of a heaven (etc.) who insist on the ("merely") imaginary nature of deity.

Eliade constantly, if rather quietly, insists on the importance of the imaginary realm. For example, in *The Quest* he points out that initiatory motifs and symbols "partake of an *imaginary* universe, and this universe is no less important for human existence than the world of everyday life" (121). And in *Images and Symbols*: "that essential and indescribable part of man that is called *imagination* dwells in realms of symbolism and still lives upon archaic myths and theologies" (19). On a slightly different note which serves to explain his meaning somewhat further, he states that

> the novel must tell something, because narrative (that is, literary invention) enriches the world no more and no less than history, although on another level. (*No Souvenirs*, 205)

The point is that imaginative, narrative creations of the human mind, which can be enormously increased by a being of infinite creativity, themselves become a conditioning factor in human experience, and one which is historically revealed to be of the greatest significance. In this way Eliade seeks to increase the ontological weight of the sacred, which is itself an argument against those scholars who have detected a reductionist tendency in his work. "Reducing" the study of religion to the categories of the sacred (i.e., the really real) and to meaning, in no way "reduces" its ontological significance, rather its whole dynamic is to *increase* the significance of religious phenomena.

This itself may provoke two objections. First, it is not the task of scholarship to increase the significance of the objects of study, but to reveal what significance they inherently possess. However, the poststructuralist thought of, for example, Roland Barthes and Jacques Derrida, has suggested strongly that significance is not an inherent characteristic of objects or events, but is a creation of human interpretation. Thus the creation of significance is precisely the aim of interpretative scholarship. Secondly, it could also be said that Eliade has ultimately failed in his aim since he has certainly not increased the ontological significance of the sacred for his critics. To those who insist on the self-evident nature of the manifest as the real, the creative hermeneutics of Eliade's history of religions must remain the unwarranted proliferation of imaginary non-entities. Although this argument is itself subjective and relativist, insisting that lack of meaning for a certain group of people indicates actual lack of meaning, it is currently impossible to refute. Only time will tell whether Eliade's detractors will have more influence than his admirers, and thus whether he will finally be seen as succeeding in increasing the significance of the sacred or otherwise.

One indication would seem to be that the characterization of the study of religion as the mere proliferation of imaginary non-entities is a deliberate restriction of imagination, the denial of meaning, the refusal of creativity and little else. If it be accepted that the creative imagination has an effective role in assessing reality, then symbols, as creative, meaningful, pre-reflective devices, are not just symbols but also effective tools of the pre-reflective imagination. Only by denying the effective role of the symbolic imagination, can you support an argument which concludes that symbols are no more than symbols and that therefore an analysis such as Eliade's is erroneous. Such an argument is either totally unimaginative (imagination not being required to see that symbols are just symbols, this is simply an observation not a creative act) or it is wrong. It could likewise be suggested that if one is capable of imagining that imaginary ideas have real effects, then the restriction of an idea capable of infinite effects to the imaginary is finally no restriction at all.

THE IMPLICIT RELIGION OF MEANING

Implicit religion as a topic of study has attracted an increasing amount of attention in works such as Thomas Luckmann's *Invisible Religion* and Andrew Greeley's *Unsecular Man: The Persistence of Religion*, and the conferences of Edward Bailey's Network for the Study of Implicit Religion have attracted a wide variety of scholars from around the world. In October and November of 1991 a major conference on this topic was organized by the University of Leiden in Holland. The very term "implicit religion" must indicate an inappropriate definition or understanding of religion whereby something thought to be non-religious is in fact religious. Its religious nature is undetected. While Eliade did not use the term he evidently recognized aspects of the "modern mind" which might be called implicitly religious. Throughout his work Eliade maintains this emphasis:

> there is no such thing as a "pure" religious fact. Such a fact is always also an historical, sociological, cultural, and psychological fact, to name only the most important contexts. (*Quest*, 19)

However,

> a religious phenomenon will only be recognized as such if it is grasped at its own level, that is to say, if it is studied as something religious. (*Patterns*, xiii)

Eliade repeatedly insists that a religious phenomenon cannot be "reduced" to one of its other aspects. This is of little assistance if one lacks a functional definition of the religious, and as Eliade "doubt[s] the value of starting with a definition of the religious phenomenon" (*Patterns*, xiv), this does seem to be the case. Even Ricketts, a very well-informed scholar on Eliade, mentions this lack of definition (*Romanian Roots*, 186). However, I have described an underlying concept of religion which is theoretically coherent in Eliade's thought, although it lacks systematic expression.

Eliade considers the recognition of and response to an exemplary pattern to be not only essential to mythic behavior but also "consubstantial with every human condition" (*Myths, Dreams, and Mysteries*, 31). By way of the connection between myth, the sacred, and religion, one can detect an understanding of the response to an exemplary pattern as religious behavior. Religion is the response to the sacred. The sacred is that which is apprehended as the real, which is expressed in "sacred history" or myth. The essential element in mythic behavior is the response to the exemplary pattern. Thus the response to an example is religious, the imitation of an exemplar is religious. By these lights the influence of any cultural form over human behavior is religious and the recognition of meaning is the religious activity *par excellence*.

It should be pointed out that such a systematic analysis of terms is analytic in the Kantian sense: it is tautological or "circular" in the reciprocal dynamic of the hermeneutical circle. Eliade was well aware of this circularity in interpretation. Nor does "interdefinability" undercut the explanatory power of a theory, for Newton's physics is also interdefinable.[7] Although this may seem an extreme and possibly procrustean reading of Eliade, it must be remembered that he insists that "non-religious man descends from *homo religiosus* and, whether he likes it or not, he is also the work of religious man" (*Sacred and the Profane*, 203), and that "an areligious society does not yet exist" (*No Souvenirs*, 163f.). It would seem that the converse applies to Eliade's constant emphasis on the concrete manifestations of

---

7. See *Patterns*, 5–6; *Myths, Dreams and Mysteries*, 176; and Adrian Marino, "Mircea Eliade's Hermeneutics," 33, in *Imagination and Meaning*, for Eliade's self-awareness in this area.

religious fact. Not only is there no such thing as a "pure" religious fact, all religious facts being also historical, psychological, and so on, but there is no such thing as a "pure" historical fact, for example. All human facts, historical, sociological, psychological, are also implicitly religious. Everything is, or has been, or could be, religious (*Patterns*, 11). But the specific areas in which we will find religious realities involve the uncritical (or mythic, see above, p. 72f) valorization of socially constructed realities and the response to exemplary models. Both of which can be seen as the response to meaning.

The fundamental interconnection of religion and the response to exemplary patterns of behavior is reinforced in an important article of 1973, "The Sacred in the Secular World." Once again Eliade insists that modern, secularized humanity still occupies a sacred dimension. The sacred is said to be part of the human mode of being in the world, the awareness of a source of values (101). What is of value is that

> so long as modern man is interested in discovering the meaning of life, that meaning can serve as a model for human life, and thus is in the same family as the archaic myth which presented the exemplary model for ritual repetition. (102)

Modern humanity "looks for being and does not immediately call it being, but meaning or goals; . . . we do not see anything religious here; we just see a man behaving as a human being" (103). But Eliade's work finally insists that this *is* religious. He writes,

> when man becomes aware of his specific mode of being in the world, he realizes that he is a mortal being, that he is created. His creation is recounted mythically in a sacred history and he realizes that he is merely the result of what happened. (101–2)

This is not necessarily to say that humanity was created by an omnipotent, omniscient creator deity. That is a specific anthropogeny. Rather, it is the realization that human existence is finite and conditioned. "Sacred history" is that narration of that conditioning that is held to best account for what humanity is and why we are so and is thus accorded a positive value. To certain people, biological evolution, as the true account of the factors which produced and conditioned humanity, is their sacred history.[8] To others sociopsychological histories seem more apt, to still others economic or theological, or combinations of several styles. "The world of meaning of modern man plays the same function that myth plays among the primitive," says Eliade, and thus he cannot believe someone immediately when he consciously says that he is not religious ("The Sacred in the Secular World," 102).

---

8.   The tendency of evolutionism to slide over into the area of the overtly religious is well documented in Mary Midgeley, *Evolution as a Religion*, and the general tendency of narrow scientific explanation to be expanded into cosmology in Toulmin.

One's initial reaction to this might be to object that this is merely an extension of inclusivist theology of Karl Rahner's "anonymous Christian" variety.[9] That is, a fallacious universalization of certain specific categories of thought. However, in Eliade's case the elevation is not of any specific or provincial categories, but of the generic, human tendency to invest experience with meaning, to find in our environment adequate sources for a coherent response. It is worthy of note that the present incumbent of the Mircea Eliade Chair at the University of Chicago, Wendy Doniger, makes a similar correlation of myth, the sacred, and meaning. "To say that a myth is a sacred story is to say that it must have a religious meaning (though it need not be a story about the gods)." Myths, she says, "are about the sorts of questions that religions ask, ... basically about meaning itself" (*Other Peoples' Myths*, 28).

As we have seen, the concept of meaning expounded in the 1973 article is directly related to human behavior, to activity rather than merely to signification. Something—a text, a narrative, or an event, some element of experience—is invested with meaning in so far as one can detect in it an exemplary model or paradigm upon which one can base one's behavior, often through repetition of the sacred act, or imitation of the sacred characteristics, as in the *imitatio Christi*. However, Eliade does not restrict such bases for behavior to clearly recognizable religious examples. He speaks with astonishment and admiration of people finding meaning in incarceration, for example, Constantin Noica, Harry Brauer and his wife, Lena Constante (*Journal*, II, 315; III, 124).

Such a theory of meaning requires careful consideration to situate it among the variety of recent theories. It is evidently similar to the theories of American pragmatists such as Charles Sanders Pierce or William James. As James has said, "to develop a thought's meaning we need therefore only determine what conduct it is fitted to produce" (*Varieties of Religious Experience*, 427). However, Eliade goes further than they, conceiving a sort of "religious pragmatism" which never reduces the thought/behavior dichotomy to a simple polarity but keeps the iterative, reciprocal interaction open as a human unity, as Adrian Marino recognizes with his text-interpreter-text, interpreter-text-interpreter cycle (*Imagination and Meaning*, 20). I would suggest, however, that the iterative cycle is somewhat more complex, involving an ongoing evolution of the interpreter, effected in part by the inter-pretation: interpreter-*interpretation*-text-*interpretation*-interpreter. Or, to couch it in slightly different terms, reader-reading-text-reading-reader.

Eliade's thought here can also be compared to that of a philosopher such as Hans Georg Gadamer, who connects hermeneutics with praxis. Richard Bernstein

---

9. See, for example, Frank Whaling, *Christian Theology and World Religions*, 87ff.; Rahner, *Schriften zür Theologie*, vol. 6, 545–54; vol. 5, 136–58; vol. 8, 187–212 (trans. as *Theological Investigations* [Baltimore: Helicon Press, 1961]).

has said that "the most intriguing and most central theme in Gadamer's under-standing of philosophical hermeneutics is the fusion of hermeneutics and praxis" (*Philosophical Profiles: Essays in a Pragmatic Mode*, 61). Gadamer argues that the three subdisciplines of the older tradition of hermeneutics (understanding, interpretation, application), are three moments of a single process. Thus genuine understanding always involves application. "Application is neither subsequent nor a merely occasional part of the phenomenon of understanding but codetermines it as a whole from the beginning" (*Truth and Method*, 289). This not only involves behavior with meaning, but does so in the same recursive, iterative fashion I have indicated above, which refuses to give either one priority.

Eliade's affinities with the phenomenological school of interpretation to which Gadamer belonged are to be expected. Yet how does he relate to, say, the deconstructionist followers of Jacques Derrida? Ioan Culianu's conclusion that for Eliade the interpretation of religious mysteries is efficacious only on condition that *one does not succeed* in deciphering the message is reminiscent of deconstruc-tionism's infinite deferral of meaning ("Mircea Eliade et La Tortue Borgne," 82).

However such affinities may be seen, one thing is quite clear: for Eliade, the "living" myth is a myth specifically in so far as "it supplies models for human behavior and, by that very fact, gives meaning and value to life" (*Myth and Reality*, 2). By that very fact also, I might add, the myth is sacred. It is the apprehension of the myth as conveying "the truth par excellence," as being the repository of the real, the true, and the meaningful which simultaneously empowers it as an exemplary model and makes it a "sacred history." Although Eliade has said that "on the archaic levels of culture, the real—that is the powerful, the significative, the living—is equivalent to the sacred" ("The Structure of Religious Symbols," 506), he has also said that there is no break between the "primitive" world and the modern West (*Myths, Dreams and Mysteries*, 38). This is revealing as regards the question of "modern man."

"Modern man," then, can fall into one of three categories: simply contem-porary humanity, which in general has no substantial distinction from traditional religious humanity; those who recognize no sacred, no real, find no meaning and thus have nothing upon which to model their behavior; or those with the specific characteristic of valorizing a specific historical situation as "the real" with an attendant devaluation of human creativity. The first category is banal and of no real significance to our topic. The second is arguably non-existent and anyway more properly the subject of clinical psychiatry. It is the third category which constitutes Eliade's unique interpretation. It is this particular "modern man" for whom "God is dead," who has undergone the "second fall" who has "lost the possibility of experiencing the sacred at the conscious level" (*Sacred, Symbolism, and the Arts*, 83). But this is by no means a prevalent condition even today, and no wonder—

when meaning is seen in this sense of exemplary behavior, one must question whether the cryptic traces in a cloud chamber at the end of a particle accelerator can effectively be perceived as more meaningful than a religious text.[10]

10.   Culianu has pointed out that "the object of this mechanism [of interpretation] is of no real importance: in the extreme, water stains on the walls will serve." ["Ce sur quoi ce méchanisme s'exercise n'a pas vraiment d'importance: à la limite, on peut se servir des tâches de moisissure sur un mur (*Incognito à Buchenwald*)." My translation.] However, it should be remembered that this is "à la limite." Such restriction is neither normal nor beneficial. ("La Tortue Borgne," 82)

CHAPTER 17

Archaic, Modern, Postmodern

Much has been said in the previous chapters about Eliade's use of the term "modern." In the attempt to make some progress beyond Eliade's implicit system of thought, however, some account should be made of the post-critical, poststructural, turn of thought often called "postmodern." In the *Religion One Index* of periodical publications on religion for 1986 there is no classification for "postmodern." In 1987 four articles appear under that heading. By 1991 the number has increased to twenty-six and decreased only slightly to twenty-three in 1992. At the national conference of the American Academy of Religion in 1993, there were two consecutive sessions on postmodernism, from the Religion and the Social Sciences Section and the Philosophy of Religion Section. After attending both of these, I was irresistibly reminded of Oscar Wilde's description of fox hunting, except that here was not the unspeakable in pursuit of the inedible, but the indefatigable in pursuit of the indefinable. Certainly the horsemanship was admirable and the accoutrements impressive, but what were we chasing? No doubt there is more than a little truth in Ihab Hassan's statement that

> at worst, postmodernism appears to be a mysterious, if ubiquitous ingredient—like raspberry vinegar, which instantly turns any recipe into *nouvelle cuisine* (173).

This is, however, "at worst." Not all considerations of the postmodern phenomena need be inconsequential as some of the above articles have proven. It is my conviction that a consideration of certain "postmodern" characteristics in the thought of Mircea Eliade occasions a substantial improvement in the understanding of both Eliade and of the recent postmodern phenomenon. Finally, the theme of initiation can be positively applied in this process of reciprocal clarification.

231

Eliade has often been criticized as an uncritical, if not sentimental, champion of "primitive," archaic, or traditional cultures.[1] It seems peculiar, in this light, to argue for a recognition of *postmodernism* in his work. Careful inspection of Eliade's writings, however, reveal his "anti-historical" tendency to be counter-modern and remarkably close to later thought which has been labelled "postmodern." It is, I believe, a more accurate appreciation of Eliade to see him as at least a precursor of postmodernism than it is to reject him as either a sentimental champion of archaic traditions or as simply anti-historical. Eliade's understanding of modernity as constituted by a specific attitude to time is of some assistance in the ongoing attempt to bring clarity to our understanding of both modern and postmodern. "The jury is still out" on postmodernism—not only do we not yet know whether it is innocent or guilty, we do not yet know what it is (or might become). I am consciously attempting to clarify Eliade's thought by means of postmodernism and postmodernism by means of his thought in the understanding that both are to some extent imaginary constructs.

ELIADE AND POSTMODERNISM

Given Eliade's understanding of modern and archaic, and his evident support for the "archaic," premodern, strategy of valorizing human experience via imaginative, non-historical means, in what way can he be "postmodern"? A standard approach to this type of query would be to establish a working definition and investigate its applicability. In the case of "postmodernism," however, this approach is more than problematic. Hassan, one of the most extensively published literary critics on the subject, has said that postmodernism is "an equivocal concept, a disjunctive category, doubly modified by the impetus of the phenomenon itself and by the shifting perceptions of its critics" (173). Denied the ability to give a neat general definition of the category, the best that can be done is to give a series, a "catena," as Hassan prefers to say, of connected specifics which indicate affinities between Eliade and nascent postmodernism.[2]

1. Eliade's analysis of the modern distinction has marked affinities with that of certain later scholars who have been connected with postmodernism. In *The*

---

1. R. F. Brown points out that "many censure Eliade's 'science' as *not value free*. . . . His overriding personal wish to recover and preserve the religious values of the archaic perspective, . . . is itself a religious program of the sort that ought not to be distorting a genuine quest for knowledge" (433). Guilford Dudley, generally a supporter of Eliade, insisted that Eliade pursues "polemics on behalf of the archaic ontology" and wrote as an "apologist for an archaic soteriology" (*Religion on Trial*, 91). Ninian Smart went as far as to suggest that Eliade institutes "a modern form of the cult of the ancestors" (*Worldviews*, 169). See also Robert Baird, *Category Formation and the History of Religions*, 87.
2. I must also insist that I am seeking the affinities between Eliade's *critical*, his self-styled "scientific," works and postmodernism rather than looking for postmodern elements in his literary work. That is quite another project.

Philosophical Discourse of Modernity, a work which has been referred to as "Habermas's Postmodern Adventure" (George A. Trey), Jürgen Habermas agrees that the clear conception of modernism began with Hegel (4). Habermas points out that "in the Christian West the 'new world' had meant the still-to-come age of the world of the future, which was to dawn only on the last day" (5). The term was applied to the contemporary age only in the modern period. It is precisely this insertion of overarching categories of value into historical time, whereas they had previously been conceived external to profane duration, which Eliade indicates in his analysis of the modern. This results in the introspective subjectivity of the modern period:

> modernity can and will no longer borrow the criteria by which it takes its orientation from the models supplied by another epoch; *it has to create its normativity out of itself*. Modernity sees itself cast back on itself without any possibility of escape. . . . The "moderns," using historical-critical arguments, called into question the meaning of imitating ancient models; in opposition to the norms of an apparently timeless and absolute beauty, they elaborated the criteria of a relative or time-conditioned beauty. (Habermas, 7–8)

The similarity to Eliade's language of paradigmatic models and exemplary acts of the gods will be apparent to readers familiar with his work (for example, *The Myth of the Eternal Return*, 35ff.; *Sacred and Profane*, 203). Habermas later states that

> the modern age . . . had attained its self-consciousness by way of a reflection that prohibited any systematic recourse to such exemplary pasts [i.e., the primitive Church and/or the Greek polis]. (30)

This is even more strikingly in accord with Eliade's analysis in which,

> among primitives . . . any human act whatever acquires effectiveness to the extent to which it exactly repeats an act performed at the beginning of time by a god, a hero, or an ancestor. (*Myth of the Eternal Return*, 22)

2. In his introduction to the SUNY series on "constructive post-modern thought," series editor David Ray Griffin indicates that "a growing sense is now evidenced that we can and should leave modernity behind" (vii). The fact is that

> *Modernity*, rather than being regarded as the norm for human society toward which all history has been aiming and into which all societies should be ushered . . . is instead increasingly seen as an aberration. A new respect for the wisdom of traditional societies is growing. (vii)

The affinities with Eliade's thought here need no further emphasis (see, for example, *Myth of the Eternal Return*, 157ff.).

3. Brian McHale (*Postmodernist Fiction*, 3–25) argues that the shift from modernism to postmodernism is the shift in emphasis from questions of epistemology to those of ontology. Eliade's emphasis on the ontological question, then, is another thing which lends weight to his postmodernism. In *Imagination and Meaning* (191–95) Eliade's consideration of "A Detail from Parsifal" reveals the importance he attaches to "the *right question*" (193). Carl Olson has accurately pointed out that

> Eliade asserts that the right question is about the nature of being, an ontological question . . . to begin to find one's way out of the labyrinth of existence involves asking the ontological question. (101)

4. In his book-length study of Eliade, Carl Olson makes the comparison between Eliade and Derrida to some effect. However, there seems to be an assumption rather than a demonstration of disagreement. Olson writes,

> when Eliade asserts that Being is, he suggests that it is present. In other words, something is because it presents itself to a subject as the present object of perceptual experience. On the other hand, Derrida argues that we cannot presuppose Being as presence. (107)

Certainly, it is fundamental to the thought of Eliade that the experience of that which is held sacred generates the idea of real being. However, could this not in fact *agree* with Derrida that "we cannot *presuppose* Being as presence?" The sacred, that which really exists, true Being, is apprehended in certain specific hierophanies which the followers of a certain religion are prepared to recognize. To others the sacred remains concealed. Eliade repeatedly states that "the sacred is an element in the structure of consciousness" (*Quest*, i; *No Souvenirs*, 1; *The History of Religious Ideas*, vol. I, xiii). Thus Being cannot accurately be presupposed to be present in anything (any more or less than it is present in everything else). The recognition or ascription of Being to certain specific phenomena is a product of existential conditioning, a *construction*, and as such is liable to deconstruction. It seems probable that Eliade agrees with Derrida that the idea of Being is a second-order phenomenon derived from personal experience rather than "the most fundamental thing that all sentient beings have in common," as Olson takes it to be (101). It further seems possible that Eliade agrees with Derrida regarding the deferral of meaning (see above, p. 229f.).

5. Although I have specifically repudiated the epithet "anti-historian" as it was applied to Eliade, the affinities which Guilford Dudley specifically recognized between Eliade's opposition to historicism and modernity and that of Michel Foucault still stand. I cannot concur with Dudley's insistence that Eliade must "relinquish . . . empirical verification" and "surrender not only his claim to

empirical justification but also his claim to being a historian."[3] Eliade's opposition to the modern conception of history as valid in and for itself does not go that far. I agree with Dudley that "historical existence for Eliade is unintelligible and empty apart from the paradigm or model that structures it" ("Anti-Historian," 57f.). History, apart from the personal history of direct experience, is not an empirical category, and even as the personal history of direct experience it requires non-empirical models to give it structure and meaning. Thus Eliade would agree with Foucault that the deference to recorded history as an exhaustive, authoritative, and canonical account of the antecedent causes which ordain our current existential condition, is vacuous if not debilitating. Of course, few would deny the epithet "postmodern" to Foucault.

6. Notably one of the very few categories which turns up in all of Hassan's "catenas" of postmodern concepts (*The Postmodern Turn*, 93, 76, 172) is that of "immanences." He has described this category as

the capacity of mind to generalize itself in symbols, intervene more and more into nature, act upon itself through its own abstractions and so become, increasingly, immediately, its own environment. (93)

This has a precise correspondence with the function of the creative imagination as outlined above (295–99). Through the creative imagination and the use of symbols, humanity (as *homo religiosus*) participates in cosmogenesis, determines its own conditioning antecedents, becomes its own environment.

7.

What does postmodernity ordinarily refer to? Apart from the sense of living through a period of marked disparity from the past, the term usually means one or more of the following: that we have discovered that nothing can be known with any certainty, since all pre-existing "foundations" of epistemology have been shown to be unreliable; that "history" is devoid of teleology and consequently no version of "progress" can plausibly be defended. (Anthony Giddens, *Consequences of Modernity*, 46)

Eliade might not openly agree that all foundations of epistemology have been shown to be unreliable. Although his subjective apprehension of the real in hierophanies certainly could be argued to provide no reliable basis for knowledge, he takes it to be self-authenticating by definition. Yet, he certainly agrees that the investiture of history with a self-contained teleology is unsatisfactory.

---

3. "Mircea Eliade as 'Anti-Historian' of Religion," 58. See also University Microfilms International version of Dudley's doctoral dissertation, "Mircea Eliade and the Recovery of Archaic Religions," 352. UMI # 73 01 378 (1972).

8. In *Postmodern Biblical Criticism*, in the chapter "Towards the Postmodern: Historical-Hermeneutical Approaches," Edgar McKnight includes several authors whom he sees as moving in that direction. Characterizing the "reconstituted historical method" of Peter Stuhlmacher, McKnight describes a form of criticism in which

> the meaning and significance of the text are not limited to those meanings that conventional historical criticism is designed to recover. Meaning is not reduced to the nexus of historical relationships. Text is not simply a historical source. (85)

In *The Two and the One* Eliade said the same thing of all religious documents: an exhaustive account of the historical examples and of the dissemination of, say, the symbol of the sacred tree would not exhaust its significance. "Quite another work would remain to be done: to establish the meaning of this symbol, what it reveals, what it shows in its quality as a religious symbol" (196–97). Like Stuhlmacher, Eliade refused to limit the religious document to historical relationships (cf. *Quest*, chapter 1).

McKnight cites Norman Gottwald as another example of this postmodern trend because he emphasizes the Hebrew Bible

> as a literary production that creates its own fictive world of meaning and is to be understood first and foremost, if not exclusively, as a literary medium, that is as words that conjure up their own imaginative reality. (*The Hebrew Bible: A Socio-Literary Introduction*, 30)

Enough has already been said on Eliade's attitude to the creative imagination; I will not belabor the point here. It is also McKnight's intention to

> show that meaning is in part a result of the creative involvement of the reader and that present conceptualizations unnecessarily limit or obscure the possibility and reality of the reader's use of imagination in interpretation. (68)

Eliade's "creative hermeneutics" (for example, "On Understanding Primitive Religion," 503; *Quest*, 61f.) undoubtedly has the same implications. It is the power which we exercise to generate meaning in creative, imaginative interaction with documents, texts, or symbols, which themselves are historical realities lacking immediate transparency.

McKnight concludes that with postmodern criticism "the limitations of historical criticism have become evident" as has "the need to move beyond any form of a conventional historical paradigm" (75). Once again, if this is postmodernism, then Eliade represents postmodern thought.

9. To utilize the description given by R. J. Zwi Werblowsky,

> Eliade's Central European origins . . . impart a special cachet to his cultural scope. The Rumanian element perhaps deserves special emphasis: a "romance" culture surrounded by Slav and Balkan cultures, and, more-

over, connected to the German and Austrian cultural heritage through its Habsburg history. Add to this the special relationship of Rumania to French culture and we get a slight idea of the complexity of Eliade's background. (135)

That very complexity lends a pluralism and decentralization to Eliade's thought which can be likened to the postmodern turn.[4] It can be argued that postmodernism has been most strongly influenced by the same strain of German Romantic thought from Goethe to Nietzsche to Heidegger (and thence to Derrida) which influenced Eliade (see above, 14, 47n.1).

10. In *The Myth of the Eternal Return*, Eliade refers to Joyce as one of two "most significant writers of our day" (the other being T. S. Eliot, 153). This led Edward J. Cronin to compose an article on "Eliade, Joyce, and the Nightmare of History" in which he outlined striking similarities between the treatment of time and history in *The Eternal Return* and in *Ulysses*. In a more recent article Brian McHale has pointed out that

> as readers recognized almost from the beginning, *Ulysses* is *double*, two distinct texts placed side by side, one of them a landmark of High Modernism, the other something else. Only lately have we learned to call this "something else" postmodernism. ("Constructing (Post)Modernism," 1–2)

In the "modern" text mobile consciousness in a stable world gives rise to "parallax," different *views* of the world, but allowing the reader a confidence as to the establishment of those views in an objective reality. According to McHale, in the "postmodern" text the "parallax of subjectivities" gives way to a "parallax of discourses" (6) which no longer affords the reader any confidence as to the external existence of an objective world, allowing "no stable landmarks 'out there'" (6). Although we do

> "persuade ourselves" that we are able to "read through" the screen of style to the "real" events, . . . it seems that different readers are differently persuaded about what those "real" events might be. (7)

Similarly, in Eliade's analysis of archaic and modern ontology, we might persuade ourselves that we can read through to the "real" behind the traditions but all we find is our own "reality." In *Images and Symbols* (28), discussing the alienation of scholars of religion from "the cultured public," Eliade recognizes that "objectivity," like "reality," is subject to fashioning and personal persuasion. Perhaps it is not surprising that one for whom language itself was a hierophany, a revelation of the real, would come to a position influenced by Saussurean linguistics which imply that

---

4. I must thank Mark Shutes of the Anthropology department of Youngstown State University for this observation.

common sense itself is ideologically and discursively constructed . . . the "obvious" and the "natural" are not *given* but are *produced* in a specific society by the ways in which the society talks and thinks about itself and its experience. (Catherine Belsey, *Critical Practice*, 3)

Whether or not this is the case, as McHale says following Mikhail Bakhtin, "a discourse implies a world. . . . discourse parallax . . . implies ontological parallax, a parallax of worlds" (11). Likewise Eliade's alternative and subjective hierophanies reveal assorted sacred spaces and times, different ontologies to different people. His juxtaposition of "archaic ontology" and modern ontology is well known (*Myth of the Eternal Return*, 34–48). What is less well recognized is the implication that there is no one *general* archaic ontology but a whole series of *specific* archaic ontologies which share the common feature of being founded upon mythical rather than historical models. "Ontological perspectivism, the parallax of discourses, and the worlds they encode, is not a characteristic structure of modernist poetics; but it is characteristic of postmodernism." (McHale, "Constructing Postmodernism," 12)

THE INTERPENETRATION OF ARCHAIC AND POSTMODERN

This is more than enough to indicate some real affinities between Eliade and postmodernism. The question is whether these affinities reveal anything of interest about either the late scholar or the nascent nomenclature. One thing which must be borne in mind is the intermingling of elements. In a relationship similar to the concepts of history we treated earlier (p. 90), archaic, modern, and postmodern mingle in Eliade's work. They are not mutually exclusive traits or tendencies. In *Ulysses*, too, the modern and postmodern combine, and, as Cronin has pointed out, Leopold Bloom "is Eliade's primitive man" (435). He "has an arsenal of protective myths" (436), and although he is "the very embodiment of the 'scientific spirit' . . . ever ready with explanations" (437), Bloom has "a potato of magical value" (437). As Cronin explains, "Molly is a paradigm, made so by the creative mythicizing of Bloom's memory" (440), which

> makes live again, in all their freshness, all his senses that were, at that one "Great Time," most acute. . . . Bloom becomes his own paradigmatic self, for it was at that moment on Howth that he achieved an identity he never after achieved, yet that, by his creative memory, he never after lost. (442)

Thus an archaic element in *Ulysses* stands revealed to complement the modern *and* the postmodern revealed by McHale. Likewise, all three elements interpenetrate in the works of Eliade, despite the unquestionable emphasis on the archaic, the modern is there, as is the postmodern. The fact is that categories such as these cannot displace each other. They are constructs of the critics and analysts, convenient fictions despite their grounding in observation or their derivation from independent sources. The postmodernism in *Ulysses*, as in Eliade, does not displace the modern, nor yet the archaic, although *in our eyes* one may eclipse the other.

INITIATION INTO A MODE OF BEING

In *Myths, Dreams and Mysteries* Eliade refers to the prevalent belief "in many religions, and even in the folk-lore of European peoples" (234) that at the moment of death individuals relive in their memory the whole of their lives, our entire lives "flash before our eyes." He homologizes individual death to cultural transformation and sees the modern world's fascination with historicity as "a sign portending [its] imminent death" (234). However, it is only in this modern culture that death is an absurd passage into Nothingness. In the religious structures of all "archaic" cultures (and it must be remembered that this includes Christianity and all conventional religions) death is intelligible as a "Great Initiation" into a "new level of being" (236). The fear of the modern world in the face of its own demise is occasioned by this (unfounded) belief that the postmodern means the death of modern culture and equates to the total loss of real order and existence, the expulsion from the ordered sacred space into chaos. Incapable of valorizing the demise of the contemporary as the advent of a new order, the self-subsistent modern world clings to its old order, and "continues to struggle for meaning" (Eagleton, "Capitalism, Modernism, and Postmodernism," 70), rejecting the postmodern as anarchy, chaos, the entry into Nothingness and the eclipse of all meaning.

Initiation rites usually involve a symbolic death and rebirth (*The Sacred and the Profane*, 133) and Eliade sees the modern world, frozen by its fear of that symbolic death and unable to believe in any rebirth, trapped in the liminal state of transition from one level to the other, caught partway through a *rite de passage*. As he explicitly describes it,

> the modern world is in the situation of a man swallowed by a monster, struggling in the darkness of its belly; or of one lost in the wilderness, or wandering in a labyrinth which is itself a symbol of the Infernal—and so he is in anguish, thinks he is already dead or upon the point of dying, and can see no way out except into darkness, Death, or Nothingness. (*Myths, Dreams and Mysteries*, 237)

This, however, need not be the case. In what Eliade describes as "archaic" thought, "the end of the world is never absolute; it is always followed by a new, *regenerated* world" (243). In this light the advent of the postmodern does *not* mean the eclipse of the modern, any more than the modern has eclipsed the archaic. (Although if modernism were no more than the restriction of reality to historical materialism, perhaps it would.)

The very self-referentiality of the modern world, its restriction of reality to actual/historical categories, seems to have led to taking the structure of individual human life as indicative or even symbolic of the structures of cultural life when we could take the structures of cultural propagation—the destruction of present structures of culture in favor of new structures which involve the old order—as indicative/symbolic of the processes of individual life. Modern humanity has become the model rather than the measure of cultural progression. Archetypal models for human life give way to human models for collective life. Periods are seen as having individual existence which will cease on the inception of the new period. "Postmodernity" is thus seen by some quite incorrectly as implying the death of modernity. In fact, destroy the modern to create the postmodern and the modern is resurrected, reincarnated, in the "new" creation.

In such thought the postmodern refusal of historicism's restriction of meaning finds pragmatic application in the reduction of individual anxiety in the face of personal death and of collective inertia in the face of cultural metamorphosis. It is that inertia which has occasioned such resistance to postmodern thought. Post-modernism might (to its insistently modern critics) seem to imply only "a refusal . . . to countenance any objective facts, any independent social structures, and their replacement by a pursuit of 'meanings'" (Gellner, 29). It is rather a refusal to countenance historicism as a self-sufficient foundation upon which to raise an adequate *Weltbilt*. To the modern who insists that historical time is the only real time and the historical/material the only real reality, this refusal is a refusal of all facts and of all significance. To those who recognize the reality of the imaginary and the significance of creativity, it could mean "the highest freedom that man can imagine: freedom to intervene even in the ontological constitution of the universe" (*Myth of the Eternal Return*, 160–61).

Although Eliade gives more credence and more space to the archaic point of view, it could be credibly argued that he was simply directing attention to what had been lost, and at what cost. His conclusion, that humanity must choose "despair or faith" (159), stems from these considerations. A parallel conclusion is that the embrace of the postmodern does not (and will not) involve the jettisoning of all meaning and significance established by the modern. Despite the fact that postmodern attitudes imply a deconstruction (and thus destruction) of the modern world, the unavoidable reconstruction of a new cosmos (unavoidable because to live we must inhabit a world, even if it is a world of discourse) will always con-stitute a resurrection of the modern world.

George Aichele points out Todorov's understanding of fantasy as a question of explanatory strategies. The "uncanny" is bizarre but elicits a "natural" explanation. The "marvelous" is also bizarre but elicits a "supernatural" explanation. The "fantastic" arises in the moment of hesitation between the two—is this to be explained naturally or supernaturally? (325). Religion is essentially fantastic in that it requires both natural and supernatural explanations, the history of Jesus and Siddartha Gautama, the miracle of the Christ and the Buddha. Human life itself is finally fantastic, a constant dynamic hesitation between the natural and the supernatural, between knowledge and imagination. In Eliade's terms, "progress" (which is more accurately the maintenance of the dynamic of the hesitation, the constant escape from history in history) requires the periodic destruction of the cosmos, a return to chaos to *initiate* a new cosmogony. This requires a constant willingness to undergo the initiatory ordeal, to embrace the deconstruction of our cosmos so that it, phoenix-like, may be built anew.

> New paradigms are not formed from the integration of new data, but rather from a relinquishing of the old paradigm (which necessarily implies an immersion in the chaos of undifferentiated perceptions), in order to come up with a new way of seeing the problem. (*Myths, Dreams and Mysteries*, 231)

Homologous—symbolically equivalent—to this is the willingness to embrace and valorize our own individual death that we may have "eternal life." The Romanian *Miorița* (*Zalmoxis*, chapter 8) and Eliade's *Iphigenia* tell that tale clearly enough. In both cases an otherwise meaningless death is valorized by reference to mythic models; the conclusion of *Isabel and the Devil's Waters* also manifests this theme. For Eliade, and for those who embrace postmodern thought, in order to escape the whale's belly, to complete the *rite de passage*, we must be willing to embrace the imagination in our own sacred history—to accept the reality of that imagination, and the construction of that reality, to accept our involvement in the cosmogony through creative imagination. Both the secular humanist and the committed religionist have contributed to the present impasse, the humanist by denying the reality of their imagination, the religionist by denying their imagination of reality. And both do so because of the modern insistence on the restriction of reality to historical time. In this light "postmodernism" becomes another in a constant series of "modes of being" opened up to us by constant hierophanies, revelations of the real, and accessible through an initiatory ordeal involving the sacrifice of some part of the old mode, in this case the sacrifice of a self-assurance and epistemic certainty which at best may have been illusory and at worst, imperialist.

CHAPTER 18

Some Final Conclusions

One aspect of Eliade's history of religions is that its autonomy springs from the central place given to the specifically religious form of consciousness. It is specifically the study of hierophany, of the apprehension of the sacred in our necessarily profane existence: the tendency to valorize certain phenomena (be they historical or conceptual, they are necessarily mythical in the sense proposed here) as "of ultimate concern," upon which we are "absolutely dependent," which constitute our proper conditioning antecedents or origins, which is the source of significance and value in all other phenomena. Properly the study of religion would become the study of the cognition of value (cf. Frederick Ferré's "The Definition of Religion"). After the struggle to evict the provincial and the biased, to remove self-interest from the academic arena of religious studies, an attempt to reconstitute the study specifically as the study of "value cognition" may seem out of step. However, it not only serves to explain the perpetual crisis of the study—any study which seeks to deny that which is its proper object must flounder hopelessly—it also promises to restore philosophical coherence and open personal involvement to a field which has suffered from the lack of both. Western philosophy has, to a certain extent, been the study of the source of value. Unfortunately due to its particular post-Hellenic lineage, it has focused exclusively on the rational sources of value, or at least rationally supportable sources. It has deliberately rejected and refused those non-, or pre-rational sources of value, classified as traditional, mythical, religious, aesthetic, and so forth and, due to the ubiquitous nature of these sources, Western philosophy has largely failed to achieve the self-consistency which is the final validating characteristic of cognitive schemes.

MYTHS IN THE STUDY OF RELIGION

The whole development of the study of religion has been beset by contemporary "mythic" valorizations such as those discussed above, implicit by virtue of their currently valid status or acceptance, mythic by virtue of their finally pre-reflective persuasion. For example, the clamor for "origins" (cf. *Australian Religions*, xiv). The etiological function of myth (possibly the mythic nature of etiology) is one of the best known, most clearly documented, and obvious factors in the field of religion; it is seen in the Book of Genesis, the introductory cosmologies of the Puranas, the explanatory, origin-stories of "primitive" myths, among others. Yet it is still not easy to look on our own contemporary search for origins and explanations as itself religious in nature. As with Barth's religion/revelation dichotomy, the tendency is to separate one's own mythic structure, the contemporary, current myth, from the recognized structures of foreign (geographically, culturally, socially, or temporally) myth. In general, myth (as an emotional, prerational persuasion or support for a specific *Weltanschauung*) will be effective if it is etiological and will be firmly separated from the mass of other myths by virtue of its acceptance as valid. My myth is not myth, any more than my religion is religion. Scientific approaches to the study of religion are also susceptible to this criticism. Although theological approaches might be accused of invalidating themselves by beginning from an assumed given of divine revelation, the scientific mind begins from the "real" given of material existence and personal experience. The confidence of empiricism becomes suspicious. "Facts" are held to be real and true because they are experienced.

The introduction of phenomenological techniques into the study of religion seems to have constituted an attempt to free the study from the worst tendencies of its own subject matter: the tendency to unquestioning adherence to and absolute valorization of an orthodoxy (the "right" opinion). This aim may be seen to have been only partially successful. While phenomenology has operated as a necessary *interimsmethode*, liberating the scholar from the despotic dictates of institutionalized religions, it has failed to liberate from the equally despotic though more insidious dictates of a currently quasi-scientific orthodoxy. (I say "quasi" advisedly since such dictates are under constant attack within the scientific fields.) This is not to propose that "science is a religion" or any such sweeping claim. Rather it is simply to affirm that the application of a scientific methodology does not negate the characteristics of *homo religiosus*.

MYTH AND SCIENCE

Assuming this attitude of even "scientific" valorization to be reflective of genuinely religious tendencies, how does it relate to Eliade's thesis of "eternal return?" While it accords with his analysis of myth as the repository of the real, the true, and the powerful, it does not appear to accord with any desire to "escape history," certainly not to return to a previous time of pure beginnings. Proponents of this approach do not hanker after a period in the past when the clear and coherent flow of thought was unclouded by the muddying effluvium of subjectivity. We do, however, infer such a period to be both potentially achievable and desirable. We "believe" in the scientific method in W. C. Smith's sense, holding it in high esteem as a means of radically changing human life, actually in the technological revolution of the past and potentially in our own academic field. This attitude fits Eliade's understanding of religion. A basic human failing is recognized and a solution is not just proposed but embraced. *Illud tempus* is a period which, although not held to have actually occurred at some time in the past, is at least a potential if the mores of truly "scientific" enquiry be followed. This does, in fact, accord with Eliade's conception of *illud tempus* as the logic of this other time is neither linear nor strictly rational, and is certainly not historical. It is by definition the time sought after, the period of our desires, the condition which would prevail should people do as they ought to do. The fact that many religious traditions have held this period to have existed in fact at some previous point is a result of a less linear conception of time itself and a less hidebound attitude to self-expression, not to mention the obvious rhetorical advantages of such a claim. The desire to stress the very real potentiality of this condition naturally leads to the expression of its actual prior existence. The expression of *illud tempus* as actually having occurred already permits a persuasive, if circular, logic in which *illud tempus* was lost because of some fault, which has led to the current undesirable period. The reversal or redemption of that fault will then lead to the "restoration" of *illud tempus*. This allows for the fault and its correction to be described from both the point of view of the "fall" it has caused and the "salvation" it could effect. The "myth of science," because of its involvement with historicism, may repudiate the circularity of this traditionally religious argument, but it eventually uses the same mythic, that is, pre-reflectively valorized, argument in which the reversal of the human fault of irrationality is seen to lead to the sought-for paradise of perfect understanding.

The very exclusivity of the objectivist/realist, "scientific" position smacks of a religious stance. To claim that this is *the* correct manner of progress which will suffer no alternative, right for all people at all times, would be an absolutist valorization of a relative position characteristic of the religious devotee subject to recent Western disapproval. Since the advent of phenomenology discouraged openly exclusivist displays of religious affiliation in the academic field, the problem has not disappeared but has become more subtle and difficult both to recognize and to avoid. Once again, the sacred has been camouflaged and it has become unrecognizable.

Furthermore, a scientific study relies on a controlled, restricted body of data or of types of phenomena. It is a specific method for the solution of specific problems which have undergone specific definition. Religion, in this interpretation, relates to the experience of human existence, the hermeneutics of human apprehensions of the real. It is what-I-am added to all others to make what-we-are, and thus the methodology developed for the solution of well-defined problems is not (and this accepts perhaps not *yet*) generally applicable. Both scientific and traditional attitudes to the religious would accept that religion includes *primarily* that which we do not understand: primordial origins, abstract concepts such as justice (theodicy) and morality, experience (as a brute fact), and existence (likewise). Scientific methodology commences from a delineated group of phenomena (radiation, chemical interactions, mechanical relations, man in society, the mental life); hence the ultimate importance to the scientific method of analysis—the division of data into coherent, restricted groups or entities—is necessarily prior to such a method. Religion is immune to such restriction *a priori* since, holistically, every element of all religious phenomena implies reference to a cosmic, self-contained, all-embracing system, the sum total of (human) existence, and thus defies final analysis into a restricted classification.

Of course, certain areas of religion can be studied in this restricted scientific manner: historically or geographically restricted phenomena and specific social or psychological effects. But the phenomena of religion as operant in contemporary experience defy such restriction. Attempts to enforce such a restriction have led to the various misappropriations of the study, the countless and costly inadequate definitions (see, for example, Hans Mol, *Identity and the Sacred*, 1f.), and the insensitivity to the personal involvement of the scholar.

It is crucial that we understand as we restrict, as each such restriction will tend to reinforce the *Weltanschauung* from which it is made. Denial of the workings of the intuitive is disastrous because it does work to considerable effect. The attempt of the scientific to be exclusive is potentially as disastrous as any other exclusivity in academic studies: it creates an orthodoxy and thence a dogma essentially opposed to the development of knowledge.

While it is frowned upon for scholars to predispose the direction of their studies by any declaration of specific religious commitment, some scholars are actively arguing for a similar predisposition along the lines of a scientific, objective predisposition. This is troublingly close to a claim of possession of The Truth such as has been held to disqualify the institutionally religious from a realistic study of the phenomena of religion. That disqualification would not apply exclusively to the institutionally religious if it were seen that the secular scientific approach can be as "religious" and "mythological" as older forms of faith. The real grounds of disqualification from the process of the apprehension of the truth is the inability to admit to the relativity of one's own apprehensions. As Eliade maintains, "ignorance is, first of all, this false identification of Reality with what each one of us *appears to be or to possess*" (*Images and Symbols*, 59). It is absolutely crucial to this understanding of Eliade to realize that he challenges the common fundamental categories of thought: objectivity, reality, history, knowledge. He is thus working from a point of view which resembles the sociology of knowledge but insists upon the creative autonomy of the human spirit and the factual possibility of escaping from the brute conditioning factors of embodied existence.

GENERAL REVELATION

The preceding position does not argue for the complete unattainabilty of truth. Rather it allows for the recognition of truth in various visions of the real. As Roger Trigg has said

> the emphasis on commitment and the dismissal of the notion of reasons for it derives in part from the contrast drawn with science. Religious belief, it is thought, is radically different from the entertaining of a scientific hypothesis. . . . [the] point is that science and religion just involve different systems of thought, and what counts as "truth" in each is radically different. (*Reason and Commitment*, 36)

Eliade's indication of the fundamental equivalence (*not* identity) of all human attitudes to the real, does more than militate against this distinction. Even though it recognizes the difference between scientific and religious truth, and between Christian and Buddhist truth, it insists on a universal humanism which also militates against the pernicious consequences of patronizing conceptual toleration in extreme relativism.

It is worth recalling that Eliade insisted that the whole of profane time and existence is itself revelatory of the reality which underlies it. This is a sentiment that the most hardline empiricists would hardly deny. Yet it is one which supports the whole of Eliade's view of the religious. Here it can be clearly seen that Eliade subscribes to a doctrine of "general revelation." Both religious revelation and scientific methodology are reactions to a real state of affairs and are descriptive of a real, although necessarily subjective, orientation. For the believer, the existence of God is a real and positive effect upon life, and for the skeptic the *explanation* for the assumed existence of God is likewise a positive and beneficial recognition of the truth. The question, "But which is *true?*" holds no real validity outside of the paradigmatic structure necessarily adopted prior to the recognition of the "truth" of each statement. The truth of each conception stands in relation to the special revelations, the hierophanies, which animate each one.

While it exceeds the scope of this study to argue for the relativization of *all* truths, the relativization of truths concerning (supposed) realities external to our embodied experience and to the empirical world is certainly not an unreasonable claim to make. Nor does this result in a final loss of all criteria of judgment concerning the validity or utility of such conflicting "truths." I believe Eliade to have accepted the criteria of geographical and temporal extent. For example, in *Zalmoxis* he speaks of the *Miorița's* capacity for adaptation to "geographical and regional realities" (240). These factors have much to say about the applicability of religious paradigms or worldviews. However, it can soon be seen that even these criteria are founded in similar and equally relative or non-justified paradigmatic assumptions. To infer that a religious worldview which was evidently acceptable

for thousands of people for thousands of years must still have much to offer to the
constantly changing human condition is not based on any apodictic logic. But
likewise to assume the superiority of the more recent materialist worldview which
succeeds in increasing the immediate physical security of a privileged few while
threatening the long-term security of the totality of global life (and does that
without securing the mental contentment of even those few) is hardly more logical.
This attitude to general revelation in which the contents of personal experience (the
scientists' experience of particle accelerators as well as the mystics' experience of
ecstasy) are open to creative interpretation capable of uncovering real and valid
meanings, preserves a meaningful access to the true and the real. One is constantly
confronted with the true and the real if only one can interpret them suitably.

RELIGION AND LITERATURE

Eliade repeatedly states that literary criticism would be a richer source of
"inspiration" for the interpretation of religion than anthropology, sociology,
psychology, and so on, thus locating both religion and its study in the world of the
arts rather than the sciences. This attitude allows for the fundamentally intuitive
basis of all methodology, whereas the "scientific" approach depends on an covert
intuitive assumption of an apodictic basis and point of departure in the empirical
method.

In *Ordeal by Labyrinth* Claude-Henri Rocquet points out that

> if the religions and masterpieces of our culture are akin, then a hermen-
> eutic stance is clearly unavoidable. Because, after all, it is obvious to
> everyone that linguistic analysis cannot exhaust our relationship with
> Rilke or Du Bellay. We all know that a poem cannot be reduced to its
> mechanics or to the historical conditions that made it possible. and if we
> do reduce it to those things, then so much the worse for us! If we under-
> stand that in the case of poetry, then why can we no longer understand it
> in the case of a religion? (138)

Eliade heartily agrees. He makes the interpretation of literary and other creative,
fictional, or poetic products of human culture (and it should be recalled that these
words all have the same fundamental meaning of human fabrication) the model for
the interpretation of religion. To say this in a slightly different way: in Eliade's
view, language itself is a hierophany. It is revelatory of the real mode of human
being in the world. One consequence of this is that

> the "sacred history" of the Primitives ought to be considered a work of
> the human mind, and not to be demythologized in order to reduce it to a
> "projection" of psychological, sociological, or economic conditions.
> Reductionism as a general method for grasping certain types of "reality"

may help to solve Western man's problems, but it is irrelevant as a hermeneutical tool. [We must] take seriously these oeuvres—in the same way we take seriously the Old Testament, the Greek tragedies, or Dante, Shakespeare, and Goethe. (*Australian Religions*, xvii)

Rocquet calls Eliade "a very reserved, very reticent person, if not actually secretive" (179), which rather conflicts with Eliade's publication of his journals. One of his stated reasons for publishing them was

> to oppose that academic superstition, which is still alive in Anglo-Saxon countries and even in the United States, which consists in a tendency to depreciate the act of the literary imagination. As though a spontaneous, free creation is valueless in comparison with a purely scientific procedure. It's a very damaging superstition.

In support of his positive valorization of the act of literary creation, Eliade refers to a statement of Bronowski that

> the step by which a new axiom is added cannot itself be mechanized. It is a free play of the mind, an invention outside the logical processes. This is the central act of imagination in science, and it is in all respects like any similar act in literature. (Preface to the English edition of *Forbidden Forest*, vi; also *Symbolism, the Sacred, and the Arts*, 155)

It is this belief in the central importance of the creative activity of the imagination which leads Eliade to

> rebel against this so-called scientific positivism of academics who claim that literary creation is no more than a game, unconnected with cognitive activity. I believe just the opposite. (*Ordeal by Labyrinth*, 179)

Evidently he homologizes the processes of creative language-use to his understanding of religion. In so doing he has produced his own creative interpretation of religious data. This interpretation reveals hitherto unrecognized significance in our experience of religious pluralism.

THE CONTEMPORARY CONDITION

> The religious life appears complex even at the most archaic stages of culture. Among the people still in the stage of food-gathering and hunting small animals (Australians, Pygmies, Fuegians etc.) the belief in a Supreme Being or "Lord of the Animals" is intermingled with beliefs and culture heroes and mythological ancestors. ("Structures and Changes in the History of Religions," 351)

Likewise, religious life must be complex now. "Western man" cannot be a unique case of "living cut off from an important part of oneself, made up of fragments of a spiritual history he is incapable of deciphering" (*Two and the One*, 14) any more than *homo religiosus* can be simply the alternative to this, or "economic man" (*Patterns*, 127) a third type. Rather we are all complexes of these potential modes of being. Perhaps Eliade would have done better to bring this out more clearly, for I am convinced he did accept it. His writings often appear more complicated than is strictly necessary.

This apparent identification of contemporary, non-technological cultures with "archaic man" has led to much criticism of Eliade's anthropological approach. It takes too much for granted to be acceptable and is rejected by most contemporary anthropologists. It was also rejected by Eliade himself (*Australian Religion*, xivf.). Modern hunter-gatherers are still just that, *contemporary* people who live in a non-technological culture, and have a cultural history correspondingly longer than their ancestors'. However, the point stands that all contemporary religion appears complex, from sophisticated technologies to self-subsistent, hunting-gathering communities.

Eliade's language is undoubtedly misleading on the point of the identification of contemporary/non-technological and "inferior" ancient societies. He speaks of "advanced cultures," "superior cultures," "more highly evolved societies, (totemistic hunters, paleo-cultivators, pastoral nomads)" ("Structures and Changes," 351, 353). He does later clarify his position on this point (in *Australian Religions*, xii n. 2), and although we might deplore the apparent value-judgment implied by such terms, it must be borne in mind that they are used to refer to extant, not extinct, cultures— Eliade was well aware that "we do not have any documents concerning an ultimate 'first phase' of the religious life of primitives" ("Structures and Changes," 352). These terms have a contemporary referent. Although it may be dubious whether they are of any historical value, insofar as they serve to understand past events, they do possess validity as regards current religious phenomena.

In the light of Eliade's attempt to understand contemporary thought, many of his theories assume renewed significance. For example, his thoughts concerning "the disappearance of the cult of the Supreme Being and the substitution of other divine figures" (354), applies just as readily to his view of the contemporary situation as to the historical. That the Supreme Being of "primitive societies" has become a *deus otiosus* upon whom people only call *in extremis* is as much expressive of the current condition in which self-professed non-religious people will call upon the god of their own cultural background only in crisis situations. Eliade cites a prayer of the Selk'nam of Tierra del Fuego—"Do not take away my child; he is too little" (355)—addressed to the normally ignored supreme Being, a *deus otiosus* in Eliade's parlance. Surely we can all recognize here the contemporary situation of modern parents, usually thoroughly "secular," who will, internally if nothing else, call upon "God" to spare the endangered life of their child, at least to make the situation meaningful, to account for "why" such terrible events must be. It is unquestionably true that modern people are just as likely to call upon the otherwise *otiose* concept of a Supreme Being in a crisis.

Much of Eliade's writing can likewise be read as more authentically expressive of contemporary humanity than of any specific historical situation, more self-expressive and symbolic than previously recognized, despite its scholarly nature. His fear of dilettantism and of reducing the academic impact of his analyses of religious phenomena by having them connected to his fictional *oeuvre*, led him to attempt to divorce the two aspects of scholarly and creative writing completely, and although he has expressed regret that he did not attempt to write "beautifully" in his scholarship, he believed that he had succeeded in separating his scholarly from his literary work in a substantial sense. However, can one person ever be so split? The suggestive mode of his fictional authorship seems to carry over into his actual work. He states that

> ultimately, what I have been doing for the last fifteen years [1945–60] is not totally foreign to literature. It may be that my research will be regarded one day as an attempt to rediscover the forgotten sources of literary inspiration. (*No Souvenirs*, 119)

It certainly seems to be the case that his *homo religiosus* functions more as a symbol of humanity in its religious mode than as any actual example of human behavior. To criticize Eliade as though his *homo religiosus* were a putative past phase of human culture, represented now by contemporary, non-literate or non-technological tribes, is to misunderstand the implications of his thought (*Australian Religions*, preface) and unavoidably generates logical fallacies.

Similarly, I would suggest that other of Eliade's assertions might be better applied as a description of the contemporary situation than as a general laws of the historical development of religions. For example,

> the disappearance of the Supreme Being from the cult indicates man's desire to enjoy a religious experience which is "stronger," more "dramatic," and, though it is often aberrant, more human. ("Structures and Changes," 357)

The move from dependence on a Supreme Being and from mythic cosmogony to more "human" religious experience expresses a discovery of greater responsibility in the existential situation of humanity. The "*aham Brahmāmī*" of the Kenopanisad, as well as modern psychological research into the active nature of cognition (and the human embodiment of God in the Incarnation), indicate this same tendency toward the authenticity of human responsibility.

RELIGIOUS BELIEF AS SIGNIFICANT

The insistence that the events of religious belief must have occurred in historical time to have significance for contemporary humanity can be seen as symptomatic of the post-Christian world's obsession with historical time. It is primarily this obsession with the significance of historical event which fuels the problems of pluralism and exclusivism in contemporary religious studies. When a religious tradition is seen as a network of significant details, of texts, rituals, buildings, institutions, traditions, and faith, it has no necessary conflict with another tradition. But when it is seen as issuing from a historical event (the truth of which cannot be disputed as this truth is the final source of the tradition's authority) then disputes concerning the historical accuracy of interpretations are all too likely. Eliade recommended accepting the existential significance of religious statements rather than challenging their historical or empirical accuracy (*Quest*, 66ff.). As Origen recognized long ago, the possibility of establishing historical apodicticity, even of factual events, is tenuous indeed. He recognized the near impossibility of "an attempt to substantiate the truth of almost any story as historical fact, even if the story is true, and to produce complete certainty about it" (Contra Celsum 1; 42, see R. M. Grant, *The Earliest Lives of Jesus*, 10ff., 65, 71; Eliade, *Myth and Reality*, 165).

One of the implications of this interpretation is the suspension of any belief in the necessarily greater significance of historically accurate description and its concomitant insistence on the relative insignificance of "mere" human creation or "fictions."[1] A steady devaluation of the products of the human imagination has accompanied the valorization of historical factuality which Eliade sees as a product of Judaeo-Christianity. It is a religious apprehension specific to one cultural tradition, although it gained ascendancy via "First World" colonialism and technological supremacy.

In this interpretation, religious rather than historical language can be seen as the language of significance. When a believer states that Jesus of Nazareth is God Incarnate, he states concisely and in traditional language, the significance of Jesus. (It should go without saying that significance is always significance *to* . . .) In these terms it is pointless for the non-believer to claim that Jesus is not *historically* God Incarnate since this is simply a statement of his or her personal affirmation of the significance of historical facticity. The *fact* remains that Jesus possesses this transcendent significance to certain people.

Unfortunately, modern believers are all too likely to confuse traditional with historical language, to attempt to restrict significance to the realm of the historical, to commit the historicist error of grounding their faith in a presumption of historical factuality, despite Kierkegaard's warning, and thus to fall prey to the terror of history. Confronted with modern technology and research techniques, claims of strict historicity are difficult to substantiate; thus a religious tradition whose significance is seen to reside in historical events of the distant past will suffer a loss

---

1. "Fiction—act of fashioning, to shape, fashion, feign—1a: something invented by the imagination or feigned; specif.: an invented story." *Webster's Ninth New Collegiate Dictionary.*

of credibility. Rather, for the academic interpreter, the significance must be seen to reside in elements present to experience: the meanings of the traditional narratives, arts, and rituals, accessible through interpretation, the ability of the institution to assist in the spiritual life of the individual and the community, and so on.

DEMYSTIFICATION, REDUCTION, FUNDAMENTALISM

Within the academic study of religion Eliade considers reductionism and "demystification" to be roughly homologous. Referring to the common belief that the village, temple, or house is situated at the center of the world, he says,

> there is no sense in trying to "demystify" such a belief by drawing the attention of the reader to the fact that there exists no Center of the World and that, in any case, the multiplicity of such centers is an absurd notion because it is self-contradictory. . . . On the contrary it is only by taking this belief seriously . . . that one succeeds in comprehending the existential situations of a man who believes that he is at the center of the world. (*Quest*, 69)

If my interpretation of Eliade's approach be allowed then such a statement can be made, *mutatis mutandis*, for all religious claims. Only by "taking seriously" (i.e., investigating the existential significance rather than challenging the historical accuracy) the various beliefs of a religion might one succeed in comprehending the existential situation of the people who hold those beliefs. The question raised here is whether this increase in mutual understanding can be seen as a valid goal for the study of religion.

Generally "demystification does not serve hermeneutics" (69), particularly when seeking to comprehend the existential situation of people who hold beliefs different from one's own. The facts are that different people experience the same events and objects as possessing different significance and articulate their existential situations in different ways. If we seek to understand these situations, to assimilate the new data, we must not focus on traditional beliefs of our own which prevent us from appreciating the significance perceived by the people under consideration (such as the identification of historical accuracy with truth). Instead, we must attempt to "take seriously" the perceptions of significance, the articulations of the existential situations. Not only does Eliade equate reduction with demystification as discussed here, he also equates it with fundamentalism. He describes the reductionist method as "the reduction of all possible significations to only one proclaimed 'fundamental'" (*Symbolism, the Sacred, and the Arts*, 6). In combination with his understanding of ignorance being primarily the false identification of reality with appearance, it can be seen that reductionism is homologized to fundamentalism in the religious sense. For Eliade there is one universal fault: the dogmatic insistence on the equation of opinion with reality.

What is finally irreducible is the religious *perspective* or attitude. Not in the sense that it cannot be analyzed into any component parts, but rather in the sense that it cannot be translated into any other perspective without an essential loss—the loss of its compelling nature to the religious believer. The viewpoint of the believer *is* the viewpoint of the believer. Accounting for one's disagreement with that viewpoint says more about oneself than it says about the believers, who are the proper object of the study of religion. Exclusive focus upon the faults, weaknesses, and inconsistencies or self-contradictions of the religious viewpoint says, "this is why *I* do not find this perspective compelling, why I am not convinced by it." Only an appreciative consideration tells the reader about the religious perspective under consideration rather than about the critic. "This is why this point of view is compelling, this why and how it makes sense." To do anything less misses its essentially religious element, its compulsion, its power, its sacrality, its cognition as reality.

Similarly, Eliade said of critics of his literary works,

> the problem posed . . . is not how to decipher the "symbolism" of the story, but, allowing that the story has "enchanted" me, has convinced me, how to interpret the message which is hidden in its reality. (Translated from the Romanian in Ricketts, "Myths for Moderns" cf. *No Souvenirs*, 308f.)

To explain why a perspective on reality, an apprehension of the sacred, a hierophany, is *not* recognized is to refuse the hierophany, to make it less than it is to the believer, and it is specifically that element of compulsion, of power, of irresistibility, which is the legitimate object of the study of religion.

Reductionist strategies are devices which may tell us a great deal about the perspective of those who embrace them, and as such they are a legitimate form of analysis. However, if our primary object is religion and its specific manifestations in forms of belief, then these strategies are incapable of revealing the innate compulsion of those forms for those who hold them and to whom Marxism, psychoanalysis, and so on are foreign ideologies. Perhaps this is why a writer such as Eliade cannot finally escape being "reductionist" himself to a certain degree in that he, too, tells his reader as much if not more about himself than he does about his subject (or object). And yet, if the compunction to believe, the internal coherence, the strengths, the power, can be communicated, then at least as much has been said about the religion in question, about the fact of its existence as a compelling perspective on reality, as has been said about the critic. It should be noted in this context that what is *sui-generis* about religion and religious studies is their concern with the origination and maintenance of intuitons of the real—not some privileged access to transcendent ontologies but the *presumption* of such access constitutive of *homo religiosus*.

No doubt such a schema is irreducibly plural, but a plurality of views of the world does not equate to no world, a plurality of foundations does not equate to no foundation, and a plurality of centers does not equate to no center. To argue that a plurality of centers equates to either an amorphous or an infinite world, to chaos or transcendence, or to argue that a plurality of foundations equates to the incommensurability of alternate *Weltbilds*, is to ignore the essentially metaphoric nature of these images (and symbols) and to refuse the compulsion of the image and symbol of the perspective. The blind men's various different descriptions of the elephant does not equate to a non-viable life form; the elephant still lives and breathes and possesses all the potentialities of a biological organism. The plurality of religious perspectives does not equate to a non-inhabitable cosmos, to chaos or incommensurability. It simply indicates a cosmos which is larger than any given perspective upon it. So the perspectives of contemporary scholars such as Segal, Wiebe, Strenski, or Penner themselves are valid objects of the study of religion, which is the study of world constructions, of cosmic plurality. Although, as examples of modern men they are in their own right fascinating, the study of the traditional systems of cosmic conceptions and their propagation is the legitimate object of the broader study of religion. A reductionist approach seeks to translate the alternative interpretation of the elephant into terms conformable to one's own experience/ interpretation. It assumes that the other interpreter is mistaken, misled, misinformed, mendacious, or malicious—anything but accurate. If he says it is a tree when I *know* it is a wall, then his misdirection must have an explanation, and one which resolves his description as a tree into what is really a wall. Thus the perspective of the other is reduced to one's own, the local is taken as the universal, the province as the empire.

THE ACADEMIC ENVIRONMENT OF RELIGIOUS STUDIES

The study of religion—far from being an undertaking of the individual scholar who then consents to publish or lecture on his or her findings—is an institutional affair. Most scholars are employed by institutions of education for the specific purpose of lecturing, of communicating their understanding of religious phenomena to students who, one way or another, pay for the privilege. The *sine qua non* of such an organization is that the lecturer is more informed about the subject than the students and that the students will thus benefit from their exposure to their lectures. This is true of all subjects. In the field of the study of religion, our fundamental position is one in which the observable facts are that throughout recorded history and across the terrestrial globe, human societies have produced systems founded in the imaginative manipulation of non-empirical elements which explain and encourage particular reactions to existential situations. Individuals react to these systems in differing ways and to differing degrees. Some devote their lives completely to the pursuits recommended by religion; many largely ignore the spiritual exhortations of their traditional cultures. It is an evident recommendation of contemporary Western cultural tradition, and one with which I agree, to critically inspect especially those recommendations which are made most strongly and with least empirical support—that is, what I have identified as myth.

However critical our assessment of the mythic traditions of our own and of other cultures may be, it can hardly be adequate to the demands of institutional education to simply acquiesce in our own inability to respond positively to the mythic valorizations of cultural traditions other than our own. We cannot respond to the inquiries of students regarding the meanings of religious phenomena with the assertion that, since they have no meaning to us, then they have no meaning. To give an example: a scholar of religion could lecture on Southeast Asian Buddhism and point out that Buddhist sanghas receive considerable charitable support from the impoverished laity, in return for which the laity receive "spiritual merit." That scholar has, after perhaps years of careful research, found no acceptable meaning to the term "spiritual merit" and thus utilizes it as an empty phrase, devoid of any meaning save as a means of persuading the peasants to part with their hard-earned material wealth. The student audience will then be confronted with a religious system at whose center resides a vacuum of insignificance. The lack of meaning of the term "spiritual merit" will evacuate the whole cultural phenomenon of inherent significance and into this vacuum will be drawn the pre-existent cultural biases of the student: perhaps the understanding that anyone who persuades another to part with material goods for a "merely" imaginary exchange is a "confidence trickster" and should be punished under law.

In order to avoid this situation, in which the bare phenomenal facts of religion become empty vessels to be filled with our own preconceived ideas, it is necessary to attempt to explicate the meaning of those facts. It is necessary to assume that those facts do have a meaning, even if we are presently utterly incapable of its recognition. (The alternative in this case is to assume that the peasants of Southeast Asia have been consistently deceived by a malicious organization for over two thousand years. Whereas, of course, some of us in the West have thrown off the oppressive yoke of superstitious ideology.) It could be argued here that if a religious phenomenon has no meaning to the scholar, especially after some time of study, then there is no meaning there. It must be accepted that in some ways this is true, but this is precisely why Eliade exhorts the scholar of religion to seek for meanings "even *if they aren't there.*" This statement seems to provoke some disgust in Ivan Strenski (*No Souvenirs,* 85; "Love and Anarchy in Romania," 392ff.). However, when it is seen in the sense of limited semantic relativism implied here, it is not as offensive as would be the *ex nihilo* creation of meaning which Strenski seems to fear. Rather, the assumption is that the religious datum in question did (or does) have meaning for the believers in question and it is the task of the interpreter to seek to expound that meaning. Thereby the whole religious structure involved in the examination will be imbued with its own significance, rather than dominated by predispositions.

In this way, both scholars and students will come to realize meanings which are new to them, rather than simply reiterating pre-existent semantic structures and relationships. In this context it is crucial to realize that, as with Eliade's analysis of symbol, the meanings of religious phenomena are polyvalent. Thus there is no singular, correct meaning to which the scholar is restricted (or to which Eliade claimed to have access, "Love and Anarchy," 401). Of course, particular meanings for particular people do exist and, insofar as they are capable of verification, they are open to debate. To return to the previous example, a scholar could be right or wrong in seeking to describe the meaning of "spiritual merit" for actual people in an actual town in Thailand.

THE AIM OF THE STUDY OF RELIGION

It is Eliade's advice that "an historian of religions must resist the temptation to predict what will happen in the near future" (*Occultism, Witchcraft and Cultural Fashions*, 67). Evidently, predictability is not a criterion of evaluation in which he puts any great store. From the context in which this statement is made, it is clear that he considers prediction to be the stock in trade of the astrologers. This is, in fact, an extremely significant statement, made in a surprisingly nonchalant manner. If the interpretations of the historian of religions cannot be verified by accurate prediction, then what is the criterion of accuracy, truth, success, or whatever it may be termed? Judging from internal evidence, I think the answer is *significance*, meaning, reality. In other words, the sacred. So the hermeneutical circle closes in the sense that the very "faculty" which recognizes the sacred per se at the outset of the process of interpretation is, finally, the same criterion which recognizes the value of the conclusion. Thus Eliade's position, too, requires some positive initial and intrinsic valorizations. It, too, is mythic to that extent; it, too, is *religious*.

To those critics of Eliade who might greet this statement with some relish, receiving it as proof that Eliade is proposing another religion among many rather than an objective way of assessing religion as a phenomena, it must be said that this is wholly consistent with his procedural assumptions. Humanity is initially seen as inherently religious. Religion is the expression of the fact of our embodied existence in the world and our constant and ongoing interaction with the reality encountered in that world. Eliade insists that "to be, or to become, human means to be religious" (*Quest*, preface). Having made such a contention, he could hardly be expected to somehow escape his own classification of humanity. Nor is the closing of the hermeneutical circle evidence of its vicious tautology. Within that circle has been inscribed all actual human experience of the world (the history) and all coherent imaginary universes which express the valorization of that experience (of religion). Empirical criteria of evaluation of religious phenomena have been suggested—their temporal and geographical extent and the ability of the religious phenomenon to generate new appraisals, new significances, new meanings which ensures this spread. This interpretation also implies a methodology which I feel to have been clearly demonstrated by this inspection of the reactions to and interpretations of the thought of Mircea Eliade. In order to understand the universes of religion, a certain critical but positive and imaginative valorization is required. If one enters on the quest for truth in the interpretation of religious data convinced that one already possesses the only infallible criterion of evaluation, be it faith in a venerable text or a particular system of pan-critical rationalism, one is hardly predisposed to recognize the true meaning of what other people have apprehended as the real, the true, and the sacred.

A PRAGMATIC PLURALISM

Eliade's system cannot support the valorization of any exclusive religion, but rather of religion itself, of religiousness, which he perceives to be a human universal. His thought is inherently, almost *a priori*, pluralist. It thus militates against "areligiousness" as a form of self-deception (typical, I may say of the "modern" consciousness which paradoxically seeks to radically dissociate itself from the very history which it valorizes so highly), but it cannot militate for any specific form of religion. It does, however, imply a series of criteria by which different forms can be compared. These include the extent to which religious belief relieves the subjective pain and suffering occasioned by the embodied experience of the human individual (the "terror of history"), which is directly related to the personally apprehended meanings and significations of that belief, which in their turn contribute to the geographical and temporal spread of specific beliefs.

The equation of the sacred and the real in the history of religions has one crucial, *a priori* assumption and intention: it places all individual human apprehensions on an initially equal level of opinion (doxa) rather than granting any one apprehension (usually one's own) a privileged access to the real. Assuming this attitude, one can never begin a study with the presumption that one knows, finally and certainly, what "the real" actually is. Not only is this in consonance with much recent critical theory concerning epistemology and the collapse of foundationalist methodologies and correspondence theories of truth, but it also allows an *a priori* sympathy with conflicting belief systems. Rather than commencing with the attitude that I know what "truth" and "reality" are, and thus that I know that beliefs which conflict with my apprehensions are positively "wrong," the historian of religion then commences with the self-knowledge of what he or she believes to be the real and the recognition that others equally believe their apprehensions to be of "the real." Given this assumption of what we might call "foundational equality," we are then quite free to apply those criteria of judgment which we have established. Hopefully, through critical and empirical methods, we can discern the significance of belief systems and their concomitant behavioral patterns without the dangerously misleading assumption that those criteria are somehow possessed of a superhuman warrant.

The whole process of thought whereby these conclusions were attained might be seen as a personal re-enactment of the developments within the history of religions, which began as a process of Christians inspecting pagans and evolved through those stages which W. C. Smith has characterized as "us/them, me/you, we/all" ("Comparative Religion—Whither, and Why?," 34). It is in order to attain to this "we/all" understanding that the scholar of religions adopts a humanist approach which concedes that no one body of people has exclusive and sole access to any divine Truth and is thus distinguished above all other people. (In making such an assumption of exclusivity, one certainly becomes the champion of a mythical belief rather than the scholar of human religiousness.) Whether exclusive access is established by way of special revelation through a traditionally venerated text or through a scientific or empirical methodology is quite inconsequential. It is the immensely destructive power of the concomitant assumption of justification thus avoided which is of consequence. In adopting such a position scholars are not deprived of all relation to truth and reality. We are forced to accept, however, that our personal relationship to the real, the sacred, is necessarily one of belief rather than one of certain knowledge.

Bibliography

I. PRIMARY SOURCES

A. Romanian Publications.

This section contains publications of Eliade's not published in English. Although some have been translated and published in French and some have been translated and provided to me by Mac Linscott Ricketts (see §D below), many have not been translated from the original Romanian, and thus I have not read them. I include this list for completeness of bibliographic reference and to give the reader a more accurate impression of Eliade's early publishing career. This section includes novels, travel writing, personal philosophy, and technical publications on the history of religions, but excludes a considerable volume in periodical publications. For these, see the Allen and Doeing bibliography of 1980.

Isabel si Apele Diavolului ("Isabel and the Devil's Waters"). Bucharest: Editura Nationala Ciornei, 1930. Unpublished English translation by M. L. Ricketts.

Soliloquii ("Soliloquies"). Bucharest: Editura Cartea cu Semne, 1932.

Intr'o mânastire din Himalaya ("In a Himalayan Monastery"). Bucharest: Editura Cartea Româneasca, 1932.

Intoarcerea din Rai ("Return from Paradise"). Editura Nationala Ciornei, 1934.

Lumina ce se Stinge ("The Light That is Failing"). Bucharest: Editura Cartea Romaneasca, 1934. Unpublished English translation by M. L. Ricketts.

Oceanografie ("Oceanography"). Bucharest: Editure Cultura Poporului, 1934.

India. Bucharest: Editura Cugetarea, 1934.

Alchimia Asiatica ("Asiatic Alchemy"). Bucharest: Editura Cultura Poporului, 1934.

Santier ("Work in Progress"). Bucharest: Editura Cugetarea, 1935.

Huliganii ("The Hooligans"). 2 vols. Bucharest: Editura Nationala-Ciornei, 1935.

Domnisoara Christina ("Mistress Christina"). Bucharest: Editura Cultura Nationala, 1936.

Sarpele ("The Snake"). Bucharest: Editura Nationala-Ciornei, 1937.

Scriere literare, morale si politice de B. P. Hasdeu ("The Literary, Moral, and Political Writings of B. P. Hasdeu"). 2 vols. Bucharest: Editura Fundatia Regala pentru Arta si Literatura, 1937.

Cosmologie si Alchimie Babiloniana ("Babylonian Cosmology and Alchemy"). Bucharest: Editura Vremea, 1937.

Nunta in Cer ("Marriage in Heaven"). Bucharest: Editura Cugetarea, 1938. Unpublished English translation by M. L. Ricketts. [This novel was translated into Italian in 1983 and won the Elba-Brignetti prize for the best novel in Italian in 1984. See Ricketts, *Romanian Roots*, 1160–78 for an English language précis of the novel.]

Fragmentarium ("Essays"). Bucharest: Editura Vremea, 1939.

Mitul Reintegrarii ("The Myth of Reintegration"). Bucharest: Editura Vremea, 1942.

Salazar si revolutia in Portugalia ("Salazar and the Revolution in Portugal"). Bucharest: Editura Gorjan, 1942.

Comentarii la legenda Mesterului Manole ("Commentaries on the Legend of Master Manole"). Bucharest: Editura Publicom, 1943.

Insula lui Euthanasius ("The Island of Euthanasius"). Bucharest: Editure Fundatia Regala pentru Arta si Literatura, 1943.

Nuvele ("Short Stories"), Madrid: Editura Destin, 1963.

(Throughout the remainder of this bibliography I have mainly restricted myself to works of Eliade available in English. However, I have included works in French where I have consulted these, and, rarely, works of importance in other languages. In this next section initial dates are of first publication, regardless of language. Brackets contain alternative titles.)

B. Non-Fiction: Books

1936 *Yoga: Essai sur les origines de la mystique Indienne.* Paris: Guenther, 1936 (This is a French translation of Eliade's Ph.D. thesis presented in Bucharest in 1933.)

1938 *Metallurgy, Magic, and Alchemy.* Paris: Guenther, 1936.

1949 *Patterns in Comparative Religion.* London: Sheed and Ward, 1958. (*Traité d'Histoire des Religions.*) Translated from the French by Rosemary Sheed. *Cosmos and History: The Myth of the Eternal Return.* Princeton: Princeton University Press, 1954. Translated from the French by Willard Trask.

1951 *Shamanism: Archaic Techniques of Ecstasy.* London: Routledge and Kegan Paul, 1964. Translated from the French by Willard Trask.

1952 *Images and Symbols: Studies in Religious Symbolism*. London: Harvill Press, 1961. Translated from the French by Philip Mairet.

1954 *Yoga, Immortality and Freedom*. London: Routledge and Kegan Paul, 1958. Translated from the French by Willard Trask. This work has considerable alterations from the earlier French publication.

1956 *The Forge and the Crucible*. London: Rider and Co., 1962 (*Forgerons et Alchimistes*.) Translated from the French by Stephen Corrin.

1957 *Myths, Dreams and Mysteries: The Encounter between Contemporary Faiths and Archaic Realities*. London: Harvill Press, 1960.
The Sacred and the Profane: The Nature of Religion. London: Harcourt Brace Jovanovich, 1959 (*Das Heilige und Das Profane*.) Translated from the French by Willard Trask.

1958 *Rites and Symbols of Initiation*. London: Harvill Press, 1958 (Birth and Rebirth.) Translated from the French by Willard Trask.

1962 *Patañjali and Yoga*. New York: Funk and Wagnalls, 1969. Translated from the French by Charles Lam Markmann.
The Two and the One. Chicago: University of Chicago Press, 1965 (*Méphisophélès et le Androgyne*.) Translated from the French by J. M. Cohen.

1963 *Myth and Reality*. New York: Harper & Row, 1963. (*Aspects du Mythe*.) Translated from the French by Willard Trask.

1967 *From Primitives to Zen: A Sourcebook in Comparative Religion*. New York: Harper & Row, 1967. English original.

1969 *The Quest: History and Meaning in Religion*. London: University of Chicago Press, 1969 (Revised as *La Nostalgié des Origins*, 1971.) English original.

1970 *Zalmoxis, the Vanishing God*. Chicago: University of Chicago Press, 1972 (De Zalmoxis à Ghengis Khan.) Translated from the French by Willard Trask.

1971 *Australian Religion*. London: Cornell University Press, 1973. English original.

1975 *Myths, Rites and Symbols: A Mircea Eliade Reader*. Edited by W. C. Beane, and W. G. Doty. New York: Harper & Row, 1975.

1976 *Occultism, Witchcraft and Cultural Fashions*. Chicago: Chicago University Press, 1976. English original.
A History of Religious Ideas, vol. I: *From the Stone Age to the Eleusinian Mysteries*. Chicago: University of Chicago Press, 1978 (Paris: Payot, 1976.) Translated from the French by Willard Trask.

1978 *A History of Religious Ideas*, vol. II: *From Gautama Buddha to the Triumph of Christianity*. Chicago: University of Chicago Press, 1982 (Paris: Payot, 1978.) Translated from the French by Willard Trask.

1978 *Ordeal by Labyrinth: Conversations with Claude-Henri Rocquet*. Chicago: Chicago University Press, 1982. Translated from the French by Derek Coltman.

1980 *What is Religion*. (Edited with David Tracy.) Edinburgh: T. and T. Clarke, 1980.
1983 *The History of Religious Ideas*, vol. III: *From Muhammad to the Age of the Reforms*. Chicago: University of Chicago Press, 1985 (Paris: Payot, 1983.) Translated from the French by Alf Hiltebeitel and Diane Apostolos-Cappadona.
1985 *Briser le Toit de la Maison*. Lausanne: Gallimard, 1985. French original.
1986 *Symbolism, the Sacred, and the Arts*. Edited by Diane Apostolos-Cappadona. New York: Crossroad, 1986. Translations from the French by Diane Apostolos-Cappadona and Frederica Adel, Derek Coltman, and from the Romanian by Mac Linscott Ricketts.
1987 *Encyclopedia of Religion* (Editor in Chief.) New York: Macmillan, 1987.
1991 *The Eliade Guide to World Religions* (with Ioan P. Couliano and Hillary S. Wiesner.) San Francisco: Harper, 1991.

C. Articles and Interviews

"Cosmical Homology and Yoga." *Journal of the Indian Society of Oriental Art* 5 (1937): 188–203.
Review of *Religion in Essence and Manifestation* by G. van der Leeuw in *Review d'Histoire de Religions* 138 (1950): 108–11.
"Techniques de l'Extase et Langages Secrets." *Confirenze di Istituto Italiano per il Medio ed Estremo Oriente*. Vol. II (1953): 1–23.
"The Yearning for Paradise in Primitive Tradition." Diogenes, 3 (1953): 18–30. Reprinted in *Daedalus* 88 (1959): 258, 261–66.
"Smiths, Shamans, and Mystagogues." *East and West* 6 (1955): 206–15.
"Les Représentations du Mort chez les Primitifs." *Temoinages. Cahier de la Pierre-qui-vire* 41 (1954): 166–74.
"La Tere-Mère et les hierogamies cosmiques." *Eranos Jahrbuch* 22 (1954).
"Mythology and the History of Religions." *Diogenes* 9 (1955): 96–113.
"The Structure of Religious Symbols." *Proceedings of the IX International Congress for the History of Religions*, Tokyo, (1958): 506–12.
"Encounters at Ascona." In *Spiritual Disciplines*, Papers from the Eranos Jahrbuch, Bollingen series, vol. 4, (1959): xvii–xxi.
"Structures and Changes in the History of Religion." In *City Invincible—A Symposium of Urbanisation and Cultural Development in the Ancient Near East*, ed. C. Kraeling and R. Adams. Chicago: University of Chicago Press, 1960.
"History and the Cyclical View of Time." *Perspectives* 5 (1960): 11–14.
"Recent Works on Shamanism: A Review Article." *History of Religions* 1 (1962): 152–86.
"Cargo Cults and Cosmic Regeneration." In *Millenial Dreams in Action*, ed. S. Thrupp. The Hague: Mouton, 1962. (Reproduces much material from *The Two and the One*, 125–40.)

"Two Spiritual Traditions in Rumania." *Arena* 11 (1963): 15–25.

"Yoga and Modern Philosophy." *Journal of General Education* 2 (1963): 124–37.

"Mystery and Spiritual Regeneration in Extra-European Religions." In *Man and Transformation: Papers from the Eranos Yearbooks*, vol. 5, ed. Joseph Campbell. New York: Pantheon, 1964, 3–26.

"Shamanism in South-East Asia and Oceania." *International Journal for Parapsychology* 6 (1964): 329–61.

"Paul Tillich and the History of Religions." In *Paul Tillich: The Future of Religion*, ed. J. C. Brauer. New York: Harper & Row, 1966.

"Initiation Dreams and Visions among the Siberian Shamans." In *The Dream and Human Societies*, ed. G. E. Grunebaum and Roger Callois. Berkeley: University of California Press, 1966, 331–40.

"In Memoriam: Paul Tillich." *Criterion* 5 (1966): 11–14.

"Briser le toit de la Maison: Symbolisme Architechtonique et Physiologie Subtile." *Studies in Mysticism and Religion*, ed. E. E.Urbach. Jerusalem: Magnes Press, 1967: 131–39. Also in Tacou, Constantin (ed.), *Mircea Eliade*. Cahiers de l'Herne no. 33. Paris: Editions de l'Herne, 1978.

"Historical Events and Structural Meaning in Tension." *Criterion* 6 (1967): 29–31.

"Marc Chagall et l'amour du Cosmos." *XXieme Siècle* 29 (1967): 137–39.

"Comparative Religion: Its Past and Future." In *Knowledge and the Future of Man*, ed. Walter J. Ong, S.J. New York: Holt, Rhinehard and Winston, 1968.

"The Forge and the Crucible: A Postscript." *History of Religions* 8 (1968): 74–88.

Preface to *Reflective Theology* by T. N. Munson. New Haven: Yale University Press, 1968.

"Notes on the Symbolism of the Arrow." In *Religions in Antiquity*, ed. J. Neusner. Leiden: E. J. Brill, 1968, 463–75.

"South American High Gods, part I." *History of Religions* 8 (1969): 338-54.

"Notes for a Dialogue." In *The Theology of T. J. J. Altizer*, ed. J. B. Cobb. Philadelphia: Westminster Press, 1970.

"South American High Gods, part II." *History of Religions* 10 (1971): 234–66.

"The Dragon and the Shaman: Notes on a South American Mythology." In *Man and his Salvation*, ed. Eric J. Sharpe and John R. Hinnells. Manchester: Manchester University Press, 1972, 99–105.

Foreword to *The Rise of Modern Mythology, 1600–1800* by R. D. Richardson. London: Indiana University Press, 1972.

"On Structural Archetypes: A Conversation Between Mircea Eliade and John Wilkinson." Unpublished paper provided by Mac Ricketts.

"Notes on the Călușari." *Journal of the Ancient Near Eastern Society of Columbia University* 5 (1973): 115–22.

"The Sacred in the Secular World." *Cultural Hermeneutics* 1 (1973): 101–13 (Renamed *Philosophy and Social Criticism* after 1978.)

"On Prehistoric Religions." *History of Religions* 14 (1974): 140–47.

"The Occult and the Modern World." *Journal of the Philadelphia Association for Psychoanalysis* 1 (1974): 195–213.

"Some Observations on European Witchcraft." *History of Religions* 14 (1975): 149–72.

"Myths and Mythical Thought." In *The Universal Myths*, ed. Alexander Eliot. New York: Meridian Books, 1990 (First published as *Myths* by McGraw Hill, 1976.)

"Sacred Tradition and Modern Man: A Conversation with Mircea Eliade." *Parabola* 1, no. 3 (1976): 74–80.

"The Myth of Alchemy." *Parabola* 3, no. 3 (1978): 6–23.

"Henri Corbin." *History of Religions* 18 (1979): 293–95.

"Some Notes on Theosophia Perennis: Ananda K. Coomaraswamy and Henry Corbin." *History of Religion* 19 (1979): 167–76.

Interview by Leslie Maitland, *New York Times*, 4 February 1979.

"History of Religions and 'Popular' Cultures." *History of Religions* 20, no. 1 (1980): 1–26.

"Indologica I." *History of Religions* 19 (1980): 270–75.

Preface to *Calus: Symbolic Transformation in Romanian Ritual* by Gail Kligman. Chicago: University of Chicago Press, 1981.

"Guiseppe Tucci (1895–1984)." *History of Religions* 24, no. 2 (1984): 157–59.

"*Homo Faber* and *Homo Religiosus*." In *The History of Religions: Retrospect and Prospect*, ed. Joseph Kitagawa. New York: Macmillan, 1985.

"American Paradise." *Art Papers* 10, no. 6 (1986).

Interview by Delia O'Hara, *Chicago* 35, no. 6 (June 1986): 147–51, 177–80.

(The following articles reappear in major works above and are included for the sake of completeness and to avoid possible confusion.)

"Durohana and the Waking Dream." *Art and Thought: A Volume in Honour of the Late Dr. Ananda K. Coomaraswamy*, 209–13. Edited by Bhasata Iyer. London: Luzac, 1947. (*Myths, Dreams, and Mysteries*, 115–22)

"La Vertu Créatrice Du Mythe." *Eranos Jahrbuch* 25 (1956): 59–85 (*The Sacred and the Profane*, chapter 2.)

"Time and Eternity in Indian Thought." In *Man and Time*, ed. J. Campbell. New York: Pantheon, 1957 (*Images and Symbols*, 57–91.)

"Bi-unité et Totalité dans la Pensée Indienne." *Acta Philosophica et Theologica*, 1958 (*Patañjali et le Yoga*, chapter 2)

"Some Methodological Remarks on the Study of Religious Symbolism." In *History of Religions: Problems of Methodology*, ed. Eliade and Kitagawa. Chicago: Chicago University Press, 1959. (Appears as "Observations on Religious Symbolism," in *The Two and the One*, chapter 5)

"Le Symbolisme des Ténèbres dans les Religions Archäics." *Polarités du Symbol, Études Carmelitains* 39 (1960): 15–28 (*Symbolism, the Sacred, and the Arts*, part I)

"Divinities, Art and the Divine." *Encyclopedia of World Art*. Vol. 4 (1961): cols. 382–87 (*Symbolism, the Sacred, and the Arts*, part II)

"The History of Religions and a New Humanism." *History of Religions* 1 (1961): 7–8 (*The Quest*, chapter 1)

"The Myths of the Modern World." *Jubilee* 8 (1961): 16–20. (*Myth and Reality*, 181–93)

"Survivals and Camouflages of Myth." *Diogenes* 41 (1963): 1–25. (*Myth and Reality*, chapter 9)

"Mythologies of Memory and Forgetting." *History of Religions* 2 (1963): 329–44. (*Myth and Reality*, chapter 7)

"The History of Religions in Retrospect, 1912–1962." *Journal of Bible and Religion* 31, no. 2 (April 1963): 98–109. (*The Quest*, chapter 2)

"Myth and Reality." In *Alienation: The Cultural Climate of Modern Man*, ed. Gerald Sykes. New York: Brazillier, 1964, 748–53. (In *Myth and Reality*, passim)

"The Quest for the Origins of Religion." *History of Religions* 4 (1964): 154–69. (*The Quest*, chapter 3)

"Archaic Myth and Historical Man." *McCormick Quarterly* 18 (Special Supplement, *Myth and Modern Man*, 1965): 23–36. (*The Sacred and the Profane*, chapter 4; *Myth and Reality*, chapters 1–2)

"Crisis and Renewal in the History of Religions." *History of Religions* 5, no. 1 (1965): 1–17. (*The Quest*, chapter 4)

"Initation et le monde modern." *Initiation*, ed. C. J. Bleeker. Leiden: E. J. Brill, 1965. (*The Quest*, chapter 7)

"The Sacred and the Modern Artist." *Criterion* 4 (Spring 1965): 22–23. ("Sur la Permanence du Sacré dans l'Art Contemporain," XXieme Siecle 24 (1964); *Symbolism, the Sacred, and the Arts*, part II)

"Myths, Dreams, and Mysteries." In *Myth and Symbol*, ed. F. W. Dillistone. London: SPCK, 1966, 35–50 (*Myths, Dreams and Mysteries*)

"Paradise and Utopia." In *Utopias and Utopian Thought*, ed. F.E. Manuel. Boston: Houghton Miflin, 1966, 35–50. (*The Quest*, chapter 6)

"Australian Religions, Part I: An Introduction." *History of Religions* 6, no. 2 (1966): 108–34. (*Australian Religions*)

"Australian Religions, Part II: An Introduction." *History of Religions* 6, no. 3 (1967): 208–35. (*Australian Religions*)

"Australian Religions, Part III: Initiation Rites and Secret Cults." *History of Religions* 7, no. 1 (1967): 61–90. (*Australian Religions*)

"Australian Religions, Part IV: The Medicine Men and Their Supernatural Models." *History of Religions* 7, no. 2 (1967): 159–83. (*Australian Religions*)

"Cosmogonic Myth and Sacred History." *Religious Studies* 2 (1967): 171–83. (Orig. lecture in French in Geneva, 1966.) (*The Quest,* chapter 5)

"Cultural Fashions and the History of Religions." In *The History of Religions: Essays on the Problem of Understanding,* ed. Joseph Kitagawa and Charles Long. Chicago: University of Chicago Press, 1967, 20–38. (*Occultism, Witchcraft, and Cultural Fashions*)

"On Understanding Primitive Religion." In *Festschrift für Ernst Benz,* ed. G. Muller and W. Zeller. Leiden: E.J.Brill, 1967. (*Australian Religion,* preface)

"Nostalgia for Paradise: Symbolism of the centre and the ritual approach to immortality." *Parabola* 1, no. 1 (1967): 6–15. (Adapted from *Images and Symbols,* chapter 1)

"Australian Religions, Part V: Death, Eschatology, and Some Conclusions." *History of Religions* 7, no. 3 (1968): 244–68. (*Australian Religions*)

"Spirit, Light, and Seed." *History of Religions* 11 (1971): 1–30. (*Occultism, Withcraft, and Cultural Fashions*)

"Zalmoxis." *History of Religions* 11 (1972): 257–302. (*Zalmoxis, the Vanishing God*)

"Literary Imagination and Religious Structure." *Criterion* 17 (1978): 30–34. (*Symbolism, the Sacred, and the Arts,* part IV)

D. Fiction

(Initial dates are of composition rather than publication.)

1924 *L'adolescent miop.* Paris: Acte Sud, 1992. (*Romanul adolescenului miop*)

1933 *Maitreyi.* Translated from the Romanian by Alain Guillermou—*La Nuit Bengali,* Lausanne: Gallimard, 1950. Translated from the French by Catherine Spencer—*Bengal Nights,* Chicago: University of Chicago Press, 1994.

1935 *Mademoiselle Christina.* Paris: L'Herne 1978. (*Domnisoara Christina*)

1936 *Andronic et le Serpente.* Paris: L'Herne, 1979. (*Sarpele*)

1939 *Iphigenia.* A play, first published as *Iphigenia: piesa in trei acte.* Valle Hermosa, Argentina: Editura Cartea Pribegnei, 1951. Also published as *Ifigenia: peisa in trei acte: cinci tablouri.* Bucharest: 1974. Unpublished English translation by M. L. Ricketts based on the revised version of the Argentinian edition.

1940 "Nights at Serampore." Translated by William Ames Coates, in *Two Strange Tales.* Boston and London: Shambala, 1986.
"The Secret of Dr. Honigberger." Translated by William Ames Coates, in *Two Strange Tales.* London: Shambala, 1986.

1943 "Men and Stones." A play. Unpublished translation by M. L. Ricketts.

1945 "A Great Man." Translated by Eric Tappe. In *Fantastic Tales.* London: Dillon's, 1969.

1952 "Twelve Thousand Head of Cattle." Co-authored with Mihai Niculescu. Translated by Eric Tappe. In *Fantastic Tales*. London: Dillon's, 1969.

1954 *The Forbidden Forest*. Notre Dame: University of Notre Dame Press, 1978. Translated by M. L. Ricketts and Mary Park Stevenson. (*Noaptea de Sanziene*)

1955 "The Captain's Daughter." Unpublished English translation by M. L. Ricketts. Original published in *La tiganci si alte povestiri*. Bucharest: Editura pentru Literatura, 1969.

1960 "With the Gypsy Girls." Translated by William Ames Coates. In *Tales of the Sacred and Supernatural*." Philadelphia: Westminster Press, 1981.

1963 "A Fourteen-Year-Old Photograph." Translated by M. Ricketts. *The Louisberg College Journal*, vol. VIII (1974): 3-15. Original published in *Nuvele*. Madrid; Colectia Destin, 1963.

The Bridge. Unpublished English translation by M. L. Ricketts.

1967 *The Old Man and The Bureaucrats*. Translated by Mary Park Stevenson. Notre Dame and London: University of Notre Dame Press, 1979. (*Pe Strada Mantuleasa*)

1970 *The Endless Column*. A play. Translated by Mary Park Stevenson. *Dialectics and Humanism* 10, no. 1 (1983): 44–88.

1971 *Two Generals' Uniforms*. Unpublished translation by M. L. Ricketts.

1974 *Incognito at Buchenwalt*. Unpublished translation by M. L. Ricketts.

1975 *The Cape*. Translated from the Romanian by M. L. Ricketts. In *Three Fantastic Novellas*. London: Forest Books, 1989.

1976 "Les Trois Grâces." Translated by M. L. Ricketts. In *Tales of the Sacred and Supernatural*. Philadelphia: Westminster Press, 1981.

1976 *Youth without Youth*. Translated by M. L. Ricketts. In *Three Fantastic Novellas*. London: Forest Books, 1989.

1979 *Nineteen Roses*. Translated by M. L. Ricketts. In *Three Fantastic Novellas*. London: Forest Books, 1989.

1980 *Dayan*. Unpublished translation by M. L. Ricketts.

1982 *In the Shadow of a Lily*. Unpublished translation by M. L. Ricketts.

E. Journals

Journal I, 1945–1955. Chicago, University of Chicago Press, 1989 (1–228 of *Fragments d'un Journal*, Paris, Gallimard, 1973.) Translated from the Romanian by M. L. Ricketts.

Journal II, 1957–1969. Chicago, University of Chicago Press, 1989 (Also published as *No Souvenirs: Journal, 1957–1969*. New York: Harper & Row, 1977 (229–571 of *Fragments d'un Journal*, with additional preface by Eliade dated 1976.) Translated from the French by Fred H. Johnson, Jr.

Journal III, 1970–1978. Chicago: University of Chicago Press, 1989 (*Fragments d'un Journal*, II, Paris, Gallimard, 1981.) Translated from the French by Teresa Lavender Fagan.

Journal IV, 1979–1985. Chicago: University of Chicago Press, 1989. Translated from the Romanian by M. L. Ricketts.

Autobiography, vol. I: *Journey East, Journey West, 1907–1938.* San Fransisco: Harper & Row, 1981.

Autobiography, vol. II: *Exile's Odyssey, 1938–1969.* Chicago: University of Chicago Press, 1988.

II. SECONDARY SOURCES

Al-George, Sergiu. "India in the Cultural Destiny of Mircea Eliade." *The Mankind Quarterly* 25 (1984): 115–35.

Allen, Douglas. "A Phenomenological Evaluation of Religious Mysticism." *Darshana International* 12 no. 3 (July 1972): 71–78 (Revised in chapter 7 of *Structure and Creativity.*)

———. "Eliade and History." *Journal of Religion* 68 (1988): 545–65.

———. "Mircea Eliade's Phenomenological Analysis of Religious Experience." *Journal of Religion* 52, no.,2 (1972): 170–86 (Also appears in *Structure and Creativity,* chapter 4.)

———. *Structure and Creativity in Religion: Hermenuetics in Mircea Eliade's Phenomenology and New Directions.* The Hague, Mouton, 1978.

Allen, Douglas and D. Doeing. *Mircea Eliade: An Annotated Bibliography.* New York and London: Garland, 1980.

Alles, G. D. "Wach, Eliade and the Critique from Totality." *Numen* 35 (1988): 108–38.

Altizer, T. J. J. "Mircea Eliade and the Death of God." *CrossCurrents* 29, no. 3 (1979): 257–68.

———. *Mircea Eliade and the Dialectics of the Sacred.* Philadelphia: Westminster Press, 1963.

———. "Mircea Eliade and the Recovery of the Sacred." *The Christian Scholar* 45, no. 4 (Winter 1962): 267–89.

Altizer, T. J. J., W. Beardsley, and J. Young (eds.). *Truth, Myth and Symbol.* Englewood Cliffs, N.J.: Prentice Hall, 1962.

Apostolos-Cappadona, Diane. "To Create a New Universe: Mircea Eliade on Modern Art." *CrossCurrents* 33, no. 4 (1982–83): 408–19.

Arcade, L. M., Ion Manea, and Elena Stamatescu (eds.). *Homo Religiosus.* Los Angeles: American-Romanian Academy of Arts and Sciences, 1990. (Selected papers from the 12th Congress of the A.R.A., Université de Paris–Sorbonne, 24–27 June 1987.)

Baird, R. D. "Normative Elements in Eliade's Phenomenology of Symbolism."
    Union Seminary Quarterly Review 25, no. 4 (1970): 505–16. Included in
    "Phenomenological Understanding: Mircea Eliade," in *Category Formation
    and the History of Religion*. The Hague: Mouton, 1971, 74–91.
Berger, A. "Anti-Judaism and Anti-Historicism in Eliade's Writings." (In Hebrew)
    Hadoar: the Jewish Histadrut of America 70 no. 25 (June 1991).
———. "Cultural Hermeneutics: the Concept of Imagination in the Phenomeno-
    logical Approaches of Henry Corbin and Mircea Eliade." *Journal of
    Religion* 66, no. 2 (1986): 141–56.
———. "Eliade's Double Approach: A Desire for Unity." *Religious Studies Review*
    11 (1985): 9–12.
———. "Fascism and Religion in Romania." *The Annals of Scholarship* 6, no. 4
    (1989): 455–65.
———. "Mircea Eliade: Romanian Fascism and the History of Religions in the
    United States." In *Tainted Greatness: Antisemitism and Cultural Heroes*,
    ed. Nancy A. Harrowitz. Philadelphia: Temple University Press, 1994.
Barbosa da Silva, A. *Phenomenology as a Philosophical Problem*. Uppsala: G. W.
    K. Gleerup, 1982.
Beane, W. C. "Introduction" and "Conclusion" in *Myths, Rites and Symbols: A
    Mircea Eliade Reader*, ed. W. C. Beane and W. G. Doty. New York: Harper
    & Row, 1975.
Bianchi, U. "Mircea Eliade and the Morphology of the Holy: Contrasting Opinions
    on the 'Holy' and on History." In *The History of Religions*. Leiden: E. J.
    Brill, 1975, 184–91.
Bolle, K. "Mircea Eliade: 1907–1986." *Epoché* 15 (1987): 3–5. This issue (105 pp.)
    was a *Festschrift* for Eliade.
Brandon, S. G. F. "Time as the 'Sorrowful Weary Wheel' and as Illusion." In
    History, Time and Deity, chapter 4, part I.
Brauer, J. C. "Mircea Eliade and the Divinity School." *Criterion* 24 (1985): 23–27.
Breu, G. "Teacher: Shamans? Hippies? They're all Creative to the World's Leading
    Historian of Religion." *People Weekly* 9, no. 12 (27 March 1978).
Brown, R. F. "Eliade on Archaic Religions: Some Old and New Criticisms."
    Sciences Religieuses 10, no. 4 (1981): 429–49.
Buchanan, J. "The Total Hermeneutics of Mircea Eliade." *Religious Studies Review*
    9 (1983): 22–24.
Bulger, Raymonde. "Maitreyi: La Nuit Bengali." Unpublished paper read to the
    annual convention of the Modern Language Association, Washington, D.C.,
    1990.
Cain, Seymour. "Mircea Eliade." *International Encyclopedia of the Social Sciences,
    Biographical Supplement*. New York: Macmillan, 1979, 18:166–72.
———. "Mircea Eliade: Attitudes towards History." *Religious Studies Review* 6,
    no. 1 (1980): 13–16.
———. "Mircea Eliade: Creative Exile." *Midstream* 1982: 50–58.

————. "Mircea Eliade, the Iron Guard, and Romanian Anti-Semitism." *Midstream* 35 (1989): 27–31.

Calinescu, M. "Between History and Paradise: Initiation Trials." *Journal of Religion* 59, no. 2 (1979): 218–23.

————. "Creation as Duty." Review article of *Autobiography II, History of Religious Ideas III*, and *Ordeal by Labyrinth. Journal of Religion* 65 (1985): 250–57.

————. "The Disguises of Miracle: Notes on Mircea Eliade's Fiction." *World Literature Today* 52, no. 4 (1978): 558–64.

————. "Imagination and Meaning: Aesthetic Attitudes and Ideas in Mircea Eliade's Thought." *Journal of Religion* 57, no. 1 (1977): 1–15.

————. "Mircea Eliade's Journals." *The Denver Quarterly* 12, no. 1 (1977): 313–15.

————. Review of *The History of Religious Ideas*, vol.I *Journal of Religion* 65 (1985): 250–57.

————. "Romania's 1930s Revisited." *Salmagundi* 97 (1993): 133–51.

Carrasco, D. and J. M. Swanberg. *Waiting for the Dawn: Mircea Eliade in Perspective.* Boulder and London: Westview Press, 1985.

Cave, John David. *Mircea Eliade's Vision for a New Humanism.* New York: Oxford University Press, 1992.

Chagnon, Roland. "Religion Cosmique, foi humaine et Christianisme chez Mircea Eliade." In *Questions actuelles sur la foi*, ed. T. Potuin and J. Richard. Montreal: Corporation et Editions Fides, 1984.

Christ, Carol. "Mircea Eliade and the Feminist Paradigm Shift." *Journal of Feminist Studies* 7 (1991): 75–94.

A Conversation with Mircea Eliade. Interview. *Encounter* (London), March 1980, 21–27.

Corless, Roger. "After Eliade, What?" *Religion* 23 (1993): 373–77.

Cronin, E. J. J. "Eliade, Joyce and the Nightmare of History." *Journal of the American Academy of Religion* 50 (1982): 435–48.

Culianu, Ioan P. *Mircea Eliade.* Assisi: Cittadella, 1977.

————. "Mahāparinirvāṇa." In *Mircea Eliade: Dialogues avec le sacré*, ed. Fernand Schwarz. Paris: Editions N.A.D.P., 1988.

————. "Mircea Eliade at the Crossroads of Anthropology." *Neue Zeitschrift für systematische Theologie und Religionsphilosophie* 27, no. 2 (1985): 123–31.

————. "Mircea Eliade Aujourd'hui." *Revue d'Études Roumaines et des Traditions Orales Méditerranéennes* 8 (1982): 39–52.

————. "Mircea Eliade et la tortue borgne." In *Homo Religiosus*, ed. L. M. Arcade, Ion Manea, and Elena Stamatescu. Los Angeles: American-Romanian College of the Arts and Sciences, 1990.

Demetrio y Radaza, F. "Mircea Eliade: His Methodology and a Critique." In *Symbols in Comparative Religion and the Georgics.* Manila: Loyola House of Studies, 1968.

Devi, Maitreyi. *It Does Not Die: A Romance*. Calcutta: Writers' Workshop Publications, 1976. Reprinted by the University of Chicago Press, 1994.

Dubuisson, Daniel. *Mythologies du XXe Siècle (Dumézil, Lévi-Strauss, Eliade)*. Lille: Presses Universitaires de Lille, 1993.

Dudley III, Guilford. *Religion on Trial: Mircea Eliade and His Critics*. Philadelphia: Temple University Press, 1977.

———. "Mircea Eliade as 'Anti-Historian' of Religion." *Journal of the American Academy of Religion* 44, no. 2 (1976): 345–59.

———. "Jung and Eliade: A Difference of Opinion." *Psychological Perspectives* 10 (1979): 38–47.

———. "Mircea Eliade and the Recovery of Archaic Religions: A Critical Assessment of Eliade's Vision and Method for the History of Religions." PhD dissertation, U.M.I. # 73 01 378 (1972).

Duerr, Hans Peter (ed.). *Die Mitte der Welt*. Frankfuhrt: Suhrkamp, 1984.

Gamwell, F. I. "Opening Remarks on the Occasion of the Establishment of the Mircea Eliade Chair in the History of Religions." *Criterion* 24, no. 3 (1985): 18–19.

Gaudette, Pierre. "La Bipartition du Monde dans la Vision Archaic: Un Theorie Incoherent de Mircea Eliade." *Laval Theologique et Philosophique* 32 (1976): 301.

Gilhus, I. S. "The Tree of Life and the Tree of Death: A study of Gnostic Symbols." *Religion* 17 (1987): 337–53.

Girardot, N. and M. L. Ricketts. *Imagination and Meaning: The Scholarly and Literary Works of Mircea Eliade*. New York: Seabury Press, 1982 (Contains a number of translations of fragments by Eliade.)

Gombrich, R. "Eliade on Buddhism." *Religious Studies* 10 (1974): 225–31.

Hamilton, K. "Homo Religiosus and Historical Faith." *Journal of Bible and Religion* 33 (1965): 213–22. Reply, D. L. Miller, 34 (1966): 305–15.

Hudson, W. M. "Eliade's Contribution to the Study of Myth." In *From Tyre Shrinker to Dragster*, ed. W. M. Hudson. Austin: Encino Press, 1968, 219–41.

Hyers, C. "Mircea Eliade: A Retrospective." *Theology Today* 44 (1987): 251–58.

Idinopulos, Thomas A. and Edward Yonan. *Religion and Reductionism: Essays on Eliade, Segal, and the Challenge of the Social Sciences for the Study of Religion*. Leiden: E. J. Brill, 1994.

Johnston, Ilinca Zarifopol. Review of *Autobiography*, vol. I. *Religious Studies Review* 9, no. 1 (1983): 11–13.

Kim, J. J. "Hierophany and History." *Journal of the American Academy of Religion* 40, no. 3 (1972): 334–48.

King, U. "A Hermeneutical Circle of Religious Ideas" (Review of *The History of Religious Ideas*). *Religious Studies* 17 (1981): 565–69.

———. "Women Scholars and the *Encyclopedia of Religion*." *Method and Theory in the Study of Religion* 2 (1990): 91–97.

Kitagawa, J. "Mircea Eliade" and "Eliade and Tillich." In *History of Religions: Understanding Human Experience*. Atlanta, Georgia: Scholars' Press, 1987.

———. "Remarks on the Mircea Eliade Chair." *Criterion* 24, no. 3 (1985): 22.

Kitagawa, J. and Charles H. Long (eds.). *Myths and Symbols: Studies in Honour of Mircea Eliade*. Chicago: University of Chicago Press, 1969.

Leach, E. "Sermons from a Man on a Ladder." *New York Review of Books*, vol. VII, 20 October 1966.

Long, C. H. "Human Centres: An Essay on Method in the History of Religions." *Soundings* 61 (1978): 400–14.

———. "The Significance for Modern Man of Mircea Eliade's Work." In *Cosmic Piety, Modern Man and the Meaning of the Universe*, ed. C. Derrick. New York: P. J. Kenedy and Sons, 1967.

Long, C. H, and K. Bolle. "Two Letters: Eliade and Politics." *Epoché* 15 (1987): 92–105.

Luyster, R. "The Study of Myth: Two Approaches." *Journal of Bible and Religion* 34, no. 3 (1966): 235–43.

McCutcheon, Russell T. "The Myth of the Apolitical Scholar." *Queen's Quarterly* 100 (1993): 642–46.

Mairet, Philip. "The Primordial Myths: A Note on the Works of Professor Eliade." *Aryan Path* 34 (1963): 8–12.

Malefijit, Annemarie de Waal. *Religion and Culture*. New York: Macmillan, 1968, 192ff.

le Manchec, Claude. "Mircea Eliade: Le chamanisme et la literature." *Review de l'Histoire des Religions* 208, no. 1 (1991): 27–48.

Manea, Norman. "Happy Guilt: Mircea Eliade, Fascism and the Unhappy Fate of Romania." *The New Republic*, 5 August 1991, 27–36.

Marino, Adrian. *L'Hermeneutique de Mircea Eliade*. Paris: Gallimard, 1981. Translated from the Romanian by Jean Gouillard.

Marty, M. "That Nice Man" (Reminiscences of Mircea Eliade). *The Christian Century* 103, no. 17 (1986): 503.

Mason, John R. *Reading and Responding to Mircea Eliade's History of Religious Ideas: the Lure of the Late Eliade*. Lampeter: Edwin Mellen Press, 1993.

Meadow, Mary Jo. "Archetypes and Patriarchy: Eliade and Jung." *Journal of Religion and Health* 31 (1992): 187–95.

Mincu, Marin and Roberto Scagno (eds.). *Mircea Eliade e L'Italia*. Milan: Jaca Book, 1987.

Mugerauer, Robert. "Mircea Eliade: Restoring the Possibilities of Place." *The Environmental and Architectural Phenomenology Newsletter* (Winter 1993): 10–12.

Munson, T. "Freedom: A Philosophical Reflection on Spirituality." *Philosophy Today* 11 (1967): 47–54.

————. *Reflective Theology, Philosophical Orientations in Religion.* New Haven: Yale University Press, 1968.

Muratore, S. "The Well at the Mind's End: On the Myth of the Collective Unconscious." *Epiphany* 8 (1988): 48–58.

Nemoianu, Virgil. "Naming the Secret: Fantastic and Political Dimensions of Charles William's and Eliade's Fiction." *Bulletin of the American-Romanian Academy of the Arts and Sciences* 4 (1983): 50–59.

————. "Wrestling with Time: Some Tendencies in Nabokov and Eliade's Later Works." *Southeastern Europe* 7, no. 1 (1980): 74–90.

Nielsen, N. "The Fundamentalist Paradigm and its Dilemmas." *King's Theological Review* 11: 55–58.

O'Flaherty, Wendy Doniger. "Remembering Eliade: 'He Loved It All.'" *The Christian Century* 103, no. 19 (1986): 540.

————. "Time, Sleep, and Death in the Life, Fiction, and Academic Writings of Mircea Eliade." *Mircea Eliade e le Religione Asiatiche,* ed. Gherardo Gnoli. Rome: Instituto Italiano per il medio ed estremo oriente, 1989.

Olson, Carl. "Theology of Nostalgia: Reflections on the Theological Aspects of Eliade's Work." *Numen* 36, no. 1 (1989): 98–112.

————. "The Fore-Structure of Eliade's Hermeneutics." *Philosophy Today* 32 1/4 (Spring 1988): 43–53.

————. "The Concept of Power in the Works of Eliade and van der Leeuw." *Studia Theologica* 42, no. 1 (1988): 39–54.

————. *The Theology and Philosophy of Eliade.* New York: St. Martin's Press, 1992.

Paden, William. "Before the Sacred became Theological: Rereading the Durkheimian Legacy." In Idinopulos, Thomas A. and Edward Yonan *Religion and Reductionism: Essays on Eliade, Segal, and the Challenge of the Social Sciences for the Study of Religion.* Leiden: E. J. Brill, 1994, 198–209.

Paus, Ansger. "The Secret Nostalgia of Mircea Eliade for Paradise: Observations on Method in the Study of Religion." *Religion* 19 (1989): 137–50.

Penner, H. H. "Bedeutung und Probleme der Religiosen Symbolik bei Tillich und Eliade." *Antaios* 9 (1967): 127–43.

Pierre, J. "Epistemologie de l'Interpretation: pour un relecture de l'oeuvre de Mircea Eliade." *Sciences Religieuses* 11, no. 3 (1982): 265–84.

————. *Mircea Eliade: Le Jour et Le Nuit.* Québec: Étitions Hurtubise, 1988.

Progoff, Ira. "Culture and Being: Mircea Eliade's Studies in Religion." *International Journal for Parapsychology* 3 (1961): 47–60.

Popescu-Cadem, C. "The M. Eliade File: Once More, the London Phase." Published as "'Dosar' M. Eliade" Din nou 'etapa' Londra." *Jurnalul Literar* (Bucharest) 2, no. 7 (November 1992). Translated by M. L. Ricketts.

Rasmusen, D. "Mircea Eliade: Structural Hermeneutics and Philosophy." *Philosophy Today* 12 (1968): 138–46. Also in, *Symbol and Interpretation*. The Hague: Martinus Nijhoff, 1974.

Ray, Richard. "Is Eliade's Metapsychoanalysis an End Run around Bultmann's Demythologization?" In *Myth and the Crisis of Historical Consciousness*, ed. L. W. Gibbs and W. Taylor Stevenson. Missoula, Montana: University of Montana Press: Scholars' Press, 1975, 57–74.

Rennie, Bryan. "The Diplomatic Career of Mircea Eliade: a Response to Adriana Berger." *Religion* 22, no. 4 (1992): 375–92. Translated by Lidia Rosu as: "Cariera diplomatica a lui M. Eliade—un raspuns Adrianei Berger," *Jurnalul Literar* 5–8 (February–March 1993): 1, 4–5.

———. "The Religious Creativity of Modern Humanity: Some Observations on Eliade's Unfinished Thought." *Religious Studies* 31, no. 2 (1995): 221–235. Translated by Raluca Podocea as: "Creativitatea religioasă umanităţii moderne," *Jurnalul Literar* 9–12 (April 1994): 4–5.

Reno, S. J. "Eliade's Progressional View of Hierophanies." *Religious Studies* 8 (1972): 153–60.

Reynolds, F. E. "A Tribute to Mircea Eliade." *Criterion* 24, no. 3 (1985): 20–21.

Ricketts, M. L. "Eliade and Altizer: Very Different Outlooks." *Christian Advocate*, October 1967: 11–12.

———. "Faţe in the *Forbidden Forest*." *Dialogue* 8 (1982): 101–19.

———. "In Defense of Eliade: Bridging the Gap between Anthropology and the History of Religions." *Religion* 1, no. 3 (1973): 13–34.

———. "Mircea Eliade and the Death of God." *Religion in Life* 36, no. 1 (Spring 1967): 40–52.

———. *Mircea Eliade: The Romanian Roots*. 2 vols. New York: Columbia University Press, 1988.

———. "The Nature and Extent of Eliade's 'Jungianism.'" *Union Seminary Quarterly Review* 25, no. 2 (1970): 211–34.

———. "On Reading Eliade's Stories as Myths for Moderns." Unpublished paper read at the Midwestern Modern Language Association, Cincinati, Ohio, 1982.

Ricoeur, P. Review of *The History of Religious Ideas*. *Religious Studies Review* 2, no. 4 (1976): 1–4.

Rudolph, K. "Mircea Eliade and the 'History of Religions'." *Religion* 19 (1989): 101–28.

Sabre, J. "The Sacred Wood in Three 20th-Century Narratives: *The Forbidden Forest* (Eliade), *Daniel Martin* (John Fowles), and *Heart of Darkness* (Joseph Conrad)." *Christian Scholars' Review* 13, no. 1 (1984): 34–47.

Saiving, V. "Androcentrism in Religious Studies." *Journal of Religion* 56 (1973): 117–97.

Saliba, J. A. "Eliade's View of Primitive Man: Some Anthropological Reflections." *Religion* 6 (1976): 150–75.

———. *Homo Religiosus in the Works of Mircea Eliade*. Leiden: E. J. Brill, 1976.

———. Review of *Australian Religion*. *Horizons* 4 (1977): 148–49.

———. Review of *The History of Religious Ideas*. *Horizons* 7 (1980): 148–49.

Schwarz, Fernand. *Mircea Eliade: Dialogues avec le sacré*. Paris: Editions N.A.D.P., 1986 (See especially Ioan Culianu, "Mahāparinirvāṇa").

Segal, R. A. "Eliade's Theory of Millenarianism." *Religious Studies* 14 (1978): 159–73.

———. Review of *Australian Religion*. *Journal for the Scientific Study of Religion* 16 (1977): 332–33.

Sharpe, E. J. "History and 'Belief': A Response to Robert Segal." *Religious Traditions* 11 (1988): 1–20.

———. Review of *Encyclopedia of Religion*. *Journal of Religion* 70, no. 3 (1990): 340–52.

———. Review of *Zalmoxis, the Vanishing God*. *Religion* 7 (1977): 105–06.

Shiner, Larry E. "Sacred Space, Profane Space, Human Space." *Journal of the American Academy of Religion* 40 (1972): 425–36.

Smart, N. "Beyond Eliade: The Future of Theory in Religion." *Numen* 25 (1978): 171–83.

———. Review of *The History of Religious Ideas*. *Journal of Religion* 60 (1980): 67–71.

———. Review of *Ordeal by Labyrinth*. *Scottish Journal of Religious Studies* 5, no. 2 (1984): 152–54.

———. Review of *The Quest*. *Religious Studies* 7 (1971): 77–79.

———. Review of *The Encyclopedia of Religion*. *Religious Studies Review* 14, no. 3 (1988).

Smith, J. Z. "The Wobbling Pivot." *Journal of Religion* 52, no. 2 (1972): 134–49.

———. "Mythos und Geschicte." In *Alcheringa oder der beginnende Zeit*, ed. Hans-Peter Duerr. Frankfurt-am-Main: Suhrkamp, 1983.

Snellgrove, D. L. Review of *Le Yoga, Immortalité et Liberté*. *Journal of the Royal Asiatic Society* (1956): 252–54.

Spariosu, Mihail. "Orientalist Fictions in Eliade's *Maitreyi*." In *Fiction and Drama in Southeastern Europe*, ed. Henrik Birnbaun and Thomas Eekman, 349–60. Columbus, OH: Slavica Publishers Incorporated, 1980.

Stancu, Zaharia. "Chaff from the Carts of the Enemy." Unpublished translation from the Romanian by M. L. Ricketts.

Stewart, M. "Royal Road towards the Centre: Fictional Hermeneutics and Hermeneutical Fiction in Eliade's Two Tales of the Occult." *Ohio Journal of Religious Studies* 6 (1978): 29–44.

Stirrat, R. L. "Sacred Models." *Man: The Journal of the Royal Anthropological Institute* 19, no. 2 (1984): 199–215.

Streng, F. "Beyond Religious Symbols and Insight: Understanding Religious Life as Processes of Valuation." *Religious Traditions* 10 (1987): 77–94.

Strenski, I. "Love and Anarchy in Romania." *Religion* 12, no. 4 (1982): 391–404.
———. "Mircea Eliade." In *Four Theories of Myth in Twentieth Century History.* London: Macmillan, 1989.
———. "Mircea Eliade: Some Theoretical Problems." In *The Theory of Myth: Six Studies*, ed. A. Cunningham. London: Sheed and Ward, 1973.
Sullivan, L. E. "Creative Writing and Imitatio Dei: The Book and the Fall." *Revista Asociatiei Culturale Internationale a Etniei Romane* 2 (March 1984): 21–22.
———. Review of *Encyclopedia of Religion. Journal of Religion* 70, no. 3 (1990): 315–39.
———. Review of *The History of Religious Ideas. Religious Studies Review* 9, no. 1 (January 1983): 13–22.
Tacou, Constantin (ed.). *Mircea Eliade.* Cahiers de l'Herne, no. 33. Paris: Editions de l'Herne, 1978.
Thornton, A. *People and Themes in Homer's Odyssey.* London: Methuen, 1970.
Tillich, P. "The Significance of the History of Religions for the Systematic Theologian." In *Paul Tillich: The Future of Religion*, ed. J. C. Brauer. New York: Harper & Row, 1966.
Tissot, G. "Camouflages et Méconaissances." *Sciences Religieuses* 10, no. 1 (1981): 45–58.
Valk, John. "The Concept of the *Coincidentia-Oppositorum* in the Thought of Mircea Eliade." *Religious Studies* 28 (1992): 31–41.
Verene, Donald Phillip. "Eliade's Vichianism: The Regeneration of Time and the Terror of History." *New Vico Studies* 4 (1986): 115–21.
Vernoff, C. E. "Mircea Eliade and the Fundamental Structure of Religious Life." *Journal of Dharma* 11, no. 2 (1986): 147–60.
Volovici, Leon. *Nationalist Ideology and Antisemitism: The Case of Romanian Intellectuals in the 30s.* New York: Pergamon Press, 1991.
Wallace, A. F. C. *Religion: An Anthropological View.* New York: Random House, 1967, 252f.
Webster, A. F. C. "Orthodox Mystical Tradition and the Comparative Study of Religion: An Experimental Synthesis." *Journal of Ecumenical Studies* 23 (1986): 621–49.
Weckman, G. "Mircea Eliade and the Role of History in Religion." *Journal of Religious Studies* (Ohio) 10, no. 2 (1983): 9–18.
Welbon, G. R. "Some Remarks on the Work of Mircea Eliade." *Acta Philosophica et Theologica* 2 (1964): 465–92.
Werblowsky, R. J. Zwi. "*In Nostro Tempore*: On Mircea Eliade." *Religion* 19 (1989): 129–36.
———. Review of *The History of Religious Ideas. History of Religions* 23 (1983): 181–87.
Whaling, F. "Mircea Eliade." In *Contemporary Approaches to the Study of Religion.* The Hague: Mouton, 1985, 214–20.

————. Review of *From Primitives to Zen. Religious Studies* 15 (1979): 421–23.

Widengren, G. "Mircea Eliade Sixty Years Old." *Numen* 14 (1967): 165–66.

Zaehner, R. C. Review of *From Primitives to Zen. Religious Studies* 3 (1968): 561–62.

————. Review of "Some Methodological Remarks." *Journal of Theological Studies* 11 (1960): 449–50.

Ziolkowski, Eric J. "Between Religion and Literature: Mircea Eliade and Northrop Frye." *Journal of Religion* 71, no. 4 (1991): 498–522.

III: OTHER WORKS CONSULTED

Aichele, George Jr. "Literary Fantasy and Postmodern Theology." *Journal of the American Academy of Religion* 59 (1991): 323–37.

Bailey, Edward. *Aspects of Implicit and Civil Religion.* As yet unpublished manuscript copy of the editorial and bibliographical sections of this projected edition.

————. "The Implicit Religion Of Contemporary Society: An Orientation and Plea for Its Study." *Religion* 13, no. 1 (1983): 69–84.

Baird, R. D. *Category Formation and the History of Religion.* The Hague: Mouton, 1971.

Bartley, W. W. *The Retreat to Commitment.* La Salle, IL: Open Court, 1984.

Belsey, Catherine. *Critical Practice.* New York: Methuen, 1980.

Berger, Peter and Thomas Luckmann. *The Social Construction of Reality.* New York: Doubleday Anchor, 1967.

Bergson, Henri. *Time and Free Will.* Trans. F. L. Pogson. New York: Macmillan, 1910.

Berlin, Isaiah. *Vico and Herder.* New York: Viking Press, 1976.

Bernstein, Richard. *Beyond Objectivism and Relativism: Science, Hermeneutics and Praxis.* Philadelphia: University of Pennsylvania Press, 1983.

Bianchi, U. *The History of Religions.* Leiden: E. J. Brill, 1975.

Bianchi, U., C. J. Bleeker and A. Bausani. *Problems and Methods of the History of Religion.* Leiden: E. J. Brill, 1972.

Bleeker, C. J. "The Future Task of the History of Religions." *Numen* 7 (1960): 221–34.

————. "The Phenomenological Method." *Numen* 6 (1959): 96–111.

Boas, F. *Tsimshian Texts.* Washington, D.C.: GPO, 1902.

Copi, Irving and Carl Cohen. *Introduction to Logic* (ninth edition). New York: Macmillan, 1994.

Cromphout, Gustaaf van. *Emerson's Modernity and the Example of Goethe.* Columbia: University of Missouri Press, 1990.

Cunningham, A. *The Theory of Myth: Six Studies.* London: Sheed and Ward, 1973.

Davis, Charles. "The Reconvergence of Theology and Religious Studies." *Sciences Religieuses* 4, no. 3 (1974): 205–21.

———. "Theology and Religious Studies." *Scottish Journal of Religious Studies* 2 (1981).

———. "Wherein There Is No Ecstasy." *Sciences Religieuses* 13, no. 4 (1984): 393–400.

Donald, Merlin. *The Origins of the Modern Mind.* Cambridge, Mass.: Harvard University Press, 1991.

Eagleton, Terry. *Literary Theory.* Minneapolis: University of Minnesota Press, 1983.

———. "Capitalism, Modernism and Postmodernism." *New Left Review* 152 (1985): 60–73.

Falck, Colin. *Myth, Truth, and Literature: Towards a True Postmodernism.* Cambridge: Cambridge University Press, 1989.

Ferré, Frederick. "The Definition of Religion." *Journal of the American Academy of Religion* 38, 1 (1970): 3–16.

Frye, Northrop. "World Enough Without Time." *The Hudson Review* 12 (1959): 423–31.

Gellner, Ernest. *Postmodernism, Reason and Religion.* New York: Routledge, 1992.

Giddens, Anthony. *The Consequences of Modernity.* Stanford: Stanford University Press, 1990.

Gleick, James. *Chaos: Making a New Science.* London: Heinemann, 1988.

Glover, David and Sheelagh Strawbridge. *The Sociology of Knowledge.* Causeway Books, 1985.

Goodenough, E. R. "Religionswissenschaft." *Numen* 6, no. 2 (1959): 77–95.

Greeley, A. M. "Mass Culture Milieu." *Worship* 33, no. 1 (1958): 19–26.

———. *The Persistence of Religion.* London: SCM, 1973.

———. *Unsecular Man: The Persistence of Religion.* New York: Schocken Books, 1985.

Gribbin, John. *In Search of Schrödinger's Cat.* New York: Bantam, 1984.

Griffin, David Ray (ed.). *Founders of Constructive Postmodern Philosophy: Peirce, James, Bergson, Whitehead, and Hartshorne.* Albany: SUNY Press, 1993.

Habermas, Jürgen. *The Philosophical Discourse of Modernity.* Cambridge, MA: MIT Press, 1987.

Hartshorne, Charles and William L. Reese (eds.). *Philosophers Speak of God.* Chicago: University of Chicago Press, 1953.

Hassan, Ihab. *The Postmodern Turn: Essays in Postmodern Theory and Culture.* Columbus: Ohio State University Press, 1987.

Hudson, W. D. "Professor Bartley's Theory of Rationality and Religious Belief." *Religious Studies* 9 (1973): 339–50.

Kirk, G. S. *Myth: Its Meaning and Function.* Cambridge: Cambridge University Press, 1970.

———. *The Nature of Greek Myths.* New York: Penquin, 1974.

Kitagawa, Joseph and Charles H. Long (eds.). *Myths and Symbols. Studies in Honor of Mircea Eliade*. Chicago and London: University of Chicago Press, 1969.

Krolick, S. "Through a Glass Darkly: What is Phenomenology of Religion?" *International Journal for the Phenomenology of Religion* 17, no. 3 (1985): 193–99.

Luckmann, T. *The Invisible Religion: The Problem of Religion in Modern Society*. London: Macmillan, 1967.

McHale, Brian. *Postmodernist Fiction*. New York: Methuen, 1987.

————. "Constructing (Post)Modernism: The Case of *Ulysses*." *Style* 24, no. 1 (1990): 1–21.

McKnight, Edgar V. *Postmodern Use of the Bible*. Nashville: Abingdon Press, 1988.

Malinowski. *Myth in Primitive Society*. Westport, Conn.: Negro University Press, 1971.

Mannheim, Karl. *Ideology and Utopia*. New York: Harcourt, 1937.

Mol, H. *Identity and the Sacred*. Oxford: Blackwell, 1976.

O'Flaherty, Wendy Doniger. *Other Peoples' Myths*. New York and London: Macmillan, 1988.

Oxtoby, Willard. "Religionswissenschaft Revisited." *Religions in Antiquity*, ed. J. Neusner. Leiden: E. J. Brill, 1968.

Pals, D. "Is Religion a *sui generis* Phenomenon?" *Journal of the American Academy of Religion* 55 (1987): 259–82.

————. "Reductionism and Belief: An Appraisal of Recent Attacks on the Doctrine of Irreducibile Religion." *Journal of Religion* 66, no. 1 (1986): 18–36.

Panikkar, Raimundo. "Have Religions the Monopoly on Religion?" *Journal of Ecumenical Studies* 11 (1974): 515–17.

————. *Worship and Secular Man*. London: Darton, Longman and Todd, 1973.

Penner, H. H. "Creating a Brahman: A Structural Approach to Religion." In *Methodological Issues in Religious Studies*, ed. R. D. Baird. Chico, Calif.: New Horizons Press, 1975.

————. "Criticism and the Development of a Science of Religion." *Sciences Religieuses* 15, no. 2 (1986): 165–75.

————. "Fall and Rise of Methodology." *Religious Studies Review* 2 (1976): 11–16.

————. "Is Phenomenology a Method for the Study of Religion?" *The Bucknell Review* 18, no. 3 (1970): 29–54.

————. "Language, Ritual and Meaning." *Numen* 32 (1985): 1–16.

————. "Myth and Ritual: A Wasteland or a Forest of Symbols?" *History and Theory* 7 8 (1968): 46ff.

————. "The Poverty of Functionalism." *History of Religion* 11 (1972): 11–91.

————. "Rationality and Religion." *Journal of the American Academy of Religion* 54 (1986): 645–71.

Penner, H. H. and Edward Yonan. "Is a Science of Religion Possible?" *Journal of Religion* 52 (1972): 107–33.

Penner, H. H. and Robert Oden. "Introduction to the Study of Religion." *Council for the Study of Religion Bulletin* 8 (1977): 89–90.

Pettazzoni, R. *Essay on the History of Religions*. Leiden: E. J. Brill, 1954.

Prigogine, Ilya and Isabelle Stengers. *Order Out of Chaos*. London: Bantam Books, 1984.

Proudfoot, Wayne. *Religious Experience*. Berkeley: University of California Press, 1985.

Ricoeur, Paul. *Freud and Philosophy*. London: Yale University Press, 1970.

———. "The History of Religions and the Phenomenology of Time Consciousness." In *The History of Religions: Retrospect and Prospect*, ed. J. Kitagawa, New York: Macmillan, 1985

———. *Time and Narrative*. Chicago: University of Chicago Press, 1984.

Rouner, Leroy S (ed.). *Religious Pluralism*. Notre Dame: University of Notre Dame Press, 1984.

Rudolph, K. "Basic Positions in Religionswissenschaft." *Religion* 11 (1981): 97–107

———. *Historical Fundamentals and the Study of Religion*. London: MacMillan, 1985.

Segal, Robert A. "Are Historians of Religion Necessarily Believers?" *Religious Traditions* 10 (1987): 71–76.

———. "Assessing Social Scientific Studies of Religion." *Council on the Study of Religion Bulletin* 13 (1982): 69–72.

———. "Candidate for the First Modern Sociologist of Religion." *Journal of the Scientific Study of Religion* 15 (1978): 365–68.

———. "The 'De-sociologising' of the Sociology of Religion." *Scottish Journal of Religious Studies* 7, no. 1 (1987): 5–28.

———. "Have the Social Sciences Been Converted?" *Journal for the Scientific Study of Religion* 24 (1985): 321–24.

———. "In Defense of Reductionism." *Journal of the American Academy of Religion* 51 (1983): 97–124.

———. "Joseph Cambell's Theory of Myth." *Journal of the American Academy of Religion* 46 (1978): 67 (abstract).

———. "The Myth-Ritualist Theory of Religion." *Journal for the Scientific Study of Religion* 19 (1980): 173–85.

———. "The Social Sciences and the Truth of Religion." *Journal of the American Academy of Religion* 48 (1980): 403–13.

———. *Explaining and Interpreting Religion: Essays on the Issue*. Vol. 16 of Toronto Studies in Religion. New York: Peter Lang, 1992.

Segal, Robert A. and Donald Weibe. "On Axioms and Dogmas in the Study of Religion." *Journal of the American Academy of Religion* 57 (1987): 591–605.

Seligman, Martin E. P. *Helplessness*. San Francisco: Freeman and Co., 1975.

Sharpe, E. J. *Comparative Religion*. La Salle, IL: Open Court, 1975.

Sheperd, William C. "Cultural Relativism, Physical Anthropology, and Religion." *Journal for the Scientific Study of Religion* 19, no. 2 (1980): 159–72.

Smart, Ninian. *The Science of Religion and the Sociology of Knowledge*. Princeton: Princeton University Press, 1973.

Smith, B. K. "Exorcising the Transcendent: Stratagems for Defining Hinduism and Religion." *History of Religion* 27, no. 1 (1987): 32–55.

————. "Sacrifice and Being: Prajāpati's Cosmic Emission and its Consequences." *Numen* 32 (1985): 71–87.

Smith, J. Z. "I am a Parrot (Red)." *History of Religion* 11 (1971): 391–413. Also appears in Map is not Territory.

————. *Map is not Territory*. Leiden: E. J. Brill, 1978.

————. *To Take Place*. Chicago: University of Chicago Press.

Smith, W. C. *Belief and History*. Charlottesville: University of Virginia Press, 1977.

————. "Comparative Religion—Whither, and Why?" In *The History of Religions: Essays in Methodology*, ed. Mircea Eliade and Joseph Kitagawa. Chicago: University of Chicago Press, 1959.

————. "On Mistranslated Booktitles." *Religious Studies* 20 (1984): 27–42.

————. "Theology and the Academic Study of Religion." *The Iliff Review* 44 (1988): 8–9.

Swidler, Leonard (ed.). *Towards a Universal Theology of Religion*. New York: Orbis Books, 1987.

Taylor, Mark C. "Toward an Ontology of Relativism." *Journal of the American Academy of Religion* 46, no. 1 (1978): 41–61.

Tillich, Paul. *Systematic Theology*, vol. I. Chicago: Chicago University Press, 1951.

Toulmin, Stephen. *The Return to Cosmology: Postmodern Science and the Theology of Nature*. Berkeley: University of California Press, 1982.

Tracy, D. "Creativity in the Interpretation of Religion: the Question of Radical Pluralism." *New Literary History* 15, no. 2 (1984): 289–309.

————. *The Analogical Imagination: Christian Theology and the Culture of Pluralism*. New York: Crossroad, 1981.

Trey, George A. "The Philosophical Discourse of Modernity: Habermas's Postmodern Adventure." *Diacritics* 19, no. 2 (1989): 67–79.

Trigg, Roger. *Reason and Commitment*. Cambridge: Cambridge University Press, 1973.

————. "Religion and the Threat of Relativism." *Religious Studies* 19 (1983): 297–310.

Wach, Joachim. *Introduction to the History of Religions*, ed. J. Kitagawa and Gregory D. Alles. New York: Macmillan, 1988.

Werblowsky, R. J. Zwi. "Marburg—and After?" *Numen* 7, no. 2 (1960): 2–3.

Werblowsky, Zwi and C. J. Bleeker (eds.). *Types of Redemption*. Leiden: E. J. Brill, 1970.

Whaling, F. (ed.). *Contemporary Approaches to the Study of Religion*. 2 vols. The Hague: Mouton, 1983.

———. *Christian Theology and World Religions*. Basingstoke, England: Marshall Pickering, 1986.

Wiebe, Donald. "The Academic Naturalization of Religious Studies." *Sciences Religieuses* 15 (1986): 197–203.

———. "Being Faithful and Being Reasonable as Mutually Exclusive: A Comment on Shein and Grean." *Ultimate Reality* 7, no. 2 (1983): 165–68.

———. "Beyond the Sceptic and the Devotee: Reductionism in the Scientific Study of Religion." *Journal of the American Academy of Religion* 52 (1984): 157–65.

———. "Explanation and the Scientific Study of Religion." *Religion* 5 (1975): 33–52.

———. "The Failure of Nerve in Religious Studies." *Sciences Religieuses* 13, no. 4 (1984): 401–22.

———. "From Religious to Social Reality: The Transformation of 'Religion' in the Academy." *Scottish Journal of Religious Studies* 12, no. 2 (1991): 127–38.

———. "Is a Science of Religion Possible." *Studies in Religion* 7, no. 1 (1978): 5–17.

———. "Is Religious Belief Problematic." *Christian Scholars' Review* 7 (1978): 23–35.

———. "Is Science Really an Implicit Religion?" *Sciences Religieuses* 18/2 (1989): 171–83.

———. "A Positive Episteme for the Study of Religion." *Scottish Journal of Religious Studies* 6, no. 2 (1985): 78–95.

———. "The Role of 'Belief' . . . ." *Numen* 26 (1979): 234–49.

———. "Theory in the Study of Religion." *Religion* 13 (1984): 283–309.

Yandell, K. "Some Varieties of Relativism." *International Journal for Philosophy of Religion* 19, no. 1 (1986): 62–85.

———. "Can There be a Science of Religion?" *Christian Scholars Review* 15, no. 1 (1986): 28–41.

Ziolkowski, T. "Religion and Literature in a Secular Age: the Critics' Dilemma." *The Journal of Religion* 59 (1979): 18–34.

APPENDIX: BRITISH PUBLIC RECORDS OFFICE INDEX OF FILES RELATING TO ELIADE.

Underlined files were referred to by Berger.
References in bold type are to files extant at the P.R.O.

1939 — no references

1940 — "On staff of Romanian Legation."
MI5 file
T5104/T6167/T7401/318/383

— "Exemption from alien restrictions."
T5878/5839/5593/377
T6167/318/383

— "Inclusion of name in diplomatic list. Activities."
T7401/T7026/318/383

— "Request by Romanian government for facilities for his return to Romania."
R8800/6850/37 in [FO 371 24996]

— "Proposed expulsion from U.K."
R7790/392/37
R7624/37

— "Portuguese visa facilities."
T6561/1522/378

— "Facilities to travel to Portugal. Activities. Attitude of H. M. Government toward."
R7858/R7698/6850/37 in [FO 371 24996]

1941 — "Departure from U.K.: effort at airport to persuade local officers of diplomatic privilege to which he was not entitled: passport etc. stamped diplomatic: so called diplomatic bag left at aerodrome."
R978/119/37
R1087/80/37 in [FO 371 29995]

[This episode is also recorded in R1061, in FO 371 29993, although this is not mentioned in the index.]

— "Use of as temporary Romanian courier."
W3239/2008/49 in [FO 371 28953]

— "Priority of passage on Plane to Lisbon."
Y171/Y 469/7311/2 650

— "Request for facilities for his departure and anti-British outlook."
R119/R283/119/37 in [FO 371 29999]

Author Index

Aichele, George, 240
Allen, Douglas, 3, 23–24, 34, 41–3, 101–102, 119, 192–93, 197–200, 202
Alles, Gregory, 41, 44, 55n. 4, 208–12
Altizer, T.J.J., 4, 27–31, 34, 216
Al-George, Sergiu, 10

Baird, Robert, 21–22, 43, 68, 183, 201–4, 222
Barbosa da Silva, Antonio, 43, 195–97
Barth, Karl, 15, 133, 244
Barthes, Roland, 225
Bartley, Wiliam Warren III, 123, 133–141
Berger, Adriana, 39n. 4, 149–59, 170
Bergson, Henri, 42–43, 79
Bernstein, Richard, 131, 228
Brown, R.F., 179–88, 232n. 1

Cain Seymour, 39n. 4, 90, 103, 147n. 4, 158–59
Calinescu, Matei, 217–18
Cassier, Ernst, 39n. 3, 47, 173, 190
Cave, John David, 43
Coleridge, Samuel Taylor, 14
Coomaraswamy, Ananda, 145
Cronin Edward J., 237–38
Culianu, Ioan, 216, 229, 230n. 10

Demetrio y Radaza, Francisco, 48–49
Derrida, Jacques, 225, 229, 237
Doniger, Wendy, 76, 228
Dubuisson, Daniel, 77, 165–76
Dudley, Guilford III, 34–35, 186–88, 222, 234–35
Dupré, Wilhelm, 45
Durkheim, Emile, 21, 173, 191, 195

Eliade, Mircea,
    analyst of contemporary, not archaic, religion, 250–51
    anti-historian or ahistorical, 101, 222
    anti-Semitism, 150–51, 159–67
    his "anti-Semitic ontology," 169
    "armchair anthropologist," 62
    arrest in connection with Iron Guard, 145–46
    author of fiction, 38n. 2, 39, 149
    bibliography, vii
    champion of an archaic religion, 81
    diplomatic status (1940–45), 143, 152–53, 157
    elitist, 82
    journals, 11
    and Jung, 7n. 2, 81
    later works as reaction against right wing politics, 165
    Master's thesis, 111
    as mystic, 174
    nationalism, 143, 151, 165, 190
    normative elements, 201–4
    objections to historicism and existentialism, 222
    ontological assumptions, 40, 197–201
    personal experience as source of his theories, 38n. 2, 39, 62, 100
    phenomenologist, 199
    philosopher, 111, 114
        in historian of religions' clothing, 140
    political involvement in 1930s and 40s, 143–177
    as reductionist, 254
    as religious, 257

287

Subject Index

amnesia, 37
anamnesis, 14n. 5
apocalypticism, 45
apostasy. *See* loss of faith
archaic, 231
  as equivalent to primitive, premodern, traditional etc., 41
  distinct from modern, 42
  ontology, 95
Archangel Michael, 144n. 1. *See also* Legion of the Archangel Michael
archetypes
  archetypal structures or acts, 7, 69, 98, 102, 105
  archetypal intuitions, 126, 147n. 5
  Eliade's archetypes as distinct from Jung's, 7n. 2
  symbols as, 56–57. *See also* exemplary patterns
authenticity, 10-11, 89, 102
  of alternative traditions, 141

big bang theory, 87
British Foreign Office
  suspicions against Eliade, 153–57
  records relating to Eliade, 152–58. *See also* appendix, p. 284
Buna Vestire (Romanian periodical), 160n. 18

camouflage
  of mysterious in the quotidian, 32
  characteristic of modern humanity, 59
  of sacred in the profane, 32, 52, 87, 215, 217–18, 220

shown by shift in meaning of "belief" and "truth," 125
center, of the world, 57
Codreanu, Corneliu Zelea, (founder of the Legion of the Archangel Michael), 144, 146, 158, 165
coincidentia oppositorum, 5, 7, 10, 11, 32–40, 58, 140
  having experiential basis in Eliade's life, 39
  a problem to be solved, 33
  as ontological assumption, 40
commitment, irrational, 141
  justified by limits of reason, 135, 138
concentration camps, 15
consciousness, hierophanies in, 17
creative hermeneutics. *See* hermeneutics, creative
Credința (Romanian periodical), 143
Criterion group, 10, 11
criticism of Eliade, 119
  as ahistorical, 222
  as fascist and anti-Semitic, 143–177
  methodological and theoretical criticisms, 179–180
  mystical, 174
  religious, 257
  theological agenda, 191–94
crucifix, symbolism of, 52
Cuvântul (Romanian periodical), 143

demystification, 253
demythologization, 74
dialectic of the sacred and the profane, 8, 27–32, 48
Dianetics (L. Ron Hubbard), 189

truth (*cont.*)
  criteria of validity of religious, 247
  related to human will, 125
  and the sacred, 74
tu quoque, 134–141

Ulysses (James Joyce), 237–38
understanding, 108
  and becoming, 108
  and meaning, 223

Viṣṇu and Narada, myth of, 36, 74
Vremea (Romanian periodical), 10, 143, 159, 163

yoga, a coincidence of opposites, 33
  empirical, 9

Zalmoxis (religious studies periodical founded
  and edited by Eliade in 1939), 145